MANAGING CYBER THREATS

Issues, Approaches, and Challenges

MANAGING CYBER THREATS

Issues, Approaches, and Challenges

Edited by

VIPIN KUMAR
University of Minnesota, U.S.A.

JAIDEEP SRIVASTAVA
University of Minnesota, U.S.A.

ALEKSANDAR LAZAREVIC
University of Minnesota, U.S.A.

 Springer

Library of Congress Cataloging-in-Publication Data

Managing cyber threats : issues, approaches, and challenges / edited by Vipin Kumar,
    Jaideep Srivastava, Aleksandar Lazarevic.
        p. cm. — (Massive computing)
        Includes bibliographical references and index.

        1. Computer networks—Security measures. 2. Computer security. 3. Data
    mining. 4. Computer crimes—Investigation. I. Kumar, Vipin, 1956– II.
    Srivastava, Jaideep. III. Lazarevic, Aleksandar. IV. Series.

    TK5105.59.M368 2005
    305.8—dc22   2005041303

    ISBN 978-1-4419-3705-6   e-ISBN 978-0-387-24230-9

Printed on acid-free paper.

9 8 7 6 5 4 3 2 1

springeronline.com

TABLE OF CONTENTS

PART IV CYBER FORENSICS

CONTRIBUTING AUTHORS

Name	Affiliation	E-mail address
Muhammad Arshad	Department of Computer Sciences Florida Institute of Technology Melbourne, FL 32901	marshad@cs.fit.edu
Vincent H. Berk	Institute for Security Technology Studies, Dartmouth College, Hanover, NH 03755	Vincent.Berk@dartmouth.edu
Philip Chan	Department of Computer Sciences Florida Institute of Technology Melbourne, FL 32901 Laboratory for Computer Science Massachusetts Institute of Technology, Cambridge, MA 02139	pkc@cs.fit.edu
Ramkumar Chinchani	Department of Computer Science and Engineering, University at Buffalo, Buffalo, NY 14260	rc27@cse.buffalo.edu
George Cybenko	Institute for Security Technology Studies, Dartmouth College, Hanover, NH 03755	gvc@dartmouth.edu

Dave DeBarr   The MITRE Corporation   debarr@mitre.org
                       Bedford, MA 01730

Yvo Desmedt   Computer Science Department,   desmedt@cs.fsu.edu
                       Florida State University,
                       Tallahassee, Florida FL 32306-4530

Tony Fountain   San Diego Supercomputer Center,   fountain@sdsc.edu
                       University of California San Diego
                       La Jolla, CA 92093-0505

Robert S. Gray   Institute for Security Technology Robert.Gray@dartmouth.edu
                       Studies, Dartmouth College,
                       Hanover, NH 03755

Robert Grossman   Laboratory for Advanced Computing, grossman@uic.edu
                       University of Illinois at Chicago
                       Chicago, IL 60607
                       Open Data Partners

Sushil Jajodia   Center for Secure Information   jajodia@gmu.edu
                       Systems, George Mason University
                       Fairfax, VA 22030-4444

Richard Kemmerer   Department of Computer Science,   kemm@cs.ucsb.edu
                       University of California, Santa
                       Barbara, Santa Barbara, CA 93106

Erin Kenneally   San Diego Supercomputer Center,   erin@sdsc.edu
                       University of California San Diego
                       La Jolla, CA 92093-0505

Vipin Kumar   Department of Computer Science and kumar@cs.umn.edu
                       Engineering, Army High Performance
                       Computing Research Center,
                       University of Minnesota
                       Minneapolis, MN 55415

Kevin Kwiat   Air Force Research Laboratory   kwiatk@af.rl.mil
                       525 Brooks Road, Rome, NY 13441

Aleksandar Lazarevic   Army High Performance Computing   aleks@cs.umn.edu
                        Research Center, University of
                        Minnesota, Minneapolis, MN 55415

Wenke Lee   College of Computing   wenke@cc.gatech.edu
                        Georgia Institute of Technology
                        Atlanta, GA 30332

Matthew V. Mahoney   Department of Computer Sciences   mmahoney @cs.fit.edu
                        Florida Institute of Technology
                        Melbourne, FL 32901

Kiran Mantha   Department of Computer Science and   kmantha@cse.buffalo.edu
                        Engineering, University at Buffalo
                        Buffalo, NY 14260

Steven Noel   Center for Secure Information   snoel@gmu.edu
                        Systems, George Mason University
                        Fairfax, VA 22030-4444

Brian O'Berry   Center for Secure Information   boberry@gmu.edu
                        Systems, George Mason University
                        Fairfax, VA 22030-4444

Xinzhou Qin   College of Computing   xinzhou@cc.gatech.edu
                        Georgia Institute of Technology
                        Atlanta, GA 30332

Jaideep Srivastava   Department of Computer Science and   srivasta@cs.umn.edu
                        Engineering, Army High Performance
                        Computing Research Center,
                        University of Minnesota
                        Minneapolis, MN 55415

Bhavani   National Science Foundation   bthurais@nsf.gov
Thuraisingham   Arlington, Virginia 22230
                        The MITRE Corporation
                        Bedford, MA 01730

Giovanni Vigna   Department of Computer Science,   vigna@cs.ucsb.edu
                        University of California, Santa
                        Barbara, Santa Barbara, CA 93106

Shambhu Upadhyaya   Department of Computer Science and   shambhu@cse.buffalo.edu
                       Engineering, University at Buffalo,
                       Buffalo, NY 14260

Jau-Hwang Wang   Dept. of Information Management   jwang@sun4.cpu.edu.tw
                       Central Police University
                       Tao-Yuan, Taiwan, ROC 333

Preface

Information technology (IT) has become the engine that drives our modern enterprises within the public and private sectors. Government agencies and businesses have become increasingly reliant on IT systems to carry out important missions and functions and to increase their productivity. However, the very same information infrastructure that has brought a high degree of agility to our society has also created a degree of fragility — which if not remedied can cause serious damage to societal and economic well-being. For example, there have been several incidents (e.g., Code-Red I & II, Nimda, and more recently the SQL Slammer and Blaster worm attacks) of large-scale, distributed denial-of-service attacks in just the last two or three years. The intention of these attacks was not simply to infect a few machines, but to affect large portions of the Internet by shutting down millions of servers and clogging the information "superhighways."

The brunt of these attacks has been borne by those responsible for computer security, and the security research and development community has come to their aid — developing a number of techniques to make it harder to launch attacks. However, this battle is becoming increasingly difficult as a number of factors are aiding the attackers as well. First, the wide adoption of the Internet by the society at large has increased the number of organizations that can be accessed through a network, making them vulnerable to attacks from anywhere in the world. Second, information systems have become significantly more powerful and more complex during the past decade with an exponential growth in features and associated capabilities. The more complex systems are, the more difficult it is to thoroughly review all of their components and ensure the absence of security holes in them. Finally, since September 11th, 2001, we have discovered that there are well-organized groups — backed by the resources of certain governments — whose express purpose is to cripple the society's information infrastructure.

Against the backdrop described above, there is a need to have a systematic and comprehensive approach to securing the society's information infrastructure, also called the "cyber infrastructure". Thus, we define *cyber threat management (CTM) as the collection of tools, techniques, policies, processes, and practices that are aimed at protecting the cyber infrastructure, and thwarting — both retro- and proactively — attacks against it.*

There are a number of challenges to existing tools and techniques for cyber threat management. First, the amount of data being generated from various network-monitoring devices is at a scale that makes human analysis essentially impossible. This requires some form of automated analysis to extract higher-level information from the monitored system, in a form and scale comprehensible to a human analyst. Second, escalating importance of cyber security in our society creates the need for new techniques for managing cyber vulnerabilities and cyber alerts that will help to improve general computer security. Finally, by integrating these new techniques with other security disciplines such as cyber forensics, more complete and comprehensive systems for cyber threat management can be achieved.

The research community must address these and various other issues, to develop tools, techniques, policies, processes, and practices, that will contain the threat against the society's cyber infrastructure, and ensure its smooth functioning. Towards this, there is a need for in-depth analyses and surveys of existing literature — a significant fraction of it carried out by universities and national laboratories, and sponsored by the defense and intelligence communities — which will help refine the societal research agenda in the area of cyber threat management. This book is one such effort towards this goal.

The contributed chapters have been organized into four parts that focus on: (i) overviews of specific sub-areas, (ii) application of data mining to cyber threat management, (iii) techniques for managing cyber vulnerabilities and alerts, and (iv) cyber forensics techniques.

The first part provides two overview articles covering the topics of cyber threats and intrusion detection systems. In Chapter 1, Thuraisingham provides an overview of various cyber threats to information systems as well as to data management systems. These threats include access control violations, unauthorized intrusions, and inference and aggregation. In addition, the chapter also discusses potential solutions and challenges in detecting such cyber threats, which include role-based access control, data mining techniques, and security constraint processing. In Chapter 2,

Lazarevic, Kumar, and Srivastava provide a detailed survey of contemporary intrusion detection techniques. They first provide a taxonomy of computer attacks and describe basic characteristics of specified attack categories. Then, they present a general architecture of intrusion detection systems and give their taxonomy, together with a short description of significant approaches belonging to different intrusion detection categories.

The second part of the book focuses on the applications of data mining techniques for handling cyber attacks. In Chapter 3, Chan, Mahoney, and Arshad propose two anomaly detection techniques that use machine learning models for characterizing normal network behavior. The first method, called LERAD (Learning Rules for Anomaly Detection) is based on a rule learning algorithm that characterizes normal behavior in the absence of labeled attack data. The second method, named CLAD (Clustering for Anomaly Detection), uses a clustering algorithm to identify outliers in network traffic data. In Chapter 4, Lee and Qin describe a novel method for security alert correlation that is based on clustering algorithm followed by causal analysis. This method is used to discover new relationships among attacks. High volume of raw alerts is first reduced by combining low level alerts based on alert attributes, and then clustering techniques are used to group these low-level alert data into high-level alerts. The method is validated on several data sets including DARPA's Grand Challenge Problem (GCP) datasets, the 2000 DARPA Intrusion Detection Scenario datasets, and the DEF CON 9 datasets. DeBarr, in Chapter 5, focuses on the use of data mining/analysis techniques for effective summarization and prioritization of network security data. Event records are aggregated by source address and period of activity in order to reduce the number of records that must be reviewed. Anomaly detection is used to identify obvious host, port, and vulnerability scans, association discovery is used to recognize common sets of events, and cluster analysis is employed to provide a synopsis of distinctive behaviors within a group of interest.

The third part provides different practical and theoretical issues of managing cyber vulnerabilities and alerts. In Chapter 6, Berk et al. present an automated system for early detection of active scanning Internet worms, soon after they begin to spread. The implemented system collects ICMP-T3 (Destination Unreachable) messages from instrumented routers, identifies message patterns that indicate malicious scanning activities, and then identifies scan patterns that indicate a propagating worm. The chapter also examines an epidemic model for worm propagation and presents simulation results that illustrate detection capabilities. In Chapter 7, Kemmerer and Vigna present STAT framework for the development of new intrusion detection functionality in a modular fashion. In the STAT framework, intrusion detection sensors are built by dynamically composing domain-specific components with a domain-independent runtime. Each sensor has the ability to reconfigure its behavior dynamically. Dynamic reconfiguration and development of deployed STAT sensors is supported by a component model, called MetaSTAT sensor control infrastructure. The final product of the STAT framework is a highly-configurable, well-integrated intrusion detection infrastructure. Upadhyaya et al. in Chapter 8, propose a novel intrusion detection system that encapsulates the user's intent by querying her or him in a proactive manner. The encapsulated intent serves the purpose of a certificate based on which more accurate intrusion detection decision can be made. The authors present the working system implemented in a university environment. In Chapter 9, Jajodia, Noel, and O'Berry describe a Topological Vulnerability Analysis (TVA) prototype tool that implements an integrated, topological approach to network vulnerability analysis. This tool automates the labor-intensive analysis that is usually performed by penetration-testing experts. The TVA prototype includes modeling of network security conditions and attack techniques (exploits). It also generates a graph of dependencies among exploits, which represents all possible attack paths without having to explicitly enumerate them. In Chapter 10, Desmedt describes a novel methodology to model computer networks as well as information infrastructures. The chapter further proposes techniques that may be used to determine which infrastructures are critical and most vulnerable. The employed methodology is based on the PERT directed graphs. Grossman, in Chapter 11, provides a short overview of alert management systems (AMSs), which are designed to screen events, build profiles associated with the events, and send alerts based upon the profiles and events. This chapter provides a brief overview of the basic AMS architecture, as well as a few examples of such systems.

The last part of the book discusses both legal and technical aspects of employing cyber forensics in real life applications. In Chapter 12, Kenneally and Fountain describe the ongoing project P^3ELE (Public-Private-Partnership Enabling Law Enforcement) at the San Diego Supercomputer Center. This project represents a research infrastructure for the management, analysis, and visualization of public and private multidimensional data. In addition, it also covers general legal (federal, law, governmental) aspects of law enforcement process. Finally, in Chapter 13, Wang introduces the basic terms of cyber forensics to the reader. First, this chapter provides an introduction and motivation for development of this field, and then it introduces the computer forensics process as well as the digital evidence in the computer systems and computer networks.

Threats to the society's cyber infrastructure, and thus to the society as a whole, have never been clearer than they are today. Equally clear are the gaps that exist in the society's ability to protect against them. However, there is a need to take stock of what our current level of understanding of the issues is. Specifically, what issues have been addressed, and to what degree have they been successful and unsuccessful?

A book such as this would certainly not be possible without the efforts of a number of people. First, we would like to thank the authors of the chapters for accepting our invitations to present their recent research work in cyber threat management and for adhering to a tight publication schedule. We would also like to thank Angela Burke and Deborah Doherty of Springer for their continuous support throughout this project. Finally, we would like to thank the National Science Foundation, the Army Research Laboratory, and the Rome Labs for supporting the research on cyber security for the editors of this book.

PART I

OVERVIEW

Chapter 1

MANAGING THREATS TO WEB DATABASES AND CYBER SYSTEMS

Bhavani Thuraisingham
The National Science Foundation and The MITRE Corporation

Abstract: This chapter provides an overview of some of the cyber threats information systems as well as data management systems and then discusses potential solutions and challenges. The threats include access control violations, unauthorized intrusions and inference and aggregation. Solutions include role-based access control, data mining techniques and security constraint processing.

Keywords: Web Databases, Cyber Threats, Data Mining, Access Control, Security, Privacy.

1. INTRODUCTION

Recent developments in information systems technologies have resulted in computerizing many applications in various business areas. Data has become a critical resource in many organizations, and therefore, efficient access to data, sharing the data, extracting information from the data, and making use of the information has become an urgent need. As a result, there have been many efforts on not only integrating the various data sources scattered across several sites, but extracting information from these databases in the form of patterns and trends has also become important. These data sources may be databases managed by database management systems, or they could be data warehoused in a repository from multiple data sources.

The advent of the World Wide Web (WWW) in the mid 1990s has resulted in even greater demand for managing data, information and knowledge effectively. There is now so much data on the web that managing it with conventional tools is becoming almost impossible. New tools and techniques are needed to effectively manage this data. Therefore, to provide interoperability as well as warehousing between the multiple data sources and systems, and to extract information from the databases and warehouses on the web, various tools are being developed.

As the demand for data and information management increases, there is also a critical need for maintaining the security of the databases, applications and information systems. Data and information have to be protected from unauthorized access as well as from malicious corruption. With the advent of the web it is even more important to protect the data and information as numerous individuals now have access to this data and information. Therefore, we need effective mechanisms for securing data and applications.

This paper will review the various threats to information systems on the web with a special emphasis on threats to database security. Then it will discuss some solutions to managing these threats. The threats include access control violations, integrity violations, unauthorized intrusions and sabotage. The solutions include data mining techniques, cryptographical techniques and fault tolerance processing techniques.

The organization of this paper is as follows. In Section 2 we provide an overview of some of the cyber threats. Much of our focus will be on threats to the public and private databases on the web. In Section 3 we discuss potential solutions. Directions are given in Section 4.

2.   CYBER THREATS

2.1   Overview

In recent years we have heard a lot about viruses and Trojan horses on the web. These security violations are costing several millions of dollars to businesses. Identity thefts are quite rampant these days. Furthermore unauthorized intrusions and inference problem and privacy violations are also occurring frequently. In this section we provide an overview of some of these threats. A very good overview of some of these threats has also been provided in [5]. We also discuss some additional threats such as threats web databases and information systems.

We have grouped the threats into two. One group consists of some vernal cyber threats, which may include threats to web databases. The second group of threats focuses more on threats to web databases. Note that we have only provided a subset of all possible threats. There are many more threats such as threats to networks, operating systems, middleware, electronic payment systems including spoofing, eavesdropping, cover channels and other malicious techniques. Section 2.2 focuses on some general cyber threats while section 2.3 discusses threats specific to web databases. It should be noted that it is difficult to group the threats so that one threat is exclusive for web databases while another is relevant only for operating systems. Threats such as access control violations are applicable both for databases and operating systems. However with databases due to complex relationships, access controls are much harder to enforce while for operating systems access controls are granted or denied at the file level. Another example is natural disasters as well as attacks to infrastructures. These attacks and disasters could damage the networks, databases and operating systems.

2.2   General Cyber Threats

In this section we discuss some general cyber threats, which are applicable to information systems including data management systems, operating systems, networks and middleware.

Authentication Violations: Passwords could get stolen and this could result in authentication violations. One may need to have multiple passwords and additional information about the user to solve this problem. Biometrics and other techniques are also being examined to handle authentication violations.

Nonrepudiation: Sender of a message could very well deny that he has sent the message. Nonrepudiation techniques will ensure that one can track the message to the sender. Today it is not difficult to track the owner of the message. However it is not easy to track the person who has accessed the web page. That is, while progress has been made to analyze web logs, it is still difficult to determine the exact location of the user who has accessed a web page.

Trojan Horses and Viruses: Trojan horses and viruses are malicious programs that can cause all sorts of attacks. In fact, many of the threats discussed in this section could be caused by Trojan horses and viruses. Viruses can spread from machine to machine and could erase files in various computers. Trojan horses could leak information from a higher level to a lower level. Various virus protection packages have been developed and are now commercially available.

Sabotage: We hear of hackers breaking into systems and posting inappropriate messages. For example, some information on the sabotage of various government web pages is reported in [5]. One only needs to corrupt one server, client or network for the problem to cascade to several machines.

Fraud: With so much of business and commerce being carried out on the web without proper controls, Internet fraud could cause businesses to loose millions of dollars. Intruder could obtain the identity of legitimate users and through masquerading may empty the bank accounts.

Denial of service and infrastructure attacks: We hear about infrastructures being brought down by hackers. Infrastructures could be the telecommunication system, power system, and the heating system. These systems are being controlled by computers and often through the Internet. Such attacks would cause denial of service.

Natural Disasters: In addition to terrorism, computers and networks are also vulnerable to natural disasters such as hurricanes, earthquakes, fire and other similar disasters. The data has to be protected and databases have to be recovered from disasters. In some cases the solutions to natural disasters are similar to those for threats due to terrorist attacks. For example, fault tolerant processing techniques are used for recovering databases from damage. Risk analysis techniques may contain the damage. In section 3 we discuss some of the solutions.

2.3   Threats to Web Databases

This section discusses some threats to web databases. Note that while these threats are mainly applicable to data management systems, they are also relevant to general information systems.

Access Control Violations: The traditional access control violations could be extended to the web. User may access unauthorized data across the web. Note that with the web there is so much of data all over the place that controlling access to this data will be quite a challenge.

Integrity Violations: Data on the web may be subject to unauthorized modifications. This makes it easier to corrupt the data. Also, data could originate from anywhere and the producers of the data may not be trustworthy. Incorrect data could cause serious damages such as incorrect bank accounts, which could result in incorrect transactions

Confidentiality Violations: Security includes confidentiality as well as integrity. That is confidential data has to be protected from those who are not cleared. Lot of work has been carried out on multilevel security where users access only the information at or below their clearance levels [1]. Statistical database techniques have also been developed to prevent confidentiality violations.

Authenticity Violations: This is a form of data integrity violation. For example consider the case of a publisher, subscriber and the owner. The subscriber will subscribe to various magazines and the owner publishers the magazines (in electronic form) and the publisher who is the third party will publish the magazines. If the publisher is not trusted, he could alter the contents of the magazine. This violates the authenticity of the document.

Various solutions have been examined to determine the authenticity of documents (see for example, [2]). These include cryptography and digital signatures.

Privacy Violations: With the web one can obtain all kinds of information collected about individuals. Also, data mining tools and other analysis tools one can make all kinds of unauthorized associations about individuals

Inference problem: Inference is the process of posing queries and deducing unauthorized information from the legitimate responses. In fact we consider the privacy problem to be a form of inference problem (see for example, [14]). Various solutions have bee proposed to handle the inference problem including constraint processing and the use of conceptual structures. We discuss some of them in the next section.

Identity Theft: We are hearing a lot about identity theft these days. The thief gets hold of one's social security number and from there can wipe out the bank account of an individual. Here the thief is posing legitimately as the owner and he now has much of the critical information about the owner. This is a threat that is very difficult to handle and manage. Viable solutions are yet to be developed. Data mining offers some hope, but may not be sufficient.

Insider Threats: Insider threats are considered to be quite common and quite dangerous. In this case one never knows who the terrorists are. They could be the database administrators or any person who may be considered to be trusted by the corporation. Background checks alone may not be sufficient to detect insider threats. Role-based access controls as well as data mining techniques are being proposed. We will examine these solutions in the next section.

The above are some of the threats. All of these threats collectively have come to be known as **cyber terrorism.** Essentially cyber terrorism is about corrupting the web and all of its components so that the enemy or adversary's system collapses. There is currently lot of funds being invested by the various governments in the US and Western Europe to conduct research on protecting the web and preventing cyber terrorism. Note that Terrorism includes cyber terrorism, bioterrroism, and violations to physical security including bombing buildings and poisoning food supplies and water supplies. In our recent book [15] we discuss terrorism and data mining solutions to counter-terrorism. In the next section we discuss data mining for detecting cyber terrorism. We also discuss some other solutions.

3.   SOLUTIONS TO CYBER THREATS

3.1   Overview

This section will discuss various solutions to handle the threats mentioned in section 2. The goals are to prevent as well as detect security violations and mitigate risks. Furthermore, damage has to be contained and not allowed to spread further. Essentially we need effective damage control techniques. The solutions discussed include securing components, cryptography, data mining, constraint processing, role-based access control, risk analysis and fault tolerance processing.

In section 3.2 we discuss solution for some generic threats. These solutions include firewalls and risk analysis. In section 3.3 we will discuss solutions for some of the threats to web databases. Note that while the solutions for generic threats are applicable for threats to web databases, the solutions for threats to web databases are also applicable for the generics threats. For example, risks analysis has to be carried out for web databases as well as for general information systems Furthermore, data mining is a solution for intrusion detection and auditing both for web databases as well as for networks. We have included them in the section on solutions for web databases, as data mining is part of data management and may be used for various threats to databases in addition to intrusions.

3.2   Solutions for General Threats

3.2.1   Securing Components and Firewalls

Various components have to be made secure to get a secure web. We need end-end-end security and therefore the components include secure clients, secure servers, secure databases, secure operating systems, secure infrastructures, secure networks, secure transactions and secure protocols. One needs good encryption mechanisms to ensue that the sender and receiver communicate securely. Ultimately whether it be exchanging messages or carrying out transactions, the communication between sender and receiver or the buyer and the seller has to be secure. We discuss encryption in more detail in section 3.2. Secure client solutions include securing the browser, securing the Java virtual machine, securing Java applets, and incorporating various security features into languages such as Java. Note that Java is not the only component that has to be secure. Microsoft has come up with a collection of products including ActiveX and these products have to be secure also. Securing the protocols include securing HTTP (hypertext transfer protocol) and the secure socket layer (SSL). Securing the web server means the server has to be installed securely as well as it has to be ensured that the server cannot be attacked. Various mechanisms that have been used to secure operating systems and databases may be applied here. Notable among them are access control lists, which specify which users have access to which web pages and data. The web servers may be connected to databases at the backend and these databases have to be secure. Finally various encryption algorithms are being implemented for the networks and groups such as OMG (Object Management Group) are envisaging security for middleware such as ORB (Object Request Broker).

One of the challenges faced by the web mangers is implementing security policies. One may have policies for clients, servers, networks, middleware, and databases. The question is how do you integrate these policies? That is how do you make these policies work together? Who is responsible for implementing these policies? Is there a global administrator or are there several administrators that have to work together? Security policy integration is an area that is being examined by researchers.

Finally, one of the emerging technologies for ensuring that an organization's assets are protected is firewall. Various organizations now have web infrastructures for internal ad external use. To access the external infrastructure one has to go through the **firewall**. These firewalls examine the information that comes into and out of an organization. This way, the internal assets are protected and inappropriate information may be prevented from coming into an organization. We can expect sophisticated firewalls to be developed in the future.

3.2.2   Cryptography

Numerous texts and articles have been published on cryptography (see for example [3]). In addition, annual cryptology conferences also take place. Yet cryptography is one of the areas that needs continuous research as the codes are being broken with powerful machines and sophisticated techniques. There are also many discussions on export/import controls on encryption techniques. This section will briefly provide an overview of some of the technical details of cryptography relevant to the web and therefore to e-commerce. Cryptography is the solution to various threats including authenticity verification as well as ensuring data integrity. It is also useful for ensuring privacy.

The main issue with cryptology is ensuring that a message is sent properly. That is, the receiver gets the message the way it was intended for him to receive. This means that the message should not be intercepted or modified. The issue can be extended to transactions on the web also. That is, transactions have to be carried out in the way they were intended to. Scientists have been working on cryptography for many decades. We hear about codes being broken during World War II. The study of code breaking has come to be known as cryptanalysis. In cryptography, essentially the sender of the message encrypts the message with a key. For example he could use the letter B for A, C for, - - - - A for Z. If the receiver knows the key, then he can decode this message. So a message with the work COMPUTER would be DPNQVUFS. Now this code is so simple and will be easy to break. The challenge in cryptography is to find a code that is difficult to break. Number theorists have been conducting extensive research in this area.

Essentially in cryptography encryption is used by the sender to transform what is called a plaintext message into cipher text. Decryption is used by the receiver to obtain the plaintext from the cipher text received. Two types of cryptography are gaining prominence; one is public key cryptography where there are two keys involved for the sender and the receiver. One is the public key and is visible to everyone and other is the private key. The sender encrypts the message with the recipient's public key. Only the recipient can decode this message with his private key. The second method is private key cryptography. Here both users have a private key. There is also a key distribution center involved. This center generates a session key when the sender and receiver want to communicate. This key is sent to both users in an encrypted form using the respective private keys. The sender uses his private key to decrypt the session key. The session key is used to encrypt the message. The receiver can decrypt the session key with his private key and then use this decrypted session key to decrypt the message.

In the above paragraphs we have discussed just cryptography. The challenge is how to ensure that an intruder does not modify the message and that the desirable security properties such as confidentiality, integrity, authentication, and nonrepudiation are maintained? The answer is in message digests and digital signatures. Using hash functions on a message, a message digest is created. If good functions are used, each message will have a unique message digest. Therefore, even a small modification to the message will result in a completely different message digest. This way integrity is maintained. Message digests together with cryptographic receipts, which are digitally signed, ensure that the receiver knows the identity of the sender. That is, the sender may encrypt the message digests with the encryption techniques described in the previous paragraphs. In some techniques, the recipient may need the public key of the sender to decrypt the message. The recipient may obtain this key with what is called a certificate authority. The certificate authority should be a trusted entity and must make sure that the recipient can legitimately get the public key of the sender. Therefore, additional measures are taken by the certificate authority to make sure that this is the case.

3.2.3   Risk Analysis

Before developing any computer system for a particular operation, one needs to study the security risks involved. The goal is to mitigate the risks or at least limit and contain them if the threats cannot be eliminated. Several papers have been published on risk analysis especially at the National Computer Security Conference Proceedings in the 1990s (see [7]). These risk analysis techniques need to be examined for cyber threats.

The challenges include, identifying all the threats that are inherent to a particular situation. For example, consider a banking operation. The bank has to employ security experts and risk analysis experts to conduct a study of all possible threats. Then they have to come up with ways of eliminating the threats. If that is not possible, they have to develop ways of containing the damage so that it is not spread further.

Risk analysis is especially useful for viruses. Once a virus starts spreading, the challenge is how do you stop it? If you cannot stop it, then how do you contain it and also limit the damage that is caused. Running various virus packages on one's system will perhaps limit the virus from affecting the system or causing serious damage. The adversary will always find ways to develop new viruses. Therefore, we have to be one step or many steps ahead of the enemy. We need to examine the current state of the practice in risk analysis and develop new solutions especially to handle the new kinds of threats present in the cyber world.

3.2.4   Biometrics, Forensics and Other Solutions

Some of the recent developments in computer security are tools for biometrics and forensic analysis. Biometrics tools include understanding handwriting and signatures as well as recognizing people from their features and eyes including the pupils. While this is a very challenging area, much progress has been made. Voice recognition tools to authenticate users are also being developed. In the future we can expect many of us to use these tools.

Forensic analysis essentially carries out post mortems just as they do in medicine. Once the attacks have occurred then how do you detect these attacks? Who are the enemies and perpetrators? While progress has been made, there are still challenges. For example, if one accesses the web pages and uses passwords that are stolen, then it will be difficult to determine from the web logs who the culprit is. That is, we still need a lot of research in the area.

Biometrics and Forensics are just some of the new developments. Other solutions being developed include smart cards, tools for detecting spoofing and jamming as well as tools to carry out sniffing. A discussion of all of these solutions is beyond the scope of this paper.

3.3   Solutions for Threats to Web Databases

3.3.1   Data Mining

Data mining is the process of posing queries and extracting patterns, often previously unknown from large quantities of data using pattern matching or other reasoning techniques (see [13]). In [15] we devote an entire book to data mining for counter-terrorism. We discus various types of terrorist attacks including information related terrorism. As mentioned in [15], by information related terrorism we essentially mean cyber terrorism. Cyber security is the area that deals with cyber terrorism. We listed various cyber attacks including access control violations, unauthorized intrusions, and denial of service in section 2 as well as in [14]. We are hearing that cyber attacks will cause corporations billions of dollars. For example, one could masquerade as a legitimate user and swindle say a bank of billions of dollars.

Data mining and web mining may be used to detect and possibly prevent cyber attacks. For example, anomaly detection techniques could be used to detect unusual patterns and behaviors. Link analysis may be used to trace the viruses to the perpetrators. Classification may be used to group various cyber attacks and then use the profiles to detect an attack when it occurs. Prediction may be used to determine potential future attacks depending in a way on information learnt about terrorists through email and phone conversations. Also, for some threats non real-time data mining may suffice while for certain other threats such as for network intrusions we may need real-time data mining.

Many researchers are investigating the use of data mining for intrusion detection. While we need some form of real-time data mining, that is, the results have to be generated in real-time, we also need to build models in real-time. For example, credit card fraud detection is a form of real-time processing. However, here models are built ahead of time. Building models in real-time remains a challenge.

Data mining can also be used for analyzing web logs as well as analyzing the audit trails. Based on the results of the data mining tool, one can then determine whether any unauthorized intrusions have occurred and/or whether any unauthorized queries have been posed. There has been much research on data mining for intrusion detection and reported at the IFIP Database Security Conferences (see [6]). This is an area we can expect to see much progress. Some interesting work on data mining for intrusion detection is given in [4].

3.3.2　Constraint Processing

We introduced the idea of security constraint processing for the inference problem. Here we define security constraints to assign security levels to the data and then developed a system to process the constraints (see [12]). We have now adapted these techniques for privacy. In a recent paper we have elaborated on privacy constraint processing [15]. Essentially privacy constraints are rules that are enforced on the data. These rules determine the level of privacy of the data. Our definition of privacy constraints follow along the lines of our work on security constraints discussed in [10]. Privacy values of the data could take a range of values including public, semi-public, semi-private, and private. Even within a privacy value we could have different levels of privacy including low-private, medium-privacy and high-private.

We have defined various types of privacy constraints. We give examples using a medical informatics database. The constraints we have identified include simple constraints, content-based constraints, context or association based constraints, release constraints and event constraints. While we use a relational database to illustrate the concepts, constraints can be defined on object as well as on XML databases.

Simple constraints assign privacy values to attributes, relations or even a database. For example, all medical records are private. Content-based constraints assign privacy values to data depending on content. For example, all financial records are private except for those who are in public office (e.g. president of the United States). Association based constraints assign privacy values to collections of attributes taken together. For example, names and medical records are private, individually they are public. That is, one can release names and medical records separately; but one cannot release them together. Furthermore, one has to be careful so that the public user cannot infer medical records for a particular person by posing multiple queries. Event constraints are constraints that change privacy values after an event has occurred. For example, after a patient has been released, some information about him or her could be made public, but while he is in the hospital information abut him or her is private. A good example was the sniper shootings that occurred in the Washington DC area in the Fall of 2002. After the victim dies, information about him or her was released. Until then the identity of the person was not available to the public. Finally release constraints assign privacy values to the data depending on what has already been released. For example, after the medical records have been released, one cannot release any information about the names or social security numbers that can form a link to the medical information.

One could define many more types of privacy constraints. As we explore various applications, we will start defining various classes of constraints. Our main purpose in [16] is to show how privacy constraints can be processed in a database management system. We call such a system a privacy enhanced database system. Our approach is to augment a database management system (DBMS) with a privacy controller. Such a DBMS is called a privacy enhanced DBMS, a high level overview of a privacy-enhanced DBMS which we well refer to as a PE-DBMS. The privacy controller will process the privacy constraints. The question is what are the components of the privacy controller and when do the constraints get processed? We take an approach similar to the approach proposed in [11] for security constraint processing. In our approach, some privacy constraints are processed during database design and the database is partitioned according to the privacy levels. Then some constraints are processed during database updates. Here, the data is entered at the appropriate privacy levels. Because the privacy values change dynamically, it is very difficult to changes then privacy levels of the data in the database in real-time. Therefore, some constraints are processed during the query operation.

The modules of the privacy controller include the constraint manager, query manager, database design tool and the update manager. The constraint manager manages the constraints. The database design tool processes constraints during database design and assigns levels to the schema. The query processor processes constraints during the query operation and determines what data is to be released. The update processors processed constraints and compute the level of the data. Details of our approach are given in [16].

3.3.3   Role-based Access Control

One of the popular access control techniques is role-based access control. The idea here is for users based on their roles are given access to certain data. For example, the engineer has access to project data while the accountant has access to financial data. The challenges include handling multiple roles and conflicting roles. For example, if one is an engineer and he cannot have access to financial data and if he also happens to be an accountant, then how can the conflict be resolved? Maintaining the consistency of the access control rules is also a challenge.

Many papers have been published on role-based access control. There is also now a conference devoted entirely to role base access control called SACMAT (see [9]). Also papers relevant to role based access control on databases have been presented at the IFIP database security conferences. It is also being examined for handling insider threats. That is, using a combination of data mining techniques to find out information about employees and granting them roles depending on their trustworthiness, one could perhaps manage the insider threat analysis problem. More work needs to be done in this area.

3.3.4   Fault Tolerant Processing Recovery and Replication

As stated earlier, the databases could be national databases that contain critical information about individuals or private corporate databases or bank databases that contain financial information. They could also be agency databases that contain highly sensitive information. When such databases are attacked, it is then possible for the enemy to obtain classified information or wipe out bank accounts. Furthermore, even if the enemy does not do anything with the data, just by corrupting the databases, the entire operation could be thwarted. Today computer systems are controlling the operation of manufacturing plants, process control plants and many critical infrastructures. Corrupting the data could be disastrous.

The fault tolerance computing community has come up with several algorithms for recovering databases and systems from failures and other problems. These techniques include acceptance testing and check pointing. Sometimes data is replicated so that there are backup copies. These techniques have to be examined for handling malicious attacks on the database and corrupting the data.

4.   SUMMARY AND DIRECTIONS

This paper has discussed various cyber threats in general and threats to web databases in particular. The threats include access control violations, sabotage, infrastructure attacks, and insider threat analysis. Next we proposed various solutions including data mining techniques and role-based access control. As we have stated, the cyber threats are very real and we need to do everything we can to detect, prevent and manage the threats. The damages have to be contained.

Various research programs are now under way to develop solutions for cyber attacks. The National Science Foundation has various programs including the Trusted Computing Program and the Data and Applications Security Program (see [8]). There are also plans to initiate an umbrella program on Cyber Trust. Other organizations like the Defense Advanced Research Projects Agency, Advanced Research and Development Activity, and the National Institute of Standards and Technology also have programs in cyber security. While several techniques have been developed, we need to ensure that these techniques scale for very large databases and large number of interconnected systems. We need end-to-end security. That is, the clients, the servers, and the infrastructures have to be secure. We must all work together to combat terrorism. We need to be many steps ahead of the enemy and thwart all attempts by the enemy to cause damage to our systems and our infrastructures.

ACKNOWLEDGEMENTS

I thank NSF and the MITRE Corporation for their support to continue my work on data mining, counter-terrorism, information security and privacy. The views and conclusions expressed in this paper are those of the author and do not reflect the policies or procedures of the National Science Foundation, the MITRE Corporation or of the US Government.

REFERENCES

[1]   Air Force Summer Study Report on Multilevel Secure Database Systems, Washington DC, 1983.

[2]   B. Carminati, E. Bertino, E. Ferrai, B. Thuraisingham, A. Gupta. Secure Third Party Publishing of XML Documents. MIT *Working Paper*, 2002.

[3]   D. Denning. *Cryptography and Data Security*. Addison Wesley, 1983.

[4]   P Dokas, L Ertoz, V. Kumar, A. Lazarevic, J. Srivastava, P. Tan. Data Mining for Intrusion Detection. *Proceedings NSF Workshop on Next Generation Data Mining*, Baltimore, MD, November 2002.

[5]   Ghosh. *E-commerce Security, Weak Links and Strong Defenses*. John Wiley, NY, 1998.

[6]   *IFIP 11.3 Database Security Conference Proceedings*, 1990-2002.

[7]   *National Computer Security Conference Proceedings*, 1990-1999.

[8]   National Science Foundation, www.nsf.gov.

[9]   *Proceedings of the Symposium on Role-based Access Control*, 2002-2003.

[10]   B. Thuraisingham. Multilevel Security for Relational Database Systems Augmented by an Inference Engine. *Computers and Security*, December 1987.

[11]   B. Thuraisingham, W. Ford, M. Collins. Design and Implementation of a Database Inference Controller. *Journal on Data and Knowledge Engineering*, December 1993.

[12] B. Thuraisingham, W. Ford. Security Constraint Processing in a Multilevel Distributed Database Management System. *IEEE Transactions on Knowledge and Data Engineering*, April 1995.

[13] B. Thuraisingham. *Data Mining: Technologies, Techniques, Tools and Trends.* CRC Press, FL, 1998.

[14] B. Thuraisingham. Data Mining, National Security and Privacy. *SIGKDD Explorations*, January 2003.

[15] B. Thuraisingham. *Web Data Mining: Technologies and Their Applications to Business Intelligence and Counter-terrorism.* CRC Press, FL, 2003.

[16] B. Thuraisingham. Privacy Constraint Processing. To be submitted to *Computers and Security*, 2003.

Chapter 2

INTRUSION DETECTION: A SURVEY

Aleksandar Lazarevic, Vipin Kumar, Jaideep Srivastava
Computer Science Department, University of Minnesota

Abstract: This chapter provides the overview of the state of the art in intrusion detection research. Intrusion detection systems are software and/or hardware components that monitor computer systems and analyze events occurring in them for signs of intrusions. Due to widespread diversity and complexity of computer infrastructures, it is difficult to provide a completely secure computer system. Therefore, there are numerous security systems and intrusion detection systems that address different aspects of computer security. This chapter first provides taxonomy of computer intrusions, along with brief descriptions of major computer attack categories. Second, a common architecture of intrusion detection systems and their basic characteristics are presented. Third, taxonomy of intrusion detection systems based on five criteria (information source, analysis strategy, time aspects, architecture, response) is given. Finally, intrusion detection systems are classified according to each of these categories and the most representative research prototypes are briefly described.

Keywords: intrusion detection, taxonomy, intrusion detection systems, data mining.

1.   INTRODUCTION

With rapidly growing adoption of the Internet, networked computer systems are playing an increasingly vital role in our society. Along with the tremendous benefits that the Internet brings, it also has its dark side. Specifically, new threats are created everyday by individuals and organizations that attack and misuse computer systems. As reported by the Computer Emergency Response Team/Coordination Center (CERT/CC) [37], the number of computer attacks has increased exponentially in the past few years (Figure 2-1). In addition, the severity and sophistication of the attacks is also growing (Figure 2-2). For example, Slammer/Sapphire Worm was the fastest computer worm in history. As it began spreading throughout the Internet, it doubled in size every 8.5 seconds and infected at least 75,000 hosts causing network outages and unforeseen consequences such as canceled airline flights, interference with elections, and ATM failures [153]. Earlier, the intruders needed profound understanding of computers and networks to launch attacks. However, today almost anyone can exploit the vulnerabilities in a computer system due to the wide availability of attack tools (Figure 2-2).

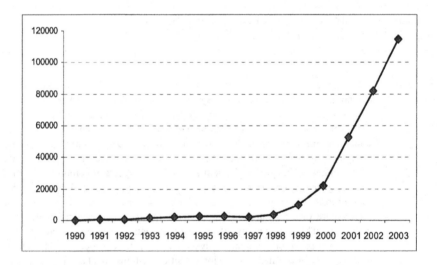

Figure 2-1. Growth rate of cyber incidents reported to Computer Emergency Response Team/Coordination Center (CERT/CC)

The conventional approach for securing computer systems is to design security mechanisms, such as firewalls, authentication mechanisms, Virtual Private Networks (VPN), that create a protective *"shield"* around them. However, such security mechanisms almost always have inevitable vulnerabilities and they are usually not sufficient to ensure complete security of the infrastructure and to ward off attacks that are continually being adapted to exploit the system's weaknesses often caused by careless design and implementation flaws. This has created the need for security technology that can monitor systems and identify computer attacks. This component is called intrusion detection and is a complementary to conventional security mechanisms.

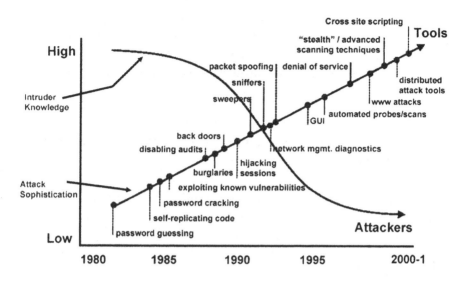

Figure 2-2. Attack sophistication vs. Intruder technical knowledge (source:
http://www.cert.org/present/internet-security-trends)

The National Institute of Standards and Technology classifies intrusion detection [15] as "*the process of monitoring the events occurring in a computer system or network and analyzing them for signs of intrusions, defined as attempts to compromise the confidentiality, integrity, availability, or to bypass the security mechanisms of a computer or network*".

Intrusions in computer systems are usually caused by attackers accessing the systems from the Internet, or by authorized users of the systems who attempt to misuse the privileges given to them and/or to gain additional privileges for which they are not authorized. An Intrusion Detection System (IDS) can be defined as a combination of software and/or hardware components that monitors computer systems and raises an alarm when an intrusion happens.

This chapter provides an overview of the current status of research in intrusion detection. It first provides an overview of different types of computer intrusions, and then introduces a more detailed taxonomy of intrusion detection systems with an overview of important research in the field. Both taxonomies are illustrated and supported with several well known examples of computer attacks and intrusion detection techniques. Several surveys in the intrusion detection have been published in the past [4, 13, 31, 55, 92, 97, 110, 114, 136]. However, the growth of the field has been very rapid, and many new ideas have since emerged. The survey in this chapter attempts to build upon these earlier surveys, but is more focused on intrusion detection projects proposed in academic institutions and research organizations than on commercial intrusion detection systems, primarily due to the lack of detailed technical information available on commercial products. The reader interested in commercial IDSs is referred to a survey of IDS products [92] and to web sites that maintain lists of such systems [57, 76].

2.   TAXONOMY OF COMPUTER ATTACKS AND INTRUSIONS

Research community in computer security has developed numerous definitions of computer attacks and intrusions. One of the most popular definitions for intrusion [181] is that it represents a *"malicious, externally induced, operational fault"*. Computer intrusions and attacks are often considered synonymous. However, other definitions of the word "attack" that differentiate it from intrusion have also been proposed in the intrusion detection literature. For example, a system can be attacked (either from the outside or the inside), but the defensive *"shield"* around the system or resource targeted by the attack may be sufficiently effective to prevent intrusion. Therefore, we may say that an attack is an intrusion attempt, and an intrusion results from an attack that has been (at least partially) successful [181].

There have been numerous attempts to categorize and classify computer attacks and intrusions [11, 112, 115, 128, 135]. Some of these attempts have provided formally developed taxonomies and specified a certain set of properties that the taxonomy should satisfy, e.g., they should be: (i) logical and intuitive [84], (ii) based on solid technical details [23], (iii) comprehensible [128], (iv) complete [5], (v) exhaustive [84, 128], (vi) mutually exclusive [84, 128], (vii) objective [108], (viii) repeatable [84, 108], and (ix) useful [84, 128]. For more details on these characteristics, the reader is referred to the above publications, as well as to Lough's PhD thesis [135].

Initial work in categorizing different aspects of computer security focused on weaknesses in computer systems and design flaws in operating systems [12], as well as functional vulnerabilities and computer abuse methods [172]. Several taxonomies that were developed later mainly focused on two issues: (i) categorization of computer misuse (i.e. attacks) and (ii) categorization of the people trying to get unauthorized access to computers (perpetrators), and the objectives and results of these attempts.

In one of earlier attempts for describing types of computer attacks, Neumann and Parker developed the SRI Computer Abuse Methods Model [165, 166, 173], which outlines about 3000 attack cases and computer misuses collected over nearly twenty years and categorizes them into the nine-level tree of attack classes. Lindqvist and Jonsson [128] extended the Neumann and Parker model by expanding several attack categories (categories 5, 6 and 7 from original nine-level tree of attacks) and by introducing the concept of dimension, which represents a basis of the attack classification. They specified two interesting criteria for system owners to perform attack classification, namely "*intrusion techniques*" and "*intrusion results*", and they called these criteria dimensions. Jayaram and Morse [96] also developed a taxonomy of security threats to networks, in which they provide five "classes of security threats" and two "classes of security mechanisms". Another significant work in computer attack taxonomies is performed by the CERIAS group at Purdue University [11, 108, 112]. Their first attempt [112] provided a classification of computer intrusions on Unix systems using system logs and colored Petri nets. Aslam [11] extended this work by providing a taxonomy of security flaws in Unix systems. Finally, Krsul [108] reorganized both previous taxonomies and provided a more complex taxonomy of computer attacks that contains four main categories (design, environmental assumptions, coding faults and configuration errors). Richardson [189, 190] extended these taxonomies by developing a database of vulnerabilities to help study of the problem of Denial of Service (DoS) attacks. The database was populated with 630 attacks from popular sites that report computer incidents. These attacks were cataloged into the categories that correspond to extensions from Aslam's taxonomy of security flaws [11] and Krsul's taxonomy of computer attacks [108]. Within the DARPA intrusion detection project, Kendall [103] developed a similar database of computer attacks that exist in DARPA intrusion detection evaluation data sets [52]. An excellent overview of these techniques as well as their extensions is provided in Lough's PhD thesis [135].

Anderson presented one of the first categorizations of attack perpetrators according to their types. He used a 2x2 table to classify computer threats into three groups (external penetration, internal penetration and misfeasance), based on whether or not penetrators are authorized to use the computer system or to use particular resources in the system [7]. One of the most influential taxonomies in categorizing attack perpetrators is the classification of types of attackers, used tools, access information, attack consequences and the objectives of the attacks, performed by CERT [84]. Researchers at Sandia National Laboratories [45] proposed a very similar taxonomy, with a few added or merged categories.

The taxonomy we provide in this survey is more general, and is obtained by examining and combining existing categorizations and taxonomies of host and network attacks published in the intrusion detection literature, and by revealing common characteristics among them. In previously published taxonomies, categories used in classification of attacks were usually either a cause of a vulnerability or the result (i.e., effect) of a vulnerability. In the taxonomy proposed here, we use traditional cause of vulnerability to specify the following categories of attacks:

- Attack type
- Number of network connections involved in the attack
- Source of the attack
- Environment
- Automation level

Attack type. The most common criterion for classifying computer attacks and intrusions in the literature is according to the attack type [84, 103]. In this chapter, we categorize computer attacks into the following classes:

– **Denial of Service (DoS) attacks**. These attacks attempt to "*shut down a network, computer, or process; or otherwise deny the use of resources or services to authorized users*" [144]. There are two types of DoS attacks: (i) operating system attacks, which target bugs in specific operating systems and can be fixed with patches; and (ii) networking attacks, which exploit inherent limitations of networking protocols and infrastructures. An example of operating system attack is teardrop, in which an attacker exploits a vulnerability of the TCP/IP fragmentation re-assembly code that do not properly handle overlapping IP fragments by sending a series of overlapping packets that are fragmented. Typical example of networking DoS attack is a "SYN flood" attack, which takes advantage of three-way handshake for establishing a connection. In this attack, attacker establishes a large number of "half-open" connections using IP spoofing. The attacker first sends SYN packets with the spoofed (faked) IP address to the victim in order to establish a connection. The victim creates a record in a data structure and responds with SYN/ACK message to the spoofed IP address, but it never receives the final acknowledgment message ACK for establishing the connection, since the spoofed IP addresses are unreachable or unable to respond to the SYN/ACK messages. Although the record from the data structure is freed after a time out period, the attacker attempts to generate sufficiently large number of "half-open" connections to overflow the data structure that may lead to a segmentation fault or locking up the computer. Other examples of DoS attacks include disrupting connections between machines thus preventing access to a service, preventing particular individuals from accessing a service, disrupting service to a specific system or person, etc. In distributed DoS (DDoS) attack, which is an advanced variation of DoS attack, multiple machines are deployed to attain this goal. DoS and DDoS attacks have posed an increasing threat to the Internet, and techniques to thwart them have become an active research area [151, 152, 154, 169, 171, 176, 226]. Researchers that analyze DoS attacks have focused on two main problems: (i) early detection mechanisms and identification of ongoing DoS activities [41, 75, 218, 235]; and (ii) response mechanisms for alleviating the effect of DoS attacks (e.g. damage caused by the attack). Response mechanisms include identifying the origin of the attack using various traceback techniques [27, 91, 195, 206] and slowing down the attack and reducing its intensity [141, 151, 248] by blocking attack packets. In addition to these two main approaches, some systems use measures to suppress DoS attacks. For example, CenterTrack [218] is an overlay network that uses selective rerouting to trace the entrance points of large flooding attack, while SOS (Secure Overlay Services) [104] employs a combination of "secure overlay tunneling, routing via consistent hashing, and filtering" to proactively prevent large flooding DoS attacks.

– *Probing (surveillance, scanning)*. These attacks scan the networks to identify valid IP addresses (Figure 2-3) and to collect information about them (e.g. what services they offer, operating system used). Very often, this information provides an attacker with the list of potential vulnerabilities that can later be used to perform an attack against selected machines and services. Examples of probing attacks include IPsweep (scanning the network computers for a service on a specific port of interest), portsweep (scanning through many ports to determine which services are supported on a single host), nmap (tool for network mapping), etc. These attacks are probably the most common ones, and are usually precursor to other attacks. The existing scan detection schemes essentially look for IP addresses that make more than N connections in T seconds. These schemes are very good at picking out fast and disperse noisy scans. Unfortunately, tools based on these techniques are quite inefficient at detecting slow/stealthy scans or scans targeted specifically at the monitored enterprise - the type of scans that analysts would really be interested in. Stealthy scans can be defined as scans that would normally not trigger typical scan alert technology. Due to these reasons, sophisticated adversaries typically attempt to adjust their scans by reducing the frequency of their transmissions in order to avoid detection. For detecting stealthy scans, there are a few recently proposed more sophisticated technique based on collecting various statistics [62, 102, 147, 191, 214, 222].

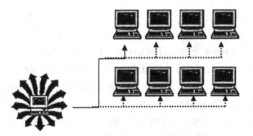

Figure 2-3. Typical scanning activity

- **Compromises.** These attacks use known vulnerabilities such as buffer overflows [38] and weak security points for breaking into the system and gaining privileged access to hosts. Depending upon the source of the attack (outside attack vs. inside attack), the compromises can be further split into the following two categories:
  - *R2L (Remote to Local) attacks*, where an attacker who has the ability to send packets to a machine over a network (but does not have an account on that machine), gains access (either as a user or as the root) to the machine. In most *R2L* attacks, the attacker breaks into the computer system via the Internet. Typical examples of R2L attacks include guessing passwords (e.g. guest and dictionary attacks) and gaining access to computers by exploiting software vulnerability (e.g. phf attack, which exploits the vulnerability of the phf program that allows remote users to run arbitrary commands on the server).
  - *U2R (User to Root) attacks*, where an attacker who has an account on a computer system is able to misuse/elevate her or his privileges by exploiting a vulnerability in computer mechanisms, a bug in the operating system or in a program that is installed on the system. Unlike *R2L* attacks, where the hacker breaks into the system from the outside, in *U2R* compromise, the local user/attacker is already in the system and typically becomes a root or a user with higher privileges. The most common U2R attack is buffer overflow, in which the attacker exploits the programming error and attempts to store more data into a buffer that is located on an execution stack. Since buffers are created to contain a specific amount of data, the additional information used by the attacker can overflow into adjacent buffers, corrupting or overwriting the valid data held in them. This data may contain codes designed to trigger specific actions, such as damaging user's files or providing the user with root access. Many approaches have recently been proposed for detection and prevention of buffer overflow attacks [49, 71], due to increased

interest in them. It is important to note that buffer overflow attacks can also belong to R2L attacks, where remote users attempts to compromise the integrity of target computer. For example, a vulnerability discovered in Microsoft Outlook and Outlook Express in July 2000 [35] allowed the attackers to simply send an e-mail message and to overflow the specific areas with superfluous data, which allowed them to execute whatever type of code they desired on the recipient's computers.

- ***Viruses/Worms/Trojan horses*** are programs that replicate on host machines and propagate through a network.
  - *Viruses* are programs that reproduce themselves by attaching them to other programs and infecting them. They can cause considerable damage (e.g. erase files on the hard disk) or they may only do some harmless but annoying tricks (e.g. display some funny messages on the computer screen). Viruses typically need human interaction (e.g. trading files on a floppy or opening e-mail attachments) for replication and spreading to other computers. One of the most well known virus examples is Michelangelo virus that infects the hard disk's master boot record and activates a destructive code on March 6, which is Michelangelo's birthday. There are various types of viruses, and classifying them is not easy as many viruses have multiple characteristics and may fall into multiple categories. The most common virus classification is according to the environment, operating system, different algorithms of work and destructive capabilities [150], although there are other categorizations based on what and how viruses infect [48, 87].
  - *Worms* are self-replicating programs that aggressively spread through a network, by taking advantage of automatic packet sending and receiving features found on many computers. Worms can be organized into several categories [105, 215, 236]:
    - *traditional worms* (e.g. Slammer [37]) usually use direct network connections to spread through the system and do not require any user interaction.
    - *e-mail (and other client application) worms*, (e.g. Melissa worm [34]) infect other hosts on the network (Internet) by exploiting user's e-mail capabilities or utilizing other client applications (e.g. ICQ – "I seek you").
    - *windows file sharing worms* (e.g. ExploreZip [221]) replicate themselves by utilizing MS Windows peer-to peer service, which is activated every time a networking device is detected in the system. This type of a worm very often occurs in

combination with other attacks, such as MS-DOS and Windows viruses.

- *hybrid worms* (e.g. Nimda [36]) typically exploit multiple vulnerabilities that fall into different categories specified above. For example, Nimda used many different propagation techniques to spread (e-mail, shared network drives and scanning for backdoors opened by the Code Red II and Sadmind worms). Success of Nimda demonstrated that e-mail and http traffic are effective ways to penetrate the network system, and that the file sharing is quite successful in replicating within the system [236].

It is important to note that some of the worms that appeared recently have also been used to launch DoS attacks [83]. For example, the erkms and li0n worms were used to deploy DDoS tools via BIND vulnerabilities [83], while Code Red was used to launch TCP SYN DoS attacks [83]. However, traditional DoS attacks typically target a single organization, while worms (e.g. SoBig.F worm) typically affect a broad range of organizations. Over the last few years, many DoS attacks have gradually mutated and merged with more advanced worms and viruses (e.g. Blaster worm in August 2003). Analysts also expect that in the future DoS attacks will be more often part of worm payloads [83].

- *Trojan horses* are defined as "malicious, security-breaking programs" that are disguised as something benign [134]. For example, the user may download a file that looks like a free game, but when the program is executed, it may erase all the files on the computer. Victims typically download Trojan horses from an archive on the Internet or receive them via peer-to-peer file exchange using IRC/instant messaging/Kazaa etc. Some actual examples include Silk Rope and Saran Wrap.

Many people use terms like Trojan horse, viruses and worms interchangeably since it is not easy to make clear distinction between them. For example, "Love Bug" is at the same time a virus, worm, and Trojan horse. It is a trojan horse since it pretends to be a love letter but it is a harmful program. It is a virus because it infects all the image files on the disk, turning them into new Trojan horses. Finally, it s also a worm since it propagates itself over the Internet by hiding in trojans that it sends out using peoples' email address book, IRC client, etc.

Number of network connections involved in an attack. Attacks can be classified according to the number of network connections involved in the attack:

- Attacks that involve *multiple network connections*. Typical examples of such attacks are DoS, probing and worms (Figure 2-3).

- Attacks that involve *a single or very few network connections*. Typical attacks in this category usually cause compromises of the computer system (e.g. buffer overflow).

Source of the attack. Computer attacks may be launched from a *single location* (*single source attacks*) or from *several different locations* (*distributed/coordinated attacks*). Most of the attacks typically originate from a single location (e.g. simple scanning), but in the case of large distributed DoS attacks or other organized attacks, multiple source locations may participate in the attack. In addition, very often distributed/coordinated attacks are targeted not only to a *single* computer, but also to *multiple destinations*. Detecting such distributed attacks typically requires the analysis and correlation of network data from several sites.

Environment. Attacks may be categorized according to the environment where they occur:

- *Intrusions on the host machine* are intrusions that occur on a specific machine, which may not even be connected to the network. These attacks are usually detected by investigating the system information (e.g. system commands, system logs). The identity of the user that performs an attack in this case is typically associated with the username, and is therefore easier to discover.

- *Network intrusions* are intrusions that occur via computer networks usually from outside the organization. Detection of such intrusions is performed by analyzing network traffic data (e.g. network flows, tcpdump data). However, such analysis often cannot reveal the precise identity of the attackers, since there is typically no direct association between network connections and a real user.

- *Intrusions in a P2P environment* are intrusions that occur in a system where connected computers act as peers on the Internet. Unlike standard "client/server" network architectures, in P2P environment, the computers have equivalent capabilities and responsibilities and do not have fixed IP address. They are typically located at "*the edges of the Internet*" [240], and actually disconnected from the DNS systems. Although P2P file sharing applications can increase productivity of enterprise networks, they can also introduce vulnerabilities in them, since they enable users to download executable codes that can introduce rogue or untraceable "backdoor" applications on users' machines and jeopardize enterprise network security.

- *Intrusions in wireless networks* are intrusions that occur between computers connected through wireless network. Detection of attacks in wireless networks is based on analyzing information about the connections in wireless networks, which is typically collected at wireless access points [126]. In general, security threats in wireless networks can be categorized into:

- *eavesdropping*, when intruder only listens for the data;
- *intrusions*, when intruder attempts to access or to modify the data;
- *communication hijacking*, when a rogue node captures the channel, poses as a rogue wireless access point and attracts mobile nodes to connect to it and then collects confidential data from them (e.g. passwords, secret keys, logon names);
- *Denial of Service (jamming) attacks*, when an attacker disturbs the communication channel with various frequency domains (cordless phones, microwave ovens), physical obstacles and disables all communication on the channel.

Automation level. Depending on the level of the attack automation, there are several categories of attacks as follows:

- *Automated attacks* use automated tools that are capable of probing and scanning a large part of the Internet in a short time period. Using these easily available tools, even inexperienced attackers may create highly sophisticated attacks (Figure 2-2). Such attacks are probably the most common method of attacking the computer systems today.
- *Semi-automated attacks* deploy automated scripts for scanning and compromise of network machines and installation of attack code, and then use the handler (master) machines to specify the attack type and victim's address.
- *Manual attacks* involve manual scanning of machines and typically require a lot of knowledge and work. Manual attacks are not very frequent, but they are usually more dangerous and harder to detect than semi-automated or automated attacks, since they give to attackers more control over the resources. Experts or organized groups of attackers generally use these attacks for attacking systems of critical importance.

3.   INTRUSION DETECTION SYSTEMS

Since the first model for intrusion detection was developed by Dorothy Denning [56] at SRI International, many intrusion detection systems (IDSs) have been proposed both in the research and commercial world. For information about these research and commercial products, the reader is referred to Web sites that contain links to them [32, 76, 149, 198, 223]. Although these systems are extremely diverse in the techniques they employ to gather and analyze data, most of them rely on a relatively general architectural framework (Figure 2-4), which consists of the following components:

- *Data gathering device* (sensor) is responsible for collecting data from the monitored system.
- *Detector* (*Intrusion Detection* (*ID*) *analysis engine*) processes the data collected from sensors to identify intrusive activities.
- *Knowledge base* (*database*) contains information collected by the sensors, but in preprocessed format (e.g. knowledge base of attacks and their signatures, filtered data, data profiles, etc.). This information is usually provided by network and security experts.
- *Configuration device* provides information about the current state of the intrusion detection system (IDS).
- *Response component* initiates actions when an intrusion is detected. These responses can either be automated (active) or involve human interaction (inactive).

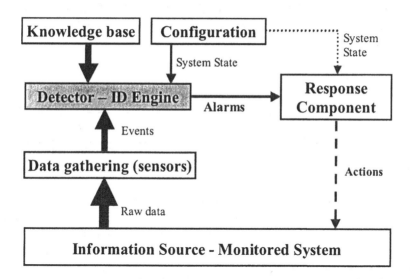

Figure 2-4. Basic architecture of intrusion detection system (IDS)

3.1 Characteristics of Intrusion Detection Systems

A number of desired characteristics for intrusion detection systems (IDSs) have been identified [55, 180], as follows:

- *Prediction performance.* In intrusion detection, simple performance measure such as prediction accuracy is not adequate. For example, the network intrusions typically represent a very small percentage (e.g. 1%) of the entire network traffic, and a trivial IDS that labels all network traffic as normal, can achieve 99% accuracy. In order to have good prediction performance, an IDS needs to satisfy two criteria: (i) it must be able to correctly identify intrusions and (ii) it must not identify legitimate action in a system environment as an intrusion. Typical measures for evaluating predictive performance of IDSs include detection rate and false alarm rate (Table 1). Detection rate is defined as the ratio of the number of correctly detected attacks and the total number of attacks, while the false alarm (false positive) rate is the ratio of the number of normal connections that are incorrectly misclassified as attacks and the total number of normal connections. In practice, it is very difficult to evaluate these two measures, since it is usually infeasible to have global knowledge of all attacks. Since detection rate and false alarm rate are often in contrast, evaluation of IDSs is also performed using ROC (Receiver Operating Characteristics) analysis [183]. ROC curve represents a trade-off between detection rate and false alarm rate as illustrated in Figure 2-5. The closer the ROC is to the left upper corner of the graph (point that corresponds to 0% false alarm and 100% detection rate), the more effective the IDS is.

Table 2-1. Evaluations of intrusions (attacks)

		Predicted connection label	
		Normal	Intrusions (Attacks)
Actual connection label	Normal connections	True Negative (TN)	False Alarm (FP)
	Intrusions (Attacks)	False Negative (FN)	Correctly detected intrusions – True Positive (TP)

- *Time Performance.* The time performance of an intrusion-detection system corresponds to the total time that the IDS needs to detect an intrusion. This time includes the *processing time* and the *propagation time*. The *processing time* depends upon the processing speed of the IDS, which is the rate at which the IDS processes audit events. If this rate is not sufficiently high, then the real time processing of security events may not be feasible. The *propagation time* is the time needed for processed information to propagate to the security analyst. Both times need to be as short as possible in order to allow the security analyst sufficient time to react to an attack before much damage has been done, as well as to stop an attacker from modifying audit information or altering the IDS itself.

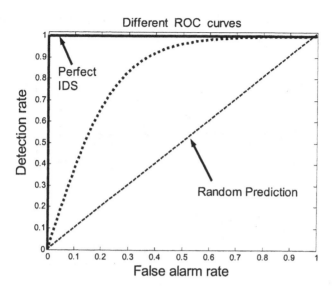

Figure 2-5. ROC Curves for different intrusion detection techniques

- *Fault tolerance.* An IDS should itself be dependable, robust and resistant to attacks, and should be able to recover quickly from successful attacks and to continue providing a secure service. This is especially true in the case of very large distributed DoS attacks, buffer overflow attacks and various deliberate attacks that can shut down the computer system and thus IDS too. This characteristic is very important for the proper functioning of IDSs, since most commercial IDSs run on operating systems and networks that are vulnerable to different types of attacks. In addition, IDS should also be resistant to scenarios when an adversary can cause the IDS to generate a large number of false or misleading alarms. Such alarms may easily have a negative impact on the availability of the system, and the IDS should be able to quickly overcome these obstacles.

3.2   Taxonomy of Intrusion Detection Systems (IDSs)

Several classifications of intrusion detection methods have been proposed in the past [4, 13, 55, 97, 110, 114, 136], but there is still no universally accepted taxonomy. In this chapter, we present a taxonomy that is based on the synthesis of a number of existing ones [13, 55]. We use five criteria to classify IDSs, as summarized in Figure 2-6.

The first criterion is *information (data) source*, which distinguishes IDSs based on the system that is monitored, i.e. source of input information (see Figure 2-4). The source information can be (i) audit trails (e.g. system logs) on a host, (ii) network connections/packets, (iii) application logs, (iv) wireless network traffic or (v) intrusion-detection and/or sensor alerts produced by other intrusion-detection systems.

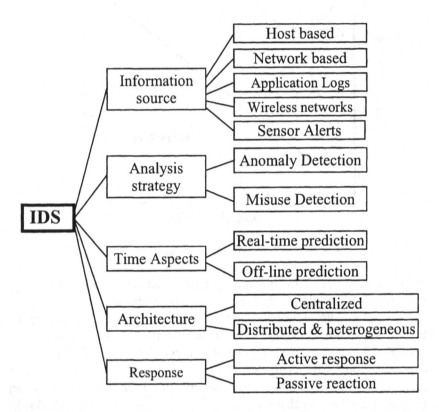

Figure 2-6. Taxonomy of intrusion detection systems according to proposed six criteria

The *analysis strategy* describes the characteristics of the detector (intrusion detection engine from Figure 2-4). When the IDS looks for events or sets of events that match a predefined pattern of a known attack, this analysis strategy is called misuse detection. When the IDS identifies intrusions as unusual behavior that differs from the normal behavior of the monitored system, this analysis strategy is called anomaly detection.

Time aspects are used to categorize the IDSs into on-line IDSs that detect intrusions in real time and off-line IDSs that usually first store the monitored data and then analyze it in batch mode for signs of intrusion.

The *architecture* of IDSs is used to differentiate between centralized IDSs that analyze the data collected only from a single monitored system and distributed IDSs that collect information from multiple monitored systems in order to investigate global, distributed and coordinated attacks.

Detection response describes the reaction of the IDS to an attack (intrusion). If the IDS reacts to the attack by taking corrective action (e.g. closing holes) or pro-active action (e.g. logging out possible attackers, closing down services), the response is called active. If the IDS only generates alarms (including paging security analysts) and does not take any actions, the response is called passive.

4. INFORMATION SOURCE

Early intrusion detection systems were largely host-based, since mainframe computers were common and all users were local to the system. In such an environment, intrusion-detection was focused only on insider threats, since interaction with outside world was quite rare. The audit information collected at the mainframe was analyzed either locally [137] or on a separate machine [204] and security-suspicious events were reported.

However, with the growth of computer networks, there has been an increasing focus on IDSs for the networked environment. Initial attempts of intrusion detection in a networked environment were focused on enabling communication among host-based intrusion-detection systems [93] and then exchanging information at several levels, either through a raw audit trail over the network [80, 204], or issuing alarms generated by local analysis [205].

In the late nineties, the intrusion detection research community debated the superiority of network-based vs. host-based approaches. However, today many systems attempt to provide an integrated tool by incorporating both variants. These IDSs are usually called hybrid IDSs. For example, in the distributed intrusion detection system (DIDS) developed by Snapp et al [205], Haystack [80, 204] is used on each host to detect local attacks, while network security monitor (NSM) [81] is employed to monitor the network. Both systems, Haystack and NSM, send information to the DIDS Director, where the final analysis is performed.

Network/host based IDSs typically analyze past network traffic and host OS activity, but they are unable to detect unauthorized use of specific applications. This caused the emergence of application-based IDSs that focus on monitoring interactions between a user and specific applications.

More recently, increasing popularity of wireless networks has caused intrusion detection researchers to focus on detecting attacks in wireless environment. Wireless network are highly sensitive and extremely insecure, as they are vulnerable to easy eavesdropping and jamming thus requiring additional security policies as well as specific intrusion detection techniques.

4.1   Host-based IDSs

Host based intrusion detection systems (IDSs) analyze users' activities and behavior on a given machine. Host-based IDSs have an advantage that they are able to work with high quality data that is typically very informative. However, depending upon the processing performed, host-based IDSs can significantly impact the performance of the machine they are running on. In addition, audit sources used in host-based intrusion analysis, can be easily modified by a successful attack, which represents another limitation of host-based IDSs. In order to alleviate these drawbacks, host-based IDSs have to process the audit trail sufficiently fast to be able to raise alarms before an attacker has an opportunity to observe and/or modify the audit trail or the intrusion-detection system itself.

There are several types of information that are typically used in host-based IDSs, e.g. (i) system commands, (ii) system accounting, (iii) syslog and (iv) security audit information.

4.1.1   System commands

System commands are a useful source of information that can be employed by host based IDSs for detecting malicious users [51, 116, 145, 193]. By analyzing system commands that users invoke in their sessions, it is possible to build user profiles, which describe users' characteristics and common behavior. Examples of such logged system commands in Unix are `ps, pstat, vmstat, getrlimit`. Information about different events provided by these commands can be very precise and informative. Since the audit information is collected as unstructured data, and has to be preprocessed before analysis.

4.1.2   System accounting

System accounting is present in both Windows and Unix operating systems. Although the interest for system accounting in Windows environment is increasing, there have not been many intrusion detection approaches that used this type of data for intrusion analysis. On the other hand, system accounting is commonly used in the Unix environment to collect information on system behavior, such as consumption of shared resources (e.g. processor time, memory, disk) by the users of the system. Data generated by system accounting can serve as a valuable and convenient source of information for IDSs [63].

There are two typical Unix accounting logs that are used for easy extraction of system behavioral information, without extensive kernel modifications often required for detailed auditing, namely: process accounting and login accounting. The standard file for storing the process accounting information is pacct or acct, while the standard file for the login accounting information is wtmp. Process accounting keeps track of information about a process at the time of process completion (e.g. user and group IDs of those that use the process, beginning and elapsed times of the process, CPU time for the process, amount of memory used). The login accounting (wtmp) system records information about users' login and logout from the system. When users successfully log in and log out or unsuccessfully attempt to login, the Unix kernel appends utmp structures to the log file.

Use of system accounting as a source of information for IDSs has several advantages. First, all Unix systems have the same format of the accounting records. Second, the time needed to store system accounting records is generally small, since information is compressed. Finally, system accounting is quite common in the modern operating systems, and it is easy to setup and use. However, using system accounting also has a few drawbacks that limit their use in security applications. First, in order to perform real time analysis of system accounting data, all historical profiles have to be compared to each currently active profile, which can be computationally intensive. This generally impacts the system load and therefore slows down potential statistical data analysis. Second, accounting is either enabled for all users or not enabled at all, and cannot be selectively activated only for particular individuals of interest. Third, system accounting logs require a large amount of disk storage, and hence, they must be periodically removed. Fourth, the accounting structures limit the length of recorded command name to only a fixed number of characters (typically eight), thus losing important information (e.g. common arguments are not recorded). Finally, the accounting data is recorded only when the application terminates, so continuously running executables such as system daemons (e.g. sendmail) are never audited (these applications have to be audited using syslogs). In such cases, it is only possible to perform off-line intrusion analysis.

Due to these drawbacks of system accounting, its use is not very common. Nevertheless, there are several systems that employ this information for intrusion detection [54, 63]. For example, the statistical and neural network modules in Hyperview [54] use system accounting only as additional information to security audit, but not as a substitute for it, while anomaly-based detection techniques in Eschrich's thesis [63] use accounting logs to identify imposters. Imposters are special class of intruders who are valid users in a system but gain illegal access to the account of other users.

4.1.3   System log information

System log data contains information that is not available at the network level, such as when users log in, when they send email, who they send email to, which ftp logs commands are issued, and which files are transferred. Capturing and collecting system log file information in a readable format is typically performed by the syslog daemon.

One of the major drawbacks of using syslog information for intrusion detection is that syslog information is not very secure, since several syslog daemons exhibit buffer overflow exploitation [33]. On the other hand, due to straightforward use of syslog, this information is widely employed by numerous network services and applications, such as `login`, `sendmail`, `nfs`, `http`, as well as security-related tools such as sudo, klaxon, or TCP wrappers [55]. For example, Swatch [78] and TkLogger [85] perform regular expression matching against system log files, search for certain patterns and take appropriate actions when they are found. These tools are especially useful for identifying things that may indicate very specific problems.

4.1.4   Security audit processing

The *security audit trails* represent records that contain all potentially important activities related to the security of the system. Since these activities are usually logged to a file in chronologically sorted order, their analysis could allow easier investigation of sequential intrusive patterns. One of the most popular security audit trails is BSM (Basic Security Module), auditing facility in Solaris operating system form Sun Microsystems Inc [219]. BSM monitors security related events and records the *"crossing of instructions executed by the processor in the user space and instructions executed in the kernel"* [219].

In general, the security audit trail can provide information about full system call traces, which includes detailed user and group identification, the parameters of system call execution, memory allocation, context switches, internal semaphores, and successive file reads that typically do not appear in the regular audit trail. In addition, advantages of using security audit data include strong user authentication, easier audit system configuration, and fine-grain parameterization of collected information [55]. On the other hand, drawbacks of using security audit trails include complex setup, intensive resource requirement and possible vulnerability to DoS attack due to filling audit file system [55].

Several research groups [77, 155, 180, 217] have been actively using security audit trails mainly for host-based intrusion detection systems. The focus of their research has been mainly to define what information the security audit trail should contain in order to increase the IDS prediction performance as well as to establish an acceptable common format for audit trail records.

4.2 Network-based information sources

With rapidly growing popularity of the Internet, there have been an increasing number of attacks aimed at the network itself (e.g. spoofing, TCP hijacking, port scanning, ping of death) that cannot be (at least not easily) detected by examining the host audit trail alone. These reasons have led to the development of specific tools that sniff network packets [161, 175, 224] in real time and facilitate searching for network attacks. In addition, by analyzing the payload of the packet, a number of typical attacks against servers can also be detected.

There are several advantages of using network based IDSs over host-based IDSs. First, network-based IDSs can be installed such that they do not have effect on existing computer systems or infrastructures. Second, they are usually more resistant than host-based IDSs, since they do not reside on the hosts that may be the targets of certain attacks. Third, the majority of network-based IDSs typically do not depend on the operating system that is used and can extract useful information at a network level (e.g. packet fragmentation). Finally, they can be installed at strategic points in a network (e.g. routers, borders) where they can be used to watch all traffic passing through these ports and therefore used to discover network attacks. However, their major drawbacks are their weak scalability, high possibility for dropping packets in fast networks under heavy load, and inability to perform intrusion detection when data is encrypted.

Network based intrusion detection systems analyze various kinds of information that are obtained by monitoring network infrastructures. Typical sources of such information are network connections/packets collected by network sniffers and management information between network devices collected due to use of Simple Network Management Protocol (SNMP).

4.2.1 Network connections and network packets

Network packet sniffers are commonly used for collecting information about events that occur on a network. Sniffers capture copies of network packets directly from the network interface and provide administrators with detailed information about the IP addresses of senders and receivers, the number of transferred packets/ bytes and other low-level information about those packets. Certain sniffers also provide protocol-level analysis of data flowing through network, packet by packet. This information is typically beneficial for administrators to diagnose and fix network related problems.

Some organizations also collect information about network events at the firewalls. There are several categories of firewalls (packet filters, circuit level gateways, application level gateways and stateful multilayer inspection firewalls [21, 231]) that all collect firewall logs and use them to detect suspicious activity and alert human analysts.

Use of network connections/packets as source of intrusion detection data has several advantages:

- There are numerous network-specific attacks (e.g. large distributed denial-of-service attacks) that cannot be detected using audit information on the host but only using information about network infrastructure.
- TCP/IP standardization of network traffic facilitates collecting, formatting and analyzing information from heterogeneous audit trail formats that come from different portions of large and complex networks.
- Using the payload information (content of the packets) can be very informative in detection of attacks against hosts.

However, using network connections/packets also has several drawbacks:

- When an intrusion has been detected, it is not straightforward to identify an attacker, since there is no direct association between network connections/packets and the identity of the user who actually performed the attack.
- If the packets are encrypted, it is practically impossible to analyze the payload of the packets, as important information may be hidden from network sniffers. In addition, if the attack signatures are not sufficiently comprehensive, it is possible to evade detection by making the contents of the packet more complex [184].

Packet sniffers can be placed at the gateways between the protected system and the outside world, or on switches within the network. Which of these is the most appropriate location, it is not always clear. Placing sniffers on switches gives better audit information but at a higher cost, due to a larger number of switches in the network. Nevertheless, networks that use switches are commonly used since they are less vulnerable to sniffer attacks [42, 184].

Network packets are the source of information used by most of the recent commercial products [8, 47, 89, 159, 160, 210, 222, 238], as well as by many projects in the research community [61, 120, 142, 174, 188, 192, 216]. Other network-based systems such as Bro [174] have been developed as network data-acquisition tools, but not as tools to directly support intrusion-detection task.

4.2.2 Simple Network Management Protocol (SNMP) information

The Simple Network Management Protocol (SNMP) is the Internet standard operations and maintenance protocol that facilitates the exchange of management information between network devices. SNMP was designed to help network administrators to manage network performance, to find and solve network problems, and to minimize resources necessary for supporting network management.

An SNMP-managed network typically consists of three components: managed devices, agents, and one or more network management systems (NMSs). A managed device corresponds to any SNMP-compliant equipment that resides on a managed network, collects management information and sends this information to NMSs using SNMP. Examples of managed devices include routers, switches, hubs, workstations, printers, etc. An agent is typically a *"network-management software"* module that resides on a managed device. The agent gathers management information from managed devices and converts that information into a format that can be passed over the network using SNMP. Finally, an NMS monitors and controls managed devices, issues requests and returns responses from devices. Information collected from NMSs can serve as a useful audit source.

One of the earliest projects that used SNMPv1 Management Information Base (MIB) for Ethernet and TCP/IP was SECURENET [212]. The SECURENET project showed that the counters maintained in the SNMPv1 MIBs could be potentially interesting as an audit source for anomaly detection techniques. SNMPv2 and SNMPv3 have also been used for security and intrusion detection [100], but the failure of SNMPv2 has lowered the interest of the intrusion-detection community in these information sources.

4.3 Application log files

Application based IDSs monitor only specific applications such as database management systems, content management systems, accounting systems, etc. An application based IDS has access to types of information that network based or host based IDSs do not have. For example, by analyzing application log files, application based IDSs can detect many types of computer attacks, suspicious activities that can be difficult to detect using host based or network based IDSs. In addition, they can be used to trace down unauthorized activities from individual users or to analyze encrypted data by employing application-based encryption/decryption services [20]. As application servers have recently become increasingly popular, application log files are used more often as an information source for intrusion detection.

In general, there are two approaches to implement application based IDSs [20]. In the first approach, IDS monitors an application and analyzes its audit log files. This post analysis allows suspicious activities in the application to be observed easily, but only after they happen. In a second, more complex approach, application based IDS is integrated into the application itself. This integration allows IDS to analyze the data at the same time the application interprets it, to detect attacks in real-time making it possible to take an immediate action.

The operation of an application based IDS in general is not impacted by the total amount of network traffic unless most of the traffic is due to the application (e.g., at a large commercial vendor sites such as Amazon.com, application-based IDSs highly depend on the network traffic).

In general, application based IDSs offer several advantages:

– *Unencrypted information*. Unlike the analyzed data at the network level, the data at the application level is not encrypted, thus giving more information for intrusion analysis to application based IDSs.
– *Prediction performance*. Since an application based IDS focuses on monitoring operations specific to the application, it is easier to define the normal and the anomalous behavior. There are certain types of information (e.g. query logs from database applications) that are available only to application based IDSs but not visible to the operating system. As a result, application based IDSs can detect intrusions that are not detectable by host-based IDSs. This results in a lower false alarm rate, as well as in higher detection rate.
– *Complete sessions*. Unlike network monitoring where network connection may be fragmented during recording, the application typically records complete transaction, and there is no inconsistency involved in the reconstruction of session records.
– *Prevention*. When an application based IDS is embedded in the application module itself, it can stop the intruder from proceeding with the attack by denying malicious operations.

However, application based IDSs have also certain limitations:

– *Performance penalty*. When an application based IDS is not a part of an application itself, it usually needs to be installed on the same host as the application. In such scenario, this installation could result in a decrease in the system performance.
– *Larger system overhead*. Since the application based IDSs have to be installed on every individual host machine, and the organization may have numerous hosts, there is a larger administration overhead.
– *Non-detectable attacks below the application layer*. Although analyzing the data at the application level allows application-based IDSs access to

encrypted information, they are not able to detect attacks that target protocols below the application layer.
- *Specific development.* Every application based IDS has to be developed for a specific application, since there is no general application-based IDS.

4.4 Wireless networks

Wireless network systems have become increasingly popular recently, mainly due to the ease of their installation and maintenance. However, this convenience comes at a price, since wireless networks pose a serious security risk. There are numerous, potentially devastating threats that have emerged in wireless networks that are more difficult to detect due to the following reasons [3, 88, 126]:
- Physical layer in wireless networks is essentially a broadcast medium and therefore less secure than in fixed computer networks. For example, an attacker that enters the wireless network, bypasses existing security mechanisms and can easily sniff sensitive and confidential information. In addition, the attacker also has access to all the ports that are regularly available only to the people within the network. In wired networks, attempts to access these ports from outside world through Internet are stopped at the firewalls. Finally, the attacker can also excessively load network resources thus causing denial of service to regular users.
- There are no specific traffic concentration points (e.g. routers) where packets can be monitored, so each mobile node needs to run an intrusion detection system.
- Separation between normal and anomalous traffic is often not clear in wireless ad-hoc networks, since the difference between compromised or false node and the node that is temporarily out of synchronization due to volatile physical movement can be hard to observe.

There are currently only a few commercial wireless IDS solutions [3, 88] in the market that try to detect a wide range of known attacks as well as identify abnormal network activities and policy violations for wireless networks. For Linux operating system, Lin et al have developed a homegrown wireless IDS [126] along with a freely available software. Other open source solutions include Snort-Wireless [208] and WIDZ [239].

4.5 Alerts from intrusion detection systems

Due to increase in a traffic volume, current commercial IDSs usually tend to produce a very large number of alarms [185]. These alarms are raised both for actual intrusions (attacks), but very often for regular behavior, thus increasing false alarm rate and overwhelming security administrator. In addition, a large distributed DoS or scanning attack may trigger multiple alarms since many network connections are involved in such attacks. This further increases the number of alarms that security analysts have to analyze. In order to decrease this number, the threshold for detecting intrusions is raised, but this can reduce the overall detection rate.

Due to these reasons, a number of researchers have attempted to develop a new generation of intrusion-detection systems that correlate information from several, "lower-level" IDSs to identify intrusions [50, 101, 168, 177, 186, 225, 229]. These IDSs employ different correlation and data-mining techniques in order to reduce both false alarm rate and the burden on the security analyst. In addition, some of these IDSs can typically provide security analysts with a summarized view of detected anomalous activities. Examples of such IDSs include distributed intrusion detection system (DIDS) [217] that correlates user identification by using information from sensors and GrIDS [225] that measures the traffic on hosts and network links and then correlates information from sensors on multiple networks. In general, there are three basic groups of alert correlation methods:

-   *Methods based on similarities between alert attributes (features)* [101, 229] compare the degree to which alerts have similar features (e.g. source IP address, destination IP address, ports), and then correlate alerts with a high degree of feature similarity.
-   *Correlation methods based on known attack scenarios* [50, 186, 225] utilize the fact that intrusions often require several actions to take place in order to succeed (e.g. to carry out a DoS attack on the DNS server, the attacker could first do an nslookup, ping, and scan port 139, and then a winnuke (sends out-of-Band data to an IP address of a windows machine)). Every attack scenario has corresponding steps required for the success of the attack. Low-level alerts from IDS(s) are compared against the predefined attack scenario before the alerts can be correlated. Major drawbacks of this method are (i) it requires that human users specify the attack scenarios and (ii) it is limited to detection of known attacks.
-   *Correlation methods based on preconditions and consequences of individual attacks* [168] work at a higher level then correlation based on feature similarities, but at a lower level then correlation based on known scenarios. Preconditions are defined as conditions that must exist for the attack to occur, and the consequences of the attack are defined as conditions that may exist after a specific attack has occurred.

5. ANALYSIS STRATEGY: MISUSE DETECTION VS. ANOMALY DETECTION

There are two primary approaches for analyzing events to detect attacks; namely misuse detection and anomaly detection. Misuse detection is based on extensive knowledge of known attacks and system vulnerabilities provided by human experts. The misuse detection approaches look for hackers that attempt to perform these attacks and/or to exploit known vulnerabilities. Although the misuse detection can be very accurate in detecting known attacks, misuse detection approaches cannot detect unknown and emerging cyber threats.

Anomaly detection, on the other hand, is based on the analysis of profiles that represent normal behavior of users, hosts, or network connections. Anomaly detectors characterize normal "legitimate" computer activity using different techniques and then use a variety of measures to detect deviations from defined normal behavior as potential anomaly. The major benefit of anomaly detection algorithms is their ability to potentially recognize unforeseen attacks. However, the major limitation is potentially high false alarm rate. Note that deviations detected by anomaly detection algorithms may not necessarily represent actual attacks, as they may be new or unusual, but still legitimate, network behavior.

Many contemporary IDSs integrate both approaches to benefit from their respective advantages [164, 167, 200, 207].

5.1 Misuse Detection

Misuse detection is the most common approach used in the current generation of commercial intrusion detection systems (IDSs). The misuse detection approaches can be classified into the following four main categories: (i) signature-based methods, (ii) rule-based techniques, (iii) methods based on state-transition analysis, and (iv) data mining based techniques.

5.1.1 Signature-based techniques

Signature-based IDSs operate analogously to virus scanners, i.e. by searching a database of signatures for a known identity – or signature – for each specific intrusion event. In signature-based IDSs, monitored events are matched against a database of attack signatures to detect intrusions. Signature-based IDSs are unable to detect unknown and emerging attacks since signature database has to be manually revised for each new type of intrusion that is discovered. In addition, once a new attack is discovered and its signature is developed, often there is a substantial latency in its deployment across networks [130]. The most well known signature-based IDSs include SNORT [207], Network Flight Recorder [167], NetRanger [47], RealSecure [89], Computer Misuse Detection System (CMDS™) [230], NetProwler [14], Haystack [204] and MuSig (Misuse Signatures) [127].

SNORT [207] is a widely used open source signature-based network IDS, which is used for performing real-time traffic logging and analysis over IP networks. Currently, SNORT has an extensive database of over a thousand attack signatures. There are three main modes in which SNORT can be configured; namely sniffer, packet logger, and network IDS. In the sniffer mode, SNORT monitors the network packets and continuously displays them on the console. Packet logger mode is used to store (log) the packets to the disk. In the network intrusion detection mode, the system analyzes network traffic for matches against a database of user defined rules and performs one of five corresponding actions:
- *Alert* – raise an alarm using the selected alert method and then log the packet;
- *Log* – log the analyzed packet;
- *Pass* – ignore the analyzed packet;
- *Activate* – generate an alert and then turn on another *dynamic* rule;
- *Dynamic* – stay inactive until turned on by an *activate* rule.

Network Flight Recorder (NFR) is a network-based IDS that also creates alerts based on rules. These rules, called "backends" in NFR terminology, contain filters (hard-coded signatures) written to trigger in response to different computer attacks. NFR includes a complete programming language, called N, designed for packet analysis and creating filters.

NetRanger [47], an IDS developed at Cisco, was introduced to intrusion detection community in November 1998. Over the years NetRanger grew into a more complex Cisco IDS [46] that provides complete intrusion protection and is a component of a SAFE BluePrint Cisco security system. NetRanger is composed of three major components: sensors, director and post office. Sensors are network appliances that analyze the network traffic using a rule-based engine, which distills large volumes of network traffic into meaningful security events, which are then forwarded to a Director. Directors are responsible for the management of security across a distributed network of sensors and can be structured hierarchically to manage large networks. Finally, the post office provides communication between NetRanger services and hosts.

RealSecure, is an earlier version of the Proventia system developed at Internet Security Systems [182]. While Real Secure was principally a signature-based IDS composed of three modules: network engines, system agents, and managers, Proventia provides a more complete security solution including: inspection firewall, antivirus protection, intrusion detection and prevention, anti-spam filters and application protection.

CMDS [230] was a predecessor of Intrusion SecureHost [90], which represents a host-based IDS that monitors and protects applications at the kernel level of operating system by building a profile of the application's normal behavior based on the *"code paths of a running program"*. NetProwler [14] is another host basd IDS that is based on "Stateful Dynamic Signature Inspection" virtual processor proposed by Anxent, which was acquired by Symantec recently. Today, NetProwler is a part of Symantec Intruder Alert IDS [220]. NetProwler collects various types of information "sniffed" from the network and then integrates them into more complex events that are matched against predefined signatures in real time. In addition, the system can install novel signatures without stopping the intrusion detection process.

The Haystack prototype [204] was one of the first signature based IDSs developed for the task of intrusion detection in a multi-user Air Force computer system. Haystack employs both misuse detection and anomaly detection strategy for detecting intrusions. The misuse detection module identifies intrusions according to behavioral constraints (rules) imposed by official security policies. On the other hand, the anomaly detection module is based on building profiles of users' behavior in the past and on constructing generic user group models that describe generic acceptable behavior for a particular group of users.

Adaptable real-time misuse detection system (ARMD) [127], developed at George Mason University, provides a high-level language for abstract misuse signatures, called MuSigs, and a mechanism to translate MuSigs into a monitoring program. With the notion of abstract events, the high-level language specifies a MuSig as a pattern over a sequence of abstract events, which is described as conditions that the abstract event attributes must satisfy. In addition, on the basis of MuSigs, the available audit trail, and the strategy costs, ARMD uses a strategy generator to automatically generate monitoring strategies to govern the misuse detection process.

Kumar and Spafford proposed a generalized framework for matching intrusion signatures based on Colored Petri Nets [113]. In this approach, every signature of an attack is represented as a Petri net, and start states and final state are used to perform signature matching.

5.1.2 Rule-based systems

Rule-based systems use a set of "if-then" implication rules to characterize computer attacks. At the early stage of intrusion detection era, rule based languages represented one of the regular methods for describing the expert's knowledge that is collected about numerous attacks and vulnerabilities. In rule-based IDSs, security events are usually monitored and then converted into the facts and rules that are later used by an inference engine to draw conclusions. Examples of such rule-based IDSs include Shadow [170], IDES [56, 95, 138, 139], NIDX [19], ComputerWatch [58], P-BEST [129], ISOA [241, 242] and AutoGuard that uses case-based reasoning [66, 67].

IDES [138] is a rule-based expert system trained to detect known intrusion scenarios, known system vulnerabilities, and site-specific security policies. IDES can also detect (i) outside attacks from unauthorized users; (ii) internal attacks from authorized users who masquerade as other users and (iii) attacks from authorized users who abuse their privileges by avoiding access controls. NIDX [19] extends the IDES model by including system dependent knowledge such as a description of file systems, and rules regarding system policies. It integrates (i) information obtained from the target computer system, (ii) user profiles built through history and (iii) intrusion detection heuristics into rules that are used to detect violations from the audit trail on the target system.

The ComputerWatch [58] data reduction tool was developed as an expert system IDS by the Secure Systems Department at AT&T. Computer Watch employs the host audit trail data to summarize system security activities and provides mechanisms for further investigation of suspicious security events by security analysts. The tool checks users' actions according to a set of rules that describe proper usage policy, and flags any suspicious action that does not match the acceptable patterns.

Production Based Expert System Toolset (P-BEST) [129] is a rule-based, forward-chaining expert system developed at SRI, and used in the EMERALD IDS [179]. The system was first deployed in the MIDAS ID system at the National Computer Security Center, and then used as the rule-based inference engine of NIDES, which is an IDES successor. P-BEST is a programmable expert system shell that consists of the definition of several fact types, and a set of inference rules on these facts. Inference rules are composed of two parts. The first part is a guard, which tests the existence of facts satisfying logical expressions; and the second part is composed of actions upon the fact base (adding, removing, modifying facts) and of calls to external functions.

ISOA (Information Security Officer's Assistant) [241, 242] is a real time IDS for monitoring security relevant behavior in computer networks. ISOA serves as the central point for real-time collection and analysis of audit information. It has two components; i.e. statistical analysis module and an expert system. These components cooperate in the automated analysis of various "concern levels". If a recognized set of indicators are matched, concern levels increase and the IDS starts to analyze the growing classes of audit events in more details to flag suspicious users or hosts.

5.1.3   State transition analysis

Intrusion detection using state transition analysis requires the construction of a finite state machine, in which states correspond to different IDS states, and transitions characterize certain events that cause IDS states to change. IDS states correspond to different states of the network protocol stacks or to the integrity and validity of current running processes or certain files. Every time when the automation reaches a state that is flagged as a security threat, the intrusion is reported as a sign of malicious attacker activity. This is the technique first proposed in USTAT (Unix State Transition Analysis Tool) [86, 178] and later in NetSTAT (Network-based State Transition Analysis Tool) [232].

USTAT, developed at UC Santa Barbara, is a real-time state transition analysis tool developed for the Unix system and based on STAT (State Transition Analysis Tool) [178]. STAT introduced the idea of representing computer attacks with high level descriptions and providing an expert system model to detect compromises. In STAT, attack scenarios are represented as states that describe security status of the system, and intrusions are detected by modeling the transition between states. The computer initially exists in a secure state, but as a result of a number of intrusions it may end up in a compromised target state. USTAT uses the C2 security audit trail data produced by the computer as the source of information about the system's state transitions. It records only those critical actions that have visible effect on the system state and must happen in order to successfully complete the penetration.

NetSTAT is a real-time network-based IDS that employs state transition analysis techniques from the STAT approach, for detecting intrusions that occur in a networked environment. The networked environment is represented by hypergraphs, where network interfaces are modeled as nodes, and hosts are modeled as edges of the hypergraph. By using state transition analysis for the states of network attacks, it is possible to automatically determine which network events have to be monitored in order to support intrusion analysis.

5.1.4   Data mining based techniques

In data mining methods for misuse detection, each instance in a data set is labeled as 'normal' or 'intrusive' and a learning algorithm is trained over the labeled data. These techniques are able to automatically retrain intrusion detection models on different input data that include new types of attacks, as long as they have been labeled appropriately. Research in misuse detection has focused mainly on classification of network intrusions using various standard data mining algorithms [16, 74, 121, 140, 202], rare class predictive models [40, 98, 99], cost sensitive modeling [99] and association rules [16, 122, 143]. Unlike signature-based intrusion detection systems, models of misuse are created automatically, and can be more sophisticated and precise than manually created signatures. The advantage of data mining based misuse detection techniques over signature-based intrusion detection systems is their high degree of accuracy in detecting known attacks and their variations.

MADAM ID [120, 122] at Columbia University was one of the first project that applied data mining techniques to the intrusion detection problem. Association rules and frequent episodes were extracted from network connection records to obtain additional features for data mining algorithms. Three groups of features are constructed, namely: content-based features that describe intrinsic characteristics of a network connection (e.g. number of packets, acknowledgments, data bytes from source to destination), time-based traffic features that compute the number of connections in some recent time interval (e.g. last few seconds) and connection based features that compute the number of connections from a specific source to a specific destination in the last N connections (e.g. $N =$ 1000). In addition to the standard features that were available directly from the network traffic (e.g. duration, start time, service), these constructed features were also used by the RIPPER algorithm to learn intrusion detection rules from DARPA 1998 data set [132, 133].

Other classification algorithms for the intrusion detection problem include decision trees [24, 202], modified nearest neighbor algorithms [246], fuzzy association rules [26, 72, 140], neural networks [30, 51, 131, 247], naïve Bayes classifiers [196], genetic algorithms [26, 145], genetic programming [158], support vector machines [65, 156], and adaptive regression splines [157]. Most of these approaches attempt to directly apply specified standard techniques to some of publicly available intrusion detection data sets [132, 133], assuming that the labels for normal and intrusive behavior are already known.

Computer intrusions, however, are much rarer than normal behavior, and in such scenarios standard classification algorithms do not perform well. Thus, some researchers have developed specially designed algorithms for handling rare classes and applied them to the problem of intrusion detection [40, 98, 99].

Finally, association patterns, often expressed in the form of frequent itemsets or association rules, have also been found to be valuable for analyzing network traffic data [16, 121, 143]. In [121], association patterns generated at different times were used to study significant changes in the network traffic characteristics at different periods of time, while in [16, 121, 143] they were used to construct a profile of the normal network traffic behavior for anomaly detection systems.

5.2   Anomaly Detection

Increase in the number of computer attacks, in their severity and complexity has raised substantial interest in anomaly detection algorithms due to their potential for recognizing unforeseen and emerging cyber activities. There are many anomaly detection algorithms proposed in the literature that differ according to the information used for analysis and according to techniques that are employed to detect deviations from normal behavior. In this section, we provide classification of anomaly detection techniques based on employed techniques into the following five groups: (i) statistical methods; (ii) rule based methods; (iii) distance based methods (iv) profiling methods and (v) model based approaches. Although anomaly detection algorithms are quite diverse in nature, and thus may fit into more than one proposed category, our classification attempts to find the most suitable category for all described anomaly detection algorithms.

5.2.1   Statistical methods

Statistical methods monitor the user or system behavior by measuring certain variables over time (e.g. login and logout time of each session). The basic models keep averages of these variables and detect whether thresholds are exceeded based on the standard deviation of the variable. More advanced statistical models also compare profiles of long-term and short-term user activities. These statistical models are used in host-based IDSs, network-based IDSs, as well as in application-based IDSs for detecting malicious viruses. Some of the first proposed anomaly detection algorithms were integrated in well known IDSs such as IDES [56, 95, 138, 139], NIDES [6], EMERALD [164, 179] and SPADE [214].

IDES [138], whose misuse detection module is explained in section 4.1.2., also has an anomaly detection module. This module characterizes normal user activity using an audit data and detects deviations from described normal user behavior. Each new audit record is processed as it enters the system, and verified against the known profile. To further distinguish unusual but authorized behavior, the prototype was extended to handle two sets of profiles for monitored subjects depending on whether the activity took place on "normal" or "suspicious" days. The security analyst defines whether working days are "normal" or not. The NIDES system [6] extends IDES by integrating results from misuse detection component with the results produced by the anomaly detection module. NIDES monitors ports and addresses and builds a statistical model of long term behavior over a period of hours or days, which is assumed to contain few or no attacks. If short-term behavior (seconds, or a few packets) differs significantly from normal, then an alarm is raised.

EMERALD [164, 179] has statistical profile-based anomaly detection module that tracks subject activity through one of four types of statistical variables: categorical, continuous, traffic intensity (e.g., volume over time), and event distribution (e.g., a meta-measure of other measures). The eBayes system [228] is a recently developed module that extends earlier anomaly detection component from the EMERALD system [164, 179] by encoding probabilistic models of normal, attack, and anomalous behavior modes with hypotheses. The eBayes system first collects basic variables of network sessions as well as derives new ones (e.g. maximum number of open connections to any unique host), and then applies probabilistic Bayesian inference to them in order to obtain a belief for the session over the states of hypotheses. For example, the session hypotheses in the eBayes TCP tree may correspond to both normal traffic modes (MAIL, FTP, etc.) and to attack scenario modes PORTSWEEP, SYNFLOOD, etc.). The eBayes builds a table of conditional probabilities for all the hypotheses and variables, which is adjusted every time the current observation is made. The eBayes has an option of detecting novel attacks by dynamically generating new hypothesis, which is obtained by adding a fake state of hypothesis and a new conditional probability table row initialized by a uniform distribution.

Similarly to eBayes, many anomaly detection techniques have been proposed recently to overcome limitations of earlier statistical anomaly detection algorithms. For example, SPADE [214] is a statistical based system, that is available as a plug-in for SNORT as a plug-in, and used for automatic detecting stealthy port scans. Unlike traditional scan detectors that look for X events in Y seconds, SPADE takes a fundamentally different approach and looks at the amount of information gained by probing. It has four different methods of calculating the likelihood of packets, of which most successful method measures the direct joint probability P(dest IP, dest Port) between destination IP address and destination port. SPADE examines TCP-SYN packets and maintains the count of packets observed on (destIP, destPort) tuples. When a new packet is observed, SPADE checks the probability of observing that packet on the (dest IP, dest Port) tuple. The lower the probability of the packet, the higher the anomaly score. However, in a real life system, SPADE gives a high false alarm rate, since all unseen (dest IP, dest Port) tuples are detected as attacks regardless whether or not they correspond to actual intrusions.

Another recently proposed statistical method employs statistical traffic modeling [29] for detecting novel attacks against networks. In this approach, a network activity model is used to detect large classes of Denial of Service and scanning attacks by monitoring the network traffic volume. By applying the KolmogorovSmirnov test on the DARPA dataset [132], it was demonstrated that, for example, normal telnet connections are statistically different from the attacks that use telnet connections.

Chi-square (χ^2) statistics have also been successfully used to detect anomalies both in host-based and network based intrusion detection. For host-based IDSs, Ye [245] proposed approach where activities on a host machine are captured through a stream of events and then characterized by the event type. For each event type, the profiles of audit events from normal behavior are defined, and then used to compute χ^2 as a measure of difference between the test audit event and the normal audit event, whereas large deviations are detected as anomalies. In network based IDS, the chi-square statistic has also been used [111] to differentiate the payload distribution (distribution of characters in the content of the network packets) in normal network packets and anomalous ones.

Some researchers have used outlier detection algorithms for anomaly detection, since outliers are typically defined as data points that are very different from the rest of the data. The statistics community has studied the concept of outliers quite extensively [17]. In these techniques, the data points are modeled using a stochastic distribution, and points are determined to be outliers depending on their relationship with this model. For example, SmartSifter [244] uses a probabilistic model as a representation of underlying mechanism of data generation, and scores each data example by measuring how large the model has changed after the learning. Smart sifter extension [243] gives positive labels to higher scored data and negative to the lower scored data, and then constructs an outlier filtering rule by applying supervised learning. Eskin's approach [64] computes the likelihood of data distribution $L_t(D)$ at some specific time interval t, removes a data example at the interval t-1 and measures the likelihood of data distribution without removed data example $L_{t-1}(D)$. The probability that removed data example is an outlier is proportional to the difference between the new likelihood $L_{t-1}(D)$ and the original one $L_t(D)$. Information theoretic measures such as entropy, conditional entropy, relative conditional entropy, information gain, and information cost [123] were also proposed for anomaly detection task. These measures were used to characterize the characteristics of an audit data set by measuring their regularity, and to build appropriate anomaly detection models according to these regularity measures. The higher regularity of audit data, the better the anomaly detection module is.

Statistic based anomaly detection techniques have also been used in detecting malicious viruses through e-mail messages. For example, the MET (Malicious Email Tracking) [22] system keeps track of email attachments as they are exchanged between users through a set of collaborating email servers that forward a subset of their data to a central data warehouse and correlation server. Only attachments with a high frequency of appearance are deemed suspicious, while the email exchange patterns among users are used to create models of normal behavior. MET system contains MET server and MET clients. MET server is used to collect data on malicious activity, store them in a database, and calculate derived statistics, while MET clients analyze email attachments across all mail domains and then detect email-based attacks.

5.2.2   Distance based methods

Most statistical approaches have limitation when detecting outliers in higher dimensional spaces, since it becomes increasingly difficult and inaccurate to estimate the multidimensional distributions of the data points [2]. Distance based approaches attempt to overcome limitations of statistical outlier detection approaches and they detect outliers by computing distances among points. Several distance based outlier detection algorithms have been recently proposed for detecting anomalies in network traffic [117]. These techniques are based on computing the full dimensional distances of points from one another [107, 187] using all the available features, and on computing the densities of local neighborhoods [25, 117]. MINDS (Minnesota Intrusion Detection System) [61] uses net-flow data to extract useful set of features to be used in anomaly detection. MINDS anomaly detection module employs an outlier detection algorithm to assign an anomaly score to each network connection. A human analyst then has to look at only the most anomalous connections to determine if they are actual attacks or other interesting behavior. MINDS anomaly detection module is used at the University of Minnesota and is also incorporated into the Interrogator architecture at the ARL Center for Intrusion Monitoring and Protection (CIMP), where network data from multiple sensors are collected and analyzed by human analysts to detect intrusions and attacks. Experiments on live network traffic at the University of Minnesota and at the ARL-CIMP have shown that MINDS is able to routinely detect various suspicious behavior (e.g. policy violations), worms, as well as various scanning activities.

In addition, in several clustering based techniques (fixed-width and canopy clustering [65]), network intrusions in DARPA 1998 evaluation data sets have been detected as small clusters when compared to the large ones that corresponded to the normal behavior.

In another interesting approach [68], artificial anomalies in the network intrusion detection data are generated around the edges of the sparsely populated data regions, thus forcing the learning algorithm to discover the specific boundaries that distinguish these regions from the rest of the data.

5.2.3   Rule based systems

Rule based systems used in anomaly detection characterize normal behavior of users, networks and/or computer systems by a set of rules. Examples of rule based IDSs include ComputerWatch [58] and Wisdom & Sense [124, 125].

ComputerWatch system [58] employs a typical rule based system that summarizes "normal" security events and then detects anomalous behavior as deviations from them. The rule system creates rules to describe proper usage policy, to check users' actions according to these rules, and to flag any action that does not match the described rule patterns. Wisdom & Sense [124, 125] employs historic audit data to produce a set of rules describing normal behavior, forming the "wisdom" of the title. These rules are then fed to an expert system that evaluates recent audit data for violations of the rules, and alerts the security analyst when the rules indicate ("sense") anomalous behavior.

Recently, Valdes [227] proposed an unsupervised technique that does not require attack free training data and detects novel scans through pattern-based anomaly detection. The model assigns network connections into one of a number of modes discovered by competitive learning. The technique is applied to port patterns in TCP sessions in simulated and real network traffic.

5.2.4   Profiling methods

In profiling methods, profiles of normal behavior are built for different types of network traffic, users, programs etc., and deviations from them are considered as intrusions. Profiling methods vary greatly ranging from different data mining techniques to various heuristic-based approaches. In this section, we provide an overview of several distinguished profiling methods for anomaly detection.

ADAM (Audit Data and Mining) [16] is a hybrid anomaly detector trained on both attack-free traffic and traffic with labeled attacks. The system uses a combination of association rule mining and classification to discover attacks in *tcpdump* data. One of the advantages of ADAM is its ability to detect novel attacks, without depending on attack training data, through a novel application of the pseudo-Bayes estimator [16]. Recently reported IDDM system [1] represents an off-line IDS, where the intrusions are detected only when sufficient amounts of data are collected and analyzed. The IDDM system describes profiles of network data at different times, identifies any large deviations between these data descriptions and produces alarms in such cases.

Human immune system has gained a lot of attention among researchers in intrusion detection community, especially when analyzing attacks at the host level [73, 119, 209]. These techniques first collect data patterns representing the appropriate behavior of the service and extract a reference table containing all the known good sequences of system calls. These patterns are then used for live monitoring to check whether the sequences generated are listed in the table or not. If they are not listed, an alarm is generated. Wespi [237] also proposed a novel technique for modeling process behavior by building a table of variable length patterns, which is based on the Teiresias algorithm. Experimental results show that the variable length pattern model is significantly better than a fixed length approach, both in reducing the number of patterns to describe the normal process behavior and in achieving better detection rates. Although the immune system approach is interesting and intuitively appealing, so far it has proven to be difficult to apply [60].

The temporal sequence learning [116] has been shown successful in profiling Unix user command line data, where user shell commands are used to build user profiles for activities during an intrusion and for activities during normal use. By comparing these profiles, it is possible to detect new types of anomalous user behavior.

Association pattern analysis has been shown to be beneficial in constructing a profile of normal network traffic behavior [61, 118, 143]. For example, Manganaris [143] used association rules to characterize the normal stream of IDS alerts from a sensor and later to distinguish between false alarms and real ones. On the other hand, MINDS [61] uses association patterns to provide high-level summary of network connections that are ranked highly anomalous in the anomaly detection module. These summaries allow a human analyst to examine a large number of anomalous connections quickly and to provide templates from which signatures of novel attacks can be built for augmenting the database of signature-based intrusion detection systems.

PHAD (packet header anomaly detection) [142] monitors network packet headers and builds profiles for 33 different fields from these headers by observing attack free traffic and building contiguous clusters for the values observed for each field. The number of clusters is pre-specified and if a new value that is observed does not fit into any of the clusters, it is treated as a new cluster and the closest two clusters are merged. The number of updates, r, is maintained for each field as well as the number of observations, n. When a new packet is being tested for anomaly, the values of all fields are checked to see if they fit into the clusters formed in the training phase. If the values for some fields do not fit into any clusters, then each of them contributes to the anomaly score value of the packet proportional to the n/r ratio for the field. ALAD (application layer anomaly detection) [142] uses the same method for calculating the anomaly scores as PHAD, but it monitors TCP data and builds TCP streams when the destination port is smaller than 1024. It constructs five features from these streams as opposed to 33 fields used in PHAD.

ADMIT (Anomaly-based Data Mining for InTrusions) [201] attempts to discriminate between masqueraders and true users on computer terminals. This task is performed by augmenting conventional password authentication measures and by continuously running a terminal-resident IDS program, which monitors the terminal usage by each user, creates an appropriate profile and verifies user data against it.

Call stack information [71] was also effectively used to detect various exploits on computer systems. The anomaly detection approach, called *VtPath*, first extracts return addresses information from the call stack and generates "abstract execution paths" between two execution points in the program. These "abstract execution paths" are then compared to the "abstract execution paths" learned during normal runs of the program.

Finally, there have also been several recently proposed commercial products that use profiling based anomaly detection techniques. For example, Antura from System Detection [222] use data mining based user profiling, while Mazu Profiler form Mazu Networks [147] and Peakflow X from Arbor networks [8] use rate-based and connection profiling anomaly detection schemes.

5.2.5   Model based approaches

Many researchers have used different types of models to characterize the normal behavior of the monitored system. In the model-based approaches, anomalies are detected as deviations for the model that represents the normal behavior.

Very often, researchers have used data mining based predictive models such as replicator neural networks [79] or unsupervised support vector machines [65, 117]. Replicator four-layer feed-forward neural network (RNN) [79] have the same number of input and output nodes. During the training phase, RNNs reconstruct input variables at the output layer, and then use the reconstruction error of individual data points as a measure of outlyingness. Unsupervised support vector machines [65, 117] attempt to separate the entire training data set from the origin, i.e. to find a small region where most of the data lies and label data points in this region as a normal behavior. In the test phase they detect deviations from learned models as potential intrusions. In addition, standard neural networks (NN) were also used in intrusion detection problems to learn a normal profile. For example NNs were often used to model the normal behavior of individual users [193], to build profiles of software behavior [74] or to profile network packets and queue statistics [122].

User Intention Identification [213] is a technique developed within the SECURENET project [212]. The goal of this technique is to model the normal behavior of users using a set of high-level tasks they have to perform on the system. These tasks are then refined into actions, which in turn are related to the audit events observed on the system. The analyzer keeps a set of tasks that each user can perform. Whenever an action occurs that does not fit the task pattern, an alarm is issued. User intention identification was also successfully used in several recently proposed approaches [43, 44].

Wagner [234] proposed to statically generate a non-deterministic finite automaton (NDFA) or a non deterministic pushdown automaton (NDPDA) from the global control flow graph of the program. The approach first computes a model of expected application behavior, built statically from program source code, then monitors program execution online at run time, and finally checks its system call trace for compliance to the model.

Specification based intrusion detection techniques have been recently proposed to produce a low rate of false alarms [199], but they have not been as effective as anomaly detection in detecting novel attacks. Hence, specification based anomaly detection [199] was designed to mitigate the weaknesses of both specification based IDSs and anomaly detection techniques and complement their strengths. The approach begins with state-machine specifications of network protocols, and augments these state machines with information about statistics that need to be maintained to detect anomalies.

Finally, anomaly detection has also been used in embedded systems [146], where Markov models were employed to determine whether the states (events) in a sequential data streams, taken from a monitored process, are normal or anomalous. It computes the probabilities of transitions between events in a training set, and uses these probabilities to assess the transitions between events in a test set.

6.   TIME ASPECTS

When considering time aspects of IDSs, we distinguish two main groups: real-time (on-line) IDSs and off-line IDSs. Real-time (on-line) IDSs attempt to detect intrusions in real-time or near real-time. They operate on continuous data streams from information sources and analyze the data while the sessions are in progress (e.g. network sessions for network intrusion detection, login sessions for host based intrusion detection). Real-time IDSs should raise an alarm as soon as an attack is detected, so that action that affects the progress of the detected attack can be taken. Most commercial IDSs claim continuous processing capability [8, 147].

Off-line IDSs perform post-analysis of audit data. This method of audit data analysis is common among security analysts who often examine network behavior, as well as behavior of different attackers, in an off-line (batch) mode. Many early host-based IDSs used this timing scheme, since they used operating system audit trails that were recorded as files [77, 155].

Off-line analysis is also often performed using static tools that analyze the snapshot of the environment (e.g. host vs. network environment), look for vulnerabilities and configuration errors and assess the security level of the current environment configuration. Examples of these tools include COPS [69] and Tiger [194] for host environments, and Satan [70] and CyberCop Scanner [163, 197] for networks. Virus detectors belong to static tools too and they scan the disks searching for patterns matching known viruses. Although static tools are very popular and broadly used by system administrators, they are typically not sufficient to ensure high security [55].

Static tools can be also specifically designed for active investigation of vulnerabilities over the Internet. For example, Tripwire [106] or ATP [233] can be used to monitor a designated set of files and to detect computer intrusions that exploited older vulnerable applications. These intrusions should also be identified and reported to the system administrator as potential security holes using other tools like COPS [69] or Tiger [194].

7.   ARCHITECTURE

There are two principal architectures that are used in IDSs, namely centralized and distributed IDSs. Most IDSs employ centralized architecture and detect intrusions that occur in a single monitored system. However, there is a recent increasing trend towards distributed and coordinated attacks, where multiple machines are involved, either as attackers (e.g. distributed denial-of-service) or as victims (e.g. large volume worms). Analysis that uses data from a single site and that is often employed by many existing intrusion detection schemes is often unable to detect such attacks. To effectively combat them, there is a need for distributed IDS and cooperation among security analysts across multiple network sites.

Unlike a centralized IDS, where the analysis of data is performed on a fixed number of locations (independent of how many hosts are being monitored), in a distributed IDS the analysis of data is performed on a number of locations that is proportional to the number of hosts that are being monitored [211]. An excellent comparison of centralized and distributed IDSs, with their advantages and drawbacks, is provided in a paper by Spafford and Zamboni [211]. Despite several drawbacks of distributed IDSs, many commercial vendors have realized the need for detecting coordinated cyber attacks from distributed locations, and adapted their systems to address these challenges [9, 162].

Starting from the first proposed distributed IDS [205], the most typical architectures of distributed IDSs assume employment of intelligent agents. There are several advantages of using mobile agent based intrusion detection systems over other approaches for distributed intrusion detection [94]. First, agents are independently running entities and can be added, removed and reconfigured without altering other components, and without restarting local IDSs. Second, agents can be tested on their own before introducing them into a more complex environment. Finally, agents can exchange information to derive more complex results than any one of them may be able to obtain on their own. Although IDSs based on mobile agents are still in their infancy and fully implemented systems are still emerging, there are many agent-based distributed IDSs [39, 109]. The typical examples include DIDS [59], AAFID [211], Argus [203], IDA [10], Micael [53].

DIDS [59] and distributed autonomous-agent NID [18] use a similar architecture that consists of a central analysis server and multiple IDS agents that communicate with each other. AAFID (autonomous agents for intrusion detection) [211] has a hierarchical design with three levels. At the lowest level, agents perform host security monitoring and data analysis. The information gathered by agents is forwarded to transceivers that distribute the information either to other agents or monitors, and control and configure agents at the second level. At the highest level, each monitor collects data from transceivers and evaluates their input. Intelligent agents in [82] employ classifier algorithms and travel among collection points, referred to as data cleaners, and uncover suspicious activities. The architecture is hierarchical, with a data warehouse at the root, data cleaners at the leaves, and classifier agents in between. A classifier agent specializes in a specific category of intrusion and is capable of collaborating with agents of another category to determine the severity level of an activity deemed suspicious. Moving the computational analysis to each collection point avoids the costly movement of information to an aggregation unit. Argus [203] employs a similar architecture with low-level agents that serve as data cleansers, and data mining agents that generate not only rules for matching a normal profile but also generate feedback for knowledge-based components. These rules can be used then to update the rule database of the NFR knowledge component [167]. Bayesian multiple hypothesis tracking was also used to more effectively analyze information provided by existing IDSs from multiple networks [28]. Hypotheses that explain the measured intrusion events are generated and stored, and then evaluated against the understanding of the sensor behavior in order to determine the likelihood of the hypotheses. The hypothesis with the greatest likelihood is assumed correct, while other hypotheses are treated as intrusions.

The Intrusion Detection Agent (IDA) system [10] is a multi-host based IDS that relies on mobile agents to trace intruders among the various hosts involved in an intrusion. IDA watches specific events that are related to various intrusions. These events are called "Marks Left by Suspected Intruder" (MLSI). If a specific MLSI is identified, IDA collects all the information related to this MLSI, analyzes this information and determines whether the MLSI is related to a real attack or not. The IDA system has a hierarchical tree structure, in which the central manager is placed at the root of the tree, while numerous agents are located at the leaves.

Micael [53] is a distributed IDS that uses autonomous mobile intelligent agents able to make various decisions in the process of intrusion detection (e.g. investigating intrusions and initiating countermeasures against them). The Micael architecture contains the following agents: (i) *headquarters*, i.e. specialized centralized agents that are responsible for creating other agents and maintaining their executable codes. They receive information about potential intrusions from *sentinel* agents and can create new *detachment* agents that will be sent to hosts when needed; (ii) *sentinels*, i.e. immobile agents that collect data about the activities on the host machines and inform *headquarter* agents about detected anomalies; and (iii) *detachments*, i.e. mobile agents that are used to face possible intrusions (hazards) by starting a detailed analysis of log files.

Applying intrusion detection techniques on a system-wide basis allows the system to be protected against general misuse, but may require significant resources. By optimizing the placement and configuration of these tools, it is possible to offer both increased protection for sensitive systems, and more context-sensitive detection, at the cost of general protection. For example, distributed IDS deployment often concentrates monitors in high-risk areas, such as network ingress points (e.g. adjacent to firewalls), or in the presence of valuable resources (such as network server farms) [148].

8.   RESPONSE

The response of IDSs to identified attacks may be either passive or active. In the most common scenario, IDSs have passive response and simply inform responsible personnel of an event, but no countermeasure is actively applied to thwart the attack. The most common method for such notifications is through pop-up windows or on-screen alerts or through recording alerts into a file. These alerts may vary from notification of alarms only to detailed information about computer attacks such as source IP address, target of the attack, specific port of interest, the tools used to perform the attack, the outcome of the attack, etc. Some products also offer remote notification through sending alarms or alerts to cellular phones and pagers carried by system security personnel. In addition, notification is often sent through e-mail messages, but this may be unsafe, as attackers may monitor email and might even block the message. Certain IDSs (e.g. Cisco IDS [46]) use SNMP traps and messages to report generated alarms to a network management system, where network operations personnel can investigate them. Passive response is often used for off-line analysis.

Alternatively, IDSs can also provide an active response to critical events, such as "patching" a system vulnerability, logging off a user, re-configuring routers and firewalls, or disconnecting a port.

Given the speed and frequency at which attacks can occur, an ideal IDS would automatically respond to computer attacks at machine speed without requiring any operator intervention. However, this is an unrealistic expectation, largely due to the difficulty in eliminating false alarms. Nevertheless, IDS products can still provide a variety of active response mechanisms that may be used at the discretion of the system administrator.

One of the most harmless, but often most productive, active responses is to collect additional information about a suspected attack and to perform damage control. This might involve increasing the sensitivity level of information sources (e.g., increasing the number of events logged by an operating system audit trail, or increasing the sensitivity of a network monitor that captures all packets). Such additional information collected can help resolve the detection of the attack (assisting the system in diagnosing whether an attack did or did not take place) thus allowing the IDS to gather information that can be used to support investigation of the attacker.

In more recent IDS tools, active responses that include countermeasure against the attacker have become increasingly popular. An example of such a tool with early countermeasure capability is NetProbe [192], which monitors a network for undesired connections and immediately terminates them. There are also other tools with similar capabilities, such as RealSecure [89], NetRanger [47], and WebStalker [204] that have options to interrupt suspicious network connections that carry attacks, to block network traffic from the hosts that are originating attacks, or to reconfigure routers and firewalls.

9. CONCLUSIONS

Intrusion detection techniques have improved dramatically over time, especially in the past few years. Initially developed to automate tedious and difficult log parsing activity, IDSs have developed into sophisticated, real-time applications with the ability to have a detailed look at traffic and to sniff out malicious activity. They can handle high-speed networks and complex traffic, and deliver detailed insight – previously unavailable – into active threats against critical online information resources. IDS technology is developing rapidly and its near-term future is very promising. It is increasingly becoming an indispensable and integral component of any comprehensive enterprise security program, since it complements traditional security mechanisms.

This chapter provides an overview of the current state of the art of both computer attacks and intrusion detection techniques. The overview is based on presented taxonomies exemplified with the most illustrative paradigms. The taxonomy of computer attacks and intrusions provides the current status and trends in techniques that attackers employ today. The taxonomy of IDSs highlights their properties and provides an overview of the past and current developments. Although a variety of techniques have been developed for detecting different types of computer attacks in different computer systems, there are still a number of research issues concerning the prediction performance, efficiency and fault tolerance of IDSs that need to be addressed. Signature analysis, the most common strategy in the commercial domain until recently, is increasingly integrated with different anomaly detection and alert correlation techniques in order to detect emerging and coordinated computer attacks.

We hope this survey provides actionable information and advice on the topics, as well as serves to acquaint newcomers with the world of IDSs and computer attacks. The information provided herein is by no means complete and we recommend further reading to the interested reader.

ACKNOWLEDGEMENTS

This work was partially supported by Army High Performance Computing Research Center contract number DAAD19-01-2-0014, NSF grant IIS-0308264, and ARDA contract number F30602-03-C-0243. The content of the work does not necessarily reflect the position or policy of the government and no official endorsement should be inferred. Access to computing facilities was provided by the AHPCRC and the Minnesota Supercomputing Institute.

REFERENCES

[1]   T. Abraham, IDDM: Intrusion Detection Using Data Mining Techniques, DSTO Electronics and Surveillance Research Laboratory, Department of Defense, Australia Technical Report DSTO-GD-0286, 2001.

[2]   C.C. Aggarwal and P. Yu, Outlier Detection for High Dimensional Data, In *Proceedings of the ACM SIGMOD International Conference on Management of Data*, Santa BArbara, CA, May 2001.

[3]   A. AirDefense, http://www.airdefense.net/products/index.html, 2004.

[4]   J. Allen, A. Christie, W. Fithen, J. McHugh, J. Pickel, E. Stoner, J. Ellis, E. Hayes, J. Marella and B. Willke, State of the Practice of Intrusion Detection Technologies., Carnegie Mellon University, Pittsburgh, PA Technical Report CMU/SEI-99-TR-028, 1999.

[5]   E. Amoroso, *Fundamentals of Computer Security Technology*, Prentice-Hall PTR, 1994.

[6]   D. Anderson, T. Lunt, H. Javitz, A. Tamaru and A. Valdes, Detecting Unusual Program Behavior Using the Statistical Component of the Next-Generation Intrusion Detection Expert System (NIDES), Computer Science Laboratory, SRI International, Menlo Park, CA Technical Report SRI-CSL-95-06.

[7]   J.P. Anderson, Computer Security Threat Monitoring and Surveillance, James P. Anderson Co., Box 42, Fort Washington, PA 19034 Technical Report Contract 79F296400, April 1980.

[8]   Arbor Networks, Intelligent Network Management with Peakflow Traffic, http://www.arbornetworks.com/products_sp.php, 2003.

[9]   ArcSight, Enterprise Security Management Software, http://www.arcsight.com/.

[10]   M. Asaka, S. Okazawa, A. Taguchi and S. Goto, A Method of Tracing Intruders by Use of Mobile Agents, In *Proceedings of the 9th Annual Conference of the Internet Society (INET'99)*, San Jose, CA, June 1999.

[11]   T. Aslam, A Taxonomy of Security Faults in the UNIX Operating System, Purdue University Master's thesis, August 1995.

[12]   C.R. Attanasio, P.W. Markstein and R.J. Phillips, Penetrating an Operating System: A Study of VM/370 Integrity, *IBM System Journal*, vol. 15, 1, pp. 102-116, 1976.

[13]   S. Axelsson, Intrusion Detection Systems: A Survey and Taxonomy, Dept. of Computer Engineering, Chalmers University Technical Report 99-15, March 2000.

[14]   AXENT Technologies, Inc, NetProwler-Advanced Network Intrusion Detection, available online at:, http://www.axent.com/iti/netprowler/idtk_ds_word_1.html, 1999.

[15]   R. Bace and P. Mell, NIST Special Publication on Intrusion Detection Systems, 2001.

[16] D. Barbara, N. Wu and S. Jajodia, Detecting Novel Network Intrusions Using Bayes Estimators, In *Proceedings of the First SIAM Conference on Data Mining*, Chicago, IL, April 2001.

[17] V. Barnett and T. Lewis, *Outliers in Statistical Data*. New York, NY, John Wiley and Sons, 1994.

[18] J. Barrus and N. Rowe, A Distributed Autonomous-Agent Network-Intrusion Detection And Response System, In *Proceedings of the Command and Control Research and Technology Symposium*, Monterey, CA, 577-586, June 1998.

[19] D.S. Bauer and M.E. Koblentz, NIDX - An Expert System For Real-Time, *Computer Networking Symposium*, 1988.

[20] T. Baving, Network vs. Application-Based Intrusion Detection, *Network and Internet Nettwork Security, Computer Science Honours*, 2003.

[21] S.M. Bellovin and W.R. Cheswick, Network Firewalls., *IEEE Communications Magazine*, vol. 32, 9, pp. 50-57, September 1994.

[22] M. Bhattacharyya, M. Schultz, E. Eskin, S. Hershkop and S. Stolfo, MET: An Experimental System for Malicious Email Tracking, In *Proceedings of the New Security Paradigms Workshop (NSPW)*, Hampton, VA, September 2002.

[23] M. Bishop, How Attackers Break Programs, and How To Write Programs More Securely, In *Proceedings of the 8th USENIX Security Symposium*, University of California, Davis, August 1999.

[24] E. Bloedorn, A. Christiansen, W. Hill, C. Skorupka, L. Talbot and J. Tivel, Data Mining for Network Intrusion Detection: How to Get Started, MITRE Technical Report, http://www.mitre.org/work/tech_papers/tech_papers_01/bloedorn_datamining, August 2001.

[25] M.M. Breunig, H.P. Kriegel, R.T. Ng and J. Sander, LOF: Identifying Density Based Local Outliers, *ACM SIGMOD Conference*, vol. Dallas, TX, May 2000.

[26] S. Bridges and R. Vaughn, Fuzzy Data Mining and Genetic Algorithms Applied to Intrusion Detection, In *Proceedings of the Twenty-third National Information Systems Security Conference*, Baltimore, MD, October 2000.

[27] H. Burch and B. Cheswick, Tracing Anonymous Packets to Their Approximate Source, In *Proceedings of the USENIX Large Installation Systems Administration Conference*, New Orleans, LA, 319-327, December 2000.

[28] D. Burroughs, L. Wilson and G. Cybenko, Analysis of Distributed Intrusion Detection Systems Using Bayesian Methods, www.ists.dartmouth.edu/IRIA/projects/ipccc.final.pdf, 2002.

[29] J. Cabrera, B. Ravichandran and R. Mehra, Statistical Traffic Modeling For Network Intrusion Detection, In *Proceedings of the 8th International Symposium on Modeling, Analysis and Simulation of Computer and Telecommunication Systems*, San Francisco, CA, August 2000.

[30] J. Cannady, Artificial Neural Networks For Misuse Detection, In *Proceedings of the National Information Systems Security Conference (NISSC'98)*, Arlington, VA, 443-456, October, 1998.

[31] J. Cannady and J. Harrell, A Comparative Analysis of Current Intrusion Detection Technologies, In *Proceedings of the Fourth Technology for Information Security Conference'96 (TIS'96)*, Houston, TX, May 1996.

[32]   CERIAS Intrusion Detection Resources, http://www.cerias.purdue.edu/coast/ids/ids-body.html, 2004.

[33]   CERT® Advisory CA-1995-13 Syslog Vulnerability - A Workaround for Sendmail, http://www.cert.org/advisories/CA-1995-13.html, September, 1997.

[34]   CERT®   Advisory   CA-1999-04   Melissa   Worm   and   Macro   Virus, http://www.cert.org/advisories/CA-1999-04.html, March 1999.

[35]   CERT® Advisory CA-2000-14 Microsoft Outlook and Outlook Express Cache Bypass Vulnerability, http://www.cert.org/advisories/CA-2000-14.html, July 2000.

[36]   CERT® Advisory CA-2001-26 Nimda Worm, http://www.cert.org/advisories/CA-2001-26.html, September 2001.

[37]   CERT® Advisory CA-2003-04 MS-SQL Server Worm, http://www.cert.org/advisories/CA-2003-04.html, 2003.

[38]   CERT® Advisory CA-2003-25 Buffer Overflow in Sendmail, http://www.cert.org/advisories/CA-2003-25.html, September, 2003.

[39]   P.C. Chan and V.K. Wei, Preemptive Distributed Intrusion Detection Using Mobile Agents, In *Proceedings of the Eleventh IEEE International Workshops on Enabling Technologies: Infrastructure for Collaborative Enterprises (WET ICE 2002)*, Pittsburgh, PA, June 2002.

[40]   N. Chawla, A. Lazarevic, L. Hall and K. Bowyer, SMOTEBoost: Improving the Prediction of Minority Class in Boosting, In *Proceedings of the Principles of Knowledge Discovery in Databases, PKDD-2003*, Cavtat, Croatia, September 2003.

[41]   C. Cheng, H.T. Kung and K. Tan, Use of Spectral Analysis in Defense Against DoS Attacks, In *Proceedings of the IEEE GLOBECOM*, Taipei, Taiwan, 2002.

[42]   W.R. Cheswick and S.M. Bellovin, *Firewalls and Internet Security - Repelling the Wily Hacker*, Addison-Wesley, ISBN 0-201-63357-4, 1994.

[43]   R. Chinchani, S. Upadhyaya and K. Kwiat, A Tamper-Resistant Framework for Unambiguous Detection of Attacks in User Space Using Process Monitors, In *Proceedings of the IEEE International Workshop on Information Assurance*, Darmstadt, Germany, March 2003.

[44]   R. Chinchani, S. Upadhyaya and K. Kwiat, Towards the Scalable Implementation of a User Level Anomaly Detection System, In *Proceedings of the IEEE Conference on Military Communications Conference (MILCOM)*, Anaheim, CA, October 2002.

[45]   J. Christy, Cyber Threat & Legal Issues, In *Proceedings of the ShadowCon'99*, Dahlgren, VA, October 26, 1999.

[46]   Cisco Intrusion Detection, www.cisco.com/warp/public/cc/pd/sqsw/sqidsz, May 2004.

[47]   Cisco Systems, Inc., NetRanger-Enterprise-scale, Real-time, Network Intrusion Detection System, http://www.cisco.com/univercd/cc/td/doc/product/iaabu/netrangr/, 1998.

[48]   cknow.com Virus Tutorial, http://www.cknow.com/vtutor/vtmap.htm, 2001.

[49]   C. Cowan, C. Pu, D. Maier, H. Hinton, J. Walpole, P. Bakke, S. Beattie, A. Grier and P. Zhang, StackGuard: Automatic Adaptive Detection and Prevention of Buffer-Overflow Attacks, In *Proceedings of the 7th USENIX Security Symposium*, San Antonio, TX, 63-77.

[50]   O. Dain and R. Cunningham, Fusing a Heterogeneous Alert Stream Into Scenarios, In *Proceedings of the ACM Workshops on Data Mining for Security Applications*, Philadelphia, PA, November 2001.

[51]   V. Dao and R. Vemuri, Computer Network Intrusion Detection: A Comparison of Neural Networks Methods, Differential Equations and Dynamical Systems, *Special Issue on Neural Networks*, 2002.

[52]   DARPA, DARPA Intrusion Detection Evaluation, http://www.ll.mit.edu/IST/ideval/pubs/pubs_index.html, 2004.

[53]   J. De Queiroz and Carmo L., MICHAEL: An Autonomous Mobile Agent System to Protect New Generation Networked Applications, In *Proceedings of the 2nd Annual Workshop n Recent Advances in Intrusion Detection*, Rio de Janeiro, Brasil, 1999.

[54]   H. Debar, M. Becker and D. Siboni, A Neural Network Component for an Intrusion-Detection System, In *Proceedings of the IEEE Computer Society Symposium on Research in Security and Privacy*, Oakland, CA, 240-250, May 1992.

[55]   H. Debar, M. Dacier and A. Wespi, Towards a Taxonomy of Intrusion Detection Systems, *Computer Networks*, vol. 31, 8, pp. 805-822, 1999.

[56]   D. Denning, An Intrusion-Detection Model, *IEEE Transactions on Software Engineering*, vol. 13, 2, pp. 222-232, 1987.

[57]   dmoz Open Security Project, Intrusion Detection Systems, http://dmoz.org/Computers/Security/Intrusion_Detection_Systems/,

[58]   C. Dowell and P. Ramstedt, The Computerwatch Data Reduction Tool, In *Proceedings of the 13th National Computer Security Conference*, Washington, DC, 1990.

[59]   N. Einwechter, An Introduction To Distributed Intrusion Detection Systems, *Security Focus*, January 2002.

[60]   D. Engelhardt, Directions for Intrusion Detection and Response: A survey, DSTO Electronics and Surveillance Research Laboratory, Department of Defense, Australia Technical Report DSTO-GD-0155, 1997.

[61]   L Ertoz, E. Eilertson, A. Lazarevic, P. Tan, J. Srivastava, V. Kumar and P. Dokas, The MINDS - Minnesota Intrusion Detection System, in *Data Mining: Next Generation Challenges and Future Directions*, A. Joshi H. Kargupta, K. Sivakumar, and Y. Yesha, Ed., 2004.

[62]   L. Ertoz, E. Eilertson, P. Dokas, V. Kumar and K. Long, Scan Detection - Revisited, Army High Performance Computing Research Center Technical Report, 2004.

[63]   S. Eschrich, Real-Time User Identification Employing Standard Unix Accounting, Florida State University PhD Thesis, Fall 1995.

[64]   E. Eskin, Anomaly Detection over Noisy Data using Learned Probability Distributions, In *Proceedings of the International Conference on Machine Learning*, Stanford University, CA, June 2000.

[65]   E. Eskin, A. Arnold, M. Prerau, L. Portnoy and S. Stolfo, A Geometric Framework for Unsupervised Anomaly Detection: Detecting Intrusions in Unlabeled Data, in *Applications of Data Mining in Computer Security, Advances In Information Security*, S. Jajodia D. Barbara, Ed. Boston: Kluwer Academic Publishers, 2002.

[66]   M. Esmaili, B. Balachandran, R. Safavi-Naini and J. Pieprzyk, Case-Based Reasoning For Intrusion Detection, In *Proceedings of the 12th Annual Computer Security Applications Conference*, San Diego, CA, December 1996.

[67]   M. Esmaili, R. Safavi-Naini and B.M. Balachandran, Autoguard: A Continuous Case-Based Intrusion Detection System, In *Proceedings of the Australian Computer Science*

Conference, Australian Computer Science Communications, Sydney, Australia, 392-401, February 1997.

[68] W. Fan, W. Lee, M. Miller, S.J. Stolfo and P.K. Chan, Using Artificial Anomalies to Detect Unknown and Known Network Intrusions, In *Proceedings of the First IEEE International conference on Data Mining*, vol. San Jose, CA, December 2001.

[69] D. Farmer, Cops Overview, http://www.trouble.org/cops/overview.html, May 1993.

[70] D. Farmer and W. Venema, Improving The Security Of Your Site By Breaking Into It, http://www.trouble.org/security/admin-guide-to-cracking.html,

[71] H. Feng, O. Kolesnikov, P. Fogla, W. Lee and W. Gong, Anomaly Detection Using Call Stack Information, In *Proceedings of the IEEE Symposium Security and Privacy*, Oakland, CA, May 2003.

[72] G. Florez, S. Bridges and R. Vaughn, An Improved Algorithm for Fuzzy Data Mining for Intrusion Detection, In *Proceedings of the North American Fuzzy Information Processing Society Conference (NAFIPS 2002)*, New Orleans, LA, June, 2002.

[73] S. Forrest, S. Hofmeyr, A. Somayaji and T. Longstaff, A Sense of Self for Unix Processes, In *Proceedings of the IEEE Symposium on Security and Privacy*, Oakland, CA, 120-128, May 1996.

[74] A. Ghosh and A. Schwartzbard, A Study in Using Neural Networks for Anomaly and Misuse Detection, In *Proceedings of the Eighth USENIX Security Symposium*, Washington, D.C., 141-151, August , 1999.

[75] T.M Gil and M. Poletto, MULTOPS: A Data-Structure for Bandwidth Attack Detection, In *Proceedings of the USENIX Security Symposium*, Washington, D.C., 23-28, July 2001.

[76] Google directory, http://directory.google.com/Top/Computers/Security/Intrusion_Detection_Systems,

[77] N. Habra, B. LeCharlier, A. Mounji and I. Mathieu, ASAX: Software Architecture and Rule-Based Language for Universal Audit Trail Analysis, In *Proceedings of the Second European Symposium on Research in Computer Security (ESORICS), Vol. 648, Lecture Notes in Computer Science, Springer-Verlag*, Toulouse, France, November 1992.

[78] S.E. Hansen and E.T. Atkins, Automated System Monitoring and Notification With Swatch., In *Proceedings of the Seventh Systems Administration Conference (LISA'93)*, Monterey, CA, November 1993.

[79] S. Hawkins, H. He, G. Williams and R. Baxter, Outlier Detection Using Replicator Neural Networks, In *Proceedings of the 4th International Conference on Data Warehousing and Knowledge Discovery (DaWaK02), Lecture Notes in Computer Science 2454*, Aix-en-Provence, France, 170-180, September 2002.

[80] Haystack Labs, Inc., Stalker, http://www.haystack.com/stalk.htm, 1997.

[81] L.T. Heberlein, G.V. Dias, K.N. Levitt, B. Mukherjee, J. Wood and D. Wolber, A Network Security Monitor, In *Proceedings of the IEEE Symposium on Research in Security and Privacy*, Oakland, CA, 296-304, May 1990.

[82] G. Helmer, J.S.K Wong, V. Honavar and L. Miller, Intelligent Agents for Intrusion Detection, In *Proceedings of the IEEE Information Technology Conference*, Syracuse, NY, 121-124, September 1998.

[83] K. Houle, G. Weaver, N. Long and R. Thomas, Trends in Denial of Service Attack Technology, CERT® Coordination Center, Pittsburgh, PA October 2001.

[84] J.D. Howard, An Analysis of Security Incidents on the Internet, Carnegie Mellon University, Pittsburgh, PA 15213 Ph.D. dissertation, April 1997.

[85] D. Hughes, TkLogger, ftp://coast.cs.purdue.edu/pub/tools/unix/tklogger.tar.Z,

[86] K. Ilgun, USTAT A Real-time Intrusion Detection System for UNIX, University of California Santa Barbara Master Thesis, 1992.

[87] Internet Guide, Computer Viruses / Virus Guide, http://www.internet-guide.co.uk/viruses.html, 2002.

[88] Internet Security Systems Wireless Products, Active Wireless Protection, An X-Force's white paper, available at: documents.iss.net/whitepapers/ActiveWirelessProtection.pdf, September 2002.

[89] Internet Security Systems, Inc., RealSecure, http://www.iss.net/prod/rsds.html, 1997.

[90] Intrusion.com, Intrusion SecureHost, white paper available at: www.intrusion.com/products/hids.asp, 2003.

[91] J. Ioannidis and S. Bellovin, Implementing Pushback: Router-Based Defense Against DDoS Attacks, In *Proceedings of the Network and Distributed System Security Symposium*, San Diego, CA, February 2002.

[92] K. Jackson, Intrusion Detection System Product Survey, Los Alamos National Laboratory Research Report, LA-UR-99-3883, June 1999.

[93] R. Jagannathan, T. Lunt, D. Anderson, C. Dodd, F. Gilham, C. Jalali, H. Javitz, P. Neumann, A. Tamaru and A. Valdes, System Design Document: Next-Generation Intrusion Detection Expert System (NIDES). SRI International Technical Report A007/A008/A009/A011/A012/A014, March 1993.

[94] W. Jansen and P. Mell, Mobile Agents in Intrusion Detection and Response, In *Proceedings of the 12th Annual Canadian Information Technology Security Symposium*, Ottawa, Canada, 2000.

[95] H.S. Javitz and A. Valdes, The SRI IDES Statistical Anomaly Detector, In *Proceedings of the IEEE Symposium on Research in Security and Privacy*, Oakland, CA, 1991.

[96] N.D. Jayaram and P.L.R. Morse, Network Security - A Taxonomic View, In *Proceedings of the European Conference on Security and Detection*, School of Computer Science, University of Westminster, UK, Publication No. 437, 28-30, April 1997.

[97] A. Jones and R. Sielken, Computer System Intrusion Detection, University of Virginia Technical Report, 1999.

[98] M. Joshi, R. Agarwal and V. Kumar, PNrule, Mining Needles in a Haystack: Classifying Rare Classes via Two-Phase Rule Induction, In *Proceedings of the ACM SIGMOD Conference on Management of Data*, Santa Barbara, CA, May 2001.

[99] M. Joshi, R. Agarwal and V. Kumar, Predicting Rare Classes: Can Boosting Make Any Weak Learner Strong?, In *Proceedings of the Eight ACM Conference ACM SIGKDD International Conference on Knowledge Discovery and Data Mining*, Edmonton, Canada, July 2002.

[100] Y.F. Jou, F. Gong, C. Sargor, S.F. Wu and W.R. Cleaveland, Architecture Design of a Scalable Intrusion Detection System For The Emerging Network Infrastructure, MCNC Information Technologies Division, Research Triangle Park, NC 27709 Technical Report CDRL A005, April 1997.

[101] K. Julisch, Mining Alarm Clusters to Improve Alarm Handling Efficiency, In *Proceedings of the 17th Annual Conference on Computer Security Applications*, New Orleans, LA, December 2001.

[102] J. Jung, V. Paxson, A. W. Berger and H. Balakrishnan, Fast Portscan Detection Using Sequential Hypothesis Testing, In *Proceedings of the IEEE Symposium on Security and Privacy*, Oakland, CA, May, 2004.

[103] K. Kendall, A Database of Computer Attacks for the Evaluation of Intrusion Detection Systems, Massachusetts Institute of Technology Master's Thesis, 1998.

[104] A.D. Keromytis, V. Misra and D. Rubenstein, SoS: Secure Overlay Services, In *Proceedings of the ACM SIGCOMM Conference*, Pittsburgh, PA, 61-72, August 2002.

[105] D. Kienzle and M. Elder, Recent Worms. A Survey and Trends, In *Proceedings of the The Workshop on Rapid Malcode (WORM 2003), held in conjunction with the 10th ACM Conference on Computer and Communications Security*, Washington, DC, October 27, 2003.

[106] G. Kim and E. Spafford, The Design and Implementation of Tripwire: A File System Integrity Checker, In *Proceedings of the ACM Conference on Computer and Communications Security, COAST*, Purdue University, IN, 18-29, November 1994.

[107] E. Knorr and R. Ng, Algorithms for Mining Distance based Outliers in Large Data Sets, In *Proceedings of the Very Large Databases (VLDB) Conference*, New York City, NY, August 1998.

[108] I.V. Krsul, Software Vulnerability Analysis, Purdue University Ph.D. dissertation, May 1998.

[109] C. Kruegel and T. Toth, Distributed Pattern Detection For Intrusion Detection, In *Proceedings of the Network and Distributed System Security Symposium Conference Proceedings, Internet Society*, Los Angeles, CA, February 2002.

[110] C. Krugel and T. Toth, A Survey on Intrusion Detection Systems, Technical University of Vienna Technical report, TUV-1841-00-11, 2000.

[111] C. Krugel, T. Toth and E. Kirda, Service Specific Anomaly Detection for Network Intrusion Detection, In *Proceedings of the ACM Symposium on Applied Computing*, Madrid, Spain, March 2002.

[112] S. Kumar, Classification and Detection of Computer Intrusion, Computer Science Department, Purdue University Ph.D. dissertation, August 1995.

[113] S. Kumar and E. Spafford, An Application of Pattern Matching in Intrusion Detection, Purdue University Technical Report, 1994.

[114] H. Kvarnstrom, A Survey of Commercial Tools for Intrusion Detection, Chalmers University of Technology, Göteborg, Sweden Technical Report, 1999.

[115] C. Landwehr, A. Bull, J. McDermott and W. Choi, A Taxonomy of Computer Program Security Flaws, *ACM Computing Surveys*, vol. 26, 3, pp. 211-254, September 1994.

[116] T. Lane and C. Brodley, Temporal Sequence Learning and Data Reduction for Anomaly Detection, *ACM Transactions on Information and System Security*, vol. 2, 3, pp. 295-331, 1999.

[117] A. Lazarevic, L. Ertoz, A. Ozgur, J. Srivastava and V. Kumar, A Comparative Study of Anomaly Detection Schemes in Network Intrusion Detection, In *Proceedings of the Third SIAM International Conference on Data Mining*, San Francisco, CA, May 2003.

[118] A. Lazarevic, J. Srivastava and V. Kumar, Cyber Threat Analysis - A Key Enabling Technology for the Objective Force (A Case Study in Network Intrusion Detection), In *Proceedings of the IT/C4ISR, 23rd Army Science Conference*, Orlando, FL, December 2002.

[119] W. Lee, S. Stolfo and P. Chan, Patterns from Unix Process Execution Traces for Intrusion Detection, In *Proceedings of the AAAI Workshop: AI Approaches to Fraud Detection and Risk Management*, Providence, RI, July 1997.

[120] W. Lee, S. Stolfo and K. Mok, Adaptive Intrusion Detection: A Data Mining Approach., *Artificial Intelligence Review*, vol. 14, pp. 533-567, 2001.

[121] W. Lee and S.J. Stolfo, Data Mining Approaches for Intrusion Detection, In *Proceedings of the USENIX Security Symposium*, San Antonio, TX, January, 1998.

[122] W. Lee and S.J. Stolfo, A Framework for Constructing Features and Models for Intrusion Detection Systems., *ACM Transactions on Information and System Security*, vol. 3, 4, pp. 227-261, 2000.

[123] W. Lee and D. Xiang, Information-Theoretic Measures for Anomaly Detection, In *Proceedings of the IEEE Symposium on Security and Privacy*, Oakland, CA, May 2001.

[124] G. Liepins and H. Vaccaro, Anomaly Detection Purpose and Framework, In *Proceedings of the 12th National Computer Security Conference*, Baltimore, MD, 495-504, October 1989.

[125] G. Liepins and H. Vaccaro, Intrusion Detection: It's Role and Validation, *Computers and Security*, pp. 347-355, 1992.

[126] Y.X. Lim, T. Schmoyer, J. Levine and H.L. Owen, Wireless Intrusion Detection and Response, In *Proceedings of the IEEE Workshop on Information Assurance*, United States Military Academy, West Point, NY, June 2003.

[127] J.L Lin, X.S. Wang and S. Jajodia, Abstraction-Based Misuse Detection: High-Level Specifications and Adaptable Strategies, In *Proceedings of the 11th IEEE Computer Security Foundations Workshop*, Rockport, MA, June 1998.

[128] U. Lindqvist and E. Jonsson, How to Systematically Classify Computer Security Intrusions, *IEEE Security and Privacy*, pp. 154-163, 1997.

[129] U. Lindqvist and P.A. Porras, Detecting Computer and Network Misuse Through the Production-Based Expert System Toolset (P-BEST), In *Proceedings of the IEEE Symposium on Security and Privacy*, Berkeley, CA, May 1999.

[130] R. Lippmann, The Role of Network Intrusion Detection, In *Proceedings of the Workshop on Network Intrusion Detection*, H.E.A.T. Center, Aberdeen, MD, March 19-20, 2002.

[131] R. Lippmann and R. Cunningham, Improving Intrusion Detection Performance Using Keyword Selection and Neural Networks, *Computer Networks*, vol. 34, 4, pp. 597-603, 2000.

[132] R. Lippmann, J.W. Haines, D.J. Fried, J. Korba and K. Das, The 1999 DARPA Off-Line Intrusion Detection Evaluation, *Computer Networks*, 2000.

[133] R.P. Lippmann, R.K. Cunningham, D.J. Fried, I. Graf, K.R. Kendall, S.E. Webster and M.A. Zissman, Results of the DARPA 1998 Offline Intrusion Detection Evaluation, In *Proceedings of the Workshop on Recent Advances in Intrusion Detection, (RAID-1999)*, West Lafayette, IN, September, 1999.

[134] J. Lo, Trojan Horse Attacks, www.irchelp.org/irchelp/security/trojan.html, April 2004.

[135]   D. Lough, A Taxonomy of Computer Attacks with Applications to Wireless Networks, Virginia Polytechnic Institute PhD Thesis, April 2001.

[136]   T. Lunt, A Survey of Intrusion Detection techniques, *Computers & Security*, vol. 12, 4, pp. 405-418, June 1993.

[137]   T. Lunt, R. Jagannathan, R. Lee, S. Listgarten, D.L. Edwards, P.G. Neumann, H.S. Javitz and A. Valdes, IDES: The Enhanced Prototype - A Real-Time Intrusion-Detection Expert System, SRI International Technical Report SRI-CSL-88-12.

[138]   T. Lunt, A. Tamaru, F. Gilham, R. Jagannathan, C. Jalali, P.G. Neumann, H.S. Javitz, A. Valdes and T.D. Garvey, A Real Time Intrusion Detection Expert System (IDES), SRI Technical report, 1992.

[139]   T.F. Lunt, Real-Time Intrusion Detection, In *Proceedings of the Thirty Fourth IEEE Computer Society International Conference (COMPCON), Intellectual Leverage*, San Francisco, CA, February 1989.

[140]   J. Luo, Integrating Fuzzy Logic With Data Mining Methods for Intrusion Detection, Department of Computer Science, Mississippi State University Master's thesis, 1999.

[141]   R. Mahajan, S. Bellovin, S. Floyd, J. Ioannidis, V. Paxson and S. Shenker, Controlling High Bandwidth Aggregates in The Network, *ACM Computer Communication Review*, July 2001.

[142]   M. Mahoney and P. Chan, Learning Nonstationary Models of Normal Network Traffic for Detecting Novel Attacks, In *Proceedings of the Eight ACM International Conference on Knowledge Discovery and Data Mining*, Edmonton, Canada, 376-385, July 2002.

[143]   S. Manganaris, M. Christensen, D. Serkle and K. Hermiz, A Data Mining Analysis of RTID Alarms, *Computer Networks*, vol. 34, 4, October 2000.

[144]   D. Marchette, *Computer Intrusion Detection and Network Monitoring, A Statistical Viewpoint*. New York, Springer, 2001.

[145]   J. Marin, D. Ragsdale and J. Surdu, A Hybrid Approach to Profile Creation and Intrusion Detection, In *Proceedings of the DARPA Information Survivability Conference and Exposition*, Anaheim, CA, June, 2001.

[146]   R. Maxion and K. Tan, Anomaly Detection in Embedded Systems, *IEEE Transactions on Computers*, vol. 51, 2, pp. 108-120, 2002.

[147]   Mazu Profiler™, An Overview, http://www.mazunetworks.com/solutions/white_papers/download/Mazu_Profiler.pdf, December 2003.

[148]   M. Medina, A Layered Framework for Placement of Distributed Intrusion Detection Devices, In *Proceedings of the 21st National Information Systems Security Conference (NISSC'98)*, Crystal City, VA, October 1998.

[149]   Meier. M. and M. Sobirey, Intrusion Detection Systems List and Bibliography, http://www-rnks.informatik.tu-cottbus.de/en/security/ids.html,

[150]   Metropolitan, Metropolitan Network BBS, Inc., Kaspersky.ch, Computer Virus Classification, http://www.avp.ch/avpve/classes/classes.stm, 2003.

[151]   J. Mirkovic, G. Prier and P. Reiher, Attacking DDoS at the Source, *10th IEEE International Conference on Network Protocols*, November 2002.

[152]   J. Mirkovic and P. Reiher, A Taxonomy of DDoS Attacks and Defense Mechanisms, *ACM Computer Communication Review*, April 2004.

[153] D. Moore, V. Paxson, S. Savage, C. Shannon, S. Staniford and N. Weaver, The Spread of the Sapphire/Slammer Worm, http://www.cs.berkeley.edu/~nweaver/sapphire/, 2003.

[154] D. Moore, G. M. Voeker and S. Savage, Inferring Internet Denial-of-Service Activity, *USENIX Security Symposium*, pp. 9-22, August 2001.

[155] A. Mounji, Languages and Tools for Rule-Based Distributed Intrusion Detection, Facult es Universitaires Notre-Dame de la Paix, Namur, Belgium Doctor of Science Thesis, September 1997.

[156] S. Mukkamala, G. Janoski and A. Sung, Intrusion Detection Using Neural Networks and Support Vector Machines, In *Proceedings of the IEEE International Joint Conference on Neural Networks*, Honolulu, HI, May 2002.

[157] S. Mukkamala, A. Sung and A. Abraham, Intrusion Detection Systems Using Adaptive Regression Splines, In *Proceedings of the 1st Indian International Conference on Artificial Intelligence (IICAI-03)*, Hyderabad, India, December 2003.

[158] S. Mukkamala, A. Sung and A. Abraham, A Linear Genetic Programming Approach for Modeling Intrusion, In *Proceedings of the IEEE Congress on Evolutionary Computation (CEC2003)*, Perth, Australia, December, 2003.

[159] NAGIOS Network Monitoring Tool, www.nagios.org, February 2004.

[160] Nessus Network Security Scanner, http://www.nessus.org/, 2004.

[161] Netflow Tools, www.netflow.com,

[162] NetForensics®, Security Information Management, http://www.netforensics.com/,

[163] Network Associates, Inc., Cybercop server, http://www.nai.com/products/security/cybercopsvr/index.asp, 1998.

[164] P. Neumann and P. Porras, Experience with Emerald to Date, In *Proceedings of the First Usenix Workshop on Intrusion Detection and Network Monitoring*, Santa Clara, CA, 1999.

[165] P.G. Neumann, *Computer Related Risks*, The ACM Press, a division of the Association for Computing Machinery, Inc. (ACM), 1995.

[166] P.G. Neumann and D.B. Parker, A Summary of Computer Misuse Techniques, In *Proceedings of the 12th National Computer Security Conference*, 396-407, 1989.

[167] NFR Network Intrusion Detection, http://www.nfr.com/products/NID/, 2001.

[168] P. Ning, Y. Cui and D. Reeves, Constructing Attack Scenarios through Correlation of Intrusion Alerts, In *Proceedings of the 9th ACM Conference on Computer & Communications Security*, Washington D.C., 245-254, November 2002.

[169] S. Nomad, Distributed Denial of Service Defense Tactics, http://razor.bindview.com/publish/papers/strategies.html, 2/14/2000.

[170] S. Northcutt, SHADOW, http://www.nswc.navy.mil/ISSEC/CID/, 1998.

[171] K. P. Park and H. Lee, On the Effectiveness of Router-Based Packet Filtering for Distributed Dos Attack Prevention in Power-Law Internets, In *Proceedings of the ACM SIGCOMM Conference*, San Diego, CA, August 2001.

[172] D.B. Parker, Computer Abuse Perpetrators and Vulnerabilities of Computer Systems, Stanford Research Institute, Menlo Park, CA 94025 Technical Report, December 1975.

[173] D.B. Parker, COMPUTER CRIME Criminal Justice Resource Manual, U.S. Department of Justice National Institute of Justice Office of Justice Programs,

Prepared by SRI International under contract to Abt Associates for National Institute of Justice, U.S. Department of Justice, contract #OJP-86-C-002., 1989.

[174] V. Paxson, Bro: A System for Detecting Network Intruders in Real-Time, In *Proceedings of the 7th USENIX Security Symposium*, San Antonio, TX, January 1998.

[175] Pcap, libpcap, winpcap, libdnet, and libnet Applications and Resources, http://www.stearns.org/doc/pcap-apps.html, 2004.

[176] T. Peng, C. Leckie and K. Ramamohanarao, Defending Against Distributed Denial of Service Attack Using Selective Pushback, In *Proceedings of the Ninth IEEE International Conference on Telecommunications (ICT 2002)*, Beijing, China, June 2002.

[177] P. Porras, D. Schanckernberg, S. Staniford-Chen, M. Stillman and F. Wu, Common Intrusion Detection Framework Architecture, http://www.gidos.org/drafts/architecture.txt, 2001.

[178] P.A. Porras and R.A. Kemmerer, Penetration State Transition Analysis: A Rule-Based Intrusion Detection Approach, In *Proceedings of the Eighth Annual Computer Security Applications Conference*, San Antonio, TX, December, 1992.

[179] P.A. Porras and P.G. Neumann, EMERALD: Event Monitoring Enabling Responses to Anomalous Live Disturbances, In *Proceedings of the 20th National Information Systems Security Conference*, Baltimore, MD., 353-365, October, 1997.

[180] P.A. Porras and A. Valdes, Live Traffic Analysis of TCP/IP Gateways, In *Proceedings of the ISOC Symposium on Network and Distributed System Security (NDSS'98)*, San Diego, CA, March 1998.

[181] D. Powell and R. Stroud, Conceptual Model and Architecture, Deliverable D2, Project MAFTIA IST-1999-11583, IBM Zurich Research Laboratory Research Report RZ 3377, Nov. 2001.

[182] Proventia™, Security's Silver Bullet? An Internet Security Systems White Paper, available at:, http://documents.iss.net/whitepapers/ProventiaVision.pdf, 2003.

[183] F. Provost and T. Fawcett, Robust Classification for Imprecise Environments, *Machine Learning*, vol. 42, 3, pp. 203-231, 2001.

[184] T.H. Ptacek and T.N. Newsham, Insertion, Evasion, and Denial of Service: Eluding Network Intrusion Detection, Secure Networks, Inc Technical Report, January 1998.

[185] Michael Puldy, Lessons Learned in the Implementation of a Multi-Location Network Based Real Time Intrusion Detection System, In *Proceedings of the Workshop on Recent Advances in Intrusion Detection (RAID 98)*, Louvain-la-Neuve, Belgium, September 1998.

[186] X. Qin and W. Lee, Statistical Causality Analysis of INFOSEC Alert Data, In *Proceedings of the 6th International Symposium on Recent Advances in Intrusion Detection (RAID 2003)*, Pittsburgh, PA, September 2003.

[187] S. Ramaswamy, R. Rastogi and K. Shim, Efficient Algorithms for Mining Outliers from Large Data Sets, In *Proceedings of the ACM SIGMOD Conference*, Dallas, TX, May 2000.

[188] M.J. Ranum, K. Landfield, M. Stolarchuk, M. Sienkiewicz, A. Lambeth and Wall E., Implementing a Generalized Tool for Network Monitoring, In *Proceedings of the Eleventh Systems Administration Conference (LISA'97)*, San Diego, CA, October 1997.

[189] T. Richardson, The Development of a Database Taxonomy of Vulnerabilities to Support the Study of Denial of Service Attacks., Iowa State University PhD Thesis, 2001.

[190] T. Richardson, J. Davis, D. Jacobson, J. Dickerson and L. Elkin, Developing a Database of Vulnerabilities to Support the Study of Denial of Service Attacks, *IEEE Symposium on Security and Privacy*, May 1999.

[191] S. Robertson, E. Siegel, M. Miller and S. Stolfo, Surveillance Detection in High Bandwidth Environments, In *Proceedings of the 3rd DARPA Information Survivability Conference and Exposition (DISCEX 2003)*, Washington DC, April 2003.

[192] P. Rolin, L. Toutain and S. Gombault, Network Security Probe, In *Proceedings of the 2nd ACM Conference on Computer and Communication Security (ACM CCS'94)*, Fairfax, VA, 229-240, November 1994.

[193] J. Ryan, M-J. Lin and R. Miikkulainen, Intrusion Detection with Neural Networks, In *Proceedings of the AAAI Workshop on AI Approaches to Fraud Detection and Risk Management*, Providence, RI, 72-77, July 1997.

[194] D. Safford, D. Schales and D. Hess, The Tamu Security Package: An Ongoing Response to Internet Intruders in an Academic Environment, In *Proceedings of the Fourth USENIX Security Symposium*, Santa Clara, CA, 91-118, October 1993.

[195] S. Savage, D. Wetherall, A. Karlin and T. Anderson, Practical Network Support for IP Traceback, In *Proceedings of the ACM SIGCOMM Conference*, Stockholm, Sweden, 295-306, August 2000.

[196] M. Schultz, E. Eskin, E. Zadok and S. Stolfo, Data Mining Methods for Detection of New Malicious Executables, In *Proceedings of the IEEE Symposium on Security and Privacy*, Oakland, CA, 38-49, May 2001.

[197] Secure Networks, Inc., Ballista Security Auditing System, http://www.securenetworks.com/ballista/ballista.html, 1997.

[198] SecurityTechNet.com Intrusion Detection Links, http://cnscenter.future.co.kr/security/ids.html, 2004.

[199] R. Sekar, A. Gupta, J. Frullo, T. Shanbhag, A. Tiwari, H. Yang and S. Zhou, Specification Based Anomaly Detection: A New Approach for Detecting Network Intrusions, In *Proceedings of the ACM Conference on Computer and Communications Security (CCS)*, Washington, D.C., November 2002.

[200] A. Seleznyov and S. Puuronen, HIDSUR: A Hybrid Intrusion Detection System Based on Real-Time User Recognition, In *Proceedings of the 11th International Workshop on Database and Expert Systems Applications (DEXA'00)*, Greenwich, London, UK, September, 2000.

[201] K. Sequeira and M. Zaki, ADMIT: Anomaly-base Data Mining for Intrusions, In *Proceedings of the 8th ACM SIGKDD International Conference on Knowledge Discovery and Data Mining*, Edmonton, Canada, July 2002.

[202] C. Sinclair, L. Pierce and S. Matzner, An Application of Machine Learning to Network Intrusion Detection, In *Proceedings of the 15th Annual Computer Security Applications Conference*, Phoenix, AZ, 371-377, December 1999.

[203] S. Singh and Kandula S., Argus: A Distributed Network Intrusion Detection System, Indian Institute of Technology Kanpur, Department of Computer Science &

Engineering, available at: http://www.cse.iitk.ac.in/research/btp2001/Argus.html Technical Report, 2001.

[204] S. Smaha, Haystack: An Intrusion Detection System, In *Proceedings of the Fourth Aerospace Computer Security Applications Conference*, 37-44, October 1988.

[205] S.R. Snapp, J. Brentano, G.V. Dias, T.L. Goan, T. Heberlein, C. Ho, K.N. Levitt, B. Mukherjee, S.E. Smaha, T. Grance, D.M. Teal and D. Mansur, DIDS (Distributed Intrusion Detection System) Motivation, Architecture, and an Early Prototype, In *Proceedings of the 14th National Computer Security Conference*, Washington, DC, 167-176, October 1991.

[206] A.C. Snoeren, C. Partridge, L.A. Sanchez, C.E Jones, F. Tchakountio, S.T. Kent and W.T. Strayer, Hash-Based IP Traceback, In *Proceedings of the ACM SIGCOMM Conference*, San Diego, CA, 3-14, August 2001.

[207] SNORT Intrusion Detection System, www.snort.org, 2004.

[208] Snort-Wireless Intrusion Detection, http://snort-wireless.org, 2003.

[209] A. Somayaji, S. Hofmeyr and S. Forrest, Principles of a computer immune system, In *Proceedings of the New Security Paradigms Workshop*, Langdale, Cumbria UK, 1997.

[210] Sourcefire, Sourcefire Real-time Network Awareness™ (RNA), http://www.sourcefire.com/products/rna.html, 2004.

[211] E. Spafford and D. Zamboni, Intrusion Detection Using Autonomous Agents, *Computer Networks*, vol. 34, pp. 547-570, 2000.

[212] P. Spirakis, S. Katsikas, D. Gritzalis, F. Allegre, J. Darzentas, C. Gigante, D. Karagiannis, P. Kess, H. Putkonen and T. Spyrou, SECURENET: A Network-Oriented Intelligent Intrusion Prevention And Detection System., *Network Security Journal*, vol. 1, 1, November 1994.

[213] T. Spyrou and J. Darzentas, Intention Modelling: Approximating Computer User Intentions for Detection and Prediction of Intrusions, In *Proceedings of the Information Systems Security*, Samos, Greece, 319-335, May 1996.

[214] S. Staniford, J. Hoagland and J. McAlerney, Practical Automated Detection of Stealthy Portscans, *Journal of Computer Security*, vol. 10, 1-2, pp. 105-136, 2002.

[215] S. Staniford, V. Paxson and N. Weaver, How to Own the Internet in Your Spare Time, In *Proceedings of the USENIX Security Symposium*, San Francisco, CA, 149-167, August 2002.

[216] S. Staniford-Chen, C.R. Crawford, M. Dilger, J. Frank, J. Hoagland, K. Levitt, C. Wee, R. Yip and D. Zerkle, GrIDS - A Graph Based Intrusion Detection System for Large Networks, In *Proceedings of the 19th National Information Systems Security Conference*, Baltimore, MD.

[217] S. Staniford-Chen, B. Tung, P. Porras, C. Kahn, D. Schnackenberg, R. Feiertag and M. Stillman, The Common Intrusion Detection Framework - Data Formats, Internet Draft Draft-ietf-cidf-data-formats-00.txt, March 1998.

[218] R. Stone, Centertrack: An IP Overlay Network for Tracking DoS Floods, In *Proceedings of the USENIX Security Symposium*, Denver, CO, 199-212, July 2000.

[219] SunSHIELD Basic Security Module Guide, http://docs.sun.com/db/doc/802-1965?q=BSM, 1995.

[220] Symantec Intruder Alert, http://enterprisesecurity.symantec.com/products/products.cfm?ProductID=171&EID=0, May 2004.

[221] Symantec Security Response, W32.ExploreZip.L.Worm, http://securityresponse.symantec.com/avcenter/venc/data/w32.explorezip.l.worm.html, January 2003.

[222] System Detection, Anomaly Detection: The Antura Difference, http://www.sysd.com/library/anomaly.pdf, 2003.

[223] Talisker's Network Security Resource, http://www.networkintrusion.co.uk/ids.htm,

[224] TCPDUMP public repository, www.tcpdump.org,

[225] S. Templeton and K. Levit, A Requires/Provides Model for Computer Attacks, In *Proceedings of the Workshop on New Security Paradigms*, Ballycotton, Ireland, 2000.

[226] B. Tod, Distributed Denial of Service Attacks, OVEN Digital, http://www.linuxsecurity.com/resource_files/intrusion_detection/ddos-faq.html, 2000.

[227] A. Valdes, Detecting Novel Scans Through Pattern Anomaly Detection, In *Proceedings of the Third DARPA Information Survivability Conference and Exposition (DISCEX-III 2003)*, Washington, D.C., April 2003.

[228] A. Valdes and K. Skinner, Adaptive, Model-based Monitoring for Cyber Attack Detection, In *Proceedings of the Recent Advances in Intrusion Detection (RAID 2000)*, Toulouse, France, 80-92, October 2000.

[229] A. Valdes and K. Skinner, Probabilistic Alert Correlation, In *Proceedings of the Recent Advances in Intrusion Detection (RAID 2001)*, Davis, CA, October 2001.

[230] J. Van Ryan, SAIC's Center for Information Security, Technology Releases CMDS Version 3.5, http://www.saic.com/news/may98/news05-15-98.html, 1998.

[231] Vicomsoft White Paper, Firewall White Paper - What Different Types of Firewalls are There?, available at:, http://www.firewall-software.com/firewall_faqs/types_of_firewall.html, 2003.

[232] G. Vigna and R.A. Kemmerer, Netstat: A Network-Based Intrusion Detection Approach, *Journal of Computer Security*, vol. 7, 1, pp. 37-71, 1999.

[233] D. Vincenzetti and M. Cotrozzi, ATP - Anti Tampering Program, In *Proceedings of the Fourth USENIX Security Symposium*, Santa Clara, CA, 79-89, October 1993.

[234] D. Wagner and D. Dean, Intrusion Detection via Static Analysis, In *Proceedings of the IEEE Symposium on Security and Privacy*, Oakland, CA, May 2001.

[235] H. Wang, D. Zhang and K. Shin, Detecting SYN Flooding Attacks, In *Proceedings of the IEEE Infocom*, New York, NY, 000-001, June 2002.

[236] N. Weaver, V. Paxson, S. Staniford and R. Cunningham, A Taxonomy of Computer Worms, In *Proceedings of the The Workshop on Rapid Malcode (WORM 2003), held in conjunction with the 10th ACM Conference on Computer and Communications Security*, Washington, DC, October 27, 2003.

[237] A. Wespi, M. Dacier and H. Debar, Intrusion Detection Using Variable-Length Audit Trail Patterns, In *Proceedings of the Recent Advances in Intrusion Detection (RAID-2000)*, Toulouse, FR, 110-129, October 2000.

[238] WheelGroup Corporation, Cisco Secure Intrusion Detection System, http://www.cisco.com/univercd/cc/td/doc/product/iaabu/csids/index.htm, 2004.

[239] WIDZ Wireless Intrusion Detection System, www.loud-fat-bloke.co.uk/articles/widz_design.pdf.

[240] D. Winer, Clay Shirky on P2P, davenet.scripting.com/2000/11/15/clayShirkyOnP2p, November 2000.

[241]   J.R. Winkler, A Unix Prototype for Intrusion and Anomaly Detection in Secure
        Networks, In *Proceedings of the 13th National Computer Security Conference*,
        Baltimore, MD, October 1990.

[242]   J.R. Winkler and L.C. Landry, Intrusion and Anomaly Detection, ISOA Update, In
        Proceedings of the 15th National Computer Security Conference, Baltimore, MD,
        October 1992.

[243]   K. Yamanishi and J. Takeuchi, Discovering Outlier Filtering Rules from Unlabeled
        Data, In *Proceedings of the Seventh ACM SIGKDD International Conference on
        Knowledge Discovery and Data Mining*, San Francisco, CA, August 2001.

[244]   K. Yamanishi, J. Takeuchi, G. Williams and P. Milne, On-line Unsupervised Outlier
        Detection Using Finite Mixtures with Discounting Learning Algorithms, In
        *Proceedings of the Sixth ACM SIGKDD International Conference on Knowledge
        Discovery and Data Mining*, Boston, MA, 320-324, August 2000.

[245]   N. Ye and Q. Chen, An Anomaly Detection Technique Based on a Chi-Square
        Statistic for Detecting Intrusions Into Information Systems, *Quality and Reliability
        Engineering International*, vol. 17, 2, pp. 105-112, 2001.

[246]   N. Ye and X. Li, A Scalable Clustering Technique for Intrusion Signature
        Recognition, In *Proceedings of the 2001 IEEE Workshop on Information Assurance
        and Security*, United States Military Academy, West Point, NY, June, 2001.

[247]   Z. Zhang, J. Li, C.N. Manikopoulos, J. Jorgenson and J. Ucles, HIDE: A Hierarchical
        Network Intrusion Detection System Using Statistical Preprocessing and Neural
        Network Classification, In *Proceedings of the IEEE Workshop on Information
        Assurance and Security*, United States Military Academy, West Point, NY, June 2001.

[248]   E. Zwicky, S. Cooper, D. Chapman and D. Ru, *Building Internet Firewalls*, 2nd
        Edition ed, O'Reilly and Associates, 2000.

PART II

DATA MINING BASED ANALYSIS
OF COMPUTER ATTACKS

Chapter 3

LEARNING RULES AND CLUSTERS FOR ANOMALY DETECTION IN NETWORK TRAFFIC

Philip K. Chan,[1,2] Matthew V. Mahoney,[1] and Muhammad H. Arshad[1]

[1]*Department of Computer Sciences, Florida Institute of Technology*

[2]*Laboratory for Computer Science, Massachusetts Institute of Technology*

Abstract: Much of the intrusion detection research focuses on signature (misuse) detection, where models are built to recognize known attacks. However, signature detection, by its nature, cannot detect novel attacks. Anomaly detection focuses on modeling the normal behavior and identifying significant deviations, which could be novel attacks. In this chapter we explore two machine learning methods that can construct anomaly detection models from past behavior. The first method is a rule learning algorithm that characterizes normal behavior in the absence of labeled attack data. The second method uses a clustering algorithm to identify outliers.

Keywords: anomaly detection, machine learning, intrusion detection

1.   INTRODUCTION

The Internet is one of the most influential innovations in recent history. Though most people use the Internet for productive purposes, some use it as a vehicle for malicious intent. As the Internet links more users together and computers are more prevalent in our daily lives, the Internet and the computers connected to it increasingly become more enticing targets of attacks. Computer security often focuses on preventing attacks using usually authentication, filtering, and encryption techniques, but another important facet is detecting attacks once the preventive measures are breached. Consider a bank vault, thick steel doors prevent intrusions, while motion and heat sensors detect intrusions. Prevention and detection complement each other to provide a more secure environment.

How do we know if an attack has occurred or has been attempted? This requires analyzing huge volumes of data gathered from the network, host, or file systems to find suspicious activity. Two general approaches exist for this problem: *signature detection* (also known as *misuse detection*), where we look for patterns signaling well-known attacks, and *anomaly detection*, where we look for deviations from normal behavior. Signature detection works reliably on known attacks, but has the obvious disadvantage of not being capable of detecting new attacks. Though anomaly detection can detect novel attacks, it has the drawback of not being capable of discerning intent; it can only signal that some event is unusual, but not necessarily hostile, thus generating false alarms. A desirable system would employ both approaches.

Signature detection methods are more well understood and widely applied. They are used in both host based systems, such as virus detectors, and in network based systems such as SNORT [32] and BRO [26]. These systems use a set of rules encoding knowledge gleaned from security experts to test files or network traffic for patterns known to occur in attacks. A limitation of such systems is that as new vulnerabilities or attacks are discovered, the rule set must be manually updated. Also minor variations in attack methods can often defeat such systems. For anomaly detection, a model of acceptable behavior can also be specified by humans as well. For example, firewalls are essentially manually written policies dictating what network traffic is considered normal and acceptable.

How do security experts discover new unknown attacks? Generally, the experts identify something out of ordinary, which triggers further investigation. Some of these investigations result in discovering new attacks, while others result in false alarms. From their experience, security experts have learned a model of normalcy and use the model to detect abnormal events. We desire to endow computers with the capability of identifying unusual events similar to humans by learning (data mining) from experience, i.e., historical data.

Since what is considered normal could be different in different environments, a distinct model of normalcy need to be learned individually. This contrasts to manually written polices of normal behavior that require manual customization in each environment. Moreover, since the models are customized to each environment, potential attackers would find them more difficult to circumvent than manually written policies that might be less customized due to inexperienced system administrators who do not change the default parameters and policies supplied by the vendors. Our goal is to learn anomaly detectors that can be customized to individual environments. This goal has a few challenges.

First, anomaly detection is a harder problem than signature detection because signatures of attacks can be very precise but what is considered normal is more abstract and ambiguous. Second, classical machine learning problems are classification tasks—given examples of different classes, learn a model that distinguishes the different classes. However, in anomaly detection, we are essentially given only one class of examples (normal instances) and we need to learn a model that characterizes and predicts the lone class reliably. Since examples of the other classes are absent, traditional machine learning algorithms are less applicable to anomaly detection. Third, research in anomaly detection uses the approach of modeling normal behavior from a (presumably) attack-free training set. However, clean data for training may not be easy to obtain. Lastly, to help humans analyze the alerts, anomaly detectors need to be able to describe the anomalies, though not as precisely as signature detectors are capable.

To meet the second challenge, we propose two methods for learning anomaly detectors: rule learning (LERAD) and clustering (CLAD). CLAD does not assume the training data are free of attacks—the third challenge. For the last challenge, our models are not black boxes. Alerts can be explained by rules that are violated in LERAD or by the centroids of the "near miss" normal clusters in CLAD. Our experimental results indicate that, though anomaly detection is a harder problem (the first challenge), our methods can detect attacks with relatively few false alarms.

This chapter is organized as follows. Section 2 contrasts related techniques in anomaly detection. Section 3 proposes the LERAD algorithm that learns the characterization of normal behavior in logical rules. Section 4 describes a clustering algorithm that can identify behavior far from the normal behavior. We summarize our findings and suggest improvements in Section 5.

2.   RELATED WORK

Anomaly detection is related to biological immunology. Forrest et al. [11] observe that part of our immune system functions by identifying unfamiliar foreign objects and attacking them. For example, a transplanted organ is often attacked by the patient's immune system because the organ from the donor contains objects different from the ones in the patient. Forrest et al. found that when a vulnerable UNIX system program or server is attacked (for example, using a buffer overflow to open a root shell), that the program makes sequences of system calls that differ from the sequences found in normal operation [12]. Forrest used n-gram models (sequences of $n = 3$ to 6 calls), and matched them to sequences observed in training. A score is generated when a sequence observed during detection is different from those stored during training. Other models of normal system call sequences have been used, such as finite state automata [34] and neural networks [13]. Notably, Sekar et al. [34] utilize program counter information to specify states. Though the program counter carries limited information about the state of a program, its addition to their model is different from typical n-gram models that rely solely on sequences of system calls. Lane and Brodley [18] use instance-based methods and Sequeira and Zaki [35] use clustering methods for detecting anomalous user commands.

A host-based anomaly detector is important since some attacks (for example, inside attacks) do not generate network traffic. However, network-based anomaly detectors can warn of attacks launched from the outside at an earlier stage, before the attacks actually reach the host. Current network anomaly detection systems such as eBayes [37], ADAM [4], and SPADE [7] model only features of the network and transport layer, such as port numbers, IP addresses, and TCP flags. Models built with these features could detect probes (such as port scans) and some denial of service (DOS) attacks on the TCP/IP stack, but would not detect attacks of the type detected by Forrest, where the exploit code is transmitted to a public server in the application payload.

Network anomaly detectors estimate the probabilities of events, such as that of a packet being addressed to some port, based on the frequency of similar events seen during training or during recent history, typically several days. They output an anomaly score which is inversely proportional to probability. Anomaly detectors are typically just one component of more comprehensive systems. eBayes is an anomaly detection component of EMERALD [24], which integrates the results from host and network-based detectors that use both signature and anomaly detection. ADAM is a Bayes classifier with categories for normal behavior, known attacks, and unknown attacks. SPADE is a SNORT [32] plug-in. Some anomaly detection algorithms are for specific attacks (e.g., portscans [36]) or services (e.g., DNS [17]).

Most current anomaly detectors use a stationary model, where the probability of an event depends on its average rate during training, and does not vary with time. However, using the average rate could be incorrect for many processes. Paxson and Floyd [27] found that many network processes, such as the rate of a particular type of packet, have self-similar (fractal) behavior. Events do not occur at uniform rates on any time scale. Instead they tend to occur in bursts. Hence, it is not possible to predict the average rate of an event over a time window by measuring the rate in another window, regardless of how short or long the windows are. An example of how a stationary model fails in an anomaly detector would be any attack with a large number of events, such as a port scan or a flooding attack. If the detector correctly identifies each packet as anomalous, then the user would be flooded with thousands of alarms in a few minutes.

Clustering and related techniques have been used to locate outliers in a dataset. Knorr and Ng [16] define an outlier as an object where a fraction p of the dataset is further than distance D from the object, where p and D are parameters specified by the users. Instead of a global perspective [16], LOF [5] uses a local perspective and locates outliers with respect to the density in the local/neighboring region. They illustrate the inability of conventional approaches to detect such outliers. LOF has two short-comings: one, their approach is very sensitive to the choice of $MinPts$, which specifies the minimum number of objects allowed in the local neighborhood (similar to k in k-NN, k-Nearest Neighbor); second, and more importantly, their approach is not well-suited for very high dimensional data such as network traffic data. Ramaswamy et al. [31] investigate the problem of finding the top n outliers. They characterize an outlier by the distance of the kth-nearest neighbor and their algorithm efficiently partitions the input space and prunes partitions that cannot contain the top outliers. Aggarwal and Yu [1] calculate the sparsity coefficient, which compares the observed and expected number of data points, in "cubes" (spatial grid cells) generated by projections on the dataset.

3. LEARNING RULES FOR ANOMALY DETECTION (LERAD)

To build a model for anomaly detection, from a probabilistic perspective, one can attempt to estimate $P(x|D_{NoAttacks})$, where x is an instance under consideration and $D_{NoAttacks}$ is a data set of instances that do not contain attacks. Since all the probabilistic estimations are based on the training data set $D_{NoAttacks}$, for notation convenience, we use $P(x)$ in lieu of $P(x|D_{NoAttacks})$. Under this model, the smaller $P(x)$ is, the more likely x is anomalous.

Each instance x is represented by values from a set of m attributes $a_1, a_2, ..., a_m$. That is, x is a tuple of values $(a_1 = v_1, a_2 = v_2, ..., a_m = v_m)$, where v_i is the value for attribute a_i. The probability $P(x)$ is hence: $P(a_1 = v_i, a_2 = v_2, ..., a_m = v_m)$ or more concisely, $P(v_i, v_2, ..., v_m)$. Using the chain rule is frequently is too computationally expensive. Some researchers assume the attributes to be independent in "Naive" Bayes algorithms [9, 6, 8]. However this assumption is usually invalid. To incorporate attribute dependence, Bayesian networks [28] model a subset of the conditional probabilities structured in networks, which are selected using prior knowledge. Recent work in Bayesian networks attempts to learn the network structures from data. However, Bayesian networks model the entire distribution of each conditional probability and could consume significant computational resources.

Instead of estimating the probability of an instance x, an alternative approach is to estimate the likelihood of values among the attributes in each instance. That is, given some attribute values, we estimate the likelihood of some other attribute values. Again, consider $v_1, ..., v_m = V$ are the values of attributes $a_1, ..., a_m$ of an instance. Let $U \subset V$, $W \subset V$, and $U \cap W = \emptyset$, we would like to estimate: $P(W|U)$. For example, consider these network packet values: $V = \{SrcIp = 128.1.2.3, DestIp = 128.4.5.6, SrcPort = 2222, DestPort = 80\}$. Further we consider $U = \{SrcIp = 128.1.2.3, DestIp = 128.4.5.6\}$ and $W = \{DestPort = 80\}$, hence $P(W|U)$ is: $P(DestPort = 80|SrcIp = 128.1.2.3, DestIp = 128.4.5.6)$.

In anomaly detection we seek combinations of U and W with large $P(W|U)$—W is highly predictive by U. These combinations indicate patterns in the normal training data and fundamentally constitute a model that describes normal behavior. If these patterns are violated during detection, we calculate a score that reflects the severity of the violation and hence the degree of anomaly. That is, the anomaly score depends on $P(\neg W|U)$, where W, though expected, is not observed when U is observed. Finding these patterns could be computationally expensive since the space of combinations is $O(d^m)$, where d is the domain size of an attribute and m is the number of attributes. In the next section we describe our proposed learning algorithm.

LERAD Algorithm

Our goal is to design an efficient algorithm that finds combinations of U and W with large $P(W|U)$ during training and uses $P(\neg W|U)$ to calculate an anomaly score during detection. The task of finding combinations of U and W is similar to finding frequent patterns in association rules [2], where U is the antecedent, W is the consequent, and $P(W|U)$ is the confidence. Algorithms for finding association rules, for example Apriori [2], typically find *all* rules that exceed the user-supplied confidence and support thresholds; consequently, a large number of rules can be generated. Checking large number of rules during detection incurs unacceptable amounts of overhead. However, our goal is different from finding association rules in two fundamental respects. First, the semantics of our rules are designed to estimate $P(\neg W|U)$. Second, we want a "minimal" set of rules that succinctly describes the normal training data. These differences are exhibited in our proposed rules and algorithm called LERAD (LEarning Rules for Anomaly Detection).

Semantics of LERAD Rules.   The semantics of LERAD rules seek to estimate $P(\neg W|U)$; in rule form, a LERAD rule is:

$$U \Rightarrow \neg W \qquad [p = P(\neg W|U)], \qquad (3.1)$$

where p denotes $P(\neg W|U)$ and reflects the likelihood of an anomaly. These rules can be considered as anomaly rules. We also extend the semantics of W. In the consequent instead of allowing a single value for each attribute, our rules allow each attribute to be an element of a set of values. For example, consider $W = \{DestPort \in \{21, 25, 80\}\}$ (instead of $W = \{DestPort = 80\}$), $P(W|U)$ is: $P(DestPort \in \{21, 25, 80\}|SrcIp = 128.1.2.3, DestIp = 128.4.5.6)$ and $P(\neg W|U)$ becomes: $P(DestPort \notin \{21, 25, 80\}|SrcIp = 128.1.2.3, DestIp = 128.4.5.6)$ or in rule form: $SrcIp = 128.1.2.3, DestIp = 128.4.5.6 \Rightarrow DestPort \notin \{21, 25, 80\}$. Given U, the set of values for each attribute in W represents all the values seen in the training data for that particular attribute. Following the above example, given $SrcIp = 128.1.2.3$

and $DestIp = 128.4.5.6$, $DestPort$ is either 21, 25, or 80 in the normal training data. This extension allows our models to be more predictive and conservative so that false alarms are less likely to occur. However, since W includes all the seen values in training, a simplistic estimation of $P(W|U)$ would yield 1 and $P(\neg W|U)$ 0. Obviously, these estimates are too extreme. Since event $\neg W$ is not observed when event U is observed during training, estimating $P(\neg W|U)$ becomes a "zero-frequency" problem [38].

Zero-frequency Problem.   *Laplace* smoothing is commonly used in the machine learning community to handle the zero-frequency problem [25, 23, 30]. One variant of the technique is to assign a frequency of one, instead of zero, to each event at the beginning. Hence, all events, observed or not, will have at least a count of one and none of the events have an estimated probability of zero. That is, the likelihood of a novel event can be estimated by: $P(NovelEvent) = \frac{|A|-r}{n+|A|}$, where $|A|$ is the size of the alphabet A of possible values, n is the total number of observed events and r is the number of unique observed events. However, *Laplace* smoothing is appropriate only for the case where A is known, and for which the *apriori* distribution over A is uniform. In general, A could be very large and unknown (for example, the set of all possible strings in the application payload), and the distribution could be highly skewed toward a few common values.

   Witten and Bell [38] proposed a few estimates for novel events in the context of data compression that are independent of alphabet size and which do not assume an *apriori* uniform distribution; one estimate is:

$$P(NovelEvent) = \frac{r}{n}. \tag{3.2}$$

This measures the average rate of novel values in the sample. Eq. 3.2 is used to estimate $p = P(\neg W|U)$ in Eq. 3.1, where n is the number of instances satisfying the antecedent U and r is the number of unique values in the attribute of the consequent W. We attempted more sophisticated estimators in initial experiments for anomaly detection, but Eq. 3.2 seems to perform as effectively as others and requires the least computation, which is advantageous in mining large amounts of data.

Randomized Algorithm.   In the previous sections we have discussed the semantics of LERAD rules and how $P(\neg W|U)$ can be estimated. We now discuss an efficient algorithm that finds combinations of U and W with low $P(\neg W|U)$ (or high $P(W|U)$). Our algorithm is based on sampling and randomization. Let D be the entire training data set, D_T and D_V be the training and validation sets respectively such that $D_T \cup D_V = D$, $D_T \cap D_V = \emptyset$, and $|D_T| > |D_V|$, and D_S is a random sample of D_T such that $D_S \subset D_T$ and

Table 3.1. Example Training Data Set $D = \{d_i\}$ for $i = 1..6$ (marked by r_k in Step 3)

d_i	a_1	a_2	a_3	a_4	in subset
d_1	1	2 (r_2)	3	4	D_S and D_T
d_2	1	2 (r_2)	3	5	D_S and D_T
d_3	2	6 (r_1)	3	5	D_S and D_T
d_4	2	7	3	5	D_T
d_5	1	2	3	4	D_V
d_6	2	8	3	4	D_V

Table 3.2. Rules (r_k) Generated by LERAD Steps 1-5

Step 1	Step 2
$r_1: * \Rightarrow a_2 = 2$	$r_1: * \Rightarrow a_2 \in \{2, 6\}$
$r_2: a_1 = 1 \Rightarrow a_2 = 2$	$r_2: a_1 = 1 \Rightarrow a_2 = 2$
$r_3: a_1 = 1, a_3 = 3 \Rightarrow a_2 = 2$	$r_3: a_1 = 1, a_3 = 3 \Rightarrow a_2 = 2$

Step 2 (rewritten in Eq.3.1 form)	Step 3
$r_1: * \Rightarrow a_2 \notin \{2, 6\} [p = 2/3]$	$r_2: a_1 = 1 \Rightarrow a_2 \notin \{2\} [p = 1/2]$
$r_2: a_1 = 1 \Rightarrow a_2 \notin \{2\} [p = 1/2]$	$r_1: * \Rightarrow a_2 \notin \{2, 6\} [p = 2/3]$
$r_3: a_1 = 1, a_3 = 3 \Rightarrow a_2 \notin \{2\} [p = 1/2]$	

Step 4	Step 5
$r_2: a_1 = 1 \Rightarrow a_2 \notin \{2\} [p = 1/2]$	$r_2: a_1 = 1 \Rightarrow a_2 \notin \{2\} [p = 1/3]$
$r_1: * \Rightarrow a_2 \notin \{2, 6, 7\} [p = 3/4]$	

$|D_S| \ll |D_T|$. D_E is a separate test/evaluation set disjoint from the training set D. Our proposed mining algorithm consists of five main steps:

1 generate candidate rules from D_S,
2 evaluate candidate rules from D_S,
3 select a "minimal" set of candidate rules that covers D_S,
4 train the selected candidate rules on D_T, and
5 prune the rules that cause false alarms on D_V

Steps 1-3 intend to select a small and predictive set of rules from a small sample D_S of the data. The selected rules are then trained on the much larger set D_T in Step 4. The validation set D_V is used to reduce overfitting in Step 5. For simplicity, we only consider rules that have only one attribute in the consequent. Further details are in [20].

Step 1.   Pairs of instances are randomly chosen from D_S. For each pair of instances, we identify the matching attribute values between the two instances. Consider d_1 and d_2 in Table 3.1 as a random pair, $a_1 = 1$, $a_2 = 2$, and $a_3 = 3$ occur in both instances. The three values are then chosen in random order, e.g., $a_2 = 2$, $a_1 = 1$, and $a_3 = 3$; and the candidate rules in Table 3.2 are generated. The first value ($a_2 = 2$) is chosen to be in the consequent (W) and the the later values are iteratively added to the antecedent (U). In r_1, $*$ is a wild card and matches anything. If the matching attribute values occur often in different instances, they will likely be found matching again in another randomly chosen pair of instances and more rules for these matching attribute values will be generated. That is, the more likely the values are correlated, the more rules will be generated to describe the correlation (duplicate rules are removed).

Step 2.   We evaluate the candidate rules on D_S. Note that the consequent in the candidate rules generated from Step 1 has only one value. In Step 2 we add values to the attribute in the consequent if more values are observed in D_S. d_1 and d_2 do not change the rules. d_3 causes r_1 is to be updated because $a_2 = 6$ in d_3; the other two rules are unchanged because the antecedents are not satisfied for d_3. The new set of candidate rules are in Table 3.2. We then write the rules in the form of Eq. 3.1 and estimate $p = P(\neg W|U)$ for each rule by using Eq. 3.2 in Table 3.2.

Step 3.   We select a "minimal" subset of candidate rules that sufficiently describe D_S. Our method is based on two heuristics. First, we prefer rules with lower $p = P(\neg W|U)$. Second, a rule can cover multiple instances in D_S, but an instance does not need to be covered by more than one rule (more details later). Hence, we sort the rules based on p and evaluate the rules in ascending order. For each rule, we mark instances that are covered by the rule. If a rule cannot mark any remaining unmarked instances, it is removed. That is, we keep rules with lower p and remove rules that do not contribute to covering instances not covered by previous rules with lower p values.

Step 4.   This step is similar to Step 2, except that the rules are updated based on D_T, instead of D_S. d_4 does not affect r_2 since its antecedent does not match. However, 7 is added to the consequent of r_1 and p is updated to 3/4 in Table 3.2. After Step 4, the rules have been trained from D_T.

Step 5.   Since all instances in the validation set D_V are normal, an alarm generated by a rule with any instance in D_V is a false alarm. To reduce overfitting, during Step 5, we remove rules that generate alarms in the validation set. Using our running example, d_5 is normal according to r_1 and r_2. However, r_1 generates an alarm for d_6 since $a_2 = 8 \notin \{2, 6, 7\}$. r_2 does not generate an alarm because $a_1 = 2$, which does not satisfy the antecedent of r_2. Hence, only r_2 remains in Table 3.2. During Step 5, to fully utilize legitimate training data in the validation set, we also update p for rules that are not removed. Hence, p for r_2 was updated to 1/3.

Anomaly Score and Nonstationary Model.   During training, a set of anomaly rules R that "minimally" describes the training data are generated and their $p = P(\neg W|U)$ is estimated. During detection, given an instance x, we generate an anomaly score if x satisfies any of the anomaly rules ($U \Rightarrow \neg W$). Let $S \subset R$ be the set of anomaly rules that x satisfies. The anomaly score is calculated as: $AnomalyScore(x) = \sum_{r_k \in S} \frac{1}{p_k}$, where r_k is a rule in S and p_k is the p value of rule r_k. The reciprocal of p_k reflects a surprise factor that is large when anomaly has a low likelihood (small p_k).

The p estimate is an aggregate over a stationary training period; however, recent events can greatly influence current events. Bursty network traffic or OS activities are common. In intrusion detection we experience that attacks cause bursty behavior as well. In order to incorporate recent novel events into our scoring mechanism, we introduce t_k which is the duration since the last novel value was observed in the consequent of anomaly rule r_k (or when r_k was satisfied). The smaller t_k is, the higher the likelihood that we will see another novel value. That is, intuitively, we are less surprised if we have observed a novel value in a more recent past. Hence, we calculate the anomaly score as:

$$AnomalyScore(x) = \sum_{r_k \in S} \frac{t_k}{p_k}. \qquad (3.3)$$

Summary of Current Results

To evaluate LERAD, we use network traffic recorded in tcpdump provided by the DARPA evaluation in 1999 [19, 15]. Week 3 inside sniffer traffic (which contains no attacks) was used for training (D) and Weeks 4 and 5 (D_E) were used for testing. The size of the validation set ($|D_V|$) was set to be 10% of the training set (D). We set $D_S = 100$ samples. LERAD was run five times with a different random seed. Attributes used in our data sets include IP addresses, port numbers, length, duration, opening and closing TCP flags, and the first 8 words of the application payload of reassembled inbound client TCP streams. LERAD is evaluated based on the number of detected attacks with at most 10 false alarms per day.

In our experiments the resulting set of rules usually contains 50 to 75 rules. Though the rule set is relatively small, LERAD, on the average, detects about 117 attacks out of 201 attacks with at most 10 false alarms per day. Under a "blind" evaluation (the test set was not available apriori), the original DARPA participant with the most detections detected 85 attacks [19]. This indicates LERAD is quite successful in finding highly predictive normal patterns. More importantly, LERAD detects about 58% of the attacks poorly detected by the original participants [19]. That is, LERAD increases the overall coverage of detectable attacks. The total computational overhead is about 30 minutes for three weeks of training and test data. Much of the overhead is in preprocessing of the raw data to generate feature values for training and testing. Training and testing on three weeks of data take less than two minutes. We also analyzed and categorized why our detected anomalies were successful in detecting attacks. The more common categories (covering about 70% of the detected attacks) are unexpected user behavior (e.g., unusual client addresses for servers) and learned (partial) attack signatures (e.g., unusual input that exploit bugs in software). Details of our findings are described in [20].

In [22] we tested LERAD on 623 hours of traffic collected on a university departmental server over a 10 week period. We first used SNORT and manual inspection to identify six attacks that evaded our gateway firewall: an inside automated port/security scan which tests for multiple vulnerabilities, three HTTP worms (*Code Red II*, *Nimda*, and *Scalper*), an HTTP proxy probe, and a DNS version probe. We evaluated LERAD using two attribute sets: TCP streams as above, and a simpler set consisting of just the first 32 pairs of bytes (i.e. 16 bit values) of inbound client IP packets. (To reduce the traffic load, we limited all packets to 16 per minute per session, and TCP up to the first payload packet). Lacking clean training data, we simply used each week's data as training for the following week. Averaged over five runs at 10 false alarms per 24 hours, the TCP version detects 2.4 attacks and the packet version detects 1.4, for a total of 3.0 (50%) after removing overlap. The probability of detection is highest for the most malicious attack (the inside scan), and lowest for the two probes.

LERAD is based on our simpler algorithms PHAD and ALAD, which use fixed rule sets [21]. PHAD was also adapted to detect attacks by modeling accesses to the Registry in the Windows OS [3].

4.   CLUSTERING FOR ANOMALY DETECTION (CLAD)

LERAD assumes the training data are free of attacks, however, making sure the data is clean could be time consuming. We propose to use a clustering approach to identify "outliers" as anomalous. Our clustering method, CLAD, is inspired by the work of [10, 29], and is related to k-NN. CLAD locates anomalies by finding local and global outliers with some restrictions, where k-NN and LOF [5] concentrate mainly on local outliers. One key difference of CLAD from other clustering algorithms is that clusters are of fixed width (radius) and allows clusters to overlap (i.e., the clusters are not mutually exclusive). This difference permits CLAD to process large amounts of data efficiently.

CLAD has two phases: Phase 1 creates the clusters and Phase 2 assigns data points to additional clusters. Fig. 3.1 illustrates the steps of the 2 phases. Given a dataset, D, Phase 1 creates clusters of fixed width, W (which will be discussed later), and assigns data points, $d \in D$, to the created clusters. If a data point is further away than width W from any existing cluster, the data point becomes the centroid of a new cluster; otherwise it is assigned to all existing clusters that

Input: Dataset D
Output: Set of clusters C

   1 initialize the set of clusters, C, to $\emptyset$
      Phase 1: Creating clusters
   2 for $d \in D$
   3   for $c \in C$
   4   if $distance(d, c) \leq W$, assign d to c
   5   if d is not assigned
   6   create cluster c' with d as the centroid and add c' to C
      Phase 2: Assigning data points to additional clusters
   7 for $d \in D$
   8   for $c \in C$
   9   if $distance(d, c) \leq W$ and d is not assigned to c
 10   assign d to c

Figure 3.1. Overall CLAD Algorithm

are not further away than W. In Phase 1 since data points can only be assigned
to existing clusters, some data points might miss assignment to clusters that are
subsequently created. Phase 2 assigns these data points to additional clusters.
So far our CLAD algorithm is basically the clustering algorithm proposed in
[10, 29], however, the methods significantly diverge on how data points are
represented for calculating distance, how the cluster width is determined, and
how the properties of outliers are decided.

Feature Vectors and Distance Function

Each data point, d, is represented by a feature vector, and a cluster, c, is
represented by its centroid, which is a data point. We use the Euclidean distance
as our distance function:

$$distance(Y_1, Y_2) = \sqrt{\sum_{j=1}^{|Y_1|}(Y_{1j} - Y_{2j})^2}, \qquad (3.4)$$

where Y_1 and Y_2 are two feature vectors, Y_{ij} denotes the jth component of Y_i,
and $|Y_i|$ denotes the length of vector Y_i.

To obtain a feature vector for a data point, we transform the data points
represented in the input attribute vectors (X_i) into our feature vectors (Y_i). We
have two types of transformation depending on whether the input attribute is
continuous or discrete. Discrete attributes are usually problematic for distance
functions. In anomaly detection since values that are observed more frequently

are less likely to be anomalous and we want distance to indicate the difference in the degree of normalcy (separating normal from abnormal behavior), we represent a discrete value by its frequency. That is, discrete values of similar frequency are close to each other, but values of very different frequency are far apart. As a result, discrete attributes are transformed to continuous attributes.

In our domain continuous attributes, including those transformed from discrete attributes, usually exhibit a power-law distribution—smaller values are much more frequent than larger values. Distances involving the infrequent large values are large and "drowns" the distances involving only small values. To reduce this problem, we use a logarithmic scale. In addition, to discount variance among values, we quantize the values using the floor operation, after taking the logarithm. Furthermore, in order to consider each attribute equally, the values of each attribute are normalized to the range [0,1]. Formally, an input attribute value, X_{ij}, is transformed to a, feature value, Y_{ij} as follows:

$$Y_{ij} = normalize(\lfloor \ln(X_{ij} + 1) \rfloor), \tag{3.5}$$

where $normalize(v_j) = (v_j - Min_j)/(Max_j - Min_j)$, v_j is a value from vector component j, and Min_j (Max_j) is the minimum (maximum) value of component j. To avoid negative and undefined values (when $0 \le X_{ij} < 1$), we add 1 to X_{ij} before taking ln.

For normalization, we also considered the number of standard deviations (SD) away from average. However, power-law distributions are one-sided and heavy-tailed, so standard deviations are not very appropriate for our purpose. Using SD for normalization resulted in noticeable degradation in performance in our experiments. Therefore, we revert to simple scaling as a means of normalization.

Cluster Width

The cluster width, W, specifies the local neighborhood of clusters that are considered close. The width is specified by the user in [29]. CLAD derives the width from the smallest distances between pairs of data points. To efficiently calculate the width, CLAD randomly draws a sample, of size $s = 1\% \times |D|$, from the entire dataset, D, and calculates the pair-wise distances. The bottom 1% of the pair-wise distances (i.e., $1\% \times s(s - 1)/2$ pairs) are considered the smallest and their average is the cluster width. That is, CLAD samples pair-wise distances and uses the average distance of the closest neighbors as W. Though CLAD has a fixed parameter of 1% for deriving W, it is much less ad hoc than asking the user to specify W, which becomes a parameter. Our parameter is similar to specifying k in k-NN methods, but our parameter is in relative percentage, which is different from the absolute count of k and is conceptually easier to specify and understand.

Density, Inter-cluster Distance, and Anomalies

To determine if a cluster is an outlier, CLAD relies on two properties of a cluster: density and distance from the other clusters. Since each cluster has the same W (and hence "area"), we define the density of cluster c_i as the number of data points, $Count_i$, in c_i. For the distance from the other clusters, we calculate the average inter-cluster distance (ICD) between c_i and the other clusters. Formally, we denote ICD_i as the ICD of cluster c_i and define ICD_i as:

$$ICD_i = \frac{1}{|C| - 1} \sum_{j=1, \neq i}^{|C|} distance(c_i, c_j) \qquad (3.6)$$

where C, as similarly defined before, is the set of clusters.

Outliers are generally *distant* and *sparse*. A cluster c_i is considered *distant* if ICD_i is more than a standard deviation away from the average ICD. From our initial experiments, we observe that the distribution of $Count$ exhibits a power-law distribution; when we use average and SD for $Count$, the average is very small and few/no clusters have $Count_i$ one SD smaller than the average. Hence, instead of using the average we use the median; a cluster c_i is considered sparse when $Count_i$ is more than one median absolute deviation (MAD) [14] smaller than the median $Count$. Interestingly, in our domain an attack could be composed of many data points (e.g., flooding attacks), and hence *dense* regions could be attacks as well. We will discuss this issue further in the next section when we evaluate CLAD. Accordingly, we define *dense* clusters, which have $Count_i$ more than one MAD larger than the median $Count$. More formally, the set of distant clusters $C_{distant}$, sparse clusters C_{sparse}, and dense clusters C_{dense}, are defined as:

$$C_{distant} = \{c_i \in C | ICD_i > AVG(ICD) + SD(ICD)\}, \qquad (3.7)$$

$$C_{sparse} = \{c_i \in C | Count_i < AVG(Count) - MAD(Count)\}, \qquad (3.8)$$

$$C_{dense} = \{c_i \in C | Count_i > AVG(Count) + MAD(Count)\}, \qquad (3.9)$$

where AVG is the average function. CLAD generates alerts for clusters that are sparse and distant, or dense and distant. Each cluster is represented by its centriod.

A *sparse* cluster/region is essentially a local outlier, i.e., it reflects how many neighbors are within W. This is similar to k-NN which computes distance to the closest k neighbors, as discussed previously. Labeling a region *distant* is equivalent to saying that the region is a global outlier.

Summary of Current Results

As with the evaluation of LERAD, we use the same DARPA 99 dataset to evaluate CLAD. Connections are similarly reassembled and the first 10 bytes

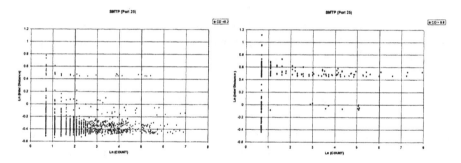

Figure 3.2. $Count$ and ICD of clusters for port 25 with CD a. $< 20\%$, b. $> 80\%$

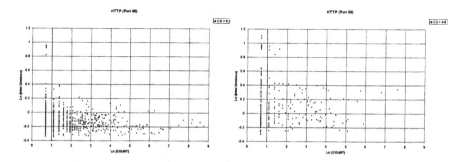

Figure 3.3. $Count$ and ICD of clusters for port 80 with CD a. $< 20\%$, b. $> 80\%$

from the application payload are in the input data. Unlike LERAD, CLAD does not require an explicit training phase, we combine the normal training data (Weeks 1 and 3) and test data (Weeks 4 and 5); the additional normal training data also help reduce the unusually high rate of attacks in the test data.

To improve effectiveness and efficiency, CLAD learns a model for each port (application protocol). For ports that are rarely used ($< 1\%$ of the dataset), we lump them into one model: "Other." Only clusters that are sparse and distant, or dense and distant trigger alerts. To make anomaly scores comparable across models, anomaly scores are normalized to the number of SD's away from the average ICD.

Density is not used in the anomaly score because it is not as reliable as ICD. This results from our analysis of how attacks are distributed between density and ICD on ports 25 and 80, which have the most traffic. Since we do not have exact labels (attack or normal) for each data point, we rely on how DARPA/LL counts an alert as a detection of an attack [19]. We define CD (counted as detection) of a cluster as the percentage of data points in the cluster, when used to trigger an alert, is counted as a detection of an attack. This is an indirect rough approximation of the likelihood of an attack present in the cluster. We plot clusters with $CD < 20\%$ ("unlikely anomalies") against

Table 3.3. Number of detections by CLAD (duplicates are removed in *Combined*)

Port	20	21	23	25	53	79	80	110	111	143	Other	*Combined*
Detections	3	14	17	33	5	8	37	2	1	3	14	76

$Count$ and ICD in Fig. 3.2a and similarly for $CD > 80\%$ ("likely anomalies") in Fig. 3.2b. Both $Count$ and ICD are in log scale. As we compare the two plots, we observe that the likely anomalies occur more often in regions with larger ICD, and the opposite for unlikely anomalies with smaller ICD. The same observation cannot be made for $Count$. This is related to the fact that some attacks can occur in dense clusters as we explained previously. For port 80 in Fig 3.3, similar observations can be made. The figures also indicate that sparse and distant, or dense and distant clusters, which we use to trigger alerts, are likely to detect attacks. Furthermore, for port 80, 96% of the clusters have $CD = 100\%$ or $< 9\%$ (similarly for port 25). This indicates that most of the clusters are near homogeneous and hence our combination of feature vectors, distance function, and cluster width can sufficiently characterize the data.

Table 3.3 shows the number of attacks detected by models learned for each port with at most 100 false alarms during the 10 day attack period in Weeks 4 and 5. The combined model detected 76 attacks, after removing duplicate detections from individual models. As mentioned perviously, the original DARPA participant with the most detections detected 85 attacks [19], which was achieved by a signature detector built by hand—unlike CLAD, which is an anomaly detector with no apriori knowledge of attacks. Compared to LERAD, CLAD detected fewer detections, but CLAD is handicapped by not assuming the availability of attack-free training data. However, we seem to detect more attacks than similar techniques [10, 29], which make similar assumptions, but we cannot claim that since the datasets are different. Further experimentation would help reduce the uncertainty.

5.   CONCLUDING REMARKS

We motivated the significance of a machine learning approach to anomaly detection and have proposed two machine learning methods for constructing anomaly detectors. LERAD is a learning algorithm that can characterize normal behavior in logical rules. CLAD is a clustering algorithm that can identify outliers from normal clusters. We evaluated both methods with the DARPA 99 dataset and show that our methods can detect more attacks than similar existing techniques.

LERAD and CLAD have different strengths and weaknesses. We would like to investigate more how one's strengths can benefit the other. Unlike CLAD, LERAD assumes the training data are free of attacks. This assumption can be relaxed by assigning scores to events that have been observed during training;

these scores can be related to the estimated probability of observing the seen events. Unlike CLAD, LERAD is an offline algorithm. An online LERAD would update the random sample used in the rule generation phase with new data by a replacement strategy, and additional rules would be constructed that consider both new and old data.

Unlike LERAD, CLAD does not aim to generate a concise model, which can affect the efficiency during detection. We plan to explore merging similar clusters in a hierarchical manner and dynamically determine the appropriate number of clusters according to the L method [33]. Also, CLAD does not explain alerts well; we plan to use the notion of "near miss" to explain an alert by identifying centriods of normal clusters with few attributes contributing much of the distance between the alert and the normal centroid. We are also investigating extracting features from the payload, as well as applying our methods to host-based data.

ACKNOWLEDGMENTS

This research is partially supported by DARPA (F30602-00-1-0603).

REFERENCES

[1] C. Aggarwal and P. Yu. Outlier detection for high dimensional data. In *Proc. SIGMOD*, 2001.

[2] R. Agrawal, T. Imielinski, and A. Swami. Mining association rules between sets of items in large databases. In *Proc. ACM SIGMOD Conf.*, pages 207–216, 1993.

[3] F. Apap, A. Honig, S. Hershkop, E. Eskin, and S. Stolfo. Detecting malicious software by monitoring anomalous windows registry accesses. In *Proc. Fifth Intl. Symp. Recent Advances in Intrusion Detection (RAID)*, 2002.

[4] D. Barbara, N. Wu, and S. Jajodia. Detecting novel network intrusions using bayes estimators. In *Proc. SIAM Intl. Conf. Data Mining*, 2001.

[5] M. Breunig, H. Kriegel, R. Ng, and J. Sander. Lof: Identifying density-based local outliers. In *Proc. SIGMOD*, 2000.

[6] P. Clark and T. Niblett. The CN2 induction algorithm. *Machine Learning*, 3:261–285, 1989.

[7] Silicon Defense. SPADE, 2001. http://www.silicondefense.com/software/spice/.

[8] P. Domingos and M. Pazzani. On the optimality of the simple bayesian classifier under zero-one loss. *Machine Learning*, 29:103–130, 1997.

[9] R. Duda and P. Hart. *Pattern classification and scene analysis*. Wiley, New York, NY, 1973.

[10] E. Eskin, A. Arnold, M. Prerau, L. Portnoy, and S. Stolfo. A geometric framework for unsupervised anomaly detection: Detecting intrusions in unlabeled data. In D. Barbara and S. Jajodia, editors, *Applications of Data Mining in Computer Security*. Kluwer, 2002.

[11] S. Forrest, S. Hofmeyr, and A. Somayaji. Computer immunology. *Comm. ACM*, 4(10):88–96, 1997.

[12] S. Forrest, S. Hofmeyr, A. Somayaji, and T. Longstaff. A sense of self for unix processes. In *Proc. of 1996 IEEE Symp. on Computer Security and Privacy*, 1996.

[13] A. Ghosh, A. Schwartzbard, and M. Schatz. Learning program behavior profiles for intrusion detection. In *Proc. 1st USENIX Workshop on Intrusion Detection and Network Monitoring*, 1999.

[14] J. Han and M. Kamber. *Data Mining: Concepts and Techniques*. Morgan Kaufmann, 2000.

[15] K. Kendall. A database of computer attacks for the evaluation of intrusion detection systems. Master's thesis, EECS Dept., MIT, 1999.

[16] E. Knorr and T. Ng. Algorithms for mining distance-based outliers in large datasets. In *Proc. VLDB*, 1998.

[17] C. Krugel, T. Toth, and E. Kirda. Service specific anomaly detection for network intrusion detection. In *Proc. ACM Symp. on Applied Computing*, 2002.

[18] T. Lane and C. Brodley. Temporal sequence learning and data reduction for anomaly detection. *ACM Trans. Information and System Security*, 1999.

[19] R. Lippmann, J. Haines, D. Fried, J. Korba, and K. Das. The 1999 DARPA off-line intrusion detection evaluation. *Computer Networks*, 34:579–595, 2000.

[20] M. Mahoney and P. Chan. Learning models of network traffic for detecting novel attacks. Technical Report CS-2002-08, Florida Inst. of Tech., Melbourne, FL, 2002. http://www.cs.fit.edu/~pkc/papers/cs-2002-08.pdf.

[21] M. Mahoney and P. Chan. Learning nonstationary models of normal network traffic for detecting novel attacks. In *Proc. Eighth Intl. Conf. on Knowledge Discovery and Data Mining*, pages 376–385, 2002.

[22] M. Mahoney and P. Chan. Learning Rules for Anomaly Detection of Hostile Network Traffic. Technical Report CS-2003-16, Florida Inst. of Tech., Melbourne, FL, 2003. http://www.cs.fit.edu/~pkc/papers/cs-2003-16.pdf.

[23] T. Mitchell. *Machine Learning*. McGraw Hill, 1997.

[24] P. Neumann and P. Porras. Experience with EMERALD to date. In *Proc. 1st USENIX Workshop on Intrusion Detection and Network Monitoring*, pages 73–80, 1999.

[25] T. Niblett. Constructing decision trees in noisy domain. In *Proc. 2nd European Working Session on Learning*, pages 67–78, 1987.

[26] V. Paxson. Bro: A system for detecting network intruders in real-time. In *Proc. 7th USENIX Security Symp.*, 1998.

[27] V. Paxson and S. Floyd. The failure of poisson modeling. *IEEE/ACM Transactions on Networking*, 3:226–24, 1995.

[28] J. Pearl. *Probabilistic Reasoning in Intelligent Systems: Networks of Plausible Inference*. Morgan Kaufmann, 1987.

[29] L. Portnoy. Intrusion detection with unlabeled data using clustering. Undergraduate Thesis, Columbia University, 2000.

[30] F. Provost and P. Domingos. Tree induction for probability-based rankings. *Machine Learning*, 2002.

[31] S. Ramaswamy, R. Rastogi, and K. Shim. Efficient algorithms for mining outliers from large data sets. In *Proc. SIGMOD*, 2000.

[32] M. Roesch. Snort – lightweight intrusion detection for networks. In *USENIX LISA*, 1999.

[33] S. Salvador and P. Chan. Learning states and rules for time-series anomaly detection. Technical Report CS-2003-05, Florida Inst. of Tech., Melbourne, FL, 2003. http://www.cs.fit.edu/~pkc/papers/cs-2003-05.pdf.

[34] R. Sekar, M. Bendre, D. Dhurjati, and P. Bollinen. A fast automaton-based method for detecting anomalous program behaviors. In *Proc. IEEE Symp. Security and Privacy*, 2001.

[35] K. Sequira and M. Zaki. ADMIT: Anomaly-based data mining for intrusions. In *Proc. KDD*, 2002.

[36] S. Staniford, J. Hoagland, and J. McAlerney. Practical automated detection of stealthy portscans. *J. Computer Security*, 2002.

[37] A. Valdes and K. Skinner. Adaptive model-based monitoring for cyber attack detection. In *Proc. RAID*, pages 80–92, 2000.

[38] I. Witten and T. Bell. The zero-frequency problem: estimating the probabilities of novel events in adaptive text compression. *IEEE Trans. on Information Theory*, 37(4):1085–1094, 1991.

Chapter 4

STATISTICAL CAUSALITY ANALYSIS OF INFOSEC ALERT DATA

Wenke Lee, Xinzhou Qin

College of Computing, Georgia Institute of Technology

Abstract: With the increasingly widespread deployment of security mechanisms, such as firewalls, intrusion detection systems (IDSs), antivirus software and authentication services, the problem of alert analysis has become very important. The large amount of alerts can overwhelm security administrators and prevent them from adequately understanding and analyzing the security state of the network, and initiating appropriate response in a timely fashion. Recently, several approaches for alert correlation and attack scenario analysis have been proposed. However, these approaches all have limited capabilities in detecting new attack scenarios. In this paper, we study the problem of security alert correlation with an emphasis on attack scenario analysis. In our framework, we use clustering techniques to process low-level alert data into high-level aggregated alerts, and conduct *causal analysis* based on statistical tests to discover new relationships among attacks. Our statistical causality approach complements other approaches that use hard-coded prior knowledge for pattern matching. We perform a series of experiments to validate our method using DARPA's Grand Challenge Problem (GCP) datasets, the 2000 DARPA Intrusion Detection Scenario datasets, and the DEF CON 9 datasets. The results show that our approach can discover new patterns of attack relationships when the alerts of attacks are statistically correlated.

Keywords: Intrusion detection, alert correlation, attack scenario analysis, time series analysis

1.   INTRODUCTION

Information security (INFOSEC) is a complex process with many challenging problems. Deploying INFOSEC mechanisms, e.g., authentication systems, firewalls, intrusion detection systems (IDSs), antivirus software, and network management and monitoring systems, is just one of the necessary steps in the security process. INFOSEC devices often output a large amount of low-level or incomplete alert information because there is a large number of network and system activities being monitored and multiple INFOSEC systems can each report some aspects of the same (coordinated) security event. The sheer quantity of alerts from these security components and systems also overwhelms security administrators. The large number of low-level or incomplete alert information can prevent intrusion response systems and security administrators from adequately understanding and analyzing the security state of the network, and initiating appropriate response in a timely fashion. From a security administrator's point of view, it is important to reduce the redundancy of alarms, intelligently integrate and correlate security alerts, construct attack scenarios (defined as a sequence of related attack steps) and present high-level aggregated information from multiple local-scale events. Correlating alerts of the related attack steps to identify an attack scenario can also help forensic analysis, response and recovery, and even prediction of forthcoming attacks.

Recently there have been several proposals on alert correlation (e.g., [4], [7], [10], [23], [26], [29]). Most of these proposed approaches have limited capabilities because they rely on various forms of predefined knowledge of attack conditions and consequences. They cannot recognize a correlation when an attack is new (previously unknown) or the relationship between attacks is new. In other words, these approaches in principle are similar to *misuse detection* techniques, which use the "signatures" of known attacks to perform pattern matching and cannot detect new attacks. It is obvious that the number of possible correlations is very large, potentially a combinatorial of the number of (known and new) attacks. It is infeasible to know *a priori* and encode all possible matching conditions between attacks. To further complicate the matter, the more dangerous and intelligent adversaries will always invent new attacks and novel attack sequences. Therefore, we must develop significantly better alert correlation algorithms that can discover sophisticated and new attack sequences.

In this paper, we study the problem of INFOSEC alert analysis with an emphasis on attack scenario analysis. The analysis mechanism is based on time series and statistical analysis. We reduce the high volume of raw alerts by combining low-level alerts based on alert attributes. Clustering techniques are used to group low-level alert data into high-level alerts. We prioritize alerts based on the relevance of attacks to the protected networks and hosts and the impacts of attacks on the mission goals. We then conduct causality analysis to correlate alerts and construct attack scenarios. We perform a series of experiments to validate our method using DARPA's Grand Challenge Problem (GCP) datasets and the DEF CON 9 datasets. Our results show that our approach can discover new patterns of alert relationships without depending on prior knowledge of attack scenarios. Our statistical approach complements other approaches in that our correlation approach does not depend on the hard-coded prior knowledge for pattern matching and can discover new attack relationships when the alerts of attacks are statistically correlated.

The emphasis of this paper is on statistical causality analysis. The remainder of this paper is organized as follows. In Section 2, we introduce Granger Causality Test, a time series analysis method. Our alert correlation steps and algorithms are presented in Section 3. In Section 4, we report the experiments and results on the GCP datasets, the 2000 DARPA Intrusion Detection Scenario datasets and the DEF CON 9 datasets. Section 5 discusses related work. We summarize our work and future work in Section 6.

2. GRANGER CAUSALITY ANALYSIS

Time series analysis aims to identify the nature of a phenomenon represented by a sequence of observations. The objective requires the study of patterns of the observed time series data. Time series analysis has been widely used in many applications, e.g., earthquake forecasting and economy analysis. In this section, we introduce time series based causal analysis, and in particular, the Granger Causality Test [11].

Time Series Analysis

A time series is an ordered finite set of numerical values of a variable of interest along the time axis. It is assumed that the time interval between con-secutively recorded values is constant. We denote a univariate time series as $x(k)$, where $k = 0, 1, \ldots, N - 1$, and N denotes the number of elements in $x(k)$.

Time series causal analysis deals with analyzing the correlation between time series variables and discovering the causal relationships. Causal anal-ysis in time series has been widely studied and used in many applications, e.g., economy forecasting and stock market analysis. Network security is an-other application in which time series analysis can be very useful. In our prior work [1, 3], we have used time series-based causality analysis for pro-active detection of Distributed-Denial-of-Service (DDoS) attacks using MIB II [28] variables. We based our approach on the Granger Causality Test (GCT) [11]. Our results showed that the GCT is able to detect the "precursor" events, e.g., the communication between Master and Slave hosts, without prior knowledge of such communication signatures, on the attacker's network before the victim is completely overwhelmed (e.g., shutdown) at the final stage of DDoS.

In this work, we apply the GCT to INFOSEC alert streams for alert correlation and scenario analysis. The intuition is that attack steps that do not have well-known patterns or obvious relationships may nonetheless have some statistical correlations in the alert data. For example, there are one or more alerts for one attack only when there are also one or more alerts for another attack. We can apply statistical causality analysis to find such alerts to identify an attack scenario. We next give some background on the GCT.

Granger Causality Test

The intuition of Granger Causality is that if an event X is the cause of another event Y, then the event X should precede the event Y. Formally, the Granger Causality Test (GCT) uses statistical functions to test if *lagged* information on a time-series variable x provides any statistically significant information about another time-series variable y. If the answer is yes, we say variable x Granger-causes y. We model variable y by two auto-regression models, namely, the Autoregressive Model (AR Model) and the Autoregressive Moving Average Model (ARMA Model). The GCT compares the residuals of the AR Model with the residuals of the ARMA Model. Specifically, for two time series variables y and x with size N, the Autoregressive Model of y is defined as:

$$y(k) = \sum_{i=1}^{p} \theta_i y(k - i) + e_0(k) \tag{4.1}$$

The Autoregressive Moving Average Model of y is defined as:

$$y(k) = \sum_{i=1}^{p} \alpha_i y(k - i) + \sum_{i=1}^{p} \beta_i x(k - i) + e_1(k) \tag{4.2}$$

Here, p is a particular lag length, and parameters α_i, β_i and θ_i ($1 \leq i \leq p$) are computed in the process of solving the Ordinary Least Square (OLS) problem (which is to find the parameters of a regression model in order to have the minimum estimation error). The residuals of the AR Model is $R_0 = \sum_{k=1}^{T} e_0^2(k)$, and the residuals of the ARMA Model is $R_1 = \sum_{k=1}^{T} e_1^2(k)$. Here, $T = N - p$.

The AR Model, i.e., Equation 4.1, represents that the current value of variable y is predicted by its past p values. The residuals R_0 indicate the total sum of squares of error. The ARMA Model, i.e., Equation 4.2, shows that the current value of variable y is predicted by the past p values of both variable y and variable x. The residuals R_1 represents the sum of squares of prediction error.

The Null Hypothesis H_0 of GCT is $H_0 : \beta_i = 0, i = 1, 2, \cdots, p$. That is, x does not affect y up to a delay of p time units. We denote g as the Granger Causality Index (GCI):

$$g = \frac{(R_0 - R_1)/p}{R_1/(T - 2p - 1)} \sim F(p, T - 2p - 1) \tag{4.3}$$

Here, $F(a, b)$ is Fisher's F distribution with parameters a and b [14]. F-test is conducted to verify the validity of the Null Hypothesis. If the value of g

is larger than a critical value in the F-test, then we reject the Null Hypothesis and conclude that x Granger-causes y. Critical values of F-test depends on the degree of freedoms and significance value. The critical values can be looked up in a mathematic table [15].

The intuition of GCI (g) is that it indicates how better variable y can be predicted using histories of both variable x and y than using the history of y alone. In the ideal condition, the ARMA model precisely predicts variable y with residuals $R_1 = 0$, and the GCI value g is infinite. Therefore, the value of GCI (g) represents the strength of the causal relationship. We say that variable $\{x_1(k)\}$ is more likely to be causally related with $\{y(k)\}$ than $\{x_2(k)\}$ if $g_1 > g_2$ and both have passed the F-test, where g_i, $i = 1, 2$, denotes the GCI for the input-output pair (x_i, y).

Applying the GCT to alert correlation, the task is to determine which hyper alerts among $B_1, B_2, \ldots, B_l$ are the most likely to have the causal relationship with hyper alert A (a hyper alert represents a sequence of alerts in the same cluster, see Section 3). For a hyper alert time series, say A, each $A(k)$ is the number of alerts occurring within a certain time period. In other words, we are testing the statistical correlation of alert instances to determine the causal relationship between alerts. For each pair of hyper alerts $(B_i, A), i = 1, 2, \ldots, l$, we compute the GCI value g_i. We record the alerts whose GCI values have passed the F-test as the candidates, and rank order the candidate alerts according to their GCI values. We can then select the top m candidate alerts and regard them as being causally related to alert A. These (candidate) relationships can be subject to more inspection by other analysis techniques such as probabilistic reasoning or plan recognition.

The main advantage of using statistical causality test such as GCT for alert correlation is that this approach does not require *a priori* knowledge about attack behaviors and how the attacks could be related. This approach can identify the correlation between two attack steps as long as the two have a high probability (not necessarily high frequency) of occurring together. We believe that there is a large number of attacks, e.g., worms, that have attack steps with such characteristics. Thus, we believe that causal analysis is a very useful technique. As discussed in [1], [3], [2], when there is sufficient training data available, we can use GCT off-line to compute and validate very accurate causal relationships from alert data. We can then update the knowledge base with these "known" correlations for efficient pattern matching in run-time. When GCT is used in real-time and finds a new causal relationship, as discussed above, the top m candidates can be selected for further analysis by other techniques.

3.   ALARM CORRELATION

In this section, we describe our framework for alert correlation and attack scenario construction. Specifically, the steps include alert aggregation and clustering, alert prioritization, alert time series formulation, alert correlation, and scenario construction.

Alert Aggregation and Clustering

One of the issues with deploying multiple security devices is the sheer amount of alerts output by the devices. The large volume of alerts makes it very difficult for the security administrator to analyze attack events and handle alerts in a timely fashion. Therefore, the first step in alert analysis is alert aggregation and volume reduction.

In our approach, we use alert fusion and clustering techniques to reduce the redundancy of alerts while keeping the important information. Specifically, each alert has a number of attributes such as *timestamp*, *source IP*, *destination IP*, *port(s)*, *user name*, *process name*, *attack class*, and *sensor ID*, which are defined in the standard document "Intrusion Detection Message Exchange Format (IDMEF)" [12] drafted by the IETF Intrusion Detection Working Group.

In alert fusion, there are two steps. First, we combine alerts that have the same attributes except timestamps. The timestamps can be slightly different, e.g., 2 seconds apart. Second, based on the results of step 1, we aggregate alerts with the same attributes but are reported from different heterogeneous sensors. The alerts varied on time stamp are fused together if they are close enough to fall in a pre-defined time window.

Alert clustering is used to further group alerts after alert fusion. Based on various clustering algorithms, we can group alerts in different ways according to the *similarity* among alerts, (e.g., [29] and [17]). Currently, based on the results of alert fusion, we further group alerts that have same attributes except time stamps into one cluster. After this step, we have further reduced the redundancy of alerts.

A *Hyper Alert* is defined as a time ordered sequence of alerts that belong to the same cluster.

For example, after alert clustering, we have a series of alerts, A_1, A_2, ..., A_n in one cluster that have the same attributes along the time axis, and we use hyper alert A to represent this sequence of alerts.

Alert Prioritization

The next phase of alert processing is to prioritize each hyper alert based on its relevance to the mission goals. The objective is that, with the alert priority rank, security analyst can select important alerts as the target alerts for further correlation and analysis. Specifically, the priority score of an alert is computed based on the relevance of the alert to the configuration of the protected networks and hosts as well as the severity of the corresponding attack assessed by the security analyst. Porras et al. proposed a more comprehensive mechanism of incident/alert rank computation model in a "mission-impact-based" correlation engine, named M-Correlator [26]. Because we focus on alert correlation and scenario analysis instead of alert priority ranking, and alert prioritization is just an intermediate step to facilitate further alert analysis, we adapted the priority computation model of M-Correlator with a simplified design.

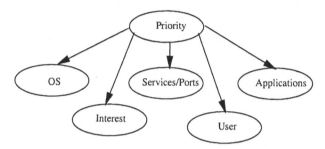

Figure 4.1. Alert Priority Computation Model

Figure 4.1 shows our priority computation model that is constructed based on Bayesian networks [25]. We use Bayesian inference to obtain a belief over states (hypotheses) of interests. A Bayesian network is usually represented as a directed acyclic graph (DAG) where each node represents a variable, and the directed edges represent the causal or dependent relationships among the variables. A conditional probability table (CPT) [25] is associated with each child node. It encodes the prior knowledge between the child node and its parent node. Specifically, an element of the CPT at a child node is defined by $CPT_{ij} = P(child\_state = j | parent\_state = i)$ [25]. The belief in hypotheses of the root is related to the belief propagation from its child nodes, and ultimately the evidence at the leaf nodes.

Specifically, in our priority computation model, the root represents the priority with two hypothesis states, i.e., "high" and "low". Each leaf node has three states. For node "Interest", its three states are "low", "medium" and "high". For other nodes, the three states are "matched", "unmatched" and "unknown". The computation result is a value in [0,1] where 1 is the highest priority score.

We denote e^k as the kth leaf node and H_i as the ith hypothesis of the root node. Given the evidence from the leaf nodes, assuming conditional independence with respect to each H_i, the belief in hypothesis at the root is: $P(H_i | e^1, e^2, \ldots, e^N) = \gamma P(H_i) \prod_{k=1}^{N} P(e^k | H_i)$, where $\gamma = [P(e^1, e^2, \ldots, e^N)]^{-1}$ and γ can be computed using the constraint $\sum_i P(H_i | e^1, e^2, \ldots, e^N) = 1$. For example, for the hyper alert of *FTP Globbing Buffer Overflow* attack, we get evidence [high, matched, matched, unknown, unknown] from the corresponding leaf nodes, i.e., Interest, OS, Services/Ports, Applications and User, respectively. As Figure 4.1 shows, the root node represents the priority of hyper alert. Assume that we have the prior probabilities for the hypotheses of the root, i.e., $P(Priority = high) = 0.8$ and $P(Priority = low) = 0.2$, and the following conditional probabilities as defined in the CPT at each leaf node, *P(Interest = high | Priority = high) = 0.70, P(Interest = high | Priority = low) = 0.10, P(OS = matched | Priority = high) = 0.75, P(OS = matched | Priority = low) = 0.20, P(Services = matched | Priority = high) = 0.70, P(Services = matched | Priority = low) = 0.30, P(Applications = unknown | Priority = high) = 0.15, P(Applications = unknown | Priority = low) = 0.15, P(User = unknown | Priority = high) = 0.10, P(User = unkown | Priority = low) = 0.10*, we then can get $\gamma = 226.3468$, therefore, *P(Priority = high | Interest = matched, OS = matched, Service = matched, Applications = matched, User = unknown) = 0.9959*. We regard this probability as the priority score of the alert. The current CPTs are predefined based on our experience and domain knowledge. It is our future work to develop an adaptive priority computation model so that the CPTs can be adaptive and updated according to specific mission goals.

To calculate the priority of each hyper alert, we compare the dependencies of the corresponding attack represented by the hyper alert against the configurations of target networks and hosts. We have a knowledge base in which each hyper alert has been associated with a few fields that indicate its attacking OS, services/ports and applications. For the alert output from a host-based IDS, we will further check if the target user exists in the host configuration. The purpose of relevance check is that we can downgrade the importance of some alerts that are unrelated to the protected domains. For example, an attacker may launch an individual buffer overflow attack against a service blindly, without knowing if the service exists. It is quite possible that a signature-based IDS outputs the alert once the packet contents match the detection rules even though such service does not exist on the protected host. The relevance check on the alerts aims to downgrade the impact of such kind of alerts on further correlation analysis. The interest of the attack is assigned by the security analyst based on the nature of the attack and missions of the target hosts and services in the protected domain.

Alert Time Series Formulation

After the above processes, we formulate each hyper alert into a univariate time series. Specifically, we set up a series of time slots with equal time interval, denoted as T, along the time axis. Given a time range H, we can have $N = H/T$ time slots. Recall that each hyper alert A represents a sequence of alerts in the same cluster in which all alerts have the same attributes except timestamp, i.e.,

$A = [A_1, A_2, \ldots, A_n]$, where A_i represents an alert in the cluster. We denote $a(k)$, where $k = 0, 1, \ldots, N - 1$, as the corresponding time series variable of hyper alert A. An element of the time series $a(k)$, denoted as a_i, is the number of alerts that fall in the ith time slot. Therefore, each element of a hyper alert time series variable represents the number of alert instances within the corresponding time slot. We currently do not use categorical variables such as port accessed and pattern of TCP flags as time series variables in our approach.

GCT Alert Correlation

The next phase of alert processing is to apply GCT for pair-wise alert correlation. Based on alert priority value and mission goals, the security analyst can specify a hyper alert as a target (e.g., alert *MstreamDDOS* against a database server) with which other alerts are correlated. The GCT algorithm is applied to the corresponding alert time series. Specifically, for a target hyper alert Y whose corresponding univariate time series is $y(k)$, and another hyper alert X whose univariate time series is $x(k)$, we compute $GCT(x(k), y(k))$ to correlate these two alerts. For the target alert Y, we compute such pair-wise correlation with all the other alerts. As described in Section 2.0, the GCT index (GCI) g returned by the GCT function represents the evidence strength if X is causally related to Y. We record the alerts whose GCI values have passed the F-distribution test as candidates of causal alerts, and rank order the candidate alerts according to their GCI values. We then select the top m candidate alerts and regard them as being causally related to alert Y. These candidate relationships can be further inspected by other techniques or security analyst based on expertise and domain knowledge. The corresponding attack scenario is constructed based on the correlation results.

In alert correlation, identifying and removing background alerts is an important step. We use *Ljung-Box* [20] test to identify the background alerts. The assumption is that background alerts have characteristic of randomness. The *Ljung-Box* algorithm tests for such randomness via autocorrelation plots. The Null Hypothesis is that the data is random. The test value is compared with critical values to determine if we reject or accept the Null Hypothesis.

However, in order to correctly remove the background alerts, expertise is still needed to verify that a hyper alert can be regarded as a background alert. In addition to expertise, we can also use other techniques, e.g., probabilistic reasoning, for further inspection and verification. This is part of our future work.

4. EXPERIMENTS

To evaluate the effectiveness and validity of our alert correlation mechanisms, we applied our algorithms to the datasets of the Grand Challenge Problem

(GCP) version 3.1 provided by DARPA's Cyber Panel program [6, 13], the 2000 DARPA Intrusion Detection Scenario SPecific datasets (LLDOS 1.0 and LLDOS 2.0.2) [21] and datasets of the DEF CON 9 Capture The Flag (CTF) [9]. In this section, we describe our experiments with an emphasis on the GCP.

The Grand Challenge Problem (GCP)

The main motivation to use the GCP datasets is that the GCP has developed multiple innovative attack scenarios to specifically evaluate alert correlation techniques. In addition to the complicated attack scenarios, the GCP datasets also include many background alerts. This makes alert correlation and scenario construction more challenging. Other datasets, e.g., DEF CON 8 Capture The Flag (CTF) [8], have relatively simple scenarios [22]. In the GCP, multiple heterogeneous security systems, e.g., network-based IDSs, host-based IDSs, firewalls, and network management systems, are deployed in several network enclaves.

GCP alerts are in IDMEF (XML) format. We implemented our alert processing system in Java. It can consume XML format alerts directly.

As described in Section 3, we first fuse and cluster raw alerts into more aggregated and *hyper alerts*. In scenario I, there are a little more than 25,000 low-level raw alerts output by heterogeneous security devices in all enclaves. After alert fusion and clustering, we have around 2,300 hyper alerts. In scenario II, there are around 22,500 raw alerts that result in 1,800 hyper alerts.

The GCP definition includes complete information about the configuration of the protected networks and hosts including services, operating systems, user accounts, etc. Therefore, we can establish a configuration database accordingly. Information of mission goals enables us to identify the servers of interest and assign interest score for corresponding alerts targeting at the important hosts. The alert priority is calculated based on our model described in Section 3.0.

In formulating hyper alert time series, as described in Section 3, we set the time slot to 60 seconds. In the GCP, the whole time range is 5 days. Therefore, each hyper alert time series $x(k)$ has a size of 7,200, i.e., k=0, 1, 2, ..., 7,199.

In GCT alert correlation, the first step is to identify and remove the background alerts. As described in Section 3.0, we apply the Ljung-Box statistical test to all hyper alerts. We select the significance level $\alpha = 0.05$. However, in order to correctly remove the background alerts, expertise is still needed to verify that a hyper alert can be regarded as background alert. In the GCP, by using this mechanism, we can identify background alerts such as "HTTP_Cookie" and "HTTP_Posts". The next step is to select the alerts with high priority values as the target alerts. In this step, we set the threshold $\beta = 0.6$. Alerts with priority scores above β are regarded as important alerts and are selected as target alerts. We then apply the GCT to correlate each target alert with other alerts from which the background alerts identified by the Ljung-Box test are already excluded.

For performance evaluation, we define two measures:

$$true\ causality\ rate = \frac{\#\ of\ correct\ causal\ alerts}{total\ \#\ of\ causal\ relationships}$$

and

$$false\ causal\ rate = \frac{\#\ of\ incorrect\ causal\ alerts}{total\ \#\ of\ causal\ alerts}$$

Here, *causal alerts* refer to the causal alert candidates output by the GCT (i.e., passing the *F-test*) w.r.t. the target alerts. In experiments of the GCP and the 2000 DARPA Intrusion Detection Scenarios, we refer to the documents with the ground truth to determine the causal relationships among the alerts.

Table 4.1. Alert Correlation by the GCT on the GCP Scenario I. Target Alert: Loki

$Alert_i$	Target Alert	GCT Index
HTTP_Java	Loki	22.25
DB_IllegalFileAccess	Loki	11.81
DB_NewClient	Loki	11.12
DB_NewClient_Target	Loki	10.84
DB_FTP_Globbing_Attack	Loki	10.84
HTTP_ActiveX	Loki	10.68

Table 4.2. Alert Correlation by the GCT on the GCP Scenario I: Target Alert: DB_NewClient

$Alert_i$	Target Alert	GCT Index
Loki	DB_NewClient	115.56
Plan_NewClient	DB_NewClient	14.50
Plan_Loki	DB_NewClient	13.06
HTTP_Java	DB_NewClient	12.84
DB_NewClient_Target	DB_NewClient	12.84
DB_FTP_Globbing_Attack	DB_NewClient	12.84
HTTP_ActiveX	DB_NewClient	12.84
DB_IllegalFileAccess	DB_NewClient	10.76

In the GCP Scenario I, there are multiple network enclaves in which attacks are conducted separately. The attack scenario in each network enclave is almost the same. We selected a network enclave as an example to show the GCT correlation results.

In this network enclave, there are a total of 370 hyper alerts. Applying the Ljung-Box test on the hyper alerts, we identify 255 hyper alerts as background alerts. According to the alert priority values calculated based on the mission-goals and relevance to the protected networks and hosts, there are 15 hyper alerts

Table 4.3. Alert Correlation by the GCT on the GCP Scenario I: Target Alert: DB_IllegalFileAccess

Alert$_i$	Target Alert	GCT Index
HTTP_Java	DB_IllegalFileAccess	22.23
DB_NewClient	DB_IllegalFileAccess	14.87
Loki	DB_IllegalFileAccess	11.24
Plan_Loki	DB_IllegalFileAccess	11.13
HTTP_ActiveX	DB_IllegalFileAccess	10.71
Plan_NewClient	DB_IllegalFileAccess	9.08

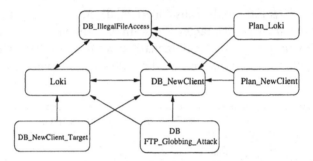

Figure 4.2. The GCP Scenario I: Correlation Graph on Database Server

whose priority values are above the threshold $\beta = 0.6$. Therefore, we have 15 hyper alerts as the target alerts, which are correlated with other alerts excluding the identified background alerts. As an example, we select three alerts that are related to the Database Server as the target alerts, i.e., *Loki*, *DB_NewClient* and *DB_IllegalFileAccess*. Alert *Loki* indicates that there is a stealthy data transfer via a covert channel. Alert *NewClient* means that a host on the network initiates a connection to a remote service that is suspicious and uncharacteristic. Therefore, alert *DB_NewClient* denotes the connection activity from the Database Server to an external suspicious site. Alert *DB_IllegalFileAccess* occurs when there is a file access (read or write) on the Database Server that violates the access policy. *DB* and *Plan* represent *Database Server* and *Plan Server* respectively. Table 4.1 shows the causal alert candidates correlated with target alert *Loki*. Table 4.2 shows the alert candidates that are causally related to target alert *DB_NewClient*. Table 4.3 shows the causal alerts related to target alert*DB_IllegalFileAccess*. Alert *DB_FTP_Globbing_Attack* indicates an *FTP Globbing buffer overflow* attack on the Database Server. Alert *DB_NewClient_Target* denotes an unusual connection activity from a host to the Database Server. Among the candidate alerts which have passed the F-test, we select the top 6 alerts according to their GCI values.

Figure 4.2 shows the correlation graph based on the correlation results of alerts *Loki*, *DB_NewClient* and *DB_IllegalFileAccess*. Here, some expert knowledge is needed to further inspect the causal alert candidates resulted from GCT correlation in order to construct the correlation graph. In this case, we do not include alerts such as *HTTP_Java* and *HTTP_ActiveX* in the scenario construction because they are not likely to be correct causal alerts. In the correlation graph, the directed edges represent the causal relationships and the arrows show the causality directions. For example, Table 4.1 shows that *DB_FTP_Globbing_Attack* is a causal alert candidate with regard to alert *Loki*. Such causal relationship is shown by a directed edge from *DB_FTP_Globbing_Attack* to *Loki* in Figure 4.2. A bi-directional edge indicates a mutual causal relationship between two alerts.

Figure 4.2 shows that there are multiple types of relationships among the alerts. First, there is a *straightforward* causal relationship that is obvious because of the nature of corresponding attacks. In Figure 4.2, we can see that alert *DB_FTP_Globbing_Attack* is causally related to alerts *Loki* and *DB_NewClient*, so is alert *DB_NewClient_Target*. Such causality indicates that the corresponding activities represented by alert *DB_FTP_Globbling_Attack* and alert *DB_NewClient_Target* cause the activities indicated by alert *DB_NewClient* and *Loki*. The fact spreadsheet in the GCP document also supports the validity of such causality. The ground truth shows that the attacker first gets root access to the Database Server using the *FTP Globbling buffer overflow* attack, then transports the malicious agent to the Database Server. The activity of agent transfer is detected by an IDS that outputs alert *DB_NewClient_Target*. The buffer overflow attack and initial malicious agent transfer are followed by a series of forthcoming autonomous attacks from/against the Database Server. Such causal relationship is obvious and can also be discovered by other correlation techniques because once the attacker obtained the root access to the victim using the buffer overflow attack, he/she can easily launch other attacks from/against the target. Therefore, a simple rule is to correlate the buffer overflow attack with other following attacks at the same target.

Some *indirect* relationships among alerts can also be discovered by the GCT correlation. As shown in Figure 4.2, we can see that alerts *Plan_Loki* and *Plan NewClient* all have causal relationship with alerts *DB_IllegalFileAccess* (triggered by activities of illegal access to files at the Database Server) and *DB NewClient* (triggered by activities of connecting to a suspicious site). It is hard to correlate them together via traditional correlation techniques because they do not have a known relationship with the target alert *DB_NewClient*. From the ground truth in the GCP document, we can see that the attacker first compromises the Plan Server and then uses that host to break into the Database Server. Alert *Plan_NewClient* indicates that the attacker downloads malicious agent from the external site to the *Plan_Server*. Alert *Plan_Loki* indicates the attacker uploads sensitive information from the *Plan_Server* to the external site.

The malicious code is later transferred to the Database Server after a buffer overflow attack against the Database Server originated from the Plan Server.

Figure 4.2 also shows a pattern of loop relationships among alerts. We can see that alerts *DB_IllegalFileAccess*, *Loki* and *DB_NewClient* have mutual causal relationships with each other. Such pattern indicates that the occurrences of these three alerts are tightly coupled, i.e., whenever we see one alert, we expect to see another one forthcoming. The fact spreadsheet validates our results. The malicious agent autonomously gets access to the sensitive files and collects data (alert *DB_IllegalFileAccess*), uploads the stolen data to an external site (alert *Loki*), then downloads new agent software (alert *DB_NewClient*) and installs it (alert *DB_IllegalFileAccess*) on the Database Server, and then begins another round of the same attack sequence. GCT correlation results show a loop pattern of causal relationship among the corresponding alerts because these activities occur together.

When we correlate each target alert with other alerts using the GCT, we have some false causal alert candidates. For example, *HTTP_Java*, *HTTP_ActiveX* in Table 4.1. Overall, in this experiment, the true causality rate is 95.06% (77/81) and the false causality rate is 12.6% (10/87) in this network enclave.

Table 4.4. Alert Correlation by the GCT on the GCP Scenario II: Target Alert: Plan_Service_Status

Alert$_i$	Target Alert	GCT Index
Plan_IIS_Generic_BufferOverFlow	Plan_Service_Status	20.21
Plan_Registry_Modified	Plan_Service_Status	20.18
IIS_Unicode_Attack	Plan_Service_Status	18.98
HTTP_Java	Plan_Service_Status	17.35
HTTP_Shells	Plan_Service_Status	16.28
HTTP_ActiveX	Plan_Service_Status	1.90

Table 4.5. Alert Correlation by the GCT on the GCP Scenario II: Target Alert: Plan_Host_Status

Alert$_i$	Target Alert	GCT Index
HTTP_Java	Plan_Host_Status	7.73
Plan_IIS_Generic_BufferOverflow	Plan_Host_Status	7.70
Plan_Registry_Modified	Plan_Host_Status	7.63
CGI_Null_Byte_Attack	Plan_Host_Status	7.56
Port_Scan	Plan_Host_Status	3.26
HTTP_RobotsTxt	Plan_Host_Status	1.67

We also use the same network enclave as an example to show our results in the GCP Scenario II. In this network enclave, there are a total of 387 hyper alerts. Applying the Ljung-Box test to the hyper alerts, we identify 273 hyper alerts as the background alerts. In calculating the priority of hyper alerts, there are 9

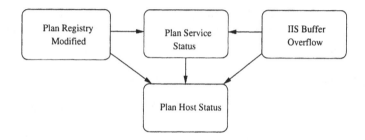

Figure 4.3. The GCP Scenario II: Correlation Graph of Plan Server

hyper alerts whose priority values are above the threshold $\beta = 0.6$. Therefore, we have 9 hyper alerts as the target alerts, which are correlated with other alerts excluding the identified background alerts. As before, based on the mission goals and alert priority, for example, we select two alerts, *Plan_Service_Status* and *Plan_Host_Status*, as the targets, then apply the GCT to correlate other alerts with them. Table 4.4 and Table 4.5 show the corresponding GCT results. We list the top 6 candidate alerts that have passed the F-test in the tables. The alerts *Plan_Host_Status* and *Plan_Service_Status* are issued by a network management system deployed on the network. The true causality rate is 93.15% (68/73) and the false causality rate is 13.92% (11/79).

After finding the candidate alerts, we construct a corresponding correlation graph as shown in Figure 4.3. This figure shows that alerts *IIS_Buffer_Overflow* and *Plan_Registry_Modified* are causally related to alerts *Plan_Service_Status* and *Plan_Host_Status*. The GCP document verifies such relationship. The attacker launches *IIS Buffer Overflow* attack against the Plan Server in order to transfer and install the malicious executable code on it. The Plan Server's registry file is modified (alert *Plan_Registry_Modified*) and the service is down (*Plan_Service_Status*) during the daemon installation. Alert *Plan_Host_Status* indicates the "down" or "up" states of the Plan Server. The states are affected by the activities of the malicious agent installed on the Plan Server. Therefore, the ground truth described in the GCP document also supports the causal relationships among the corresponding alerts. These relationships are represented by directed edges pointing to *Plan_Host_Status* from *IIS_Buffer_Overflow*, *Plan_Registry_Modified* and *Plan_Service_Status* in Figure 4.3.

However, the correlation result in the GCP Scenario II is not comprehensive enough to cover the complete attack scenarios. By comparing the alert streams with the GCP document, we notice that many malicious activities in the GCP Scenario II are not detected by the IDSs. Therefore, there are some missing intrusion alerts. In our approach, we depend on alert data for correlation and scenario analysis. When there is a lack of alerts corresponding to the intermediate attack steps, we cannot construct the complete attack scenario. In practice,

IDSs or other security mechanisms can miss some attack activities. We will study how to deal with the "missing" attack steps in alert analysis and scenario construction.

2000 DARPA Intrusion Detection Scenarios

In order to validate our approach using more case studies and compare with the results of other approaches (e.g., [23]), we also applied our algorithms to the 2000 DARPA Intrusion Detection Scenario datasets of LLDOS 1.0 and LLDOS 2.02. Compared with GCP, the attack scenarios in LLDOS 1.0 and LLDOS 2.02 are simpler. In both scenarios, the attacker performs a series of attacks and eventually launches a DDoS attack. In this section, we report our experimental results.

LLDOS 1.0.   In LLDOS 1.0, the attack series include *IP scan*, *port scan*, *sadmind buffer overflow attack*, *DDoS daemon installation* and *DDoS attack*. The network traffic is collected from the DMZ and from the inside part of the evaluation network, denoted as "inside network" [21]. We use Snort [27], a popular IDS, to detect intrusions in the network traffic of the "inside network" and correlate the Snort alerts.

Snort outputs around 1,200 raw alerts. Alert fusion and clustering result in 30 hyper alerts of which 12 hyper alerts are regarded as target alerts for further analysis. For convenience, we denote the following: *subnet1* : 172.16.115.0/24, *subnet2* : 172.16.113.0/24, *subnet3* : 172.16.112.0/24, *host_A* : 172.16.115.20, *host_B* : 172.16.112.10, *host_C* : 172.16.112.50, *host_D* : 131.84.1.31, *host_E* : 172.16.115.87, *host_F* : 172.16.113.50, *host_G*: 172.16.113.105, *host_H* : 172.16.113.148, *host_I* : 172.168.112.10, *host_J* : 172.168.112.105, *host_K* : 172.168.112.194.

As described in Section 3, we go through the steps of alert correlation and apply GCT to the alerts.

We first select alert *Mstream attack* that corresponds to the *Mstream* DDoS attack as the target alert, and apply GCT to correlate it with other alerts. Based on the correlation results, we select a causal alert as the next correlation target alert. For example, after each GCT correlation, we select the causal alert that is related to *host_B* (selecting *host_A* or *host_C* produces similar causal relationships that make up the attack paths) as the target alert for the next GCT correlation. Table 4.6 to Table 4.10 show the corresponding GCT correlation results with regard to the selected target alerts, i.e., *DDoS_Zombie_Host_B*, *rsh_root_Host_B*, *sadmind_Buffer_Overflow_Host_B* and *rpc_portmap_sadmind_Host_B*. We construct the attack scenario graph based on the GCT correlation results and alert analysis.

Figure 4.4 shows the DDoS attack scenario discovered in the "inside network" of LLDOS 1.0. The true causality rate is 96.81% and the false causality rate is 3.95%. In this experiment, Snort does not output alerts for the attacker's

Table 4.6. DDoS Attack: Target Alert: ms stream attack

$Alert_i$	Target Alert	GCT Index
DDoS_Zombie_Host_A	Mstream_attack	200.55
DDoS_Zombie_Host_B	Mstream_attack	198.67
DDoS_Zombie_Host_C	Mstream_attack	193.51

Table 4.7. DDoS Attack: Target Alert: $DDoS\_Zombie\_Host\_B$

$Alert_i$	Target Alert	GCT Index
rsh_root_Host_A_Src	DDoS_Zombie_Host_B	308.32
rsh_root_Host_B_Src	DDoS_Zombie_Host_B	298.67
rsh_root_Host_C_Src	DDoS_Zombie_Host_B	296.12
rsh_root_Host_A_Target	DDoS_Zombie_Host_B	289.07
rsh_root_Host_B_Target	DDoS_Zombie_Host_B	285.32
rsh_root_Host_C_Target	DDoS_Zombie_Host_B	283.45

Table 4.8. DDoS Attack: Target Alert: rsh_root_Host_B

$Alert_i$	Target Alert	GCT Index
rsh_Host_B_Src	rsh_root_Host_B_Target	189.32
sadmind_BufferOverflow_Host_B	rsh_root_Host_B_Target	182.37
sadmind_BufferOverflow_Host_C	rsh_root_Host_B_Target	179.54
sadmind_BufferOverflow_Host_A	rsh_root_Host_B_Target	176.21
rsh_root_Host_A_Target	rsh_root_Host_B_Target	150.32

activities of installing the DDoS software on the hosts. Alerts *rsh_root_Host_A_Src*, *rsh_root_Host_B_Src*, *rsh_root_Host_C_Src*, *rsh_root_Host_A_Target*, *rsh_root_Host B_Target* and *rsh_root_Host_C_Target* are corresponding to the attacker's activities of transferring DDoS software to the hosts. Our correlation mechanism can correctly correlate them with the alerts *DDoS_Zombie* that represent the the detection of the attacker controlling the slave hosts to launch the DDoS attack. Figure 4.4 shows that our correlation mechanism can correctly correlate attack alerts and construct the DDoS scenario that is the same as the results of [23].

LLDOS 2.0.2. In LLDOS 2.0.2, the scenario is more complicated than that of LLDOS 1.0. The attacker probes for host information using DNS HINFO instead of the *IP Sweep* and *rpc port scan*. In addition, the attacker compromises one host first from which he/she continues to compromise other hosts. In LLDOS 1.0, the attacker attacks each host individually.

We use Snort to detect the intrusions in the "inside network" traffic and analyze the output alerts. Snort outputs 870 raw alerts. We aggregate raw alerts and get 26 hyper alerts. We identify 8 hyper alerts as target alerts. For convenience, we denote *Host_A* : 172.16.115.20, *Host_B* : 172.16.112.50,

Table 4.9. DDoS Attack: Target Alert: sadmind_Buffer_Overflow_Host_B

$Alert_i$	Target Alert	GCT Index
sadmind_BufferOverflow_Host_A	sadmind_BufferOverflow_Host_B	230.32
rpc_portmap_sadmind_Host_G	sadmind_BufferOverflow_Host_B	212.37
rpc_portmap_sadmind_Host_C	sadmind_BufferOverflow_Host_B	209.25
rpc_portmap_sadmind_Host_B	sadmind_BufferOverflow_Host_B	201.12
rpc_portmap_sadmind_Host_A	sadmind_BufferOverflow_Host_B	198.65
rpc_portmap_sadmind_Host_E	sadmind_BufferOverflow_Host_B	176.83

Table 4.10. DDoS Attack: Target Alert: rpc_portmap_sadmind_Host_B

$Alert_i$	Target Alert	GCT Index
ipScan_Subnet3	rpc_portmap_sadmind_Host_B	218.32
rpc_portmap_sadmind_Host_A	rpc_portmap_sadmind_Host_B	192.37
rpc_portmap_sadmind_Host_F	rpc_portmap_sadmind_Host_B	176.65
ipScan_Subnet2	rpc_portmap_sadmind_Host_B	156.15
ipScan_Subnet1	rpc_portmap_sadmind_Host_B	141.78
rpc_portmap_sadmind_Host_E	rpc_portmap_sadmind_Host_B	132.39

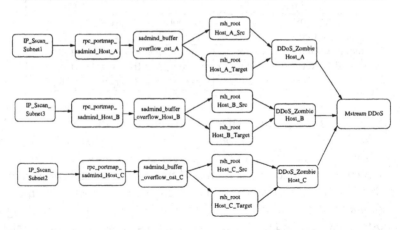

Figure 4.4. LLDOS 1.0: DDoS Attack Scenario in the "inside network"

Host_C : 172.16.117.132, *Host_D* : 172.16.115.87, *Host_E*: 172.16.115.44, *Host_F* : 172.16.113.207, *Host_G* : 131.84.1.31.

Table 4.11. DDoS Attack: Target Alert: Mstream_attack_Host_G

$Alert_i$	Target Alert	GCT Index
DDoS_Zombie_Host_B	Mstream_attack_Host_G	387.19

We first select alert *Mstream_attack_Host_G* as the target alert for correlation. Table 4.11 shows the GCT correlation results. From the result, we con-

Table 4.12. DDoS Attack: Target Alert: *DDoS_Zombie_Host_B*

$Alert_i$	Target Alert	GCT Index
sadmind_BufferOverflow_Host_B	DDoS_Zombie_Host_B	272.31
web_cgi_redirect_Host_D	DDoS_Zombie_Host_B	265.04
ftp_PassOverflow_Host_B	DDoS_Zombie_Host_B	265.04
web_cgi_redirect_Host_C	DDoS_Zombie_Host_B	251.57
web_cgi_redirect_Host_E	DDoS_Zombie_Host_B	230.19

Table 4.13. DDoS Attack: Target Alert: sadmind_BufferOverflow_Host_B

$Alert_i$	Target Alert	GCT Index
ftp_PassOverflow_Host_A	sadmind_BufferOverflow_Host_B	225.30
web_cgi_iis_fpcount_Host_F	sadmind_BufferOverflow_Host_B	217.19
web_cgi_finger_Host_C	sadmind_BufferOverflow_Host_B	187.19

Table 4.14. DDoS Attack: Target Alert: ftp_PassOverflow_Host_B

$Alert_i$	Target Alert	GCT Index
sadmind_BufferOverflow_Host_B	ftp_PassOverflow_Host_B	265.31
ftp_PassOverflow_Host_A	ftp_PassOverflow_Host_B	253.42
web_cgi_finger_Host_C	ftp_PassOverflow_Host_B	213.19

tinue to choose alert *DDoS_Zombie_Host_B* as the correlation target. Table 4.12 shows the correlation results. Snort outputs some false positive alerts related to *Web CGI*, such as alert *web_cgi_redirect*, *web_cgi_iis_fpcount* and *web_cgi_finger*. These alerts are unrelated to the DDoS attack scenario. Further inspecting the alert information can easily filter out these alerts. The inspection and analysis is based on expert knowledge. Therefore, in Table 4.12, we only have interests in alerts *sadmind_BufferOverflow_Host_B* and *ftp_PassOverflow_Host_B* and select them as the target alert for correlation. The results are shown in Table 4.13 and Table 4.14. Table 4.15 shows the GCT correlation results with regard to alert *ftp_PassOverflow_Host_A*.

Figure 4.5 shows the attack scenario in the "inside network". The true causality rate is 97.34% and false causality rate is 4.89%. As Snort does not output alerts corresponding to the attacker's activity of using DNS HINFO to probe the host, we cannot retrieve the first step in the DDoS scenario, i.e., the stage of probe is missed. We use the dash-line to represent the missing stage. The LL-DOS 2.0.2 document shows that attacker first compromises *Host_A* from which he/she continues to compromise *Host_B* using *sadmind buffer overflow* attack, and then uses *ftp* to transfer the DDoS software to *Host_B*. We can see such sequence of steps in Figure 4.5. In the figure, alert *ftp_Pass_Overflow_Host_B* corresponds to the activity of DDoS software transfer. Figure 4.5 shows that

Table 4.15. DDoS Attack: Target Alert: ftp_PassOverflow_Host_A

Alert$_i$	Target Alert	GCT Index
sadmind_BufferOverflow_Host_A	ftp_PassOverflow_Host_A	481.01
web_cgi_iis_fpcount_Host_F	ftp_PassOverflow_Host_A	387.51

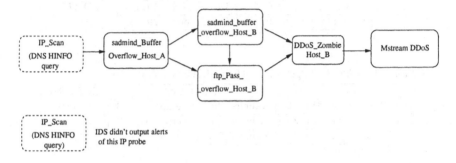

Figure 4.5. LLDOS 2.0.2: DDoS Attack Scenario in the "inside network"

we can construct the DDoS attack scenario correctly based on GCT alert correlation.

DEF CON 9 Capture The Flag

As another case study, we applied our algorithms on the DEF CON 9 Capture The Flag (CTF) datasets. We use Snort to analyze the network traffic and output alerts for analysis. The DEF CON 9 CTF datasets are collected on 7 subnets. However, some datasets in subnet *Eth0* are corrupted. Therefore, we do not include them in our analysis. Because there is no information available about the network topology and host configuration, we cannot fully apply our model of alert priority computation on the datasets. Therefore, we select the target alerts for correlation based on domain knowledge.

As an example, we report results of alert analysis for *subnet 4*. Snort outputs more than 378,000 raw alerts. Scanning related alerts account for 91% of the total alerts. Alert *ICMP Redirect Host* accounts for about 3% of the total and alert *MISC Tiny Fragments* accounts for 5.9% of the total. Other alerts include Buffer Overflow, DDOS, DOS, DNS, TFTP, SNMP and Web-related attacks.

Applying our alert fusion and clustering algorithms, we can reduce the redundancy of low-level alerts dramatically, in particular, scanning alerts. The number of concrete high-level hyper alerts is about 1,300. We apply the Ljung-Box test with the significance level $\alpha = 0.05$ to all hyper alerts, and identify 754 hyper alerts as background alerts. For convenience, we denote the following: *Host_A* : 10.255.100.250, *Host_B* : 10.255.30.201, *Host_C* : 10.255.30.202, *Host_D* : 10.255. 40.237.

We first select the alert *DDOS Shaft Zombie* targeting at *Host A*, and apply the GCT to correlate it with other alerts. Based on the correlation results, we select a causal alert as the next correlation target alert. For example, after each GCT correlation, we select the causal alert that is oriented from *host C* as the target alert for the next GCT correlation. Table 4.16 through Table 4.18 show the corresponding GCT correlation results with regard to the selected target alerts, i.e., *DDoS Zombie Host A*, *FTP Command Overflow Host C Src*, and alert *FTP CWD Overflow Host C Src*. We construct the attack scenario graph based on GCT correlation results and alert analysis.

Table 4.16. DefCon 9: Target Alert: DDOS Shaft Zombie Host A

$Alert_i$	Target Alert	GCT Index
FTP Command Overflow Host B Src	DDOS Shaft Zombie	13.43
FTP User Overflow Host B Src	DDOS Shaft Zombie	12.98
FTP Command Overflow Host C Src	DDOS Shaft Zombie	11.43
WEB-CGI ScriptAlias Access	DDOS Shaft Zombie	11.12
TFT GetPasswd Host B Src	DDOS Shaft Zombie	10.88
FTP Aix Overflow Host B Src	DDOS Shaft Zombie	10.83
EXPERIMENTAL MISC AFS Access	DDOS Shaft Zombie	10.70
FTP CWD Overflow Host D Src	DDOS Shaft Zombie	10.68
WEB-CGI Wrap Access	DDOS Shaft Zombie	10.54
FTP Command Overflow Host D Src	DDOS Shaft Zombie	10.35
FTP CWD Overflow Host C Src	DDOS Shaft Zombie	9.87
FTP OpenBSDx86 Overflow Host D Src	DDOS Shaft Zombie	7.86
WEB-CGI WebDist Access	DDOS Shaft Zombie	7.54

Table 4.17. DefCon 9: Target Alert: FTP Command Overflow Host C Src

$Alert_i$	Target Alert	GCT Index
Scan NMAP TCP	FTP Command Overflow Host C Src	11.27
ICMP Ping NMAP	FTP Command Overflow Host C Src	10.93
WEB-MISC Perl Command	FTP Command Overflow Host C Src	10.75
Xmas Scan	FTP Command Overflow Host C Src	10.23
RPC Portmap Request	FTP Command Overflow Host C Src	10.17
FIN Scan	FTP Command Overflow Host C Src	10.13
NULL Scan	FTP Command Overflow Host C Src	10.11

Figure 4.6 shows the attack scenario targeting *Host A* according to the network activities in subnet 4. We can see that the attackers first launch a series of port scanning, e.g., *NMAP* and *RPC Portmap*. Then multiple *FTP Buffer Overflow* attacks are launched against the target in order to get root access. The attackers also launch some Web-related attacks against the target. There are also some other attack scenarios that our algorithms are able to find; many of them are *port scanning* followed by *Buffer Overflow* attacks.

Table 4.18. DefCon 9: Target Alert: FTP_CWD_Overflow_Host_C_Src

Alert$_i$	Target Alert	GCT Index
Scan_NMAP_NULL	FTP_CWD_Overflow_Host_C_Src	12.72
ICMP_Ping_NMAP	FTP_CWD_Overflow_Host_C_Src	12.12
WEB-MISC_Perl_Command	FTP_CWD_Overflow_Host_C_Src	11.87
Xmas_Scan	FTP_Command_Overflow_Host_C_Src	11.63
SYN FIN_Scan	FTP_CWD_Overflow_Host_C_Src	11.27
NULL_Scan	FTP_CWD_Overflow_Host_C_Src	10.92

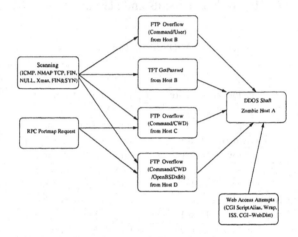

Figure 4.6. DefCon 9: A scenario example of victim Host A

Discussion

In our experiments, the results from the GCP and the 2000 DARPA Intrusion Detection Scenarios show that our approach can correlate alerts that have statistical causal relationships. However, as the GCP results show, we have false causal alert candidates resulted from GCT correlation that can result in false scenarios. One reason is that a large amount of background alerts can increase the false correlations. For example, we have a relatively high false causality rate in the GCP because the GCP has a lot of background alerts. Another reason is that, in our experiments, we do not have and use any training data sets. Therefore, it is different from traditional anomaly detection in which training data is used to construct the baseline that can reduce the false positive rate. In the DEF CON 9 dataset, our approach also finds some reasonable scenarios. Because of the nature of the DEF CON 9 dataset, we cannot comprehensively evaluate the success rate of our alert correlation method.

The key strength of our approach is that it can discover new alert correlations. Another advantage of our approach is that we do not require *a priori* knowledge about attack behaviors and how attacks are related when finding candidate alert correlations. In addition, our approach can also reduce the workload of security analysts in that they can focus on the causal alert candidates output by the GCT for further analysis. They do not have to assess all alerts and investigate all possible correlations. This is especially helpful when an attack is in progress and the security analysts need to figure out the attack scenarios in a timely fashion.

The time series used in our approach is based on the alert count instead of other categorical variables such as port access and pattern of TCP flag. The intuition is that if two attacks are related or have causal relationships, their occurrences should be tightly correlated because the causal attack triggers the resulting attack. Some experimental work and theoretical analysis have been presented in [1], [3], [2]. However, it is important to consider categorical variables when constructing attack scenarios. We will address this issue in our future work.

One challenge to our approach is background alert identification. Using the Ljung-Box test cannot cover all the background alerts. The limit of our approach is that we still need expert knowledge to further inspect the causal alert candidates resulted from GCT alert correlation when constructing attack scenarios. Human intervention has limits in automating attack scenario constructions. In future work, we will develop new correlation algorithms, in particular, probabilistic reasoning, and will integrate other existing correlation algorithms, e.g., *prerequisite-consequence* approach, for alert correlation in order to reduce the false correlation rate and improve the accuracy of scenario analysis.

5.   RELATED WORK

Recently, there have been several proposals on alert correlation and attack scenario analysis.

Porras et al. design a "mission-impact-based" correlation system, named M-Correlator [26]. The main idea is to evaluate alerts based on security interests and attack relevance to the protected networks and hosts. Related alerts are aggregated and clustered into a consolidated incident stream. The final result of the M-Correlator is a list of rank ordered security incidents based on the relevance and priority scores, which can be further analyzed by the security analyst. This approach focuses on the incident ranking instead of attack scenario analysis. The security analyst needs to perform further correlation analysis.

Valdes and Skinner [29] develop a probabilistic-based alert correlation mechanism. The approach uses similarities of alert attributes for correlation. Measures are defined to evaluate the degree of similarity between two alerts. Alert aggregation and scenario analysis are conducted by toughening or relaxing the similarity requirement in some attribute fields. However, it is difficult for this approach to correlate alerts that do not have obvious (or predefined) similarities in their attributes.

In the approach proposed by Debar and Wespi [7], alert clustering is applied for scenario construction. Two reasoning techniques are used to specify alert relationships. Backward-reasoning looks for *duplicates* of an alert, and forward-reasoning determines if there are *consequences* of an alert. These two types of relationships between alerts are predefined in a configuration file. The main limitation of this approach is that it relies on the predefined duplicate and consequence relationships between alerts.

Goldman et al. [10] build a correlation system that produces a correlation graph, which indicates the security events that aim to compromise the same security goal, with IDS alerts as the supporting evidence of the security events. The reasoning process is based on the predefined goal-events associations. Therefore, this approach cannot discover attack scenarios if the attack strategy or objective is not known.

Some other researchers have proposed the framework of alert correlation and scenario analysis based on the pre-condition and post-condition of individual alerts [4], [5], [23]. The assumption is that when an attacker launches a scenario, prior attack steps are preparing for later ones, and therefore, the consequences of earlier attacks have a strong relationship with the prerequisites of later attacks. The correlation engine searches for alert pairs that have a consequences and prerequisites match and builds a correlation graph with such pairs. There are several limitations with this approach. First, a new attack may not be paired with any other attack because its prerequisites and consequences are not yet defined. Second, even for known attacks, it is infeasible to predefine all possible prerequisites and consequences. In fact, some relationships cannot be expressed naturally in rigid terms.

Our approach differs from prior work in that it focuses on discovering *new* and *unknown* attack strategies. Instead of depending on the prior knowledge of attack strategies or pre-defined alert pre/post-conditions, we correlate the alerts and construct attack scenarios based on statistical and temporal relationships among alerts. In this respect, our approach is analogous to *anomaly detection* techniques.

We also notice that alert correlation has been a research topic in network management for decades. There are several well-known approaches such as case-based reasoning system [19], code-book [18], and model-based reasoning systems [16, 24]. In network management system (NMS), event correlation focuses on alarms resulted from network faults, which often have fixed patterns. Whereas in security, the alerts are more diverse and unpredictable because the attackers are intelligent and can use flexible strategies. We nevertheless can borrow ideas in NMS event correlation for INFOSEC data analysis.

6. CONCLUSION AND FUTURE WORK

In this paper, we presented an approach for correlating INFOSEC alerts and constructing attack scenarios. We developed a mechanism that aggregates and clusters raw alerts into high level hyper-alerts. Alert priority is calculated and ranked. The priority computation is conducted based on the relevance of the alert to the protected networks and systems. Alert correlation is conducted based on the Granger Causality Test, a time series-based causal analysis algorithm. Attack scenarios are analyzed by constructing a correlation graph based on the GCT results and on alert inspection. Our initial results have demonstrated the potential of our method in alert correlation and scenario analysis. Our approach can discover new attack relationships as long as the alerts of the attacks have statistical correlation. Our approach is complementary to other correlation approaches that depend on hard-coded prior knowledge for pattern matching.

We will continue to study statistical-based approaches for alert correlation, and develop algorithms to detect background alerts, develop techniques to integrate categorical variables such as patterns of TCP flags, and study how to reduce false causality rate. We will also develop other correlation algorithms, in particular, probabilistic reasoning approaches, to integrate multi-algorithms for alert correlation and scenario analysis. We will also study how to handle missing alerts of attack steps in scenario analysis. One approach may be to insert some hypothesis alerts and look for evidence to either support or degrade the hypothesis from other sensor systems. We will validate our correlation algorithms on alert streams collected in the real world.

ACKNOWLEDGMENTS

This research is supported in part by a grant from DARPA (F30602-00-1-0603) and a grant from NSF (CCR-0133629). We thank João B.D. Cabrera of Scientific Systems Company for helpful discussions on time series analysis and Granger-Causality Test. We also thank Giovanni Vigna of University of California at Santa Barbara, Alfonso Valdes of SRI International and Stuart Staniford of Silicon Defense, as well as the anonymous reviewers for their valuable comments and suggestions.

REFERENCES

[1] J. B. D. Cabrera, L. Lewis, X. Qin, W. Lee, R. K. Prasanth, B. Ravichandran, and R. K. Mehra. Proactive detection of distributed denial of service attacks using mib traffic variables - a feasibility study. In *Proceedings of IFIP/IEEE International Symposium on Integrated Network Management (IM 2001)*, May 2001.

[2] J. B. D. Cabrera and R. K. Mehra. Extracting precursor rules from time series - a classical statistical viewpoint. In *Proceedings of the Second SIAM International Conference on Data Mining*, pages 213–228, Arlington, VA, USA, April 2002.

[3] J.B.D. Cabrera, L.Lewis, X. Qin, W. Lee, and R.K. Mehra. Proactive intrusion detection and distributed denial of service attacks - a case study in security management. *Journal of Network and Systems Management*, vol. 10(no. 2), June 2002.

[4] S. Cheung, U. Lindqvist, and M. W. Fong. Modeling multistep cyber attacks for scenario recognition. In *Proceedings of the Third DARPA Information Survivability Conference and Exposition (DISCEX III)*, Washington, D.C., April 2003.

[5] F. Cuppens and A. Miège. Alert correlation in a cooperative intrusion detection framework. In *Proceedings of the 2002 IEEE Symposium on Security and Privacy*, pages 202–215, Oakland, CA, May 2002.

[6] DAPRA Cyber Panel Program. DARPA cyber panel program grand challenge problem (GCP). http://ia.dc.teknowledge.com/CyP/GCP/, 2003.

[7] H. Debar and A. Wespi. The intrusion-detection console correlation mechanism. In *4th International Symposium on Recent Advances in Intrusion Detection (RAID)*, October 2001.

[8] DEFCON. Def con capture the flag (ctf) contest. http://www.defcon.org. Archive accessible at http://wi2600.org/mediawhore/mirrors/shmoo/, 2000.

[9] DEFCON. Def con capture the flag (ctf) contest. http://www.defcon.org. Archive accessible at http://smokeping.planetmirror.com/pub/cctf/defcon9/, 2001.

[10] R.P. Goldman, W. Heimerdinger, and S. A. Harp. Information modleing for intrusion report aggregation. In *DARPA Information Survivability Conference and Exposition (DISCEX II)*, June 2001.

[11] C.W.J. Granger. Investigating causal relations by econometric methods and cross-spectral methods. *Econometrica*, 34:424–428, 1969.

[12] IETF Intrusion Detection Working Group. Intrusion detection message exchange format. http://www.ietf.org/internet-drafts/draft-ietf-idwg-idmef-xml-09.txt, 2002.

[13] J. Haines, D. K. Ryder, L. Tinnel, and S. Taylor. Validation of sensor alert correlators. *IEEE Security & Privacy Magazine*, January/February, 2003.

[14] J. Hamilton. *Time Series Analysis*. Princeton University Press, 1994.

[15] A.J. Hayter. *Probability and Statistics for Engineers and Scientists*. Duxbury Press, 2002.

[16] G. Jakobson and M. D. Weissman. Alarm correlation. *IEEE Network Magazine*, November 1993.

[17] K. Julisch and M. Dacier. Mining intrusion detection alarms for actionable knowledge. In *The 8th ACM International Conference on Knowledge Discovery and Data Mining*, July 2002.

[18] S. Kliger, S. Yemini, Y. Yemini, D. Oshie, and S. Stolfo. A coding approach to event correlations. In *Proceedings of the 6th IFIP/IEEE International Symposium on Integrated Network Management*, May 1995.

[19] L. Lewis. A case-based reasoning approach to the management of faults in communication networks. In *Proceedings of the IEEE INFOCOM*, 1993.

[20] G.M. Ljung and G.E.P. Box. On a measure of lack of fit in time series models. In *Biometrika* 65, pages 297–303, 1978.

[21] MIT Lincoln Lab. 2000 DARPA intrusion detection scenario specific datasets. http://www.ll.mit.edu/IST/ideval/data/2000/2000_data_index.html, 2000.

[22] P. Ning, Y. Cui, and D.S. Reeves. Analyzing intensive intrusion alerts via correlation. In *Proceedings of the 5th International Symposium on Recent Advances in Intrusion Detection (RAID)*, October 2002.

[23] P. Ning, Y. Cui, and D.S. Reeves. Constructing attack scenarios through correlation of intrusion alerts. In *9th ACM Conference on Computer and Communications Security*, November 2002.

[24] Y. A. Nygate. Event correlation using rule and object based techniques. In *Proceedings of the 6th IFIP/IEEE International Symposium on Integrated Network Management*, May 1995.

[25] J. Pearl. *Probabilistic Reasoning in Intelligent Systems: Networks of Plausible Inference*. Morgan Kaufmann Publishers, Inc, 1988.

[26] P. A. Porras, M. W. Fong, and A. Valdes. A Mission-Impact-Based approach to INFOSEC alarm correlation. In *Proceedings of the 5th International Symposium on Recent Advances in Intrusion Detection (RAID)*, October 2002.

[27] Snort. http://www.snort.org.

[28] W. Stallings. *SNMP, SNMPv2, SNMPv3, and RMON 1 and 2*. Addison-Wesley, 1999.

[29] A. Valdes and K. Skinner. Probabilistic alert correlation. In *Proceedings of the 4th International Symposium on Recent Advances in Intrusion Detection (RAID)*, October 2001.

Chapter 5

UNDERSTANDING NETWORK SECURITY DATA: USING AGGREGATION, ANOMALY DETECTION, AND CLUSTER ANALYSIS FOR SUMMARIZATION

Dave DeBarr
The MITRE Corporation

Abstract: This chapter discusses the use of off-line analysis techniques to help network security analysts at the ACME Corporation review network alert data efficiently. Aggregation is used to summarize network events by source Internet Protocol (IP) address and period of activity. These aggregate records are referred to as meta-session records. Anomaly detection is then used to identify obvious network probes using aggregate features of the meta-session records. Cluster analysis is used for further exploration of interesting groups of meta-session records.

Keywords: Intrusion Detection, Aggregation, Anomaly Detection, Cluster Analysis, Data Mining

1.   INTRODUCTION

Intrusion detection analysts at the ACME Corporation[1] spend much of their time reviewing network security data. They analyze alerts from Network-based Intrusion Detection Systems (NIDS) in order to determine an appropriate response. Possible "actions" include: ignoring the alert, checking the target server to ensure appropriate security patches have been applied, adding/modifying firewall rules, or removing a compromised host from the network (for further investigation/clean-up).

---

[1] Not their real name.

Unfortunately, the network sensors generate an enormous amount of data. For example, over the course of a week, the NIDS sensors generated over 35,000 alerts. To investigate these alarms, the analysts usually look at other traffic from the same source IP address around the same time period. Pre-aggregating this contextual information in summary form is a useful time-saving step for the analysts.

There have been many projects involving the use of data mining for intrusion detection. Typically, these projects focus on mining either network packet data or individual audit records in order to make inferences. This chapter focuses on the use of meta-session records instead of individual event records. These aggregate records summarize network events by source IP address and period of activity, thus reducing the amount of data to be reviewed and providing contextual information for individual alerts. We also demonstrate the use of anomaly detection to identify "obvious" (though often otherwise undiscovered) probes, and the use of cluster analysis to explore groups of similar meta-session records.

2.   THE ACME NETWORK

Figure 5-1 depicts the general layout of the ACME Corporate network.

The network is divided into three zones. The "Internet" zone is external to the ACME Corporation. The "De-Militarized" Zone (DMZ) contains ACME's public servers; supporting protocols such as Domain Name Services (DNS), the Simple Mail Transfer Protocol (SMTP), the Hyper Text Transfer Protocol (HTTP), and the File Transfer Protocol (FTP). The "intranet" zone contains ACME's private servers and workstations.

There are three major types of network-based sensors: NIDS, firewalls, and event loggers. The NIDS sensors monitor network packet traffic, employing user-defined signatures to generate alerts. For example, an HTTP request containing the string "/root.exe" generates a "CodeRed root.exe" alert. The alerts are considered to be high-priority events because they are typically generated by malicious activity. Although the external NIDS may also generate alerts, these external alerts are used only for context information. Often, the firewalls will block the malicious activity.

The firewalls employ user-defined rules to determine if network data should be passed, dropped, or rejected; but only drops or rejects generate event records. A "Drop" message indicates that data has been discarded without notifying the sender, while a "Reject" message indicates that data has been discarded and the sender has been notified explicitly. Because the firewall event data rarely requires action on the part of the network security analyst, these are considered to be low priority events.

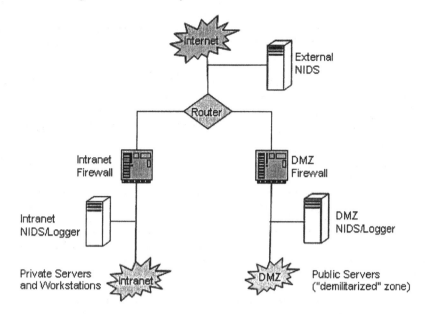

Figure 5-1. The ACME Corporate Network

The event loggers are used to identify User Datagram Protocol (UDP) exchanges and Transmission Control Protocol (TCP) connections seen "inside" the ACME Corporate network. A "TCP attempt" message indicates the event logger has seen TCP activity, while a "UDP attempt" message indicates the event logger has seen UDP activity. These loggers provide useful context information. For example, a connection from a host that generated alerts from the external NIDS, or drops/rejects from the firewall, may warrant further investigation.

The event records from each sensor are collected in a centralized database. Each event record contains 16 elements:

1. Sensor Location: "Intranet", "DMZ", or "External"
2. Sensor Type: "NIDS", "firewall", or "logger"
3. Priority: "1" for high-priority alert, "2" for low-priority alert, "3" for firewall drops/rejects, "4" for event logger records
4. Event Type: descriptive label for the event; e.g. "Drop", "Reject", "TCP attempt", "UDP attempt", "WEB-IIS CodeRed v2 root.exe access", etc.
5. Event Start Date and Time: year, month, day, hour, minute, and second for the first packet of the event
6. Duration: number of seconds between the first and last packets of the event
7. Source IP Address

8. Source IP Address Type: "E" for external, "R" for reserved (e.g. 1.1.1.1), "P" for private (e.g. 10.0.0.1), "M" for multicast, "I" for intranet, or "D" for DMZ

9. Source IP Address Subtype: "N" for ACME network addresses, "B" for ACME broadcast addresses, "O" otherwise.

10. Destination IP Address

11. Destination IP Address Type: "E", "R", "P", "M", "I", or "D" (see "Source IP Address Type" for meanings)

12. Destination IP Address Subtype: "N", "B", or "O" (see "Source IP Address Subtype" for meanings)

13. Protocol: "I" for Internet Control Message Protocol (ICMP), "T" for TCP, "U" for UDP, or "O" for other

14. Source Port or ICMP Type: an integer representing the source port for TCP or UDP protocol events, or an integer representing the message type for ICMP packets (e.g. ICMP type 3 messages indicate data has been prohibited from reaching an intended destination)

15. Destination Port or ICMP Code: an integer representing the destination port for TCP or UDP protocol events, or an integer representing the message code for ICMP packets (e.g. ICMP type 3 messages with code 13 indicates that communication has been administratively prohibited)

16. Common Destination Port Flag: indicates the destination port is considered to be common (e.g. TCP ports 21, 25, 53, 80, etc; or UDP ports 53, 111, 161, 162, etc.)[2]

A subset of the attributes for some sample events is shown in Table 5-1. These events are shown in the order they were recorded by the sensors.

Table 5-1. Abbreviated Sample of Network Security Event Data

Sensor	Priority	Event	Protocol	Source	Destination
DMZ Firewall	3	Drop	UDP	External 192.0.2.176	DMZ 192.168.242.175:500
External NIDS	2	WEB-IIS cmd.exe access	TCP	External 192.0.2.176	DMZ 192.168.242.175:80
DMZ NIDS	1	WEB-IIS cmd.exe access	TCP	External 192.0.2.176	DMZ 192.168.242.175:80
DMZ NIDS	1	WEB-IIS ISAPI .ida attempt	TCP	External 192.0.2.176	DMZ 192.168.242.175:80

The firewall event is considered low priority, because the firewall actually blocked access to UDP port 500; but the alerts from the DMZ NIDS are a possible cause for concern. An external host was able to send likely malicious HTTP requests to a server on the DMZ. Fortunately, this particular server is not vulnerable to this particular exploit; but it's useful to

[2] The SANS "Top 20" Vulnerabilities list was used to identify "common" ports

identify other activity from the same host, surrounding the time of the alert. This is where aggregation helps.

3. AGGREGATION

Event records are aggregated by source IP address and period of activity for two major reasons:
1. to provide contextual information for alerts to be reviewed
2. to reduce the number of records to be reviewed

A 30 minute time-out period is used to aggregate events from the same source IP address. Using the sample data from Table 5-1: if the next event occurs 31 minutes after the fourth event, the next event would generate a new meta-session record. Because the aggregation engine is designed to operate on a stream of event data, a 60 minute timeout is used to generate intermediate output for long-running periods of activity (thus freeing up memory used to maintain state for the meta-session). Each meta-session record includes the following elements:
1. Source IP Address (including Type and Subtype information)
2. Time Range
3. Destination IP Address Range
4. Destination IP Address Count
5. Maximum Number of Common Ports per Destination Address
6. Count of Event Types
7. Priority of Highest Priority Event
8. Perimeter Crossing Count: for example, the number of events from an external source seen on the DMZ or intranet
9. Event List: a list containing up to 5 distinct event types, sorted by priority

Table 5-2 shows the meta-session record corresponding to the events shown in Table 5-1. The maximum priority for the events was one (Max Pri). Two of the events from the external IP address were recorded on the DMZ (Crossing Count). There was only one destination address (Dst Addr Count), but two "common" ports were targeted (Max Ports). The three event types are listed in the far right-hand column, with the firewall message also indicating the destination port.

Table 5-2. Abbreviated Example of a Meta-Session Record

Source	Max Pri	Crossing Count	Dst Addr Count	Max Ports	Event Types	Event List
External 192.0.2.176	1	2	1	2	3	WEB-IIS cmd.exe access WEB-IIS ISAPI .ida attempt Drop (udp:500)

By aggregating the event records into meta-session records, we were able to aggregate 7,560,570 event records generated over the course of a week into 914,241 meta-session records, a reduction of more than 87%[3] with the added benefit of providing instant context for those alerts that need to be reviewed. Less than 10% of the meta-session records covered an hour of activity, and only 35 of the meta-session records contained more than 5 types of events. Using anomaly detection for the aggregate features allows for easy detection of intrusive probes that might otherwise be missed by an analyst or the network sensors.

4.   ANOMALY DETECTION

Anomaly detection involves identifying unusual values, but the keys to using anomaly detection effectively revolve around monitoring relevant variables and setting appropriate detection thresholds. As Stefan Axelsson points out in his survey of intrusion detection systems, "The problems with [anomaly detection] rest in the fact that it does not necessarily detect undesirable behaviour, and that the false alarm rates can be high."

In order to identify network probes, three variables can be monitored independently:
1. Destination IP Address Count: an unusually large destination address count is likely to indicate the meta-session contains host scanning behavior; i.e. the source host is looking for active hosts connected to the destination network
2. Maximum Number of Common Ports per Destination Address: an unusually large port count is likely to indicate the meta-session contains port scanning behavior; i.e. the source is looking for active services running on a particular host
3. Count of Event Types: an unusually large count of event types is likely to indicate the meta-session contains vulnerability scanning behavior; i.e. the source is testing for susceptibility to a variety of known exploits

In order to identify "normal" values for the "Destination IP Address Count" and the "Maximum Number of Common Ports per Destination Address", we restricted our profiling efforts to meta-session records that contained *no* firewall drops/rejects or NIDS alerts. In order to identify "normal" values for the "Count of Event Types", we included the NIDS

---

[3] Although the techniques discussed in this paper can be applied to events where the source IP address is an ACME host, all results reported in this chapter pertain to events where the source IP address belongs to an external host (for privacy reasons).

alerts as well (allowing us to quickly identify those meta-sessions involving more focused attacks).

The histogram in Figure 5-2 illustrates the distribution of destination IP address counts for a week's worth of these meta-session records. The most noticeable feature of this graph is the presence of multiple peaks, indicating a mixture of distinctive behaviors within the observed data. The majority of these meta-sessions have very few destination IP addresses. In fact, over 99% of these meta-sessions have less than 10 destination IP addresses.

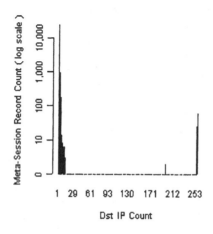

Figure 5-2. Distribution of Destination IP Address Count Values

A model-based clustering algorithm, known as MCLUST, was used to generate a mixture model for this data. The initial model was built using a random sample of two-sevenths of the meta-session records from the first week; and the Bayesian Information Criterion (BIC) measure was used to determine the number of components in the data. Using the sample data provided and a fixed-width variance for each component (like the K-means clustering algorithm), two components were identified: one group of meta-sessions with mean value 1.13 and the other group with mean value 248.40.

By determining the mean and standard deviation of the log likelihood of the data for each of the next four weeks of data, we were able to generate a test for continued efficacy of this model. Any future log-likelihood values falling at least three standard deviations below the mean log-likelihood value would indicate the model needs to be rebuilt. In our example, the cut-off threshold is -73,634 (keep in mind that we're talking about the log-likelihood of observing tens of thousands of values).

A sample from each of the two groups from the week of training data was reviewed to determine if they contained host scans. As you might suspect, the group with the smaller number of destination IP addresses per meta-session did not appear to contain any host scans, while the group with the larger number of destination IP addresses per meta-session appeared to contain only host scans! To identify host scans, we want to flag values that would not be likely to be considered similar to the values found in our "normal" group (the one without host scans). Because the maximum *possible* value for a member of group one is 124, we chose 124 as our threshold value; i.e. meta-sessions with more than 124 destination addresses are labeled as suspected host scanning episodes.

As mentioned earlier, the 101 meta-session records belonging to the group with the larger mean appeared to have been generated by host scans that did not trip any rules on either a firewall or a NIDS! These scanning episodes were directed against 3 subnets within the DMZ. They included 44 scans for UDP port 38293 (Norton Anti-Virus), 20 scans for TCP port 1433 (Microsoft SQL Server), and 14 scans for TCP port 21 (FTP). Although these particular scans do not appear to have resulted in successful exploits, it might be prudent to add firewall rules to restrict requests to valid servers only.

To estimate performance of our host scan detection test, we selected a random sample of data from the entire population of meta-session records for a sixth week of data (remember, we used 1 week of data for training and 4 weeks of data for validation). The results are shown in Table 5-3.

Table 5-3. Host Scan Test Results for a Random Sample of Meta-Sessions

		Predictions	
		Not Host Scan	Host Scan
Actuals	Unknown	5	0
	Not Host Scan	91	0
	Host Scan	3	1

The estimated detection rate for the test is 25% (95% confidence interval: 1%-81%), while the estimated false alarm rate is 0% (95% confidence interval: 0%-98%). Unfortunately, there were not enough host scans present in the sample to get smaller confidence intervals around the estimated detection and false alarms rates; but there were enough samples to provide a better estimate of the base rate for host scans. The estimated base rate for host scans is 4% (95% confidence interval: 1%-10%).

The 124 address threshold seems a bit high, and it will obviously miss some host scans; but there's almost always a trade-off between the detection rate and the false alarm rate. For our purposes, we have chosen to emphasize minimizing the false alarm rate. In the future, if firewalls are able to provide an automated response to temporarily block the sources of suspected host scans, we believe this will also require an emphasis on minimizing the false alarm rate.

The 3 host scans that our test misclassified appeared to be the result of worm activity involving attempted connections to apparently randomly selected IP addresses. These meta-sessions involved attempted connections to only one or two hosts, but other meta-session records indicated sporadic efforts to contact different addresses within the ACME network. The "unknown" values appear to be the result of back scatter or chaff, a consequence of a third party's use of spoofed addresses. To get a better estimate of the false alarm rate (a smaller confidence interval), we reviewed a random sample of 30 of the 624 suspected scans from this same week of test data.

Good news: all 30 of the suspected host scans appear to be host scans. This gives us an estimated false alarm rate of 0%, with a 95% confidence interval ranging between 0 and 12%. As a note of interest, 4 of these 30 scans all targeted the same TCP port in IANA's unassigned range; and all 4 of these scans made it past the firewall. This might be indicative of a new trojan port that requires a new firewall rule.

Unlike the number of destination addresses, the distribution of values for the maximum number of common ports per destination address appeared to have only one component. Nevertheless, we employed a similar strategy for building a model that can be tested for changes in the future. The change detection threshold for this model was also established as a log-likelihood value that falls three standard deviations below the mean for the next four weeks of data (-21,050). The values for the maximum number of common ports appear to have a tighter distribution than the values for the number of destination addresses. The mean value for the two-sevenths random sample from the first week of data was 0.68. Because we're only monitoring ports with common vulnerabilities, some meta-sessions actually have a value of zero for the maximum number of common ports per destination address.

To identify a threshold value for detecting port scans, we used a heuristic based on the survival function of the exponential probability distribution. We took the mean value of the test sample, plugged it into the following equation, and solved for X.

$$Exp(-X/B) = 1/N$$

where
- B is the mean value for the "normal" (training) sample
- N is the number of meta-session records in our training sample

Meta-sessions targeting more than 6 common ports for any destination address were labeled as port scans, but there appeared to be very few port scans in our data. In fact, there were no port scans found in the earlier sample of 100 meta-session records used for testing; so our estimated base rate for port scans is 0%, with a 95% confidence interval between 0 and 4%.

The seven meta-sessions in the test data that were labeled as port scanning episodes appear to have been labeled correctly, so our estimated false alarm rate is again 0%, but our 95% confidence interval is between 0 and 41%! This broad confidence interval is one of the pitfalls of using real-world data to estimate performance, but it does preclude the difficulties of attempting to "manufacture" representative test data. The only note of interest for the port scan test data was the presence of two hosts from the same source network targeting ports on the same destination address.

Like the values for the maximum number of common ports per destination address, the values for the number of event types also had a unimodal distribution. The mean of the two-sevenths sample from the first week of data was 1.12, and the change detection threshold for the resulting model was a log-likelihood of -22,076. To identify a threshold value to detect vulnerability scans, we used the same heuristic based on the survival function of the exponential probability distribution (solving the equality mentioned earlier for X). Meta-sessions with more than 10 event types were identified as vulnerability scans.

Vulnerability scans appeared to be *very* scarce in the test data. There were no vulnerability scans in the earlier sample of 100 test records. In fact, only one meta-session was labeled as a vulnerability scan in the entire test set. This record was indeed a vulnerability scan. The source appeared to be trying to identify the type of platform for the destination host, and then the source launched a series of exploit attempts against the secure shell port.

For all three types of anomaly detection tests, we tended to error on the side of caution by emphasizing the minimization of false alarms; but the heuristics could easily be adjusted to maximize the detection rate. The labels are not mutually exclusive (for example, an attacker could conduct a host scan, followed by a port scan and a vulnerability scan in the same meta-session); but the flagged records can be easily prioritized by reviewing suspected vulnerability scans, followed by port scans, then host scans. Within these groupings, the individual meta-sessions can be ordered by the maximum number of events per host; i.e. giving priority to meta-sessions that involved a scan followed by focus on a particular host.

5.   CLUSTER ANALYSIS

While unusual observations may be indicative of activity that requires our attention, the opposite is often true as well. Very common activities typically do not require intervention on the part of the network security analyst. Grouping meta-sessions can be useful for analyzing data in bulk. For example, one week of data contained a total of 1,731 meta-sessions involving only "ICMP Destination Unreachable (Communication Administratively Prohibited)" messages. In order to review these meta-sessions, it's useful to group together meta-sessions with similar characteristics.

We used the Partitioning Around Medoids (PAM) algorithm to summarize groups of meta-sessions with similar characteristics. Because PAM uses medoids rather than means to represent each group of observations, it is more robust than the K-means clustering algorithm. Medoids are records whose average dissimilarity to all other records in the group is minimal. A medoid can be thought of as a prototype for the group it represents.

The average silhouette value was used to identify the optimal number of clusters for summarizing a set of meta-session records. The silhouette value is near one for a record that fits well with its cluster, and near negative one for a record that does not fit well with its assigned cluster.

To cluster meta-session records, we use the continuous attributes of the meta-session record (eliminating variables with no variance and the variate with the smallest variance for each pair of correlated variables). For the "ICMP Destination Unreachable", we used the following attributes to build the model:

- number of events observed on the Intranet
- number of events observed on the DMZ
- number of seconds between the first and last events of the meta-session
- number of destination IP addresses

To measure the dissimilarity between any two meta-session records, we used the Euclidean distance for vectors containing normalized values for the attributes mentioned above. The optimal model for the "ICMP Destination Unreachable" meta-sessions had 6 partitions, with the average silhouette value for this model being 0.71. The medoids for this model are listed in Table 5-4.

Table 5-4. Prototypes for the "ICMP Destination Unreachable" Meta-Session Groups

Group	Member Count	Intranet Records	DMZ Records	Time Range	Destination Count
1	1,288	0	1	1	1
2	131	0	3	1,282	2
3	9	0	16	1,411	14
4	14	1	0	1	1
5	4	3	0	1	3
6	285	0	14	21	1

The largest group, group one, consists of single "ICMP Destination Unreachable" replies directed toward DMZ hosts, while the smallest group, group five, consists of multiple "ICMP Destination Unreachable" messages directed toward intranet hosts (a relatively rare occurrence).

A principal components projection of the meta-session records is shown in Figure 5-3. The groups are shown by elliptical rings. Although much of the variance of the values is lost when projecting from the initial set of four variables down to two variables for plotting, a diagram such as this makes it easy to visualize outliers. Group 5 appears off to itself in the upper right-hand corner, because it's unusual for intranet hosts to receive "ICMP Destination Unreachable" replies.

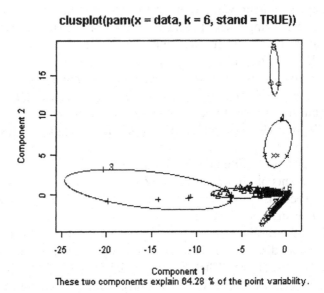

Figure 5-3. Plot of Cluster Analysis Results

In this particular instance, the 1,731 meta-session records can be effectively summarized by a list of 6 prototypes, allowing the analyst to focus attention on groups of interest.

Cluster analysis can also be used to group together meta-session records with event lists that are similar, but not exactly the same. Over the course of a week, there were only 26 distinct event lists that appeared in 168 or more meta-sessions; however, there were 4,830 distinct event lists that appeared in less than 168 meta-sessions. For example, there was only one meta-session with the following single-item event list:

• WEB-CGI /cgi-bin/ access

To find similar meta-sessions, we grouped the infrequent events lists by again using the PAM algorithm. This time, however, we measured the distance between two meta-sessions by using the Jaccard dissimilarity coefficient for the tokens in the event lists. For example, the dissimilarity value between the following single-item event lists would be 0.50, because they only share two of the four distinct tokens.

- WEB-CGI /cgi-bin/ access
- WEB-CGI calendar access

The 4,830 distinct event lists formed a total of 47 groups in the optimal model, where the average silhouette value was 0.36 (not perfect, but still useful for summarization purposes). The group containing the "WEB-CGI /cgi-bin/ access" event is listed in Table 5-5.

Table 5-5. Sample Grouping of Meta-Session Records with Infrequent Event Lists

Event List Id	Highest Priority Event	Number of Meta-Sessions	Event[1]	Event[2]
1	1	1	WEB-CGI /cgi-bin/ access	
2	2	1	WEB-CGI calendar access	
3	2	1	WEB-CGI calendar access	WEB-CGI register.cgi access
4	2	1	WEB-CGI calendar access	WEB-MISC intranet access
5	2	1	WEB-CGI calendar access	TCP Attempt (tcp:53)
6	2	1	WEB-CGI phf access	
7	2	1	WEB-CGI register.cgi access	
8	2	1	WEB-CGI swc access	

The prototype of this group is event list number 2. The prototype event list and the highest priority for the list can be used to represent each group of meta-sessions. Again, this summarized view allows both a reduction in data and an increase in understanding. Comparing the group in Table 5-5 to the group in Table 5-6, it is easy to see there are indeed significant differences between the two groups. The first row in Table 5-6 is the prototype for this small group.

Table 5-6. Contrast Grouping of Meta-Session Records with Infrequent Event Lists

Event List Id	Highest Priority Event	Number of Meta-Sessions	Event[1]	Event[2]	Event[3]
1	1	1	NNTP AUTHINFO USER overflow attempt	P2P GNUTella GET (tcp:119)[4]	
2	1	1	NNTP AUTHINFO USER overflow attempt	P2P GNUTella GET (tcp:119)	TCP attempt (tcp:119)

6.   CONCLUSIONS

This chapter describes the use of aggregation for data reduction, anomaly detection for probe identification, and cluster analysis for summarization. The techniques demonstrated are independent of the specific sensors used to generate the network security data. The only requirements for the data included the presence of IP address and port information, along with distinctive labels for alerts generated by the NIDS.

By using aggregation, we are able to replace many individual event records with a single aggregate record. For example, consider the "script kiddie" who simply tries to launch an exploit against every possible address in your network. The flow of individual alerts to the console could be overwhelming. A single meta-session record can be used to replace these alerts, and anomaly detection can be used to flag the meta-session as a host scanning episode.

A simple form of anomaly detection can be used to discover probes that may not generate alerts. For instance, a single week of data contained over a 100 host scans that were missed by both the firewalls and the NIDS. By monitoring relevant variables, with the desired emphasis on minimizing false alarms, it's possible to use anomaly detection effectively for identifying probes.

Cluster analysis is useful for grouping together similar records for review. By providing effective summaries, it allows an analyst to focus attention on only those groups requiring further investigation.

Although the work described here illustrates a potentially useful approach to anomaly detection, further work is needed to improve the

---

[4] This is actually a false alarm, the result of a signature searching for the string "GET".

detection rate. One possible approach might involve building a probe classification model, using multiple features from the meta-session records simultaneously. Active learning could be used to minimize the amount of labeled data required to perform the classification task.

ACKNOWLEDGEMENTS

The research discussed in this chapter was conducted at MITRE with the help of many people, including (but not limited to): Eric Bloedorn, Lisa Talbot, Bill Hill, David Wilburn, Josh Gray, Clem Skorupka, and Dan Ellis.

REFERENCES

[1]   S. Axelsson, Intrusion Detection Systems: A Taxonomy and Survey. *Technical Report No 99-15*, Chalmers University of Technology: Department of Computer Engineering, 2000.

[2]   D. Barbara, J. Couto, S. Jajodia, L. Popyack, and N. Wu, ADAM: Detecting Intrusion by Data Mining, *Proceedings of the 2001 IEEE Workshop on Information Assurance and Security*, 2001.

[3]   J. Campione, et al., SANS/FBI Top 20 List: The Twenty Most Critical Internet Security Vulnerabilities, Version 3.23, May 2003. <http://www.sans.org/top20/>

[4]   C. Fraley and A. Raftery, MCLUST: Software for Model-Based Clustering, Discriminant Analysis and Density Estimation, *Technical Report No 415*, University of Washington: Department of Statistics, 2002.

[5]   S. Jajodia and D. Barbara, *Applications of Data Mining in Computer Security* (Advances in Information Security, Volume 6), Kluwer Academic Publishers, 2002.

[6]   L. Kaufman and P. Rousseeuw, *Finding Groups in Data: An Introduction to Cluster Analysis*, John Wiley & Sons, 1990.

[7]   A. Lazarevic, L. Ertoz, V. Kumar, A. Ozgur, and J. Srivastava, A Comparative Study of Anomaly Detection Schemes in Network Intrusion Detection, *Proceedings of the Third SIAM Conference on Data Mining*, 2003.

[8]   W. Lee, S. Stolfo, and K. Mok, A Data Mining Framework for Building Intrusion Detection Models, *Proceedings of the 1999 IEEE Symposium on Security and Privacy*, 1999.

[9]   R. Lippmann, J. Haines, D. Fried, J. Korba, and K. Das, The 1999 DARPA Off-Line Intrusion Detection Evaluation, *Computer Networks*, 579 - 595, October 2000.

[10]   SANS Institute, TCP/IP and tcpdump Pocket Reference Guide, June 2002, http://www.sans.org/resources/tcpip.pdf.

[11]   R. Thomas, Bogon List, Version 2.0, www.cymru.com/Documents/bogon-list.html, April 2003.

[12]   W. Venables and B. Ripley, *Modern Applied Statistics with S*, Fourth edition, Springer Verlag, 2002.

PART III

TECHNIQUES FOR MANAGING
CYBER VULNERABILITIES
AND ALERTS

Chapter 6

EARLY DETECTION OF ACTIVE INTERNET WORMS

Vincent H. Berk, George V. Cybenko, and Robert S. Gray

Institute for Security Technology Studies, Thayer School of Engineering, Dartmouth College

Abstract: An active Internet worm is malicious software that autonomously searches for and infects vulnerable hosts, copying itself from one host to another and spreading through the susceptible population. Most recent worms find vulnerable hosts by generating random IP addresses and then probing those addresses to see which are running the desired vulnerable services. Detection of such worms is a manual process in which security analysts must observe and analyze unusual network or host activity, and the worm might not be positively identified until it already has spread to most of the Internet. In this chapter, we present an *automated* system that can identify active scanning worms soon after they begin to spread, a necessary precursor to halting or slowing the spread of the worm. Our implemented system collects ICMP Destination Unreachable messages from instrumented routers, identifies message patterns that indicate malicious scanning activity, and then identifies scan patterns that indicate a propagating worm. We examine an epidemic model for worm propagation, describe our ICMP-based detection system, and present simulation results that illustrate its detection capabilities.

Keywords: Security, Worms, Propagation Models, Detection, Active Response

1. INTRODUCTION

An active Internet worm is malicious software (or malware) that autonomously spreads from host to host, actively searching for vulnerable, uninfected systems. The first such worm was the 1988 Internet worm, which spread through vulnerable Sun 3 and VAX systems starting on November 2, 1988. [17], This worm exploited flaws in the sendmail and fingerd code of that time, and through the rsh service and a password-cracking library, also exploited poor password policies. The worm collected the names of target hosts by scanning files, such as .rhosts and .forward, on the local machine, and then attempted to infect those hosts through the finger, sendmail, and password-guessing exploits.

Although the exact number of infected machines is unclear, the worm infected enough machines to disrupt normal Internet activity for several days due to high network traffic and CPU loads.

Recent examples of active worms include Code Red v2, which exploited a flaw in Microsoft's Internet Information Services and infected 360,000 machines [12], and Sapphire/Slammer, which exploited a flaw in Microsoft's SQL Server and infected 75,000 machines [11]. Code Red, Sapphire/Slammer and most other recent active worms find vulnerable machines by generating random (or pseudo-random) IP addresses and then probing to see if the desired vulnerable service is running at those addresses. Compared to the 1988 Internet, the modern Internet has so many hosts that random probing is an effective way to find vulnerable machines. The 1988 worm would have needed years (or even centuries) to find even one *existing* machine if it had used random probing.

In addition to using random probing, most recent worms probe as quickly as possible, so that the worm can spread to most vulnerable machines before system administrators have time to shut down infected machines and repair the exploited security hole. In fact, since current response is entirely manual, a worm only has to spread faster than human response time to succeed. Sapphire/Slammer, the fastest spreading worm to date, far exceeded human response time by infecting most vulnerable machines within five minutes of its launch [11]. Clearly, if the Internet community wants to halt the spread of a worm, rather than simply cleaning up afterward, some form of automated detection and response is needed. Here, we will focus on the problem of *detection*, and present an automated system that can identify active scanning worms soon after they begin to spread. Worm authors, when faced with such a detection system, might switch from address scanning to stealthier techniques for identifying potential targets, including the older, but effective, techniques of the 1988 worm. For this reason, we also will give a brief overview of potential techniques for detecting slow-moving or stealthy worms.

In the rest of this chapter, we present background on Internet worms and a model for their propagation, describe the architecture of our prototype worm-detection system, DIB:S/TRAFEN, and examine simulation results that illustrate the system's detection performance. Finally, we examine future directions for both worm authors and worm defenders.

2.   WORMS AND THEIR PROPAGATION

The first step in detecting an active worm is to understand how active worms propagate, and to develop a general propagation model that can be used as the starting point for detection algorithms. First, we compare active worms with other types of malware, and then we present an epidemic model for worm propagation.

Worms and Viruses

Over the last several years, there has been frequent discussion of the difference between viruses and worms. In the early days after the 1988 Internet worm, Eichin et al. [7] referred to this new event as an "Internet virus", stating that it bore no resemblance to the biological equivalent of a worm. Today, however, most experts refer to it as the "Morris worm", indicating that biological equivalence no longer dictates the terminology. Figure 6.1 is an inheritance graph showing current, commonly accepted relationships in terminology. Viruses and worms are both part of the larger category of malicious code. A related member of the malicious-code group is rootkits and backdoors, pieces of software often installed on compromised systems by hackers to enable them to easily regain control of the machine in the future. Rootkits are associated with the so-called "auto-rooters", pieces of software that offer a nice GUI to the hacker, making computer intrusion child's play. A disturbing detail is that many of these tools can perform multiple attacks (exploits) with various target selection strategies, eliminating the need for any understanding from the hacker. The tools often are easier to use than most security products.

Another related member of the malicious-code family is spyware, software that ships and installs with bona fide programs and relays information from the user's computer back to a data center without the user's explicit consent. This implies that the user often is not aware that spyware programs are present on the system, increasing the risk that private, or even privileged, information might be stolen. Spyware is gaining more attention lately, largely because software packages are increasing in size and complexity, making detection of spyware much more difficult. In addition, spyware programs tend to remain on the system even when the program to which it was originally attached is removed.

Where other malicious code is intended for controlled use, viruses and worms are designed to propagate without control. This makes them very dangerous, since there are no bounds on their spread, and their workings are fully decen-

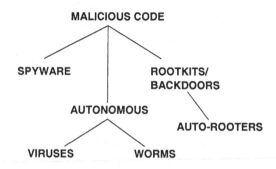

Figure 6.1. A partial hierarchy of malicious code (or malware).

tralized. Where rootkits and backdoors provide the hacker with full control of a system, worms and viruses need to be fully autonomous, following the same algorithm over and over again for each newly infected system. There is no reason, however, why the two cannot be combined. creating a massively (self-) propagating piece of malware that leaves backdoors for the hacker to enter all infected systems at will. Regarding terminology, worms and viruses can be viewed as separate types of autonomous malware (as we prefer and depict in Figure 6.1), or viruses can be viewed as a broad category of which worms are a special case. Whether worms are their own category or a subcategory has little effect on the discussion of their properties, so we leave it to the reader to form their own opinion.

The difference between worms and viruses lies in their method of propagation. In short, viruses require carriers, where worms facilitate their own propagation. Worms often use an attack strategy that actively selects targets and opens connections to those targets. The worm then launches an exploit, and, if successful, propagates by copying its code to the new system and then running that code. The new system now is infected and will behave the same as the system that infected it, resulting in two copies of the worm, both looking for new systems to infect. This spread continues until most vulnerable systems are infected, or until a built-in timer stops the propagation and switches the worm to another mode, such as a massive Distributed Denial of Service (DDOS) attack using all the infected systems as drones.

In contrast to worms, viruses need a carrier to propagate. Traditionally, viruses bind to executable files, the system boot sector, or both. This ensures that the virus is loaded into memory at boot time, or whenever a program is loaded. Once active in memory, the virus binds to the operating system and tries to infect the boot sector and every program that is run. This will guarantee its spread, since infected executables that are run on clean systems will infect the boot-sector of that system, leading to subsequent infection of that system's other programs as well. This technique requires executable files to be shared between computers, imposing a natural limit on how fast the virus can spread. Recently, however, viruses have been designed to piggy-back on bona fide communication mechanisms such as email. Email viruses often rely on the recipient to open the email and run the attached viral executable, which, in turn, will attempt to send itself to all e-mail address in the user's address book. This is the reason that such viruses often come from your best friend. Virus writers use many techniques to hide the actual virus from the user, such as embedding the viral code inside a screensaver or game. A more sophisticated approach is to include a macro in the e-mail that will run the viral code as soon as the e-mail is opened (without the user having to open the viral attachment itself). This approach, however, requires an email client that understands and automatically interprets and runs such macros. Email viruses, with or without automatic execution of the viral attachment, show propagation patterns very similar to those of active worms.

Worm Spread

The propagation pattern and autonomous behavior that classifies worms leads to a clearly identifiable three-step algorithm: (1) target selection, (2) infection attempt, and (3) code propagation (when the infection attempt succeeds). Intuitively, the faster a worm can identify and infect new vulnerable targets, the faster it can propagate. This is important, since historically it seems that slow and "silent" worms do significantly worse than fast and "loud" worms, in terms of the peak number of infected systems. The major reason for the success of fast worms is the minimal response time that they provide to take appropriate countermeasures. Successful response mainly depends on human factors, since it usually involves system administrators learning about new worm events, and then identifying and patching or removing any vulnerable systems in their networks. Given the limits of human response time, the initial propagation of a new worm can proceed unobstructed, giving fast worms the chance to reach a "critical mass", namely, infect enough systems to create and sustain an epidemic. In the next section, we will back these intuitive explanations with some basic epidemiology.

The target-selection algorithm is crucial to the success of a worm, and worm authors have shown stunning creativity in this part. Proposed or observed approaches include (1) random (directed or hitlist), (2) sniffing, and (3) name (email addresses, system files, DNS). In addition, many worms have combined these three techniques with varying results. The most common, and easily implemented, algorithm is random generation of target IP addresses. This method has gained popularity on the IPv4 Internet, since the IPv4 Internet is densely populated. Selecting a random IP address has a high chance (between 5% to 15%) of hitting an existing machine. A larger address space, like IPv6, would mitigate this problem since it would take *years* to even find a populated IP address by random scanning.

To improve the chance of finding vulnerable machines, many worm authors employ techniques in which they direct the random target selection. By preferring address ranges that are densely populated or address ranges that are suspected to contain a large number of *vulnerable* machines, the worm can propagate significantly faster. As an example of the latter case, the vulnerability that the worm exploits might be typical of home computers. The worm author would attempt to identify up front which target ranges hold the most home computers (dial-up and cable-modem ISPs) and then program the worm to prefer targets in those address ranges. Alternatively, the worm can be programmed to select targets only from a list of *known* targets. This approach usually is called "hitlist propagation", and is most effectively used as an initial propagation method before defaulting to random propagation [18]. Such a hitlist would contain IP addresses that are known to be vulnerable systems, and thus would need to be constructed before the worm was released. Construction of hitlists can be done slowly over the course of months by randomly scanning the Internet. To avoid attacking the same system multiple times during propagation, the list can be split in half every time a worm instance propagates. One half is kept by the infecting system, while the other half is given to the newly infected system. Hitlists are an effective way of establishing a critical mass of infected systems.

Scanning activity can be difficult to hide, since intrusion-detection and traffic-monitoring systems can notice the pattern of one machine actively connecting to many other machines. A technique that has been frequently discussed, although not used in implemented worms yet, is passively sniffing the network (or inspecting application-level traffic) to identify reachable IP addresses that likely are running a service that the worm can exploit. As an example, a contagion worm might have two exploits, one for Web clients and one for Web servers. [18]. A copy of the worm on a Web server attempts to infect any Web client that requests a page, while a copy of the worm on a Web client attempts to infect any Web server to which the client connects. Fortunately, this approach is applicable only for some services, since the worm must see enough traffic to build up a reasonably sized set of potential targets. For example, if the worm only had an exploit for Web servers and was passively sniffing the network to identify other Web servers, it might see little or no traffic for any Web server other than the one already infected, particularly given the prevalence of switched Ethernet. On the other hand, a worm exploiting a vulnerability in email servers will have a better chance of succeeding, since email servers contact *each other* to exchange email. As long as users on the local network make moderate to heavy use of email, the worm will be able to identify a significant number of email servers that it can attempt to infect. As an added bonus for the worm author, such an email worm would be equally successful in densely or sparsely populated address spaces.

When the address space is only sparsely populated, random scanning (even to construct a hitlist) can be an impossible task, and thus other methods need to be employed. In addition to the passive network sniffing discussed above, a worm can use DNS names rather than IP addresses to identify systems. When a top-level domain name is acquired, DNS servers often will reveal the names of the associated mail exchange server and Web server. Even if these names are not obtainable directly from the DNS system, the worm author can make an educated guess as to what the names of existing systems would be. Imagine that the worm acquired the domain *exampledomain.com*. A logical naming scheme would suggest that *www.exampledomain.com* would be the Web server and *mail.exampledomain.com* would be the mailserver. A list of other names would include *www1, ns, ns1, dns, dns1, nameserver, ftp, smtp, pop3 or skywalker*. Names from Greek mythology also are very popular. The worm author's creativity can be endless, and techniques that have been used for many years in password crackers also can be used to construct hostnames. If a site has a hostname *sparc09*, for example, it is worth trying *sparc01, sparc02, ... sparc99* as well. Additionally, hostnames can be gleaned from many other sources. The 1988 worm [7] used the *.rhosts* file to obtain hostnames of other systems in the network. Similarly, most operating systems maintain small name databases as a backup for when the DNS system fails. Other sources can be email addresses, which have the basic structure *username@domainname*, and provide domain names for the process above. Obtaining the addresses or names of potential targets from information stored on the currently infected machine often is called topological scanning. [18] Although most worms today use some form of random target selection, the introduction of IPv6 means that it is no longer the guaranteed fastest way to propagate. Future worms most likely will employ combinations of the above techniques to facilitate their propagation. In addition, viruses that use normal network traffic as a carrier will become increasingly popular, since they do not need to select their own targets.

After a target is selected, the worm will attempt to infect it. If successful, the worm will run a copy of itself on the newly compromised system. The two general approaches to code propagation are the use of a central repository or the use of cloning. Although a central repository allows more control (since it is contacted at every propagation), it is also at risk of counter attack, effectively stopping worm propagation. Therefore, most worms are simply cloned when propagated. Evolutions of the central-repository technique, however, or programming worm copies to create their own peer-to-peer network for command distribution, will provide significant control capabilities for hard-to-stop worms [18].

Epidemics

To get a feel for the factors that govern worm (as well as virus) propagation, most researchers take to the classic epidemiological equations. These models describe biological epidemics quite well, and have proven to be very applicable to their cyber equivalents. We will introduce these models here and refer to further reading for a more in-depth coverage of the topic.

In its most basic form, the behavior of a single host is described by the SIR (Susceptible-Infective-Recovered) model as shown in Figure 6.2. For a given worm, the S-state (susceptible) indicates the host is vulnerable to that worm. The I-state (infective) indicates that the host is infected and spreading the worm. The R-state (recovered/removed) means that the host is not (or no longer) of interest to the epidemic. The reasons for being in the R-state may vary, most often the host simply was not vulnerable to the worm in the first place, or the host was patched (whether infected or not). Alternatively, the host might be disconnected from the network, either to prevent infection or further propagation. For any worm, only a marginal portion of all the hosts are vulnerable, i.e., in the group of susceptibles S. The majority of Internet-connected hosts will be in the R-group, and not be involved in the spread of the epidemic. The transitions between the states are given below, keeping in mind that the transitions apply to the state of a host for one particular infection only:

$S \rightarrow I$ (infection)
$I \rightarrow R$ (patching or disconnection)

And furthermore:

$S \rightarrow R$ (uninfected system patched)
$I \rightarrow S$ (infection removed, but system not patched)
$R \rightarrow S$ (susceptible system reconnected to the network)
$R \rightarrow I$ (infected system reconnected to the network)

The first two transitions are the most common case, and account for the majority of the total number of state transitions made during an epidemic. They model the infection of vulnerable systems (S→I transition), and the patching or removal of infected systems (S→R transition). Many systems generally are not vulnerable to a certain worm attack, and such systems do not change state and largely remain in their R-group. The classic epidemic equations from Kermack and McKendrick focus on these two transitions (see Daley and Gani [6]) for modeling the spread of an infection in continuous time. The population N is constructed from the three groups S, I, and R, which change over time as defined by $s(t)$, $i(t)$, and $r(t)$, where t_0 is the time at which the infection begins. Note that $N = s(t) + i(t) + r(t)$, meaning that the population size is assumed constant, which is acceptable considering that we defined R to contain disconnected, not just patched, systems. The population changes over time can be defined as

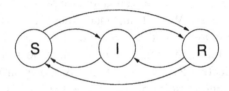

Figure 6.2. The SIR (Susceptibles-Infectives-Recovered) model is probably the most popular way of identifying the groups in an epidemic, and its transitions form the basis for a broad range of mathematical models.

$$(a) \quad \frac{\mathrm{d}s}{\mathrm{d}t} = -\beta si \qquad (b) \quad \frac{\mathrm{d}i}{\mathrm{d}t} = \beta si - \gamma i \qquad (c) \quad \frac{\mathrm{d}r}{\mathrm{d}t} = \gamma i \qquad (6.1)$$

The parameter β models the transition S→I and γ models the transition I→R. Intuitively, β is the likelihood of one particular infected system contacting (and infecting) one particular susceptible system in $\mathrm{d}t$ time. Likewise, γ is the likelihood that one particular infected system is patched or disconnected in $\mathrm{d}t$ time. Putting a number to these factors is not easy since it is different for each worm. The general principals discussed in the previous section, however, lead to some guidelines. First, the rate at which a worm can infect new systems is limited by the rate at which it can contact other systems (which determines β). This rate is either limited by parallelism or by bandwidth, whichever reaches its limit first, and these factors are determined by the capabilities of the infected host and the target-selection algorithm of the worm. The most effective propagation would be when the worm uses up all the bandwidth that the host has to offer, thus, the closer a worm can approach this limit, the better its chances are for fast propagation. There are several factors involved that make this easier or harder. The first factor is the protocol that the worm uses to propagate. When the worm uses a fire and forget protocol (like UDP), it most easily can use all of the bandwidth since it never has to wait for a return packet. When a connection-oriented protocol (such as TCP) is used, however, the worm will need to wait for an acknowledgment from the target host before it can send the attack data. The choice is not always up to the worm author since most services (and hence most vulnerabilities) are built using connection-oriented protocols.

The latency between initiation and acknowledgment, however, can be filled with connection requests to other potential targets when the worm interleaves them properly. With appropriate programming, which may include the worm generating its own connection requests and bypassing the operating system's network stack, the worm can hide most of the latency associated with connection-oriented protocols. For example, one thread in the worm would craft requests packets, transmit those packets, and log the outstanding connection in a table, while a second thread constantly would check (sniff) for return packets and attempt to match them with the entries in the table. Every several seconds the worm traverses the entire table to fault connection requests that have not had a response within a *worm-defined* timeout period. By making this table sufficiently large, the worm should be able to fill the available bandwidth without needing to run thousands of concurrent copies of itself on the infected host. Although such an approach makes the worm more complex and more difficult to implement correctly, the added burden might be well worth the increased propagation speed.

Given this discussion, the average time that each connection takes can be calculated as

$$\tau = r \times t_{latency} + (1 - r) \times t_{timeout} \qquad (6.2)$$

where r is the reachability based on the target-selection algorithm. A perfect hitlist would give $r = 1$, and random target selection on the current Internet would give $r \approx 0.1$.

When a worm does use a hitlist for initial propagation, the worm would have two different values for β, one value for the hitlist part of the propagation, and a second smaller value for the remaining (random) part of the propagation. In addition, I_0 (the initial number of infected systems) for the second part would be the number of infected systems after the hitlist propagation is complete. For completely random target selection, β can be defined as

$$\beta = \frac{1}{N} \times \frac{\alpha}{\tau} \qquad (6.3)$$

where N is the size of the address space (2^{32} in case of IPv4) and α is the number of concurrent scanning threads. In the case of a worm that implemented a fully parallel scan through the construction of its own request packets, α might be defined quite high (even if the worm itself only used the two threads described above). In the equations, dt is the same as the unit of τ, meaning that if τ is calculated in seconds, dt in Equations 6.1 also is in seconds. For a perfect hitlist (where every IP address is indeed a susceptible host), we instead could define β as:

$$\beta = \frac{1}{S_0} \times \frac{\alpha}{\tau} \qquad (6.4)$$

where S_0 is the number of systems that are initially susceptible (assuming that the hitlist holds *all* susceptible systems). The second factor $\frac{\alpha}{\tau}$ essentially calculates the average number of successful connections a single infected host can complete in dt time (not all of those are necessarily susceptibles). When network bandwidth is the limiting factor, rather than worm parallelism, the second factor can be replaced with a division of the available network bandwidth by the size of the infection packetstream.

The γ parameter (the I→R transition) can be harder to model since it mostly depends on actions of the system administrator. (See Figure 6.3.) It will take security personnel some time to discover a newly launched worm, and then they will need to analyze the worm and possibly write a patch. System administrators then must learn about, download, and install the new patch. Another option for system administrators is the disconnection of infected machines from the network. Both processes, patching and disconnection, are hard to model, and likely are not governed by a fixed rate. Note that in the Kermack and McKendrick model, the transition is dependent only on the current size of the

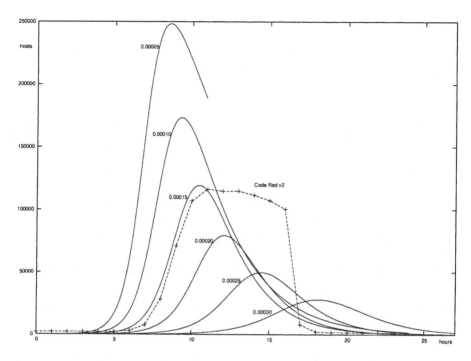

Figure 6.3. Spread of Code Red v2 versus the epidemic equations for different values of γ. The vertical axis represents the total number of infected systems at any given time, and the horizontal axis is the time in hours. Parameter β was calculated based on Equations 6.2 and 6.3 and the characteristics of Code Red v2 on a per-second basis: Code Red v2 used 100 concurrent scanning threads ($\alpha = 100$), with an average reachability of $r = \frac{1}{10}$ and a default timeout on no response of 21 seconds (based on the default Windows NT timeout, exponential back-off with 3 retries after 3, 6, and 12 seconds). This gives (6.2) $\tau = \frac{1}{10} \times 1 + (1 - \frac{1}{10}) \times 21 = 19$. The address space was IPv4, and thus $N = 2^{32}$ gives (6.3) $\beta = \frac{1}{2^{32}} \times \frac{100}{19} = 1.23 \times 10^{-9}$. Notice how the total number of systems infected (surface area under the graphs) decreases with higher values for γ. Code Red v2 data was collected at TRIUMF Canada (http://www.triumf.ca), which generously made the data available to us for this research.

group of infected systems, which could be too simple a dependency to model the behavior of security personnel and system administrators.

Additional Transitions. The other transitions in the SIR model are interesting for further study. The S→R transition models uninfected systems that are vulnerable to the worm under consideration, but get patched or disconnected before they are infected. Although this process might be underway before the worm is launched (i.e., a patch for the worm's exploit is available a priori), only its effect on the worm should be modeled. Patching that occurs before the worm is released simply decreases S_0. Below is an extended set of differential equations taking into account all six transitions from the graph:

$$\frac{ds}{dt} = -\beta si - \eta i + \zeta r + \theta i \tag{6.5}$$

$$\frac{di}{dt} = \beta si - \gamma i + \varepsilon r - \theta i \tag{6.6}$$

$$\frac{dr}{dt} = \gamma i - \varepsilon r - \zeta r + \eta i \tag{6.7}$$

The S→R transition is governed by the parameter η and is taken to be dependent on the size of the group of infectives over time. This is parallel to the I→R transition, and indicates that administrators will patch uninfected systems, as well as infected ones, with greater urge as the worm propagates. It can be argued, however, that it should be multiplied by the size of the group of susceptibles as well, since the chance that administrators patch or disconnect uninfected systems decreases as there are fewer systems uninfected. The I→S transition (represented by θ) also is taken to increase and decrease as the group of infected systems grows and shrinks. This means that the larger the group of infected systems, the greater the number of systems that will be cleaned, but not patched. A good example of this was the propagation of the Code Red v2 worm. Although Code Red v2 could be removed from a system by rebooting, the system would be susceptible to re-infection after the reboot. The R→S transition (ζ in the equations) is most likely due to uninfected, yet susceptible, systems being taken off-line and then reconnected to the network later. The R→I transition (modeled by ε) will be small, representing the infected systems that are taken off-line and later reconnected, allowing them to continue spreading the infection. One final note on these four transitions is their relative insignificance compared to β and γ. Even for very small values of θ, ε and ζ, the equations can be unrealistically imbalanced. The interested reader is encouraged to try different values for all parameters and see how the epidemic curve behaves.

3.   RESPONSE

The best way to respond to an epidemic is to prevent it in the first place. History has shown, however, that there have always been unpatched vulnerabilities. Moreover, with software getting more and more complex, it is unlikely that this will change. Software vendors put significant effort into distributing patches to mend security holes in their software, but not nearly enough users install such patches promptly. Often people are not aware of security updates, and many others get tired of the continuous stream of updates, inadvertently leading to disregard. Patching does decrease the size of the pool of susceptibles, however, effectively limiting the damage any worm can do. The most obvious solution would seem to be automated patching services, although the necessary basis of trust is lacking. Few security experts would trust *another* piece of software to secure the system, arguing that such a service would itself be a target for attack.

The scenario is clear; once the security service is compromised, specifically the central server from where the patches actually come, the attackers can distribute a patch that installs a vulnerability that later can be exploited in a massive worm attack. It would even be possible to distribute the initial copies of the worm though such a service and use it as the initial group of infectives, creating a very broad critical mass. Needless to say, such a situation would be devastating.

Thus, although automated patching does have its place, automated response after the worm is launched must be a critical part of an effective defense. When we consider the epidemic equations, the two parameters that govern the majority of all transitions are β and γ. An epidemic can be reduced by either lowering β or increasing γ. Figure 6.3 shows how increasing the value of γ reduces the number of hosts affected by the epidemic (surface area under the graph). We now will discuss several ways of influencing these parameters as a form of active response to worms.

Increasing γ. A common way of avoiding communication with infected systems is the "blacklist". This is a technique often used within the security community to filter out IP addresses that have shown aggressive behavior in the recent past. A similar technique could be used to collect IP addresses of systems that are known infectives. This list would grow as the worms propagate. Routers and firewalls across the world would have to implement filtering rules to disallow traffic from any of these IP addresses. This effectively cuts infected systems off the network by blocking them from communicating, therefore increasing γ. The R-group will increase, and there will be relatively more disconnected, infected systems than normal. Problems with this approach are the implementation requirements. Moore et al. [13] conclude that practically all of the Internet's major connections need to employ blacklist filters for this technique to be effective. In addition, the list of blocked IP addresses needs to be continually updated and, as the list grows, it will incur a significant load on all the participating routers and firewalls. Additionally, a fast and accurate detection system needs to be in place to determine which systems should be added to the blacklist. Another common problem that this technique poses is the ability for attackers to perform a DOS attack on arbitrary hosts or networks. Attackers can spoof malicious traffic, making it seem like it came from a particular network, and get the worm response system to blacklist or filter out all traffic from that network, effectively disconnecting it from the Internet.

Reducing β. Since β governs the growth of the worm, worm authors will try to maximize β to speed up the propagation, the security community, in turn, must try to minimize it. A technique that has been discussed by Williamson [19] is to reduce the number of new connections that a host may initiate per timeslice. A connection is counted as new when it connects to an IP address that it was not communicating with in the recent past. Known IP addresses (i.e., those with which a machine communications often, such as mail or DNS servers) are stored in a list of a given size and will never incur a delay. For the unknown IP addresses, however, the connection limit is imposed incrementally. A worm, which created a list of hundreds of IP addresses to contact, would incur a delay between itself and the previous connection request. The connection limit is suggested at five new connections per second, which is the effective scanning speed of the Code Red v2 worm, meaning that only the fastest of worms will be hindered.[1] An additional argument for implementing this method is the minimal overhead it puts on the system, while putting a direct limit to β. Some server systems, however, would suffer badly from this method, since they usually have more active outbound connections. Consider, for example, DNS or email servers, both of which will connect to many other systems based on the name queries or email messages sent by the users. A similar difficulty is encountered on multi-user systems, where multiple users are logged on at the same time. This technique works better on "static" servers like webservers that mainly listen for incoming connections. Additionally, it may be possible for a worm to circumvent the rate-limiting mechanisms by crafting packets instead of traversing the TCP/IP stack.

A second technique is "traffic content filtering". It is based on the idea that routers and/or firewalls will test all traffic flowing through against a set of known, viral signatures. When a malicious signature is detected, the packet is dropped, effectively limiting the propagation of malicious code and decreasing β. The technique, however, requires very elaborate signatures and matching on port/protocol combinations, since the sheer volume of traffic traveling through large routers creates a fair possibility that smaller signatures would be matched in regular, bona fide traffic. As Moore et al. discuss [13], for application during a new worm event, this approach requires the signature to be generated as early as possible. Signature-capable routers would need to be in widespread use, as well as a mechanism to quickly and securely distribute new signatures. Once again, this defense system allows for a DOS attack when an attacker is able to insert a falsified signature that would block all traffic for a particular service. In addition, this system would put a tremendous overhead on critical network routers on the Internet, since signature matching (especially when the pool of signatures is large) is very processor intensive. Combined with the need to re-assemble each fragmented packet, to avoid overlooking fragmented attacks, this cure might be difficult to deploy widely.

Conclusion. The general mantra for this section is the need for very early detection of new worm events. Whatever the response will be, it will never be useful if the alert and classification come too late. Considering that the Sapphire/Slammer worm [11, 1] propagated in just several minutes, it is clearly not humanly possible to generate the alerts. Although automated alert and response systems would be up to the task, they are at the risk of becoming the target themselves, potentially being more dangerous than any regular worm could ever be. It seems, therefore, that there will always remain a delicate balance between human interaction and machine automation. We can envision a system in which the monitoring and detection is done automatically, such that alerts and signatures are generated for a human first responder to assess. Next the human responder can decide which (if any at all) of the active response mechanisms to activate, allowing an appropriate response to the event.

4. EARLY DETECTION OF SCANNING WORMS

Our prototype system for detecting scanning worms collects ICMP Destination Unreachable (or ICMP-T3) messages from instrumented routers, aggregates these messages to identify scanning activity, and then looks for patterns of scanning activity that indicate a propagating worm. The system, whose architecture is shown in Figure 6.4, has two major components, the Dartmouth ICMP BCC: System or DIB:S, which aggregates the ICMP-T3 messages into scans alerts, and our Tracking and Fusion Engine or TRAFEN, which identifies propagating worms based on their scanning activity. TRAFEN, which uses a Multiple Hypothesis Tracking [16] (MHT) framework, assigns likelihoods to sets of alerts or observations that appear to be correlated, thus forming tracks of related observations. By defining the likelihood functions so that observations are highly correlated only if they appear to represent worm activity, TRAFEN can quickly and accurately detect a scanning worm. In this section, we present background on ICMP-T3 messages, describe the DIB:S and TRAFEN components, and examine the detection capabilities of the prototype system.

ICMP-T3 Messages and Instrumented Routers

When a source machine attempts to contact a nonexistent or unreachable machine, an Internet router, somewhere between the source machine and the target network, will determine that the packets can go no farther. This router, if configured to do so, will send an ICMP-T3 message to the source machine. Scanning worms, through the process of probing randomly selected IP addresses, will attempt to contact many unreachable or nonexistent machines, such as machines protected by a firewall or addresses from an unassigned part of the Internet. If this scanning activity produces enough ICMP-T3 messages, we can infer the presence of a propagating worm through its unique scanning pattern, specifically, the growth in scanning activity as the worm infects more and more machines.

Table 6.1 shows the responses we received when we probed selected address ranges on the Internet. The data, which was obtained for a separate project, is skewed slightly, since we scanned only populated address ranges. Many address ranges simply are unassigned, and contain no reachable machines at all. The two most significant numbers are the high response rates (25% average) and the

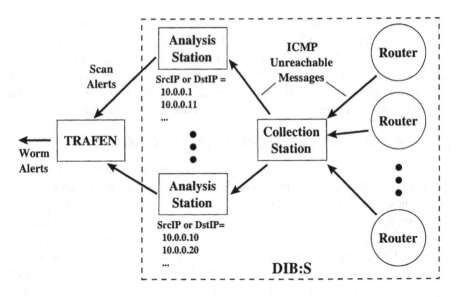

Figure 6.4. The combined DIBS:S and TRAFEN system. ICMP Unreachable messages with the same source or destination address are sent to the *same* analysis station.

	PING 24.[0-128]/16		PING [209-211].[32-64]/16		TCP/80 [209-211].[32-64]/16	
Requests	1628977	100%	6487973	100%	1171298	100%
No response	1258388	77.3%	4911425	75.7%	800636	68.4%
Echo replies	244445	15.0%	636135	9.8%	37707	3.2%
ICMP-T3	77361	4.7%	398841	6.0%	104555	8.9%
Other	48783	3.0%	550472	8.5%	228400	19.5%

Table 6.1. Responses to random probing on the Internet - ICMP echo request on the 24.0/16 - 24.128/16 networks. ICMP echo and TCP port 80 request on the 209.32-64/16 - 211.32-64/16 networks

numbers of ICMP-T3 messages returned (6.2% average). The latter number, although seemingly low, means that a significant fraction of scan attempts will produce an ICMP-T3 message at some router. Thus, if we can collect and analyze ICMP-T3 messages from multiple, distributed routers, we will have enough messages to detect a worm's unique scanning activity.

Due to privacy concerns, we have chosen *not* to sniff for ICMP-T3 messages, but instead to ask network providers and other organizations to forward the ICMP-T3 messages from their routers to our analysis systems. These forwarded messages are essentially a Blind Carbon Copy (BCC) of the original ICMP-T3 message, which is a legitimate action since the generating router was a participant in the original conversation. Although site policy may require that no response be sent to the source machine, the router can remain silent to the outside world while still sending the ICMP-T3 messages to the analysis systems. In particular, there was no response to 75% of our probes, but many of these probes may have gone through routers that were instructed to silently ignore unsolicited traffic. These routers could easily forward ICMP-T3s to the analysis systems, while still dropping the original packet without a response to the sender. [2] This approach allows broader coverage, while still respecting the security policies of individual organizations. We currently provide router patches for the LINUX kernel to provide the ICMP-T3 forwarding ability.

ICMP-T3 messages come in several different flavors, [14] two of which are of particular interest for detecting scanning activity: Network Unreachable (Code 0) and Host Unreachable (Code 1). A router generates a Network Unreachable message when a desired network cannot be reached. This might happen when a packet is sent to an IP address that resides in an unassigned portion of the Internet address space. Far more commonly, a router generates a Host Unreachable message when a router cannot find the addressed host in its network. This might happen when the packet could be routed to the correct network, but the router responsible for that network could not locate a machine in its network that bears the requested IP address.

The feature that makes analyzing ICMP-T3 messages useful is their message body. When a router builds a Destination Unreachable message, it includes the IP header, and at least the first eight bytes of the body of the *original message* (i.e., the message that provoked the ICMP-T3 response) as the payload of the ICMP-T3 message. For TCP and UDP, this includes the source and destination port numbers. Scanning systems thus will reveal both their IP address and their target port.

DIB:S

The primary task of DIB:S is to collect ICMP-T3 data and identify blooms of scanning activity. The instrumented routers, described in the previous section, send carbon copies of their ICMP-T3 messages to one or more collectors, which, in turn, will forward the messages to one or more analyzers. Each analyzer is assigned an IP address range within which it will look for scanning activity, and more analyzers can be spawned dynamically as needed (with appropriate updates to the assigned address ranges). When an ICMP-T3 message arrives at a collector, the collector extracts the embedded content, sends one copy of the message to the analyzer associated with the embedded source IP address, and sends another copy to the analyzer associated with the embedded destination IP address. Depending on the number of analyzers and the particular source and destination IP addresses, the two copies might go to the same analyzer, in which case only one copy is actually sent. An analyzer will see all information about a specific range of IP addresses, regardless of the routers from which the information came. Organizing the analysis by source and destination address, rather than the generating router, is critical, since randomly scanning worms will hit many different networks, and the resulting ICMP-T3 messages will come from many different routers. Thus, the scanning activity is much more visible when viewed across routers, rather than at a single router.

The analyzers keep a history of the ICMP-T3 messages received for a particular IP address over the last Δt seconds. DIB:S will generate alerts in six cases. Only two are relevant to worm detection – in the last Δt seconds, on the same port p and using the same protocol P, one host has *contacted* N different IP addresses (Case 1), or one host has been *contacted by* N different IP addresses (Case 2). These are classical scanning patterns, both observed during worm propagation, although Case 2 also can indicate a failed server for which requests keep arriving. The other four cases, which involve one machine contacting another *single* machine N times or on N different ports, generally are not observed during worm propagation, but instead during service failure or manual attacks. The DIB:S alerts contain the case number, the embedded source and destination IP address, the protocol, and, if available, the source and destination port numbers. Analyzers will not issue the *same* alert twice within Δt seconds, If one IP address is scanning two different ports, however, DIB:S will issue two separate alerts.

The proper values for the parameters N and Δt depend on the number of participating routers, but several general things can be said. A lower value of N increases the chances of false positives, and any value below $N = 4$ makes the system unusable. Although higher values will lead to more accurate detection, the moment of detection will be later, possibly *too* late. Experimentation has shown that $5 \leq N \leq 15$ gives the best results. Similarly, smaller values for Δt will give a very inaccurate view of events, since alerts on fast scanning IP addresses will be frequently re-issued, and slower-scanning worms will not be detected at all. Higher values of Δt, however, put a serious performance penalty on the analysis system since each packet has to be remembered for a longer time. Proper values during experimentation were determined to be $300 \leq \Delta t \leq 14400$. We will consider these two parameters in more detail in a later section.

TRAFEN

TRAFEN (TRacking And Fusion ENgine) was not implemented specifically for the detection of active worms, but instead is a prototype process query system [3]. A process query system (PQS) is a software system that allows users to interact with multiple data sources in new and powerful ways. In a traditional DBS, users express queries as constraints on the field values of records stored in a database or arriving from a sensor network, as allowed by SQL and its variants for streaming data. In contrast, a PQS allows users to define *processes*, and to make queries against databases and real-time sensor feeds by submitting those process definitions. The PQS parses the process description and performs sequences of queries against the available data sources, searching for evidence that instances of the specified process or processes exist. Depending on the capabilities of the PQS and the problem domain, the process description might be specified as a rulebase, a Kalman filter [4], a Hidden Markov Model [15], or any of a number of other representations. A major innovation of the PQS concept is the virtual process-description machine that it presents to the programmer. Such a system abstracts away the details of observation collection, management, and aggregation, and allows the developer to focus on the task of defining and implementing an appropriate process description.

TRAFEN parses the process model, subscribes to the required event streams dynamically, and then uses traditional tracking algorithms to match incoming events with the process model, most commonly using an implementation of Reid's multiple hypothesis tracking (MHT) algorithm [16]. Reid's algorithm keeps multiple *hypotheses*, where each hypothesis is a set of *tracks* of related events. Each event is represented only once in each hypothesis, and each hypothesis aims to represent an accurate view of the world. Each new incoming event (in our case the DIB:S alerts) is added to every track in every hypothesis, thus creating an exponential number of new hypotheses. Next, the process query is used to assign a likelihood, representing the accuracy of the track under the current process model, to all the tracks in all the hypotheses. The likelihood of each hypothesis then is calculated as the combined likelihood of its tracks. Finally, the hypotheses are ranked by likelihood, and only the topmost hypotheses are kept, with the rest pruned to keep the exponential growth under control.

To apply TRAFEN to a particular problem domain, the developer must define an XML message format for the observations, and must provide (1) a definition of "process state", and (2) a function that measures the *likelihood* that particular observations are correlated (i.e., the likelihood that an observation is related to a previously established track). For our active-worm detection, the observations are the scan alerts from the DIB:S analyzers, and for simplicity, the probability assigned to a track is the probability that the track represents a worm. TRAFEN subscribes to the DIB:S Alert stream and picks out the Case 1 and Case 2 alerts (since those are the most relevant for worm detection). TRAFEN passes the filtered observations to a dynamically loaded, simplified version of Reid's Multiple Hypothesis Tracking algorithm [16]. The tracking algorithm, if it is receiving the first observation ever, will create a one-observation track with a very low probability. The low probability reflects the fact that a single observation of scanning activity does not by itself indicate a worm. For subsequent observations, the MHT algorithm iterates through each active hypothesis and each track inside the hypotheses. For each track, it calculates the likelihood that the observation is related to a track, or, in other words, that a scan represents a continuation of the worm scanning activity represented in the track.

The likelihood calculation, then, is the heart of the MHT algorithm, and in our current implementation, is essentially rule-based. After initial experiments, we arrived at three straightforward rules. *Rule 1:* If a machine scans the same port, using the same protocol, as the machines already in a particular track, the type match is *high* (0.9); otherwise the type match is *low* (0.1). This rule captures the fact that an active worm typically scans for and exploits one particular vulnerable service, although the rule could be extended easily to take into account those worms that scan two or more *related* service ports. *Rule 2:* If a machine performs a scan only a short period of time after a previous series of scans, the time match should be higher than if the scans occur farther apart, which captures the fact that an active worm must scan continuously if it wants to propagate quickly. We assign a time match of 1.0 if the new scan occurs 10 seconds or less after a previous scan, a time match of 0.0 if a new scan occurs 300 seconds or more after a previous scan, and a time match scaled linearly between 0 and 1 if the scan is between 10 and 300 seconds after the previous scan. Although the exact thresholds have little effect on tracking performance, these thresholds are best for fast-moving worms. *Rule 3:* Finally, if the type match is low, the overall likelihood that the new scan is related to the tracked scans is set low, again 0.1. Two scans on different destination ports likely do not represent the same active worm, no matter how closely together those two scans occur in time. If the type match is high, the overall likelihood is set between 0.675 and 0.925, scaled linearly according to the time match. Again, the exact values of 0.675 and 0.925 do not have a significant effect on tracking performance, as long as the high end of the range is greater than our worm detection threshold in later sections. Since the probability of an initial single-observation track is set to a low value, and since the *track* likelihood is a moving average of these individual likelihoods, the rules ensure that it takes several observations for the track probability to increase significantly, reflecting the fact that only a series of scans can indicate a worm.

Overall, the TRAFEN framework allowed us to produce a working worm detector (given the DIB:S input) in only a few hours, and provides the flexibility to extend the tracking system later through more complex models. Next, we will examine the detection performance of the current ruleset, and discuss extensions to the current DIB:S/TRAFEN system.

Simulating Worms

DIB:S and TRAFEN currently are deployed at Dartmouth College, with in-strumented Dartmouth routers sending their ICMP-T3 messages to our DIB:S installation. This initial local deployment is not enough to analyze the detection performance of the system, however, and we turn to simulated worms for that purpose. We developed two different worm simulations, one small-scale and one large-scale. The small-scale simulation allows us to run hundreds of worms through the DIB:S/TRAFEN system in rapid succession, allowing us to explore the parameter space and fine-tune the system for specific environments. The large-scale simulation is essentially the same, but it simulates a worm propagating over the *entire* Internet, allowing system evaluation under more realistic conditions. The volume of ICMP-T3 messages generated in the large-scale simulation can be massive, and take significantly longer to run through the DIB:S/TRAFEN system. The large-scale simulation verifies the results obtained with the small-scale simulation, however.

Small-Scale Worm Simulation Our small-scale worm simulator is designed to run worms on address spaces of one million addresses or less. The number of reachable hosts and the number of susceptible hosts is configurable, and each susceptible host is simulated individually. We assume that each reachable system is reachable from all connected hosts, using a given latency distribution, and we do not explicitly simulate routers. Instead, the generation of ICMP-T3 messages is done based on address ranges. For example, when the router coverage is set to 10%, ICMP-T3 messages are generated for a fixed 10% of the addresses (and only for those addresses within the 10% that do not correspond to a reachable host). For a random address probe, the simulation first checks whether the address is associated with a vulnerable host, then whether it is associated with a reachable host, and finally, if not reachable, whether the address is covered by an instrumented router. When the probe hits a vulnerable host, the worm propagates to that host, and the newly infected host starts scanning as well. In our experiments, typical network parameters are a space of $10^5 - 10^6$ addresses of which 5-15% are reachable and 100-1000 hosts are vulnerable. The only worm-specific parameter is the worm's scan rate, and the worm selects random target addresses uniformly distributed through the address space, with the random seed for each worm instance derived from the current (simulated) time and the address of the infected machine.

Large-Scale Worm Simulation The large-scale worm simulator, developed by fellow ISTS Researchers Michael Liljenstam, Yougu Yuan, BJ Premore, and David Nicol [10], aims to be an accurate representation of the current Internet. The address space contains 2^{32} addresses and is subdivided into *Autonomous Systems* between which simulated BGP-routers route traffic. The simulation is divided into two tiers, the macroscopic level and the microscopic (or network) level. The BGP-routers are simulated at the macroscopic level, where a stochastic version of the epidemic model is used to model the total flow of infection packets *between* autonomous systems. At this level, only the size of the flow and the source of the flow (a distribution of autonomous systems) is simulated. Then, for several representative (1-128) autonomous systems, the actual networks and the infected, susceptible, and reachable hosts are simulated at the microscopic or packet level. The ICMP-T3 messages are generated at the border of participating autonomous systems, under the assumption that those autonomous systems are connected by a single gateway. The actual IP addresses of the infected systems are used to ensure accurate simulation of the expected traffic. The ICMP-T3 forwarding routers only look at arriving scan packets, sending ICMP-T3 messages to a real DIB:S/TRAFEN system when a scan hits an IP address that was not represented by an actual host. The generation of ICMP-T3 messages is rate limited at 3 per second per router.

Detection Capabilities

Small-Scale Worm Simulation. Figure 6.5 shows the detection performance of DIB:S and TRAFEN for a simulated Sapphire/Slammer worm. The y-axis is the percentage of vulnerable machines that are infected at the time of worm detection, and the x-axis is the router coverage. Each line in the graph corresponds to a different network size. For each network size, 75% of the addresses were unreachable, 25% of the addresses were reachable, and 0.1% of the addresses were reachable *and* vulnerable. For example, for a network size of 500,000 unique addresses, 375,000 addresses are unreachable, 125,000 are reachable, and 500 are vulnerable. The reachable 25% corresponds to our observed data from the scans of selected *populated* address ranges, while the vulnerable 0.1%, although large, corresponds to a vulnerability in Web, mail, database, or other widely installed software. Each data point in the graphs is an average across ten simulated worms, and each simulated worm probed 100 target addresses per infected machine per second, slightly lower than, but consistent with, the average Sapphire/Slammer scan rate. DIB:S had to receive $N = 5$ ICMP-T3 messages for the same IP address before issuing a scan alert to TRAFEN, and DIB:S maintained a history window of $\Delta t = 300$ seconds. Each simulation run continued until the worm infected all vulnerable machines, and TRAFEN was assumed to have detected the worm as soon as the probability of a track containing the relevant scanning activity went above a likelihood threshold of 0.9, a constant value used in all experiments.

As seen in Figure 6.5, the detection performance improves significantly as the router coverage increases from 1% to 2%, but then levels off at different, roughly constant, values for the different network sizes. For a network size of 500,000, for example, the infection percentage starts at a peak of 5% when the router coverage is 0.5, but drops quickly to around 2% as the coverage increases. The straightforward reason is that, for router coverages of 2% and higher, DIB:S receives enough ICMP-T3 messages to reliably detect the scanning activity of the *first* few infected machines. Thus, at these higher coverages, the detection

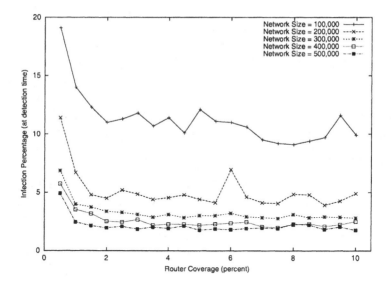

Figure 6.5. Detection performance with the small-scale simulation. The x-axis is the router coverage, and the y-axis is the percentage of vulnerable machines already infected at the time that an active worm is detected.

always will take place within a fixed number of infected machines, no matter whether the coverage is 2% or 10%. For router coverages below 2%, however, DIB:S will not receive enough ICMP-T3 messages to reliably detect all scanning activity, and correspondingly more machines will be infected before DIB:S can conclude that a worm is present. The critical message of this graph is that router coverage of 2% provides just as good detection performance as higher coverages, meaning that we need only a modest number of instrumented routers, and that we need only transmit and process a manageable volume of ICMP-T3 messages.

In addition, the detection performance improves as the network size increases. The explanation is simply that DIB:S detection performance is dependent not so much on the percentage of machines infected so far, but on the absolute number of infected machines and the amount of scanning activity that the worm generated while infecting those machines. Overall, in terms of our ability to detect the worm early and eventually protect the largest *percentage* of vulnerable, but not yet infected, machines, we can keep the router coverage fixed, and still do better and better as the network size increases. Alternatively, for a larger network, we can achieve the same detection performance with a smaller router coverage.

Large-Scale Simulation. The large-scale simulation allows us to explore these network-size results further. The large-scale simulation used 2^{32} addresses, and instrumented routers were placed at the border of class-B sized networks. Each of those class-B networks were assumed to have 50% unused address space, and each router was rate limited at 3 ICMP-T3 messages per second. Two worms were simulated for router coverages varying from 1 class-B participating router up to 64 class-B participating routers, The first worm, a simulated version of Code Red v2, scanned at a rate of 5.65 scans per second with a population of 380,000 susceptible hosts, and the second worm, a simulated version of Sapphire/Slammer scanned at a rate of 4000 scans per second with a population of 120,000 susceptible hosts. The DIB:S parameters were $N = 5$ and $\Delta t = 7200$ for the Code Red v2 worm, and $N = 5$ and $\Delta t = 3600$ for the Slammer/Sapphire worm. The higher values of Δt are necessary since the number of instrumented routers is small compared to the size of the address space. Although the number of incoming ICMP-T3s was very large, the chances that one infected system hits the small group of participating routers several times is minimal. Therefore, accurate detection over time requires larger values for Δt. The lower Δt value for Sapphire/Slammer allowed faster simulation runs, but did not affect detection performance. Finally, for simulation convenience, the recovery parameter γ was set to 0.

Figure 6.6 shows the resulting detection performance as a function of router coverage. For 2 class-B instrumented routers (which corresponds to a 0.003% router coverage), Code Red detection occurs at 0.2% infection of the susceptible population, dropping to 0.03% for 16 class-B networks. For 4 class-B networks, Slammer detection occurs at 0.01% infection of the susceptible population, dropping to 0.005% for 16 class-B networks. The drastic increase in detection performance compared to Code Red v2 is due to the vastly increased scanning speed of the Sapphire/Slammer worm, and the smaller number of susceptibles (i.e., more scans were necessary to find one vulnerable system). An important note, however, is that TRAFEN *failed* to detect the Slammer worm with a coverage of 1 or 2 class-B networks, since at these coverages, even the overwhelming scanning activity of Slammer did not cause those routers to generate enough ICMP-T3 messages (due to the ICMP-T3 rate limiting).

The simulations for the Code Red v2 worm were run again with a simulated background noise of 1.41 coincidental random probes on the worm's target port per class-B network per second, which corresponds to the background noise observed at the start of the real Code Red v2 worm infection. In other words, participating routers would see, on average, 1.41 unrelated scan packets per second, and thus might generate ICMP-T3s that have no connection with the propagating worm. The results, also shown in Figure 6.6, show that this modest noise level does not affect detection performance. Similar noise results have been obtained for Slammer/Sapphire, although not yet with the large-scale simulation.

N and Δt. There are many parameters within the DIB:S and TRAFEN systems that affect detection performance. Two of the most important are

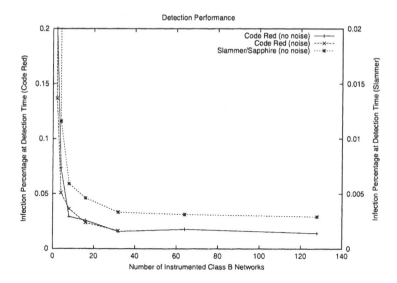

Figure 6.6. Detection performance for the Internet-scale simulated Code Red v2 and Sapphire/Slammer worms.

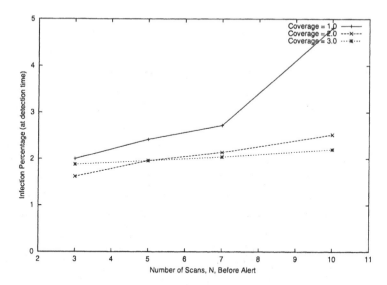

Figure 6.7. Detection performance for different values of N, the number of ICMP-T3 messages required for the generation of a scan alert.

N, the number of ICMP-T3 messages per generated DIB:S alert, and Δt, the size in seconds of the DIB:S history window. Figure 6.7 shows the detection performance for a small-scale Sapphire/Slammer simulation as a function of N, while Figure 6.8 shows the detection performance as a function of Δt. For both

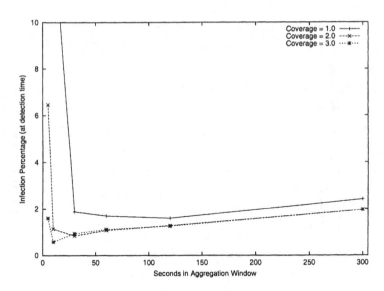

Figure 6.8. Detection performance for different values of Δt, the length, in seconds, of the history window over which ICMP-T3 messages are aggregated.

graphs, the network size is 500,000, and the number of vulnerable machines is 500. When N is varied, Δt is held fixed at 300 seconds, and when Δt is varied, N is held fixed at five ICMP-T3 messages per alert. In Figure 6.7, we see that detection performance decreases as N increases, particularly when the router coverage is only 1%. At lower coverages and higher values of N, DIB:S might not see enough ICMP-T3 messages to actually generate an alert, and scanning activity will go unreported. In Figure 6.8, we see that detection performance is very poor for the lowest values of Δt, and then after an initial improvement decreases steadily as Δt increases. The very poor performance is due to the fact that when the history window is too small, ICMP-T3 messages will age out before enough messages are received to produce an alert. The steady decrease in performance after the initial improvement is arguably illusory, since when Δt is small, DIB:S will generate multiple scan alerts for the same source address, whereas when Δt is large, DIB:S will generate only one scan alert per source address (during the worm's initial propagation). Although the multiple alerts per source address drive the track probability in TRAFEN above the detection threshold quite quickly, multiple scans from the *same* source address are not, in fact, a reliable indicator of worm activity. They could merely indicate an intense, but manual, scanning effort. In the current system, therefore, Δt must be kept high enough to avoid "duplicate" alerts within too short a time period.

Future Extensions

The current ruleset is simple enough that it can lead to false positives. Although our experiments have shown that *random* scanning noise does not affect detection performance, not all scanning noise is random. For example, attackers constantly scan TCP port 80 looking for vulnerable Web servers. If many of these scans coincidentally occur within seconds of each other, TRAFEN incorrectly will detect a worm that exploits Web servers. The goal of an improved TRAFEN ruleset is to quickly detect an exponential increase in scanning activity (i.e., detect the worm) without incorrectly classifying non-exponential behavior as exponential (i.e., avoid false positives). We must detect the worm even if it is spreading slowly, and we must separate simultaneous exponential and non-exponential processes in case a worm and a human attacker coincidentally are targeting the same port at the same time. There are several modeling techniques that can be used to detect a wide range of worms while still minimizing false positives, but we are particularly interested in Hidden Markov Models [15], which (loosely speaking) allow a system to infer the state of an unobservable generation process through statistical properties of the observed effects of that process. Hidden Markov or other models could be defined for the scanning activity associated with worms, machine failures, and the simultaneous, but unrelated, activity of individual attackers. The MHT algorithm then could hypothesize about the type (worm, host failure, coincidental) of the observed scanning activity, rather than just the likelihood that the scanning activity represents a worm. Additionally, these new models can be applied at different time scales, allowing detection of worms spreading at arbitrary rates, thus removing the time dependency which currently makes DIB:S/TRAFEN most effective only for fast spreading worms.

Simultaneously, we are working to deploy additional instrumented routers within the networks of selected partners. As seen with the large-scale simulation results, a coverage of 4 to 16 class-B networks is enough for accurate detection. Achieving such coverage may be administratively difficult, but is entirely achievable with the cooperation of only a few medium- to large-sized organizations. Alternatively, large portions of the Internet address space are unassigned. If these unassigned address ranges were routed to a system that provided no response to the sender, but merely forwarded appropriate alerts to DIB:S/TRAFEN, we would gain significant data with minimal risk of "noise". Unassigned address ranges never should be contacted in normal Internet communication.

In terms of scalability, if DIB:S is installed at a single, central location, the network bandwidth will limit the number of incoming ICMP-T3 messages. This limit is not as serious as it might appear, however. Even with 64K instrumented routers covering 4 *Class-A* networks, for example, the routers would generate only approximately 200 Mbps of ICMP-T3 messages (at a three per second ICMP-T3 rate limit). In addition, if 200 Mbps is too much network traffic for a single collector site for some reason, DIB:S can be distributed almost to an arbitrary degree. Instrumented routers can send their ICMP-T3 messages to "nearby" collectors, and the analyzers, each of which is in charge of a particular address range, can be distributed throughout the Internet.

ICMP-T3 messages are not the only data source that can provide indications of worm activity. Although ICMP messages are particularly attractive since they indicate scanning activity that spans multiple independent networks, scan reports and other information from firewalls, intrusion-detection systems and even host-based sensors also can be fed into the DIB:S/TRAFEN system, serving as a useful complement to the ICMP-T3 data. The ICMP-T3 messages can provide useful additional information themselves, since passive OS fingerprinting[3] would allow DIB:S to infer the type of the operating system that is performing the scan, adding to the hypothesis-generation ability of TRAFEN. Two scans originating from a Linux and Windows machine respectively, for example, most likely do not belong to the same worm.

Finally, regardless of how effective an early warning system is, there is no use in detecting a worm unless something can be done. This can be as little as informing system administrators or as much as having a framework in place that will automatically reconfigure firewalls. and IDS systems as the epidemic is occurring. Automated response will be a critical topic of future work, both for our group and many others. Even so, early warning is always worthwhile.

5.   FUTURE

Computers increasingly are taking on the role of home appliances, integrating such services as game and DVD playing, digital television recording and playback, Internet-based telephony, and traditional personal and home-office computing. In addition, software from a small number of companies is finding its way into more and more products, increasing the likelihood that a software vulnerability will affect a large number of systems. Finally, broadband Internet now is commonplace in many homes, increasing the number of connected systems. With more connected computer systems, often with higher bandwidth, and with more widely deployed software, worm and virus authors will continue to have an ideal environment for their malicious code. There will remain a desperate need for diversity in software and operating systems, decreasing the likelihood of massively homogeneous vulnerabilities.

The increase in connectivity also has prompted a shortage in available IP address space. Although this shortage mostly has been mended with Network Address Translation (NAT), eventually a more structural solution will be needed. Increasing the address space will bring with it the nice property that random scanning for vulnerable IP addresses will become nearly impossible, requiring a significant change in the way authors write their worms. As an example, consider IPv6, which offers 128 bits of address space versus the 32 bits available in IPv4, and Code Red v2, which we analyzed for IPv4 in Figure 6.3. We limit ourselves to propagation within a single IPv6 site, which has 2^{64} possible IP addresses. We assume 2^{16} responding machines, of which $1/100^{th}$ are vulnerable. We pick $\gamma = 0$, so that there is no recovery or removal and the worm is free propagate. This makes $r(t)$ a constant, leading to $s(t) + i(t) = M$ being a constant as well, and effectively rewrites the epidemic-model equations [6]:

$$\frac{di}{dt} = \beta si = \beta(M - i)i \tag{6.8}$$

This also is known as the logistic growth equation, and it represents a worst-case epidemic in which there are no recoveries or disconnects, and each infective stays infective forever. Propagation speed will be higher than in a realistic scenario, but the equation allows us to define the absolute limit on propagation speed. Citing Daley and Gani [6] once more for the integral over $(0, t)$, we have

$$i(t) = \frac{i_0 M}{i_0 + (M - i_0)e^{-\beta M t}} \tag{6.9}$$

We can use this formula to find out how fast a worm would spread in the fastest scenario, given ideal connectivity and no countermeasures. To do so, we set

$$i(T_\varepsilon) = \varepsilon M \tag{6.10}$$

where ε is the fraction of susceptibles infected (for example we could define T_{END} by taking $\varepsilon = 0.95$). Replacing the left-hand side of Equation 6.10 with Equation 6.9, and performing straightforward algebraic manipulation – i.e., moving terms to isolate e and then inverting, simplifying, and taking the natural log of both sides – we have

$$T_\varepsilon = \frac{1}{\beta M} \times \ln\left(\frac{\varepsilon(M - i_0)}{i_0(1 - \varepsilon)}\right) \tag{6.11}$$

Looking at Equations 6.8 and 6.11, we note two important properties. First, realizing that $\mathcal{O}(\beta) \gg \mathcal{O}(M)$ and that $\mathcal{O}(M) \approx \mathcal{O}(i)$, it is clear that the propagation time will be mostly dependent on β. Second, the relationship between propagation time and β is a linear one. If β is doubled, $\frac{di}{dt}$, which is the propagation speed, also doubles. If the speed is doubled, the time it will take for all hosts to be infected will be halved. The linear relationship with β, as well as M, also can be clearly seen from Equation 6.11. Now we can fill in the numbers for Code Red v2 in IPv4 space, assuming the initial number of infected hosts is 10, and we are looking for how long it takes to infect 95% of all susceptible hosts. Remembering that $\beta = 1.23 \times 10^{-9}$ (see the caption of Figure 6.3), we have a time in seconds of

$$T_{0.95} = \frac{1}{1.23 \times 10^{-9} \times 360000} \times \ln \left(\frac{0.95 \times (360000 - 10)}{10 \times (1 - 0.95)} \right)$$

which is $30220/3600 = 8.4$ hours, a good approximation of what we can read from Figure 6.3 and thus verifying our equations. Now we fill in the numbers for the Code Red v2 worm propagating within one IPv6 site. First, we calculate r: $r = 2^{16}/2^{64} = 2^{-48} \approx 10^{-15}$. We obtain τ by filling in Equation 6.2: $\tau = 10^{-15} \times 1 + (1 - 10^{-15}r) \times 21 \approx 21$. Finally, we obtain β by filling in equation 6.3: $\beta = \frac{1}{2^{64}} \times \frac{100}{21} \approx 2.5814 \times 10^{-19}$. With $M = 2^{16}/100 \approx 655$, the time to reach 95% propagation is:

$$T_{0.95} = \frac{1}{2.5814 \times 10^{-19} \times 655} \times \ln \left(\frac{0.95 \times (655 - 10)}{10 \times (1 - 0.95)} \right)$$

which gives 4.2057×10^{16}, or over 1.3 billion years, and confirms the intuition that an enlarged address space will pose a significant challenge to randomly propagating worms.

This undoubtedly will lead to new and improved target selection techniques, most of which were already discussed in the *Worms and Viruses* section. We will mention two of them again, however, and suggest probable detection strategies. To acquire IP addresses of hosts running a vulnerable service the worm could sniff the network wire for traffic from that service. Mail and DNS servers will be most vulnerable to this approach, since they constantly communicate between peers. One possible way of detecting such a worm is by inserting bogus communication into the network. By spoofing non-existent IP addresses and so making fake queries to all the services in the network, sniffing worms can be provoked to connect to these non-existent machines. The challenge would be to make the fake communication look as real as possible, ensuring that the worm could not distinguish between real and false events. Worms attempting to connect to the non-existent addresses would provoke ICMP-T3 messages, which could be fed into the DIB:S/TRAFEN system.

The DIB:S/TRAFEN system also can be used in the case of DNS exploration. As noted before, worms can gain hostnames by probing DNS servers and potentially trying whole ranges of possibly related hostnames (recall the example with *sparc01, sparc02, ... sparc99*). DIB:S could be configured to receive notification of all failed DNS queries, as a blind carbon copy from name servers. The analogy is simple: one IP address attempted to contact many *host-names* on many different networks (and failed). This would be a clear bloom, and TRAFEN soon would detect the worm when multiple hosts show the same behavior. It will be difficult to infer what service the worm was exploiting, however, unless the DNS server occasionally responded with bogus IP addresses, provoking ICMP-T3 generation.

Finally, worms will begin to use some of the same polymorphism techniques as the most advanced viruses, such as encrypting and permuting basic code blocks on each propagation, making signature-based detection more difficult. Thus, inferring the existence of worms through their secondary network traffic (such as ICMP-T3 messages), rather than using signatures, always will be an important detection strategy, even for *previously seen* worms.

6. RELATED WORK

In 1991, Jeffrey Kephart and Steve White already were working on analytical models of computer viruses and the epidemics they cause [9]. The SIS model that they described still makes sense in the active-worm arena, and can be expanded easily to include I-R and R-S transitions. Other researchers, such as Moore, Shannon, Voelker and Savage [13] and Zou, Gong and Towsley [21], start from the same equations of Kermack and McKendrick [6] as we do, and arrive at related, but distinct, worm-propagation models. These models differ in how and if they include certain transitions and worm characteristics, but are able to make similar predictions about how long it will take a worm to spread through the Internet. In all of these models, the parameters governing the transitions are still basic. The formula we use for β, for example, does not take into account the dynamics of a saturated network, which was the primary limiting factor on the Sapphire/Slammer worm. It remains to be seen if there is a proper way to model the effect of Internet topology.

Systems such as NetBait [5] and Kerf [2] allow system administrators to pose complex queries against distributed attack data. These systems, however, cannot detect previously unseen attacks (for which no signatures are available), and do not support real-time detection. On the other hand, Zou, Gao, Gong, and Towsley have developed an approach based on Kalman filters for automatically detecting worms based on their scanning activity. [20]. This work places ingress and egress scan monitors at key network points, and collects the resulting scan alerts. A Kalman filter, which has the advantage of being robust to missing scan data, is applied to the scan alerts (for a particular port) to see if the pattern of scanning activity matches their SIR-based model of worm propagation. For an address space with 2^{32} addresses (i.e., the Internet), monitoring coverage of $2^{17}/2^{32}$, and 500,000 vulnerable machines, their system can detect a simulated Code Red worm, and predict its overall infection rate, as soon as the worm infects approximately 5% of the vulnerable machines. From the standpoint of our work, the Kalman filter has several attractive features compared to our current ruleset, and could be a plug-in replacement for that ruleset within the TRAFEN framework.

Both signature-based and anomaly-based [8] intrusion-detection systems can detect worm scans and probes. These systems, however, see only the network traffic that reaches a particular network boundary, and thus might not recognize a scan or probe as evidence of a propagating worm. Some systems collect and analyze data from *distributed* intrusion-detection sensors, and can provide more insight into worm activity than stand-alone systems. Scans still might be overlooked, however, if they hit any individual network only a few times. By collecting ICMP-T3 messages from a broadly deployed set of instrumented routers, DIB:S can detect a scan even if that scan never hits an individual network more than once. On the other hand, distributed intrusion-detection systems could provide additional data for TRAFEN.

7.   CONCLUSION

Most current worms identify vulnerable machines through random probing of the address space, as the Internet becomes more and more densely populated with machines, such worms will be able to spread faster and faster. Fortunately, it is possible to quickly detect such worms by looking for unusual patterns in different kinds of network traffic. In this chapter, we explored the use of ICMP-T3 messages for worm detection. When a connection request is made to an IP address that is not populated by an actual system, routers along the path may return ICMP Destination Unreachable messages (ICMP-T3). The system we developed, DIB:S/TRAFEN, collects ICMP-T3 messages forwarded from participating routers, and looks for the distinct, bloom-like connection pattern that worm-infected hosts exhibit while they are randomly scanning for targets. Using both small-scale and large-scale simulated worms, we demonstrated that our system is capable of detecting propagating worms early in their lifetime. In particular, the large-scale simulation indicates that a router coverage of 16 class-B networks is enough to detect worms that spread at Code Red v2 and Sapphire/Slammer rates before 0.03% of the vulnerable machines are infected. These results, particularly since they involve a router coverage that would be achievable in the real Internet, are extremely promising. When DIB:S/TRAFEN is fully deployed on the real Internet, it will be able to detect active worms early enough to take meaningful defensive action.

Detection is only half of the solution, however, and significant additional research is needed to develop active-response systems that can slow or stop the spread of a detected worm. In addition, we can expect worm authors to write more worms that use alternatives to random probing, requiring the inclusion of new data sources into the DIB:S/TRAFEN system, or requiring entirely new detection approaches (such as "tricking" a worm into attempting to infect a dummy server or client). Finally, it is important to note that diversity in operating systems and server software, as well as appropriate maintenance and patching procedures, mitigates the total damage that any individual worm can do.

ACKNOWLEDGMENTS

Supported under Award Number 2000-DT-CX-K001 (S-2) from the Office of Justice Programs, National Institute of Justice, Department of Justice, with additional support from DARPA under Contract Number F30602-00-2-0585. Points of view in this document are those of the authors and do not necessarily represent the official position of the United States Department of Justice.

Notes

1. This number is easily calculated, see the subscript of Figure 6.3, as well as observed from the actual worm in our test environment.

2. RFC 1812 section 5.2.7.1 states that routers *should be able* to generate ICMP-T3s, not that they *should* generate them.

3. Michael Zalewski wrote some of the first passive-fingerprinting code, which is available at $http://www.stearns.org/pOf/$.

REFERENCES

[1] Microsoft SQL Sapphire Worm Analysis Technical Report, eEye Digital Security, 2003. Available at http://www.eeye.com/html/Research/Flash/AL20030125.html.

[2] J. Aslam, S. Bratus, R. Peterson, D. Rus, B. Tofel, The Kerf Toolkit for Intrusion Analysis Dartmouth College, In review, 2003.

[3] V. H. Berk, W. Chung, V. Crespi, G. Cybenko, R. Gray, D. Hernando, G. Jiang, H. Li, Y. Sheng, Process Query Systems for Suerveillance and Awareness In *Proceedings of the 7th World Multifconference on Systems, Cybernetics and Informatics (SCI 2003)*, Orlando, FL, July 2003.

[4] R. G. Brown, P. Y.C. Hwang, *Introduction to Random Signals and Applied Kalman Filtering*, John Wiley & Sons, 1983.

[5] B. N. Chun, J. Lee, H. Weatherspoon, Brent N. Chun and Jason Lee and Hakim Weatherspoon, Netbait: A Distributed Worm Detection Service, Available at http://netbait.plainlab.org, 2003.

[6] D.J. Daley, J. Gani, *Epidemic Modeling* Cambridge University Press, 1999.

[7] M. W. Eichin, J. A. Rochlis, With Microscope and Tweezers: An Analysis of the Internet Virus of November 1988, In *Proceedings of the 1989 IEEE Computer Society Symposium on Security and Privacy*, May 1989.

[8] W. Fan, M. Miller, S. Stolfo, W. Lee, P. Chan, Using artificial anomalies to detect known and unknown network intrusions, In *Proceedings of the First International Conference on Data Mining*, November 2001.

[9] J. O. Kephart, S. White, Directed-Graph Epidemiological Models of Computer Viruses, In *Proceedings of the 1991 IEEE Computer Society Symposium on Research in Security and Privacy*, May 1991.

[10] M. Liljenstam, Yougu Yuan, B. J. Premore, D. Nicol, A Mixed Abstraction Level Simulation Model of Large-Scale Internet Worm Infestations, In *Proceedings of Tenth IEEE/ACM International Conference on Modeling, Analysis and Simulation of Computer and Communications Systems (MASCOTS 2002)*, October 2002.

[11] D. Moore, V. Paxon, S. Savage, C. Shannon, S. Staniford, N. Weaver, The Spread of the Sapphire/Slammer Worm, Technical Report, CAIDA, 2003.

[12] D. Moore, C. Shannon, J. Brown, Code Red: A case study on the spread and victims of an Internet worm, In *Proceedings of the Second Internet Measurement Workshop (IMW 2002)*, November 2002.

[13] D. Moore, C. Shannon, G. M. Voelker, S. Savage, Internet Quarantine: Requirements for Containing Self-Propagating Code, In *Internet Quarantine: Requirements for Containing Self-Propagating Code*, April 2003.

[14] J. Postel, RFC 792: Internet Control Message Protocol, volume 792 of *Request for Comments*. 1981.

[15] L. R. Rabiner, A Tutorial on Hidden Markov Models and Selected Applications in Speech Recognition, In *Proceeding of the IEEE*, 77, Num 2:257–286, 1989.

[16] D. B. Reid, An algorithm for tracking multiple targets, *IEEE Transactions on Automatic Control*, AC-24:843–854, december 1979.

[17] E. H. Spafford, The Internet Worm: Crisis and Aftermath, *Communications of the ACM*, 32(6), June 1989.

[18] S. Staniford, V. Paxson, N. Weaver, How to Own the Internet in Your Spare Time, in *Proceedings of the 11th USENIX Security Symposium (Security '02)*, San Franciso, CA, August 2002.

[19] M. Williamson, Throttling Viruses: Restricting propagation to defeat malicious mobile code, Technical Report 172, HP Labs Bristol, 2002.

[20] C. Zou, L. Gao, W. Gong, D. Towsley, Monitoring and Early Warning for Internet Worms, Technical Report TR-CSE-03-01, University of Massachusetts at Amherst, 2003.

[21] C. Zou, W. Gong, D. Towsley, Code Red Worm Propagation Modeling and Analysis, in *Proceedings of the 9th ACM Conference on Computer and Communication Security (CCS 2002)*, Washington, DC, November 2002.

Chapter 7

SENSOR FAMILIES FOR INTRUSION DETECTION INFRASTRUCTURES

Richard A. Kemmerer and Giovanni Vigna

Reliable Software Group, Department of Computer Science, University of California Santa Barbara

Abstract: Intrusion detection relies on the information provided by a number of *sensors* deployed throughout a protected network. Sensors operate on different event streams, such as network packets and application logs, and provide information at different abstraction levels, such as low-level warnings and correlated alerts. In addition, sensors range from lightweight probes and simple log parsers to complex software artifacts that perform sophisticated analysis. Therefore, deploying, configuring, and managing, a large number of heterogeneous sensors is a complex, expensive, and error-prone activity.

Unfortunately, existing systems fail to manage the complexity that is inherent in today's intrusion detection infrastructures. These systems suffer from two main limitations: they are developed *ad hoc* for certain types of domains and/or environments, and they are difficult to configure, extend, and control remotely.

To address the complexity of intrusion detection infrastructures, we developed a framework, called STAT, that overcomes the limitations of current approaches. Instead of providing yet another system tailored to some domain-specific requirements, STAT provides a software framework for the development of new intrusion detection functionality in a modular fashion.

According to the STAT framework, intrusion detection sensors are built by dynamically composing domain-specific components with a domain-independent runtime. The resulting intrusion detection sensors represent a software family. Each sensor has the ability to reconfigure its behavior dynamically. The reconfiguration functionality is supported by a component model and by a control infrastructure, called MetaSTAT. The final product of the STAT framework is a highly-configurable, well-integrated intrusion detection infrastructure.

Keywords: Security, Intrusion Detection, Intrusion Detection Infrastructures, Intrusion Detection Frameworks, Software Engineering, STAT.

1. INTRODUCTION

In recent years, networks have evolved from a mere means of communication to a ubiquitous computational infrastructure. Networks have become larger, faster, and highly dynamic. In particular, the Internet, the world-wide TCP/IP network, has become a mission-critical infrastructure for governments, companies, financial institutions, and millions of everyday users.

The surveillance and security monitoring of the network infrastructure is mostly performed using Intrusion Detection Systems (IDSs). These systems analyze information about the activities performed in computer systems and networks, looking for evidence of malicious behavior. Attacks against a system manifest themselves in terms of events. These events can be of a different nature and level of granularity. For example, they may be represented by network packets, operating system calls, audit records produced by the operating system auditing facilities, or log messages produced by applications. The goal of intrusion detection systems is to analyze one or more event streams and identify manifestations of attacks.

Event streams are used by intrusion detection systems in two different ways, according to two different paradigms: *anomaly detection* and *misuse detection*. In anomaly detection systems [14, 17, 7, 34], historical data about a system's activity and specifications of the intended behavior of users and applications are used to build a profile of the "normal" operation of the system. Then, the intrusion detection system tries to identify patterns of activity that deviate from the defined profile. Misuse detection systems take a complementary approach [21, 23, 28, 20, 13]. Misuse detection systems are equipped with a number of attack descriptions (or "signatures") that are matched against the stream of audit data looking for evidence that the modeled attack is occurring. Misuse and anomaly detection both have advantages and disadvantages. Misuse detection systems can perform focused analysis of the audit data and they usually produce only a few false positives, but they can detect only those attacks that have been modeled. Anomaly detection systems have the advantage of being able to detect previously unknown attacks. This advantage is paid for in terms of the large number of false positives and the difficulty of training a system with respect to a very dynamic environment.

The intrusion detection community has developed a number of different tools that perform intrusion detection in particular domains (e.g., hosts or networks), in specific environments (e.g., Windows NT or Solaris), and at different levels of abstraction (e.g., kernel-level tools and alert correlation systems). These tools suffer from two main limitations: they are developed *ad hoc* for certain types of domains and/or environments, and they are difficult to configure, extend, and control remotely.

In the specific case of signature-based intrusion detection systems, the sensors are equipped with a number of attack models that are matched against a stream of incoming events. The attack models are described using an *ad hoc*, domain-specific language (e.g., NFR's N-code [27]). Therefore, performing intrusion detection in a new environment requires the development of both a new system and a new attack modeling language. As intrusion detection is applied to new and previously unforeseen domains, this approach results in increased development effort.

Today's networks are not only heterogeneous; they are also dynamic. Therefore, intrusion detection systems need to support mechanisms to dynamically change their configuration as the security state of the protected system evolves. The configuration and management of a large number of sensors raises multiple issues.

One issue is the static configuration of the data sources used for analysis. The *ad hoc* nature of existing IDSs does not allow one to dynamically configure a running sensor so that new event streams can be used as input for the security analysis. This is a limitation because new attacks may have manifestations in event streams that are not currently analyzed by a specific IDS. Being bound statically to a single source of events may result in limited effectiveness.

A second issue is the static configuration of the attack models used for analysis. Most existing intrusion detection systems (e.g., [28]) are initialized with a set of signatures at startup time. Updating the signature set requires stopping the IDS, adding new signatures, and then restarting execution. Some of these systems provide a way to enable/disable some of the available signatures, but few systems allow for the dynamic inclusion of new signatures at execution time.

A third issue is the relatively static configuration of responses in existing intrusion detection systems. In most cases it is possible to choose only from a specific subset of possible responses. In addition, to our knowledge, none of the systems allows one to associate a response with *intermediate* steps of an attack. This is a severe limitation, especially in the case of distributed attacks carried out over a long time span.

Finally, managing a large number of sensors requires an effective control infrastructure. Most systems provide some sort of management console that allows the Security Administrator to remotely tune the configuration of specific sensors. This reconfiguration procedure is mostly performed manually and at a very low level. This task is particularly error-prone, especially if the intrusion detection sensors are deployed across a very heterogeneous environment and with very different configurations. The challenge is to determine if the current configuration of one or more sensors is valid or if a reconfiguration is meaningful.

This chapter describes a framework for the development of intrusion detection systems, called STAT, and a sensor control infrastructure, called Meta-STAT, which have been developed to address the issues above and to overcome the limitations of existing approaches.

The STAT framework includes a domain-independent attack modeling language and a domain-independent event analysis engine. The framework can be extended in a well-defined way to match new domains, new event sources, and new responses. The framework has been used by the authors to develop a number of different intrusion detection systems, from a network-based intrusion detection system, to host-based and application-based systems, to alert correlators.

The resulting set of intrusion detection systems can be seen, in Software Engineering terms, as a *software family*. Members of the family share a number of features, including dynamic reconfigurability and a fine-grained control over a wide range of characteristics [33]. The STAT framework is the only known framework-based approach to the development of intrusion detection systems. Our experience with the framework shows that by following this approach it is possible to develop intrusion detection systems with reduced development effort, with respect to an *ad hoc* approach. In addition, the approach is advantageous in terms of the increased reuse that results from using an object-oriented framework and a component-based approach.

The configuration of sensors in the STAT family can be controlled at a very fine grain using the MetaSTAT infrastructure. MetaSTAT provides the basic mechanisms to reconfigure, at run-time, which input event streams are analyzed by each sensor, which scenarios have to be used for the analysis, and what types of responses must be carried out for each stage of the detection process. In addition, MetaSTAT supports the explicit modeling of the dependencies among the modules composing a sensor so that it is possible to automatically identify the steps that are necessary to perform a reconfiguration of the deployed sensing infrastructure.

The result of applying the STAT/MetaSTAT approach is a "web of sensors", composed of distributed components integrated by means of a communication and control infrastructure. The task of the web of sensors is to provide fine-grained surveillance inside the protected network. The web of sensors implements *local surveillance* against both outside attacks and local misuse by insiders in a way that is complementary to the mainstream approach where a single point of access (e.g., a gateway) is monitored for possible malicious activity. Multiple webs of sensors can be organized either hierarchically or in a peer-to-peer fashion to achieve scalability and to be able to exert control over a large-scale infrastructure from a single control location.

This chapter is structured as follows. Section 2 introduces the STAT framework. Section 3 presents a family of intrusion detection systems developed using the framework. Section 4 describes the MetaSTAT control infrastructure, shared by all the IDSs in the family. Section 5 presents relevant related work. Finally, Section 6 draws some conclusions.

2. THE STAT FRAMEWORK

The *State Transition Analysis Technique* [10] is a methodology to describe computer penetrations as *attack scenarios*. Each attack scenario is represented as a sequence of transitions that characterize the evolution of the security state of a system. In an attack scenario *states* represent snapshots of a system's security-relevant properties and resources. A description of an attack has an "initial" starting state and at least one "compromised" ending state. States are characterized by means of *assertions*, which are predicates on some aspects of the security state of the system. For example, in an attack scenario describing an attempt to violate the security of an operating system, assertions would state properties such as file ownership, user identification, or user authorization. *Transitions* between states are annotated with *signature actions* that represent the key actions that if omitted from the execution of an attack scenario would prevent the attack from completing successfully. For example, in an attack scenario describing a network port scanning attempt, a typical signature action would include the TCP segments used to test the TCP ports of a host.

The characterization of attack scenarios in terms of states and transitions allows for an intuitive graphic representation by means of *state transition diagrams*. Figure 7.1 shows a state transition diagram for a pedagogical example of a STATL attack scenario specification. The attack scenario detects a Trojan horse attack, where an apparently benign program (e.g., an MP3 player) is first downloaded by a user (first transition), and then installed and executed (second transition). The Trojan horse program contains "hidden" functionality (the warriors hidden in the Trojan horse) that allows the creator of the program to take control of the user's account. When executed, the Trojan horse opens a network connection back to an attacker controlled host that is outside the local network, and it waits for commands to be executed (third transition). When the scenario reaches the final state (represented as a double circle) the attack is considered completed. Note that even though this scenario is fairly representative of this type of attack, it is not to be considered a complete, detailed specification.

In the early 1990s, the State Transition Analysis Technique was applied to host-based intrusion detection, and a system, called USTAT [8, 9, 25], was developed. USTAT used state transition representations as the basis for rules to interpret changes in a computer system's state and to detect intrusions in real-time. The changes in the computer system's state were monitored by leveraging the auditing facilities provided by security-enhanced operating systems,

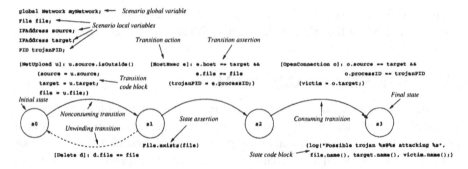

Figure 7.1. A sample state transition diagram of an attack scenario. The attack is a very sim-plified version of a Trojan horse installation attack. The first transition is fired when the upload of a file from a host outside the local network is detected. The second transition fires when the same file is executed. The final transition fires when the program being executed opens a network connection to another host.

such as Sun Microsystems' Solaris equipped with the Basic Security Mod-ule (BSM) [30]. The first implementation of USTAT clearly demonstrated the value of the STAT approach, but USTAT was developed in an *ad hoc* way and several characteristics of the first USTAT prototype were difficult to modify or to extend to match new environments (e.g., Windows NT/2000).

During the 90s, the focus of intrusion detection shifted from the host and its operating system to the network and the protocols used to exchange data. Therefore, the natural evolution of state transition analysis was its direct appli-cation to networks. The NetSTAT intrusion detection system was the result of this evolution [32]. NetSTAT was aimed at real-time state-transition analysis of network data. The NetSTAT system proved that the STAT approach could be extended to new domains. However, NetSTAT was also developed *ad hoc*, by building a completely new IDS that would fit the new domain.

In 1998, both NetSTAT and USTAT were used to participate in a DARPA-sponsored intrusion detection evaluation effort. The evaluation exercises in-cluded off-line analysis of audit logs and traffic dumps provided by the MIT Lincoln Laboratory [19] and the installation of the systems in a large testbed at the Air Force Research Laboratory (AFRL) [3, 4]. Intrusion detection systems from a number of universities, research centers, and companies were tested with respect to different classes of attacks, including port scans, remote com-promise, local privilege escalation, and denial-of-service attacks. A detailed description of the attacks used in the MIT Lincoln Laboratory evaluation can be found in [16]. In both efforts the STAT-based systems performed very well and their combined results scored at the highest level in the evaluations.

Participating in this event gave strong positive feedback on the research that had been performed so far, and it also gave new insights into the STAT ap-proach. In particular, running NetSTAT and USTAT at the same time revealed a number of similarities in the way attack scenarios were represented and in the runtime architecture of the systems. A closer analysis of the mechanisms used by the STAT-based systems to match attack scenarios against a stream of events suggested that the STAT-based IDSs could be redesigned as a family of systems that leverages an object-oriented framework.

The approach taken was to factor-out the mechanisms and techniques used by the intrusion detection analysis and to design an extension process that would support the development of intrusion detection systems for many different target environments. The result of this redesign was the *STAT Framework*. The STAT Framework consists of a domain-independent language, called *STATL*, and a runtime for the language, called the *STAT Core*. These elements can be extended following a well-defined process to match a specific target domain. Section 2.1 presents STATL, Section 2.2 describes the STAT Core, and Section 2.3 describes the framework extension process.

2.1 STATL

A STATL specification is the description of a complete attack scenario. The attack is modeled as a sequence of steps that bring a system from an initial safe state to a final compromised state. This modeling approach is supported by a state/transition-based language. One of the advantages of this approach is that state/transition specifications can be represented graphically by means of state transition diagrams (STDs). Therefore, even though STATL is primarily a text-based language, the STATL development environment includes a graphic editor that allows one to directly visualize the STD representing an attack scenario.

2.1.1 STATL Overview. The STATL language provides constructs to represent an attack as a composition of *states* and *transitions*. States are used to characterize different snapshots of a system during the evolution of an attack. Obviously, it is not feasible to represent the complete state of a system (e.g., volatile memory, file system); therefore, a STATL scenario uses variables to record just those parts of the system state needed to define an attack signature (e.g., the value of a counter or the ownership of a file). A transition has an associated *action* that is a specification of the event that can cause the scenario to move to a new state. For example, an action can be the opening of a TCP connection or the execution of an application. The space of possible relevant actions is constrained by a *transition assertion*, which is a filter condition on events that could possibly match the action. For example, an assertion can require that a TCP connection is opened with a specific destination port or that an application being executed should be part of a predefined set of security-critical applications.

It is possible for several occurrences of the same attack to be active at the same time. A STATL attack scenario, therefore, has an operational semantics in terms of a set of *instances* of the same scenario *prototype*. The scenario prototype represents the scenario's definition and global environment, and the scenario instances represent attacks currently in progress.

The evolution of the set of instances of a scenario is determined by the type of transitions in the scenario definition. A transition can be *consuming*, *nonconsuming*, or *unwinding*. A nonconsuming transition is used to represent a step of an occurring attack that does not prevent further occurrences of attacks from spawning from the transition's source state. Therefore, when a nonconsuming transition fires, the source state remains valid, and the destination state becomes valid too. An example of a nonconsuming transition is given in Figure 7.1. The transition between states s1 and s2 represents the execution of a file. This step does not invalidate the previous state, that is, another execution of the program may occur. Semantically, the firing of a nonconsuming transition causes the creation of a new scenario instance. The original instance is still in the original state, while the new instance is in the destination state of the fired transition. In contrast, the firing of a consuming transition makes the source state of a particular attack occurrence invalid. Semantically, the firing of a consuming transition does not generate a new scenario instance; it simply changes the state of the original one. The transition between states s2 and s3 in Figure 7.1 is an example of a consuming transition. The transition is fired when the executed Trojan program opens a connection. This invalidates state s2. It is no longer necessary to check if the program is opening a network connection since the program has already been identified as a Trojan. Unwinding transitions represent a form of "rollback" and they are used to describe events and conditions that invalidate the progress of one or more scenario instances and require the return to an earlier state. The transition between states s1 and s0 in the example in Figure 7.1 is an unwinding transition. The deletion of the uploaded file invalidates the condition needed for the attack to complete, and, therefore, the scenario instance is brought back to the previous state before the file was created.

2.1.2   STATL Syntax.   This section presents STATL's syntax. It also includes fragmentary examples for each of the syntax rules. In the syntax rules, literal keywords are in **boldface** and other literal text is enclosed in single quotes. Optional items are enclosed in square brackets '[', ']', items that may appear zero or more times are enclosed in curly braces '{', '}'. Alternatives are separated by '|' and grouped with parentheses where necessary to indicate associativity. Examples may include ellipses (...) to indicate that details have been left out; the ellipses are not part of STATL.

Lexical Elements. STATL identifiers consist of letters, digits, and the underscore character '_', and start with a letter. For example host_name and IPaddr2 are identifiers. STATL identifiers are case-sensitive, so IPaddress is different from IPAddress. STATL compound identifiers use standard object-oriented dot notation, as in "object.attribute". STATL keywords are reserved words and may not be used as identifiers. For example, since scenario is a keyword, it may not be used as a variable name.

STATL includes two kinds of comments: any text between "/*" and "*/" (except "*/"), including the delimiters, is a comment. Any text following "//" to the end of the line, including the "//" marker, is a comment. Whitespace may appear anywhere in a STATL specification except within tokens (keywords, identifiers, and multiple-character operators).

Data Types. STATL includes several built-in types: int and u_int in various sizes, bool, string, timeval (for timestamps), and timer. It also includes arrays, plus containers vector, set, list, and map. It is not possible to define new data types within a STATL scenario. Application-specific types must be defined within the application-specific extension library (see Section 2.3). For example, network-based scenarios may use different types than host-based scenarios, but both use int and timeval.

Scenario. A scenario uses zero or more libraries of application-specific types, events, functions, and predicates. A scenario has a name, may have parameters, may contain constant and variable declarations, and most importantly, contains the states and transitions that define the "attack signature" – what to match and what to do with matches. A scenario may also define supporting functions to be used in state and transition assertions and code blocks:

Scenario ::=
    { **use** *LibraryID* {',' *LibraryID*} ';' }
    scenario *ScenarioID*
    [*ScenarioParameters*]
    '{'
        [*FrontMatter*]
        {*State* | *Transition* | *NamedAction*}
    '}'
    { *FunctionDefinition* }

A scenario must have at least one transition and two states – the initial state and a final state. The initial state must have no incoming transitions, and final states have no outgoing transitions. Scenario parameters are specified as a list of comma-separated typed identifiers:

ScenarioParameters ::=

    '(' *Parameter* {',' *Parameter*} ')'
Parameter ::= *Type ParameterId*

Example:

```
scenario example (string host, int count)
{ ... }
```

The example scenario has two parameters, host and count. Parameters are accessible by the scenario instances as global constants.

Front Matter.   Scenarios may declare constants and variables:

Front Matter ::=
    {(*ConstDecl* | *VarDecl*)}

ConstDecl ::=
    const *Type ConstId* { '[' [*size*] ']' } '=' *InitialValue* ';'
VarDecl ::=
    [**global**] *Type VarId* { '[' [*size*] ']' } ['=' *InitialValue*] ';'

A variable declared "global" is shared by all instances of the scenario. A variable not declared "global" is instantiated privately in each instance of the scenario. Variables may be assigned initial values.

Example:

```
use tcpip;
scenario example
{
  const int bufsize = 1024;
  global int count = 0;
  Host server;
  ...
}
```

This example declares a constant integer bufsize with value 1024 and declares a global variable count with initial value 0. This variable will be shared by all instances of the scenario. That is, if a scenario instance increments the count variable, the update is seen by all other instances of the scenario. The variable declaration in the example also includes a variable named server of type Host (a type defined in the network-based language extension called tcpip). Because server is a local variable (i.e., its declaration does not contain the keyword **global**), each instance of the scenario will have its own copy of server.

State.   "State" is one of the two fundamental concepts in STATL. States have names so they can be referred to in transitions and in the graphical representation of the scenario (i.e., in the STD). Each state may have an assertion and a code block, but these elements are optional:

State ::=
>   [**initial**]
>   **state** *StateId*
>   '{'
>>   [*StateAssertion*]
>>   [*CodeBlock*]
>   '}'

Exactly one state must be designated as the initial state. When a scenario plugin is loaded into an IDS a first instance is created in the initial state.

The state assertion, if present, is tested before entry to the state, after testing the assertion of the transition that leads to the state. A state's assertion is implicitly True if none is specified. A state's code block is executed after the incoming transition's assertion and the state's assertion have been evaluated and found to be True and after the incoming transition's code block (if it exists) is executed.

Example:

```
scenario example
{
  const int threshold = 64;
  int counter;
  ...
  initial
  state s1 { }
  ...
  state s3
  {
    counter > threshold
    { log("counter over threshold limit"); }
  }
  ...
}
```

In this example state s1 is designated as the initial state. It has neither an assertion nor a code block. State s3 has an assertion and a code block. The assertion specifies that the value of local variable counter is greater than the value of constant threshold. The code block calls the built-in procedure log to write a message to the IDS's log file.

Transition.   "Transition" is the second of the two fundamental concepts in STATL. Each transition has a name and must indicate the pair of states that it connects. Transitions may have the same source and destination state; that is, loops are allowed. In addition, a transition must specify a type, must specify an event type to match, and may have a code block:

Transition ::=
    transition *TransitionID* '(' *StateId* '->' *StateId* ')'
    (**consuming** | **nonconsuming** | **unwinding**)
    '{'
        ('[' *EventSpec* ']' | *ActionId*)
        [':' *Assertion*]
        [*CodeBlock*]
    '}'

A transition's event is specified either directly (see section on EventSpecs) or by reference to a named signature action (see section on NamedSigAction). In the former case the transition's assertion is just the assertion in the transition. In the latter case, if the named signature action includes an assertion and the transition also includes an assertion, then the resulting assertion is the conjunction of the two assertions. An example is given later, after named signature actions are defined.

A transition's code block is executed after evaluating the transition's assertion and the destination state's assertion, and before executing the destination state's code block. More precisely, the order of evaluation of assertions and the execution of code blocks, after matching an event type (defined later), is as follows:

1 evaluate the transition assertion. If True, then

2 evaluate the state assertion. If True, then

3 execute the transition code block, possibly modifying local and global environments, and then

4 execute the state code block, possibly modifying local and global environments[1].

Transitions are deterministic, which means that every enabled transition fires if its assertion and the destination state's assertion are satisfied. A transition's code block may perform any computation supported by STATL and the IDS extension in use, but is typically used to copy event field values into the global or local environment for later reference.

Example:

```
use bsm, unix;
```

```
scenario example
{
  int userid;
  ...
  transition t2 (s1 -> s2)
    nonconsuming
  {
    [READ r] : r.euid != r.ruid
    { userid = r.euid; }
  }
  ...
}
```

In this example, t2 is a nonconsuming transition that leads from state s1 to state s2. The event spec indicates that the transition should match events of type READ, with a filter condition specifying that the euid and ruid fields of the event must differ for the transition to fire. The transition's code block copies the euid field of event r into the local variable userid for later reference. Note that this scenario uses both bsm and unix extensions, which define BSM events and UNIX-related abstractions, respectively.

EventSpec. "Event specs" are the essential elements of transitions. They specify what events (signature actions) to match and under what conditions.

EventSpec ::= (BasicEventSpec [SubEventSpec]) | TimerEvent

BasicEventSpec ::= EventType EventId

SubEventSpec ::= '[' EventSpec { ',' EventSpec } ']'
EventType ::= **ANY** *|*
      ApplEventType '(' ApplEventType {'|' ApplEventType } ')'

An event spec is either a basic event spec optionally followed by a subevent spec, or it is a timer event. A *basic event spec* identifies the built-in meta-event "type" ANY, which matches any event, or an application-specific event type (e.g., READ) or a disjunction of application-specific event types (e.g., (UDP | TCP)), and a name that will be used to reference the matching event. A basic event spec identifying a single type matches an event of the same type only. A basic event spec that is the disjunction of two or more event types matches an event of any of the types in the disjunction. A subevent spec identifies a set of event specs. Subevent specs enable complex, tree-structured event patterns. A subevent spec matches a set of subevents if each event spec in the subevent spec matches one of the events in the set.

Example:

```
[(READ | WRITE) access] :
```

```
        access.euid != access.ruid
```

Example:

```
[IP d1 [TCP t1]] :
     (d1.src == 192.168.0.1) && (t1.dst == 23)
```

The first example is a USTAT event spec that matches read or write events in which the effective and real user-ids differ. The second example is a NetSTAT event spec (with a subevent spec) that matches any IP datagram containing a TCP segment, with source IP address 192.168.0.1 and destination port 23.

The built-in meta-event type ANY is effectively the same as disjunction over all application-specific event types, but is easier to specify (and more efficient to implement as a special case).

NamedSigAction.   A named signature action has a name and specifies an event spec:

NamedSigAction ::=
    action *ActionId*
    '{'
         ('[' *EventSpec* ']' | *ActionId*)
         [':' *Assertion*]
    '}'

Named signature actions may be used to improve clarity and maintainability when multiple transitions have identical or similar actions; for example, having the same action type but slightly different assertions. In such cases the common part can be factored out, put into a named signature action, and then used in the similar transitions.

Example:

```
use bsm, unix;
scenario example
{
  ...
  action a1
  {
    [WRITE r] : r.euid != 0
  }

  transition t1 (s1 -> s2)
  {
    a1: r.euid != r.ruid
  }

  transition t2 (s1 -> s3)
  {
    a1: r.euid == r.ruid
```

```
  }
  ...
}
```

In this example transitions t1 and t2 both use named signature action a1 as their event spec, but with different assertions. This is equivalent to:

```
use bsm, unix;
scenario example
{
  ...
  transition t1 (s1 -> s2)
  {
    [WRITE r] : (r.euid != 0) && (r.euid != r.ruid)
  }

  transition t2 (s1 -> s3)
  {
    [WRITE r] : (r.euid != 0) && (r.euid == r.ruid)
  }
  ...
}
```

CodeBlock. Transitions and states may have code blocks that are executed after the corresponding transition and state assertions have been evaluated and found to be True. A code block is a sequence of statements enclosed in braces:

CodeBlock ::=
    '{'
        {*statement*}
    '}'

The statements in a codeblock can be assignments, *for* and *while* loops, *if-then-else*, procedure calls, etc. Semantically, the statements in a STATL code block are executed in order, in the context of the global and local environments of the scenario instance in which the code block is executed.

Timers. Timers are useful to express attacks in which some event or set of events must (or must not) happen within an interval following some other event or set of events. Timers can also be used to prevent "zombie" scenarios – scenarios that have no possible evolution – from wasting memory resources.

Timers are declared as variables using the built-in type timer. There are both local and global timers. All timers must be explicitly declared. Timers are started in code blocks using the built-in procedure timer_start. Timer expiration is treated as an event, and these events may be matched by using "timer events" as transition event specs.

Example:

```
scenario example
```

```
{
  timer t1;

  state s1
  {
    { timer_start(t1, 30); }
  }

  transition expire (s1->s2)
  { [timer t1] }
  ...
}
```

The code block of state s1 starts timer t1, which will expire in 30 seconds (i.e., at a time 30 seconds later than the timestamp on the event that led to state s1). The timer event timer t1 matches the expiration of the timer named t1. When timer t1 expires, transition expire will fire, leading to state s2.

Starting a timer that is already "running" resets that timer. A single timer may appear in multiple transitions; every enabled transition that has timer t as its event spec fires when the timer expires.

Assertions. Assertions appear as filter conditions in states and in event specs (which are the matching element of transitions). STATL assertions are built up from literal constants, variable and constant names, function calls, and common arithmetic and relational operators. A STATL assertion is evaluated at runtime in the context of the global and local environments of the scenario instance where it is evaluated.

Assertions may use, but may not change, the value of any name in the global or local environment. In addition, transition assertions may refer to the events named in the event spec and to the fields of those events.

2.2   STAT Core

The STAT Core module is the runtime for the STATL language. The Core implements the concepts of state, transition, timer, etc. In addition, the Core performs the event processing task, which is the basic mechanism used to detect intrusions by matching event streams against attack scenarios.

The STAT Core module has an event-based multi-threaded architecture (see Figure 7.2). Events are sent to or received from the Core through four separate event queues.

- The *control queue* is used to send control events to the Core. These events modify the Core's behavior or its configuration (e.g., by requesting the activation of a new attack scenario).

- The *info queue* is used by the Core to publish control-related information, such as the result of a reconfiguration request. The events in this

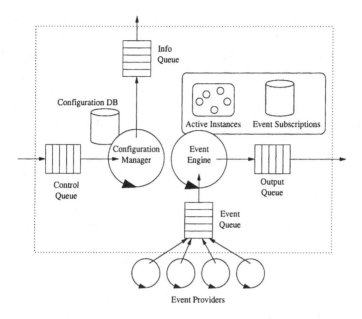

Figure 7.2. The STAT Core Architecture.

queue are used by external components (e.g., a MetaSTAT Proxy, see Section 4) to monitor the status of a Core component.

- The *input queue* is the source of the event stream for the intrusion detection analysis. Multiple external Event Providers (see Section 2.3) can contribute events to this queue.

- The *output queue* is used by the Core to publish events related to the intrusion detection process, such as detection alerts. This event queue can be connected to the input event queue of another Core component to realize a multi-core pipelined architecture.

The most important task of the Core is to keep track of active attack instances, which are called, in STATL terms, scenario instances. The Core maintains a data structure for each scenario instance. The data structure contains the current state of the scenario, its local environment, and the list of transitions that are are enabled, that is, the transitions that may possibly fire. These transitions have an associated action and a corresponding assertion, which, together, represent the subscription for an event of interest. The set of all current event subscriptions for all the active scenario instances is maintained by the Core in an internal database.

The Event Engine component of the Core is responsible for extracting events from the input queue and matching each event against the active event subscriptions. For each matching event subscription the tuple ⟨*scenario, transition, event*⟩ is inserted in the set of transitions to be fired. There are three separate sets depending on the type of transition: nonconsuming, consuming, and unwinding.

Once all the enabled transitions have been collected, the transitions are fired one by one. First, nonconsuming transition are fired. When a nonconsuming transition of a scenario instance is fired, a new scenario instance is created. The original instance becomes the *parent* of the new instance which, in turn, becomes one of the original instance's *children*. The child instance has a copy of the parent's local environment and a copy of the parent's timers. The state of the child instance is set to the destination state of the transition that fired. Then, the destination state code fragment is executed in the context of the child instance. If the destination state is a final state the child instance is removed. Otherwise, for each outgoing transition of the destination state a subscription for the associated event is inserted in the event subscription database.

After all the nonconsuming transitions have been fired, consuming transitions are fired. In the most common case, the instance state is changed to the destination state, previous subscriptions are canceled, and new subscriptions for the events associated with the transitions outgoing from the new state are inserted in the event spec database. Then, the destination state code is executed. If there are multiple enabled consuming transitions to be fired associated with the same scenario instance, then for each transition firing, except for the last one, a *clone* of the scenario instance is created. A cloned instance differs from a child instance in that a clone instance has the same parent as the original instance. After the creation of the clone, the execution process follows the steps of the previous case. Another special case is represented by a scenario instance that is in a state that can be the destination of an unwinding transition, that is an *unwindable state*. In this case, if the instance has any descendants, it is possible that at some time in the future one of the descendants may want to unwind to the ancestor instance as it is in its current state. If the instance's state changes because of the firing of a consuming transition, the system would reach an inconsistent state. To avoid this, a clone instance is created and the original instance is put in an *inactive status*. In the inactive status, the current subscriptions of the instance are removed and they are not replaced with new subscriptions. The instance will be restored to an active status if one of the children actually unwinds to the instance in the specified state.

After both consuming and nonconsuming transitions have been fired, the Core proceeds to fire the unwinding transitions. The firing of an unwinding transition with respect to a scenario instance has the effect of undoing the steps that brought the scenario instance to its current state. This means that other scenario instances may be affected by the unwinding procedure. More precisely, if we consider an unwinding transition from state S_x to state S_y we have to

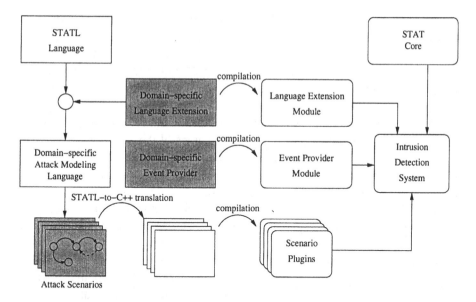

Figure 7.3. The STAT Framework extension process. The grayed boxes are the modules that need to be developed to extend the framework. The other components are generated automatically through either translation or compilation.

remove all the instances that were created by the series of events that brought the unwinding instance from state S_y to state S_x. In the Core, this is achieved by traversing back the parent/child chain until an instance in state S_y is found. Then the instance subtree rooted in the last visited instance is removed.

After all the transitions have been fired, the Configuration Manager component takes control of the Core. If a new control message is found in the control queue, the necessary reconfiguration of the Core is performed, and then the event processing is resumed in the new configuration.

2.3 STAT Extensions

The STATL language and the Core runtime are domain-independent. They do not support any domain-specific features that may be necessary to perform intrusion detection analysis in particular domains or environments. For example, network events such as an IP packet or the opening of a TCP connection cannot be represented in STATL natively. Therefore, the STAT Framework provides a number of mechanisms to extend the STATL language and the runtime to match the characteristics of a specific target domain.

The framework extension process is performed by developing subclasses of existing STAT Framework C++ classes. The framework root classes are STAT_Event, STAT_Type, STAT_Provider, STAT_Scenario, and ST-AT_Response. In the following paragraphs, the extension process is presented in detail. A graphic description of the extension process is given in Figure 7.3.

The first step in the extension process is to create the events and types that characterize a target domain. A STAT event is the representation of an element of an event stream to be analyzed. For example, an IP event may be used to represent an IP datagram that has been sent on a link. The event stream is composed of IP datagrams and other event types, such as Ethernet frames and TCP segments. All event types must be subclasses of the STAT_Event class. Basic event types can be composed into complex tree structures. For example, it is possible to use a tree of events to express encapsulation, such as Ethernet frames that encapsulate IP datagrams, which, in turn, contain TCP segments.

All of the types used to describe the components of an event and other auxiliary data structures must be subclasses of the STAT_Type class. For example, the IPAddress class is a type used in the definition of the IP event, and, therefore, it is a subclass of STAT_Type.

A set of events and types that characterize the entities of a particular domain is called a *Language Extension*. The name comes from the fact that the events and types defined in a Language Extension can be used when writing a STATL scenario once they are imported using the use STATL keyword. For example, if the IP event and the IPAddress type are contained in a Language Extension called tcpip, then by using the expression use tcpip it is possible to use IP events and IPAddress objects in attack scenario descriptions.

The events and types defined in a Language Extension must be made available to the runtime. Therefore, Language Extensions are compiled into dynamically linked libraries (i.e., a ".so" file in a UNIX system or a DLL file in a Windows system). The Language Extension libraries are then loaded into the runtime whenever they are needed by a scenario.

Attack scenarios are written in STATL, extended with the relevant Language Extensions. For example, a signature for a port scanning attack can be expressed in STATL extended with the tcpip Language Extension. STATL attack scenarios are then automatically translated into a subclass of the STAT_Scenario class. Finally, the attack scenarios are compiled into dynamically linked libraries, called *Scenario Plugins*. When loaded into the runtime, Scenario Plugins analyze the incoming event stream looking for events or sequences of events that match the attack description.

Once Language Extensions and Scenario Plugins are loaded into the Core it is necessary to start collecting events from the environment and passing them to the STAT Core for processing. The input event stream is provided by one or more *Event Providers*. An Event Provider collects events from the external environment (e.g., by obtaining packets from the network driver), creates STAT events as defined in one or more Language Extensions, and inserts these events into the event queue of the STAT Core.

Event Providers are created by subclassing the STAT_Provider framework class. This class defines a minimal set of methods for initialization/finalization of a provider and the retrieval of events from the environment. An Event Provider component is compiled into a dynamically linked library. An Event Provider library module can be loaded into the STAT Core at runtime. Once a Provider has been loaded, it has to be activated with specific parameters. The activated Event Provider will then start collecting events from the external environment. A single Event Provider can be activated in many instances and many different Event Providers can be loaded and activated at one time. Each activation of an Event Provider is associated with a dedicated thread. The thread uses the functions defined in the Event Provider module to retrieve events from the environment and insert them into the Core event queue for processing.

A runtime equipped with Language Extensions, Scenario Plugins, and Event Providers represents a functional intrusion detection system. In addition, the STAT Framework also provides classes that define *Response Modules*. A Response Module is created by subclassing the STAT_Response class. A Response Module contains a library of actions that may be associated with the evolution of a scenario. For example, a network-based response action could reset a TCP connection, or it could send an email to the Network Security Officer. Response Modules are compiled into dynamically linked libraries that can be loaded into the runtime at any moment. Functions defined in a Response Module can be associated with any of the states defined in a Scenario Plugin that has been loaded in the runtime. This mechanism provides the ability to associate different types of response functions with the intermediate steps of an intrusion.

Figure 7.4 presents the high-level class structure of the STAT Framework. The classes in the top part of the hierarchy are the STAT Framework classes. The lower part of the hierarchy is represented by the classes used to create a simple network-based intrusion detection system. The Language Extension Module is created by extending STAT_Event with subclasses IP, UDP, and TCP, which represent instances of the corresponding protocol units. The STAT_Type class is subclassed by IPAddress and Port, which are used to represent IP addresses and TCP/UDP ports, respectively. NetSniffer is an Event Provider (a subclass of STAT_Provider) that reads the packets sent on a network link and creates instances of the IP, UDP, and TCP events. The three subclasses UDPFlood, RemoteBufferOverflow, and Portscan extend the framework with descriptions of three network-based attacks. Finally, the subclass NetworkResponse contains network-specific response functions such as firewall reconfiguration directives and TCP connection shutdown.

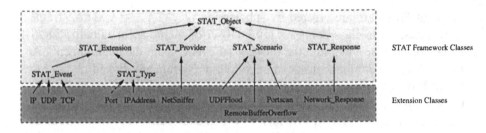

Figure 7.4. The STAT Framework class hierarchy.

3. THE STAT FAMILY

The framework described in the previous section has been used to develop a number of STAT-based intrusion detection systems. These IDSs are constructed by extending the STAT runtime with a selection of Language Extensions, Event Providers, Scenario Plugins, and Response Modules.

To be more precise, we developed an application, called *xSTAT*, that acts as a generic wrapper around the STAT Core runtime. xSTAT can be configured with different components. For example, xSTAT may load a network-centered Language Extension (e.g., the `tcpip` extension described in Section 2), a network-based Event Provider, and some network attack scenarios. The resulting system would be a network-based intrusion detection system, similar to Snort [28] or ISS RealSecure [13]. Note that loading a different set of components would create a completely different IDS. In addition, the STAT Framework has been ported to a number of platforms, including Linux, Solaris, Windows NT/2000/XP, FreeBSD, and MacOS X. Therefore, it is possible to create IDSs for these platforms by recompiling the necessary components.

By extending the STAT runtime with different modules it is possible to produce a potentially unlimited number of IDSs. In the past few years, we concentrated on the most important applications of intrusion detection, and we developed a family of intrusion detection systems based on the STAT Framework. The following subsections give a brief description of the current toolset.

3.1 USTAT

USTAT was the first application of the STAT technique to host-based intrusion detection. Even though the type of analysis that is performed on the event stream has mostly remained unchanged, the tool architecture has been completely re-designed [25]. USTAT performs intrusion detection using BSM audit records [30] as input. The record contents are abstracted into events described in a BSM-based Language Extension. USTAT also uses a UNIX-centered Language Extension that contains the definitions of a number of UNIX entities, such as user, process, and file. USTAT uses a BSM-based Event

Provider that reads BSM events as they are produced by the Solaris auditing facility, transforms them into STAT events, and passes them to the STAT Core. The events are matched against a number of Scenario Plugins that model different UNIX-based attacks, such as buffer overflows and access to sensitive files by unprivileged applications.

3.2   NetSTAT

NetSTAT is a network-based IDS composed of a network-centered Language Extension, an Event Provider that collects traffic from traffic dumps or network links, and a number of scenarios that describe network-based attacks, such as scanning attacks, remote-to-local attacks, and traffic spoofing. NetSTAT is similar to other network-based intrusion detection systems. However, it has some unique features that are the result of being part of the STAT family. For example, NetSTAT scenarios can be written in a well-defined language that has a precise semantics [5]. In addition, it is possible to perform stateful analysis that takes into account the multi-step nature of some attacks. This is in contrast to most existing network-based intrusion detection systems, which are limited to the analysis of single packets and do not provide a well-defined language for the description of multi-step scenarios.

3.3   WebSTAT and logSTAT

WebSTAT and logSTAT are two systems that operate at the application level. They both apply STAT analysis to the events contained in log files produced by applications. More precisely, WebSTAT parses the logs produced by Apache web servers [1], and logSTAT uses UNIX syslog files as input. In both cases, Language Extension modules that define the appropriate events and types have been developed, as well as Event Providers that are able to parse the logs and produce the corresponding STAT events.

3.4   AlertSTAT and afedSTAT

AlertSTAT is a STAT-based intrusion detection system whose task is to fuse, aggregate, and correlate alerts from other intrusion detection systems. Therefore, AlertSTAT uses the alerts produced by other sensors as input and matches them with respect to attack scenarios that describe complex, multi-step attacks. For example, an AlertSTAT scenario may identify the following three-step attack. The first step is a scanning attack detected by a network-based intrusion detection system, such as Snort or NetSTAT. This is followed by a remote buffer overflow attack against a Web Server (as detected by WebSTAT). Next, an alert produced by a host-based intrusion detection system (e.g., USTAT) located on the victim host indicates that the Apache process is trying to access the /etc/exports file on the local machine. The resulting alert is an aggregated report that conveys a much higher level view of the overall attack process.

AlertSTAT operates on alerts formatted according to the IETF's Intrusion Detection Message Exchange Format (IDMEF) proposed standard [2]. The application is built by composing an IDMEF-based Language Extension with an Event Provider that reads IDMEF events from files and/or remote connections and feeds the resulting event stream to the STAT Core. A number of attack scenarios have been developed, including the detection of complex scans, "many-to-one" and "one-to-many" attacks, island hopping attacks, and privilege escalation attacks.

Another correlator, called *afedSTAT*, has also been developed. The afedSTAT IDS uses the events contained in a database of alerts, called AFED, which was developed by the Air Force Research Labs. In this case, the Event Provider is a format translator. More precisely, the Event Provider used in afedSTAT reads events from the database and transforms them into IDMEF events as specified by the IDMEF Language Extension. As a consequence, it was possible to reuse all of the scenarios developed for AlertSTAT in the analysis of the AFED data without change.

3.5   WinSTAT and LinSTAT

WinSTAT and LinSTAT are two host-based systems similar to USTAT. WinSTAT uses the event logs produced by Windows NT/2000/XP. LinSTAT uses the event logs produced by the Snare Linux kernel module [12]. These two systems are an interesting example of component reuse to implement similar functionality in different environments/platforms. The Event Providers for USTAT, LinSTAT, and WinSTAT are obviously different. However, some of the entities used in scenarios are the same, and so are some of the scenarios (e.g., a scenario that detects privileged access from unprivileged applications).

3.6   AodvSTAT and AgletSTAT

The versatility of the STAT Framework was tested in developing very different systems. A well-defined framework extension process is not only a good way to develop a family of systems; it is also useful to produce proof-of-concept prototypes in a short amount of time. This is the case for two systems, called AodvSTAT and AgletSTAT. AodvSTAT is an IDS that interprets AODV [24] protocol messages and detects attacks against ad hoc wireless networks. AgletSTAT is an IDS that analyzes the events generated by a mobile agent system, called *Aglets* [18], and detects attacks that exploit mobile agents.

3.7 Family Issues

Developing a family of systems using an object-oriented framework has a number of advantages. First, the members of the program family benefit from the characteristics of the common code base. For example, all of the STAT applications use extended versions of STATL, and, therefore, they all have a well-defined language to describe attack scenarios. Second, it is possible to embed command and control functionality within the shared part of the framework. As a consequence a single configuration and control paradigm can be used to control a number of different systems. This is an issue that is particularly relevant for the domain of intrusion detection, and it is explained further in Section 4. Third, by factoring-out the commonalities between members of the family, it is possible to reuse substantial portions of the code. Finally, the use of a framework-based approach reduces the development time and allows one to build complete intrusion detection systems in a small amount of time.

4. METASTAT

MetaSTAT is an infrastructure that enables dynamic reconfiguration and management of the deployed STAT-based IDSs. MetaSTAT is responsible for the following tasks:

- **Route control messages to STAT sensors and other MetaSTAT instances.** MetaSTAT components can remotely control STAT-based sensors [2] through control messages. These messages may also cross the boundary of a web of sensors if the infrastructure security policy allows one to do so.

- **Collect, store, and route the alerts produced by the managed sensors.** Alerts about ongoing attacks are collected in a database associated with a single web of sensors. In addition, MetaSTAT components and STAT-based sensors can subscribe for specific alerts. Alerts matching a subscription are routed to the appropriate MetaSTAT endpoints. Alerts can also be sent across webs of sensors, to support high-level correlation and alert fusion.

- **Maintain a database of available modules and relative dependencies.** Every STAT component is stored in a *Module Database* together with meta-information, such as the dependencies with respect to other modules and the operational environment where the module can be deployed.

- **Manage sensor reconfiguration.** MetaSTAT uses the Module Database and the information regarding the components that are active or installed

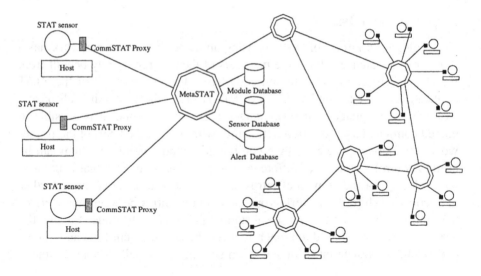

Figure 7.5. Architecture of a web of sensors.

at each STAT-based sensor as the basis for controlling the sensors and planning reconfigurations of the surveillance infrastructure.

4.1   Control Infrastructure

The high-level view of the architecture of the STAT-based web of sensors is given in Figure 7.5. MetaSTAT uses a communication infrastructure, called *CommSTAT*, to route messages and alerts between the different MetaSTAT endpoints in a secure way. CommSTAT messages are based on the IDMEF format, which defines two events, namely Heartbeat and Alert. This original set of events has been extended to include STAT-related control messages that are used to control and update the configuration of STAT sensors. For example, messages to ship a Scenario Plugin to a remote sensor and have it loaded into the Core have been added, as well as messages to manage Language Extensions and other modules.

MetaSTAT-enabled sensors are connected to a *MetaSTAT proxy*, which serves as an interface between the MetaSTAT infrastructure and the sensors. The proxy application performs preprocessing of messages, authentication of the MetaSTAT endpoints, and integration of third-party applications into the MetaSTAT infrastructure. When receiving messages from a *MetaSTAT controller*, the proxy passes the control message on to the connected sensors, which execute the control command. Three different classes of control messages are supported:

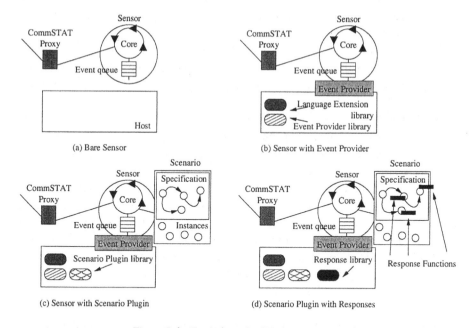

Figure 7.6. Evolution of a STAT-based sensor.

- **Install/uninstall messages.** An install message copies a software component to the local file system of a sensor, and an uninstall message removes the component from the file system.

- **Load/unload messages.** A load message instructs a sensor to load a STAT module into the address space of the sensor. After the processing of the message is completed the loaded module is available for the sensor to use. An unload message removes an unused module from the address space of a sensor.

- **Activate/deactivate messages.** An activate message starts an instance of a previously loaded STAT module. The activate message supports the passing of parameters to a STAT module. It is common to activate several instances of the same module with different parameters. A deactivate message stops the execution of an instance.

The configuration of a STAT sensor can be changed at run-time through control directives sent by the MetaSTAT controller to the proxy component responsible for the sensor. A set of initial modules can be (and usually is) defined at startup time to determine the initial configuration of a sensor. In the following paragraphs, an incremental configuration of a STAT-based sensor will be described to better illustrate the role of each sensor module, provide a hint of the high degree of configurability of sensors, and describe the dependencies between the different modules.

When a sensor is started with no modules, it contains only an instance of the STAT Core waiting for events to be processed. The Core is connected to a proxy, which, in turn, is connected to a MetaSTAT controller instance. This initial "bare" configuration, which is presented in Figure 7.6 (a), does not provide any intrusion detection functionality.

The first step is to provide a source of events. To do this, an Event Provider module must be loaded into the sensor and then activated. This is done through MetaSTAT by requesting the shipping of the Event Provider shared library to the sensor, and then requesting its loading and activation. An Event Provider relies on the event definitions contained in one or more Language Extension modules. If these are not available at the sensor's host, then they have to be installed and loaded. Once both the Event Provider and the Language Extensions are loaded into the sensor, the Event Provider is activated. As a consequence, a dedicated thread of execution is started to execute the Event Provider. The provider collects events from an external source, filters out those events that are not of interest, transforms the remaining events into event objects (as defined by a Language Extension), and then inserts the event objects into the Core input queue. The Core, in turn, consumes the events and checks if there are any STAT scenarios interested in the specific event types. At this point, there are no scenarios, and, therefore, there are no events of interest to be processed. This configuration is described in Figure 7.6 (b).

To start doing something useful, it is necessary to load one or more Scenario Plugins into the Core and activate them. To do this, first a Scenario Plugin module, in the form of a shared library, is installed on the sensor's host. A scenario may need the types and events of one or more Language Extension modules. If these are not already available at the destination host then they are installed and loaded. Once all the necessary components are available, the scenario is loaded into the Core and activated, specifying a set of initial parameters. When a Scenario Plugin is activated, an initial scenario prototype is created. The scenario prototype contains the data structures representing the scenario's definition in terms of states and transitions, a global environment, and a set of activation parameters. The prototype creates a first instance of the scenario. This instance is in the initial state of the corresponding attack scenario. The Core analyzes the scenario definition and subscribes the instance for the events associated with the transitions that start from the scenario's initial state. At this point the Core is ready to perform event processing, as shown in Figure 7.6 (c).

As a scenario evolves from state to state, it may produce some output. A typical case is the generation of an alert when a scenario completes. Another example is the creation of a *synthetic event*, which is a STAT event that is generated by a scenario plugin and inserted in the Core event queue. The event is processed like any other event and may be used to perform forward chaining of scenarios.

Apart from logging (the default action when a scenario completes) and the production of synthetic events (that are specified internally to the scenario definition), other types of responses can be associated with scenario states using *response modules*. Response modules are collections of functions that can be used to perform any type of response (e.g., page the administrator, reconfigure a firewall, or shutdown a connection). Response modules are implemented as shared libraries. To activate a response function it is necessary to install the shared library containing the desired response functionality on the sensor's host, load the library into the Core, and then request the association of a function with a specific state in a scenario definition. This allows one to specify responses for any intermediate or final state in any attack scenario. Each time the specified state is reached by any of the instances of the scenario, the corresponding response is executed. Responses can be installed, loaded, activated, and removed remotely using the MetaSTAT component. Figure 7.6 (d) shows a response library and some response functions associated with particular states in the scenario definition.

At this point, the sensor is configured as a full-fledged intrusion detection system. Event providers, scenario plugins, language extensions, and response modules can be loaded and unloaded following the needs of the overall intrusion detection functionality. As described above, these reconfigurations are subject to a number of dependencies that must be satisfied in order to successfully load a component into the sensor and to have the necessary inputs and outputs available for processing. These dependencies are managed by the MetaSTAT component, and they are discussed in the next section.

4.2   Sensor Reconfiguration

The flexibility and extendibility supported by the STAT-based approach is a major advantage: the configuration of a sensor can be reshaped in real-time to deal with previously unknown attacks, changes in the site's policy, different levels of concern, etc. Fine-grained configurability requires careful planning of module installation and activation, and this activity can be very complex and error-prone if carried out without support. For this reason the MetaSTAT component maintains a database of modules and their associated dependencies and a database of the current sensor configurations. These databases provide the support for consistent modifications of the managed web of sensors. In the following, the term *module* is used to denote language extensions, event providers, scenario plugins, and response modules. The term *external component* is used to characterize some host facility or service that is needed by an event provider as a source of raw events or by a response function to perform some action. External components are outside the control of MetaSTAT. For example, a BSM event provider needs the actual BSM auditing system up and running to be able to access audit records and provide events to the STAT Core.

Dependencies between modules can be classified into *activation* dependencies and *functional* dependencies. Activation dependencies must be satisfied for a module to be activated and run without failure. For example, consider a scenario plugin that uses predicates defined in a language extension. The language extension must be loaded into the Core before the plugin is activated. Otherwise, the plugin activation will fail with a run-time linking error. Functional dependencies are associated with the *inputs* of a module. The functional dependencies of a module are satisfied if there exist modules and/or external components that can provide the inputs used by the module. Note that a module can successfully be activated without satisfying its functional dependencies. For example, suppose that a scenario plugin that uses BSM events has been successfully activated, but there is no BSM event provider to feed BSM events to the Core. In this case, the scenario is active but completely useless. The inputs and outputs of the different module types, and the relative dependencies are summarized in Table 7.1.

Module	Inputs	Outputs	Activation Dependencies	Functional Dependencies
Event Provider	External event stream	STAT events	Language Extension modules	External components
Scenario Plugin	STAT events, synthetic events	Synthetic events	Language Extension modules	Scenario plugins, Event providers
Response Module	Parameters from plugin	External response	Language Extension modules	External components
Language Extension	None	None	Language Extension modules	None

Table 7.1. Input and output, and dependencies of STAT sensor modules.

Information about dependencies between modules is stored in MetaSTAT's *Module Database*.

Determining the functional dependencies on other modules requires that two queries be made on the Module Database. The first query gets the inputs required by the module. The second query determines which modules are generating the inputs that were returned from the first query. The results returned from the second query identify the modules that satisfy the functional dependencies of the original module. The functional dependencies on external components are modeled explicitly by the database. In addition to dependencies, the Module Database also stores information such as version and OS/architecture compatibility information.

The Module Database is used by MetaSTAT to automatically determine the steps to be undertaken when a sensor reconfiguration is needed. Since sensors do not always start from a "bare" configuration, as shown in Figure 7.6 (a), it is usually necessary to modify an existing sensor configuration. Therefore, the MetaSTAT component maintains a second database called the *Sensor Database*, which contains the current configuration for each sensor. This database is updated at reconfiguration time by querying the current configuration of the sensor.

To be more precise, the term *configuration* is defined as follows: *A STAT sensor configuration is uniquely defined by a set of installed and activated modules and available external components.* The term *installed* is used to describe the fact that a module has been transferred to and stored on a file system accessible by the sensor and in a location known by the sensor. The term *activated* is used to describe the fact that a *module* has been dynamically loaded in a sensor as the result of a control command from MetaSTAT. The term *loaded* has the same meaning as *activated* in relation to language extension modules.

A configuration can be *valid* and/or *meaningful*. A configuration is valid if all activated modules have all their activation dependencies satisfied. A configuration is meaningful if the configuration is valid and all functional dependencies are also satisfied.

4.3   Reconfiguration Example

To better describe the operations involved in a reconfiguration and the support provided by MetaSTAT, an example will be used.

Suppose that the Intrusion Detection Administrator (IDA) noted or was notified of some suspicious FTP activity in a subnetwork inside the IDA's organization. Usually, the IDA would contact the responsible network administrator and would ask him/her to install and/or activate some monitoring software to collect input data for further analysis. The IDA might even decide to login remotely to particular hosts to perform manual analysis. Both activities are human-intensive and require considerable setup time.

MetaSTAT supports a different process in which the IDA interacts with a centralized control application (i.e., the MetaSTAT console) and expresses an interest in having the subnetwork checked for possible FTP-related abuse. This request elicits a number of actions:

1 The scenario plugins contained in the Module Database are searched for
   the keyword "FTP". More precisely the IDA's request is translated into
   the following SQL query:

```
SELECT module_id, name, os_platform, description
  FROM Module_Index
  WHERE (name LIKE '%ftp%' OR
         description LIKE '%ftp%')
    AND type="plugin";
```

The following information is returned:

module_id	name	os_platform	description
module_1	wu-ftpd-bovf	Linux X86	BOVF attack against ftpd
module_2	ftpd-quote-abuse	Linux X86	QUOTE command abuse
...	...	...	...
module_9	ftpd-protocol-verify	Linux X86	FTP protocol verifier

The IDA selects the `wu-ftp-bovf` and `ftpd-quote-abuse` scenario plugins for installation.

2 The Module Database is examined for possible activation dependencies.
   The `wu-ftp-bovf` activation dependencies are determined by the following query:

```
SELECT dep_module_id FROM Activation_Dependency
  WHERE module_id="module_1";
```

The query results (not shown here) indicate that the scenario plugin requires the `ftp` language extension. This is because events and predicates defined in the `ftp` extension are used in states and transitions
of the `wu-ftp-bovf` scenario. A similar query is performed for the
`ftpd-quote-abuse` scenario plugin. The query results indicate that
the `syslog` language extension is required by the plugin.

3 The Module Database is then searched for possible functional dependencies. For example in the case of the `wu-ftp-bovf` scenario the
   following query is executed:

```
SELECT input_id FROM Module_Input
  WHERE module_id="module_1";
```

The query returns an entry containing the value FTP_PROTOCOL. This means that the wu-ftp-bovf scenario uses this type of event as input. Therefore, the wu-ftp-bovf scenario plugin has a functional dependency on a module providing events obtained by parsing the FTP protocol. A similar query indicates that the ftpd-quote-abuse plugin has a functional dependency on a provider of SYSLOG events.

4 These new requirements trigger a new search in the Module Database to find which of the available modules can be used to provide the required inputs. SYSLOG events are produced by three event providers: syslog1, syslog2, and win-app-event. The FTP_protocol events are produced, as synthetic events, by the ftp-protocol-verify scenario.

5 Both the syslog1 and syslog2 event providers require an external source, which is the syslog facility of a UNIX system. In particular, syslog2 is tailored to the *syslogkd* daemon provided with Linux systems. Both event providers have an activation dependency on the syslog language extension. The win-app-event event provider is tailored to the Windows NT platform. It depends on the NT event log facility (as an external component) and relies on the NT event log language extension (winevent). The ftp-protocol-verify is a network-based scenario and, as such, requires a network event provider that produces events of type STREAM, which are events obtained by reassembling TCP streams. The scenario has two activation dependencies; it needs both the tcpip and the ftp language extensions. The first is needed because STREAM events are used in the scenario's transition assertions. The second is needed to be able to generate the FTP_protocol synthetic events.

6 Events of type STREAM are produced by an event provider called netproc. This event provider is based on the tcpip language extension, and requires, as an external component, a network driver that is able to eavesdrop traffic.

7 At this point, the dependencies between the modules have been determined (see Figure 7.7). The tool now identifies the sensors that need to be reconfigured. This operation is done by querying the Sensor Database to determine which hosts of the network under examination have active STAT-based sensors. The query identifies two suitable hosts. Host lucas, a Linux machine, has a bare sensor installed. Host spielberg,

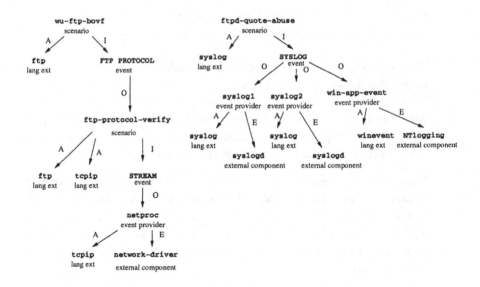

Figure 7.7. Dependency graph for scenarios wu-ftp-bovf and ftpd-quote-abuse. In the figure, arrows marked with the letter "A" are used to represent activation dependencies. Arrows marked with "I" represent the relationship between a module and the input events required. Arrows marked with an "O" represent the relationship between an event type and the module that produce that type of event as output. Arrows marked with "E" represent a dependency on an external component.

another Linux machine, runs a STAT-based sensor equipped with the netproc event provider, the tcpip language extension, and some scenario plugins. Both hosts provide the network driver and UNIX syslog external component. The tool decides (possibly with intervention from the IDA) to install the ftpd-quote-abuse scenario on lucas and the wu-ftp-bovf scenario on spielberg.

8 The syslog language extension is sent to lucas, and it is installed in the file system. This is done using the following CommSTAT messages:

```
<x-stat-extension-lib-install id="1">
    <extension_lib name="syslog" version="1.0.1">
        [... encoded library ...]
    </extension-lib>
</x-stat-extension-lib-install>

<x-stat-extension-lib-activate id="2">
    <extension_lib name="syslog" version="1.0.1">
    </extension-lib>
</x-stat-extension-lib-activate>
```

The `syslog2` event provider is sent, installed, and loaded in the sensor by means of similar commands. At this point syslog events are being fed to the Core of the sensor on host `lucas`. The `ftpd-quote-abuse` scenario plugin is sent to the host, installed on the file system, and eventually loaded into the Core.

9 The `ftp` language extension is sent to host `spielberg`. The `tcpip` language extension is already available, as is the `netproc` event provider. Therefore, the `ftp-protocol-verify` scenario plugin can be shipped to host `spielberg`, installed, and loaded into the Core. The scenario starts parsing STREAM events and producing FTP_PROTOCOL synthetic events. As the final step, the `wu-ftpd-bovf` scenario is shipped to host `spielberg`, installed, and loaded into the Core, where it immediately starts using the synthetic events generated by the `ftp-protocol-verify` scenario.

After the necessary reconfigurations are carried out, the IDA may decide to install specific response functions for the newly activated scenarios. A process similar to the one described above is followed. Response modules, in the form of shared libraries, may be installed on a remote host and linked into a sensor. Additional control commands may then be used to associate states in a scenario with the execution of specific functions of the response module.

5. RELATED WORK

Object-oriented frameworks are "sets of cooperating classes that make up a reusable design for a specific class of software" [6]. Generally, frameworks are targeted for specific domains to maximize code reuse for a class of applications [15]. The STAT Framework is targeted for the development of event-based intrusion detection systems. In this context, the use of a framework differs from traditional approaches [11, 29], because all of the components that are developed as part of the framework are highly independent modules that can be composed (almost) arbitrarily through dynamic loading into the framework runtime. In addition, the framework extension process is not limited to the creation of a domain-specific intrusion detection system. The same process produces products for different domains, depending on the events, types, and predicates defined in the Language Extensions. The product of the STAT Framework is a family of intrusion detection systems.

The concept of program families was introduced by Parnas in [22] and has received considerable attention from the Software Engineering community ever since. Unfortunately, the criteria, methodologies, and lessons learned in developing software families in a number of fields have not been applied to intrusion detection. Even though in recent years the focus of intrusion detection has moved from single-domain approaches (e.g., network-based only) to multi-domain approaches (e.g., correlation of alerts from both network-level and OS-level event analysis), this change of focus has not been matched by a corresponding shift in development methodology. As a consequence, while IDS are becoming more common, their development is still characterized by an *ad hoc* approach. Notable examples are SRI's Emerald [26, 20], ISS RealSecure [13], and Prelude [31]. All of these toolsets include a number of different sensor components and high-level analysis engines. For example, Emerald has a host-based intrusion detection system, two network-based analyzers, and a correlation/aggregation component. Even though the toolset covers a number of different domains, there is no explicit mechanism in the Emerald approach that is exclusively dedicated to support the extension of the system to previously uncovered domains. The same limitation appears in both RealSecure, which is a mainstream commercial tool, and Prelude, which is an open-source project.

6. CONCLUSIONS

The STAT Framework is an approach for the development of intrusion detection systems based on the State Transition Analysis Technique. This chapter described the framework, the corresponding extension process, and the result of applying the framework to develop a family of systems.

The work reported in this chapter makes contributions in several areas. By using object-oriented frameworks and by leveraging the properties of program families it was possible to manage the complexity of implementing intrusion functionality on different platforms, environments, and domains. The framework supports efficient development of new intrusion detection sensors because the main mechanisms and the semantics of the event processing are implemented in a domain-independent way. Therefore, the IDS developer has to implement only the domain/environment-specific characteristics of the new sensor. Practitioners in the field of intrusion detection can certainly gain from the lessons learned. Hopefully, they will use the STAT framework or adapt a component-based software family approach for their own development.

Two areas where the reported work contributes to previous work in the component and framework communities is in leveraging the architecture to have a common configuration and control infrastructure and in having the attack specification language tightly coupled with the application development. STAT-based intrusion detection systems that operate on different event streams (e.g., OS audit records and network packets) and at different abstraction levels (e.g., detection and correlation) share a similar architecture and similar control primitives. As a consequence, a single configuration and control infrastructure can be used to manage a large number of heterogeneous components.

Language Extension modules extend the domain-independent STATL core language to allow users to specify attack scenarios in particular application domains. The same Language Extension modules are compiled and used by the runtime core for recognizing events and types. Because it is the same Language Extension module for both, the user automatically gets an attack specification language along with his/her intrusion detection system. In addition, because the attack specification languages are an extension of the STATL core language, a user does not need to learn a new language style when setting up attack scenarios for a new intrusion detection application.

The STAT tools and the MetaSTAT infrastructure have been used in a number of evaluation efforts, such as the MIT/Lincoln Labs evaluations and the Air Force Rome Labs evaluations, in technology integration experiments, such as DARPA's Grand Challenge Problem (GCP) and the iDemo technology integration effort. In all of these very different settings, the STAT tools performed very well by detecting attacks in real-time with very limited overhead. In most cases, the STAT tools were run and compared with other tools from both the research and the commercial worlds. The positive feedback received from the organizers of these evaluation efforts provided a particularly significant comparison of the STAT toolset performance with respect to other state-of-the-art intrusion detection technologies.

The STAT Framework, the MetaSTAT infrastructure, and the STAT-based tools are open-source and publicly available at the STAT web site *http://www.-cs.ucsb.edu/~rsg/STAT.*

ACKNOWLEDGMENTS

This research was supported by the Army Research Office, under agreement DAAD19-01-1-0484, by the Defense Advanced Research Projects Agency (DARPA) and Rome Laboratory, Air Force Materiel Command, USAF, under agreement number F30602-97-1-0207, and by the National Security Agency's University Research Program, under agreement number MDA904-98-C-A891. The U.S. Government is authorized to reproduce and distribute reprints for Governmental purposes notwithstanding any copyright annotation thereon.

The views and conclusions contained herein are those of the authors and should not be interpreted as necessarily representing the official policies or endorsements, either expressed or implied, of the Army Research Office, the Defense Advanced Research Projects Agency (DARPA), the National Security Agency (NSA), or the U.S. Government.

Notes

1. An alternative would be to execute the transition codeblock before evaluating the state assertion. However, this would require backtracking to undo environment changes when the state assertion is not satisfied. Otherwise, the environment could be changed for "partially" fired transitions, which would be semantically unsatisfactory.

2. In the remainder of this chapter an instance of an intrusion detection system may be referred to as a sensor.

REFERENCES

[1] *Apache 2.0 Documentation*, 2001. http://www.apache.org/.

[2] D. Curry and H. Debar. Intrusion Detection Message Exchange Format: Extensible Markup Language (XML) Document Type Definition. draft-ietf-idwg-idmef-xml-06.txt, December 2001.

[3] R. Durst, T. Champion, B. Witten, E. Miller, and L. Spagnuolo. Addendum to "Testing and Evaluating Computer Intrusion Detection Systems". *CACM*, 42(9):15, September 1999.

[4] R. Durst, T. Champion, B. Witten, E. Miller, and L. Spagnuolo. Testing and Evaluating Computer Intrusion Detection Systems. *CACM*, 42(7):53–61, July 1999.

[5] S.T. Eckmann, G. Vigna, and R.A. Kemmerer. STATL: An Attack Language for State-based Intrusion Detection. *Journal of Computer Security*, 2002.

[6] E. Gamma, R. Helm, R. Johnson, and J. Vlissides. *Design Patterns*. Addison-Wesley, 1995.

[7] A.K. Ghosh, J. Wanken, and F. Charron. Detecting Anomalous and Unknown Intrusions Against Programs. In *Proceedings of the Annual Computer Security Application Conference (ACSAC'98)*, pages 259–267, Scottsdale, AZ, December 1998.

[8] K. Ilgun. USTAT: A Real-time Intrusion Detection System for UNIX. Master's thesis, Computer Science Department, University of California, Santa Barbara, July 1992.

[9] K. Ilgun. USTAT: A Real-time Intrusion Detection System for UNIX. In *Proceedings of the IEEE Symposium on Research on Security and Privacy*, Oakland, CA, May 1993.

[10] K. Ilgun, R.A. Kemmerer, and P.A. Porras. State Transition Analysis: A Rule-Based Intrusion Detection System. *IEEE Transactions on Software Engineering*, 21(3):181–199, March 1995.

[11] Taligent Inc. Building Object-Oriented Frameworks. White Paper, 1994.

[12] Intersect Alliance. Snare: System Intrusion Analysis and Reporting Environment. http://www.intersectalliance.com/projects/Snare, August 2002.

[13] ISS. Realsecure 7.0. http://www.iss.net/, August 2002.

[14] H. S. Javitz and A. Valdes. The NIDES Statistical Component Description and Justification. Technical report, SRI International, Menlo Park, CA, March 1994.

[15] R. Johnson and B. Foote. Designing Reusable classes. *Journal of Object-Oriented Programming*, 1(2):22–35, June/July 1988.

[16] K. Kendall. A Database of Computer Attacks for the Evaluation of Intrusion Detection Systems. Master's thesis, MIT, June 1999.

[17] C. Ko, M. Ruschitzka, and K. Levitt. Execution Monitoring of Security-Critical Programs in Distributed Systems: A Specification-based Approach. In *Proceedings of the 1997 IEEE Symposium on Security and Privacy*, pages 175–187, May 1997.

[18] D. Lange and M. Oshima. *Programming and Deploying Java Mobile Agents with Aglets.* Addison-Wesley, 1998.

[19] R. Lippmann, D. Fried, I. Graf, J. Haines, K. Kendall, D. McClung, D. Weber, S. Webster, D. Wyschogrod, R. Cunningham, and M. Zissman. Evaluating Intrustion Detection Systems: The 1998 DARPA Off-line Intrusion Detection Evaluation. In *Proceedings of the DARPA Information Survivability Conference and Exposition, Volume 2*, Hilton Head, SC, January 2000.

[20] P.G. Neumann and P.A. Porras. Experience with EMERALD to Date. In *First USENIX Workshop on Intrusion Detection and Network Monitoring*, pages 73–80, Santa Clara, California, April 1999.

[21] NFR Security. *Overview of NFR Network Intrusion Detection System*, February 2001.

[22] D.L. Parnas. The Design and Development of Program Families. *IEEE Transactions on Software Engineering*, March 1976.

[23] V. Paxson. Bro: A System for Detecting Network Intruders in Real-Time. In *Proceedings of the 7th USENIX Security Symposium*, San Antonio, TX, January 1998.

[24] C.E. Perkins and E.M. Royer. Ad hoc on-demand distance vector routing. In C. Perkins, editor, *Ad hoc Networking*. Addison-Wesley, 2000.

[25] P.A. Porras. STAT – A State Transition Analysis Tool for Intrusion Detection. Master's thesis, Computer Science Department, University of California, Santa Barbara, June 1992.

[26] P.A. Porras and P.G. Neumann. EMERALD: Event Monitoring Enabling Responses to Anomalous Live Disturbances. In *Proceedings of the 1997 National Information Systems Security Conference*, October 1997.

[27] M.J. Ranum, K. Landfield, M. Stolarchuck, M. Sienkiewicz, A. Lambeth, and E. Wall. Implementing a Generalized Tool for Network Monitoring. In *Eleventh Systems Administration Conference (LISA '97)*. USENIX, October 1997.

[28] M. Roesch. Snort - Lightweight Intrusion Detection for Networks. In *Proceedings of the USENIX LISA '99 Conference*, November 1999.

[29] G. F. Rogers. *Framework-Based Software Development in C++*. Prentice-Hall, 1997.

[30] Sun Microsystems, Inc. *Installing, Administering, and Using the Basic Security Module.* 2550 Garcia Ave., Mountain View, CA 94043, December 1991.

[31] Y. Vandoorselaere. Prelude, an Hybrid Open Source Intrusion Detection System. http://www.prelude-ids.org/, August 2002.

[32] G. Vigna and R.A. Kemmerer. NetSTAT: A Network-based Intrusion Detection Approach. In *Proceedings of the 14th Annual Computer Security Application Conference*, Scottsdale, Arizona, December 1998.

[33] G. Vigna, R.A. Kemmerer, and P. Blix. Designing a Web of Highly-Configurable Intrusion Detection Sensors. In W. Lee, L. Mè, and A. Wespi, editors, *Proceedings of the 4th International Symposiun on Recent Advances in Intrusion Detection (RAID 2001)*, volume 2212 of *LNCS*, pages 69–84, Davis, CA, October 2001. Springer-Verlag.

[34] C. Warrender, S. Forrest, and B.A. Pearlmutter. Detecting intrusions using system calls: Alternative data models. In *IEEE Symposium on Security and Privacy*, pages 133–145, 1999.

Chapter 8

ENCAPSULATION OF USER'S INTENT: A NEW PROACTIVE INTRUSION ASSESSMENT PARADIGM

Shambhu Upadhyaya, Ramkumar Chinchani, Kiran Mantha
Department of Computer Science and Engineering, University at Buffalo

Kevin Kwiat
Air Force Research Laboratory

Abstract: Few practical implementations of anomaly detection systems are currently known. Major hindrances in this regard are poor accuracy of detection and excessive false positives. While some of the reasons may be attributed to theory and technology, a major factor that is overlooked is the user. We propose a novel approach that brings the user into the loop by querying him for his session intent in a proactive manner. This encapsulated intent serves the purpose of a certificate based on which more accurate intrusion detection decisions can be made.

Keywords: Anomaly detection, Intrusion detection, Misuse detection, Role based access control, User intent

1. INTRODUCTION AND MOTIVATION

The field of computer security is concerned with enforcing a code of proper conduct in the digital domain. The various facets of computer security are prevention, detection and mitigation. Preventive measures, such as firewalls, form the first line of defense. However, they may not be adequate to contain every possible attack. It is, therefore, essential to detect those attacks that have breached this line of defense and initiate additional countermeasures. The process of detecting attacks is called *intrusion detection*, and a program that performs this task is called an *intrusion detection system* (IDS).

Intrusion detection systems can be categorized as either *misuse* detection or *anomaly* detection systems. Misuse detection techniques look for very specific patterns of attacks, but their effectiveness is limited to the database of patterns or signatures of known attacks. On the other hand, anomaly detection approaches rely on defining a reference line for normalcy and flagging any significant deviations as intrusive activity. A downside of this approach is that determining proper thresholds for normalcy and intrusions is very difficult.

Many important lessons have been learned in conjunction with the advances that have been made in intrusion detection. Intrusion detection is primarily a process of decision-making based on systemic audit data that is gathered from probes, which are placed at strategic points in a computer system or network. An operating system on a computer can offer multiple interfaces through which users can interact with the computer, as illustrated in Figure 8.1. A user may execute commands locally on a shell, which consequently invokes the system call subsystem. Users may also access the computer remotely by utilizing the networking subsystem. Unfortunately, these very channels of interaction with a computer may be misused to launch attacks; hence, security systems have to be deployed at these points. External network-level attacks are perhaps the

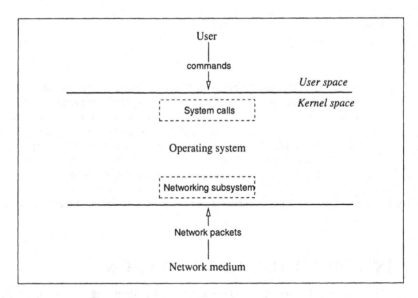

Figure 8.1. Multiple Interfaces Provided by an Operating System

most common type of attacks and they have been well-studied. Consequently, a gamut of techniques and tools are currently available such as firewalls, network intrusion detection systems and security audit tools. On the system call interface, the threat manifests mainly in the form of mobile code, malicious users, insiders and masqueraders. In order to combat the problem of malicious mobile code and users, solutions such as proof carrying code and sandboxing have been proposed. In contrast, few solutions have been offered for the threat posed by insiders and masqueraders. Traditional rule-based misuse detection systems are not very successful, because it is not possible to define signatures accurately for every user. Due to their ability to construct specific statistical models, anomaly detection approaches are considered more promising. However, practical implementations of anomaly detection systems are not common due to issues involving data collection and processing, learning time and high false positive/negative rate.

In this chapter, we propose a novel methodology to tackle these issues and lay the groundwork for the implementation of a practical anomaly detection system. The first step of our intrusion detection technique is generation of a run-time plan for the user. The user is then monitored for any significant deviation from this plan. This plan is composed of verifiable *assertions* that are automatically generated on the basis of a few system usage inputs provided by the user at the beginning of a session. These inputs are obtained in a controlled manner through some form of user interface. Once an assertable plan is generated, the user will be monitored throughout the session to see how closely he conforms to the plan. Any significant deviation from the plan is construed as an intrusion.

This approach is based on sound principles of signature analysis that have been successfully used in concurrent monitoring of processor operation for fault tolerance. Besides, the new approach offers several advantages. First of all, this does away with audit trail analysis. Audit trails are generally huge and the analysis and filtering out of useful information is expensive ([14]). Also, the assertable plan based on encapsulation of owner's intent attaches a greater significance to the semantics of user's operations and also can take into account user dynamics and any intended changes in the user behavior. Therefore, no special learning is needed as is the case with other statistics based systems. The analysis is done at a much higher level of abstraction compared to kernel level monitoring ([11]). This can lead to the detection of intricate and subtle attacks. Since on-line monitoring can potentially lower the latency of detection, our scheme can be combined with any recovery schemes for effective damage containment and restoration of service.

2. BACKGROUND AND RELATED WORK

Intrusion detection techniques have been devised at various levels, i.e., using audit data sampled deep inside the system, system call level and in some cases at the user level. Some aspects of these techniques are similar to our approach.

Rule Based

When certain attack patterns and their security implications are known, it is possible to derive their signatures, and arrive at rules to detect and disallow such activity. Due to the ease of implementation and reasonably high accuracy, this is one of the commonly used techniques for intrusion detection and prevention. These rules form a security policy and they may be derived and enforced ([9]; [2]; [10]; [21]; [29]) at various levels. The rules may govern various aspects such as packet formats, network activity, system usage, program and user behavior, etc.

Program Behavior Based

Of particular interest is ([10]) where intended program behavior is specified in terms of assertions. These assertions are, in general, rules which govern what a program can or cannot do. This approach is feasible for a small number of programs but does not scale well in real world settings where there are a large number of programs available for use. The concept of assertions that we speak of is very similar to this idea except that our specifications are at various levels. The technique discussed in ([7]) constructs program behavior profiles and compares the run-time activity against this profile. Various models based on automatons and state transitions ([29]) exist to model program behaviors.

User Behavior Based

The work that is closest to our approach is ([25]) that speaks about modeling user intent based on system audit data. This technique was not very effective primarily because of the amount of information collected and the problem of ambiguity resolution at that level. The work discussed in ([13]) attempts to model user behavior statistically by observing the operations and commands that he uses, and detect any deviations from this profile. The problem is tackled from an AI perspective. However, considering the large number and variety of operations and commands, detection becomes infeasible and inaccurate. Another notable work ([3]) uses keystroke monitoring to identify users and then differentiates between legitimate users and intruders. However, ([12]) discounts this technique as being impractical due to the myriad ways of expressing the same attack at the keystroke level. Aliasing has also been cited as a reason for the defeat of this technique.

Role Based Access Control

Role based access control (RBAC) mechanism ([6]) defines a sandbox based on the user-id and associated privileges. Roles are assigned to each user and he can make only those transactions for which he has the required privileges. This mechanism is similar to our approach in way of defining the bracket of allowed activity. However, RBAC is successful when the transactions that can be made are few and clearly defined. Hence, it finds good applications in databases.

Real-time Detection

Quite a few techniques claim to achieve real-time detection. This is true when the data set is small or the instance of the problem is small ([10]; [9]). In other cases, even if the data is large, they may be able to detect intrusions rapidly but have to do it offline resulting in slower response times. Some other previous works such as a more powerful version of NADIR ([8]) called UNICORN accepts audit logs from Cray Unix called UNICOS, Kerberos and common file systems. It then analyzes them and tries to detect intruders in real-time. However, since these audit logs can be large, significant computing power has to be devoted to process them, defeating the very goal of real-time intrusion detection.

Distributed and Concurrent Schemes

DIDS ([23]) is a distributed intrusion detection system which looks at and correlates the connections on multiple machines to the initial login. GrIDS ([26]) is a graph based intrusion detection system that collects data about activities on computers and network traffic between them. This graph is then used to detect large-scale automated or coordinated attacks in real-time. The computer science lab at SRI International has completed a project called EMERALD (Event Monitoring Enabling Response to Anomalous Live Disturbances) ([19]). This project has developed a distributed monitoring scheme which uses a combination of a signature engine and a profiler engine within the monitor for intrusion detection. It is possible to draw some parallels from the domain of fault tolerance such as the concept of system level check for concurrent error detection ([1]). It is now a well accepted theory that faults can be detected by using verifiable assertions placed at strategic points in the real-time system. These assertions are similar to the rules and other invariants specified for system behavior for intrusion detection. The research group at Purdue has developed an adaptive network monitoring scheme using autonomous agents. Their approach ([24]) is distributed in the sense that one agent is used per node instead of a monolithic entity. The agent is somewhat similar to the monitor of EMERALD ([19]). This architecture also uses a hierarchical approach like EMERALD.

Masqueraders and Insider Threats

The problem of insiders and masqueraders is a serious one with few solutions. The work of ([16]) is a recent attempt at trying to solve the problem using anomaly detection via truncated command lines. Though they report some success, they admit that such success is limited only to their data set and the results may not even be replicable. This work also compares and contrasts other known statistical techniques to solve the problem. We argue that it is neither feasible nor practical to solve the problem using only statistical methods because of the number of possibilities.

3.   GUIDELINES

On the basis of the rich experience provided by these recent research efforts, we have identified some guidelines to achieve our goal of a practical online anomaly detection system. We also present arguments in support of these guidelines.

GUIDELINE 1 *Use the principle of least privilege to achieve better security.*

The principle of least privilege ([6]) implies that security is achieved only at the loss of certain freedom. A user's operations should be restricted to the extent that it is just sufficient for him to perform his jobs without hindrance.

GUIDELINE 2 *Use mandatory access control wherever appropriate.*

Mandatory access controls [1] are rules that govern the access to objects and resources. This principle supplements Guideline 1 when there is a conflict of interest between the user's freedom and achieving better security.

Both of these guidelines serve an additional purpose. In general, data collection and processing is central to an anomaly detection technique. It is often the case that audit data gathered by sensors or probes contains noise, which interferes with the construction of accurate statistics. By setting appropriate restrictions and rules for system usage, this noise can be reduced. This requirement is stated as Guideline 3.

GUIDELINE 3 *The data used for intrusion detection should be kept simple and small.*

This has several implications. If the data is kept small and simple, it becomes possible to effectively sift through it for information regarding attacks. The processing and storage overheads are reduced significantly. More importantly, this reduces false positives and facilitates lower detection latency. Since our focus is user-level intrusion detection, data collection is done at higher levels in the system such as commands and system calls, rather than low levels such as a filesystem and networking subsystems.

GUIDELINE 4 *Intrusion detection capabilities are enhanced if environment specific factors are taken into account.*

No single intrusion detection can sufficiently cater to all the security needs. The parameters used to collect information are very dynamic and highly environment specific. A lot of anomaly based intrusion detection systems do not take into consideration the environmental factors. The expectation that anomaly based systems will perform well irrespective of the environment has been proven to be unrealistic ([15]). In order to achieve similar efficacy in detection, such systems should be flexible enough so that their parameters can be configured to reflect the environment they are deployed in.

4. METHODOLOGY OVERVIEW

Intrusion Model and Assumptions

Any activity at the user level is initiated by programs executed on some user's behalf. We classify malicious user activity into the following categories.

- System abuse and access violations

  A user after logging into a system may execute commands that lower the overall quality of service or attempt to access resources that he is not authorized to.

- Identity theft attacks

  An attacker can assume the identity of a legitimate user through a compromised password or physically joining an open session of an authenticated user.

In our definition of a distributed system, we include a network of computers that service users on the basis of an account and a password. Further, we assume that the users on different machines have the same user-id although the passwords could be distinct. This model precludes the monitoring of web surfing and anonymous ftp activities. No specific topology is assumed for the network. All communications between nodes are by message passing and the network is assumed to be stable. This model makes our intrusion detection approach unique in that all intrusions are abstracted as happening through well-defined user sessions which are invoked through a user-id and password submission. The problem of intrusion detection simply transforms into monitoring these well-defined user sessions. We also assume that a user session on a node is of finite length.

Basic Principle

Our technique of intrusion detection using verifiable assertions is firmly based on the principle of control flow checking in fault tolerance ([18]; [22]; [28]). In control flow checking, an analysis prior to compilation of the program is done to generate a control flow graph of the application. Signatures or assertions are embedded into the instruction stream at compile time to generate a reference graph. At run-ime, signatures generated from the execution of instructions are monitored and at designated intervals, the run-time signatures are compared with predetermined signatures of the reference graph. Any discrepancy between the run-time signatures and the expected signatures indicates an error. Both instruction level bit errors and control flow errors are detected by this scheme. Though the control flow checking concept can be extended to intrusion detection, instruction-level models are not applicable here because instruction-level control flow variations may not indicate attacks occurring at higher levels. Accordingly, we use a different approach for the derivation of a reference graph as described below.

In our intrusion detection scheme, the user starts a session on a computer in a standard way, that is, by logging in. The system then encapsulates his intent as a session-scope. This is an approximate summary of his intended system usage. Once the scope-file is submitted, the user is allowed to continue with his session. Meanwhile the system translates the scope-file into a set of verifiable statements. When no ordering of events is considered on the activities of the user, the set is simply a table of verifiable statements. It has no control flow information as such.

The verifiable statements give a mechanism for monitoring the user behavior. These statements are generated automatically by reading the scope-file and interpreting the user inputs properly. An important component of our verifiable statements is the subject field. The subject field is generated from the user-id and other unique identifications such as the IP address of the workstation, tty number of the terminal being used etc. All such information will be coded into the subject field. For instance, a user may wish to open multiple login sessions. As long as such intent is expressed in the scope-file, a more general subject coding can be done for this user in order to allow him to work from different terminals or set up multiple login sessions. There is only one monitor process per user even though multiple sessions are opened.

When the user is in session, his operational commands are checked to see if they are the ones he originally intended to execute. Any significant deviation from the plan is an indication of potential intrusive activity.

The flow diagram of Figure 8.2 represents the basic principle of our new approach and by itself has limited usage. While extensions are easily conceivable for improved performance ([27]), we retain our basic framework for ease of presentation of the scheme. Some of the techniques used to minimize false alarms and to build robustness to this basic monitoring scheme will be discussed later.

User Intent Encapsulation

Actively querying a user for computational intent may initially appear as a departure from traditional techniques and an avoidable annoyance, but there are some definite benefits. When an online IDS is installed on a computer system,

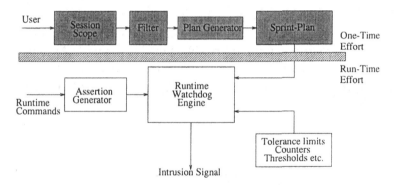

Figure 8.2. Flow Diagram of Intrusion Detection

it makes decisions regarding the current user activity, which may or may not be contested by a user. Figure 8.3 illustrates the various scenarios.

IDS decision:
Is the current user activity intrusive?

		Yes	No
		Yes	No
User consent: Does the user agree?	Yes	True Positive	True Negative
	No	False Positive	False Negative

Figure 8.3. Different Scenarios Corresponding to an IDS' Decisions and a Monitored User's Response to Those Decisions

The four regions, shaded and unshaded, represent the "hits" and "misses" of an IDS' detection mechanism. Perfect intrusion detection is achieved if all the decisions of the IDS lie in the shaded regions without exception. However, that is seldom the case. Misuse detection techniques are generally accurate in detecting known attacks, but they are not complete. On the other hand, although anomaly detection approaches claim to be complete, they are not very accurate on the account of statistical methods being used. Even when the IDS is very accurate, a decision can be wrong simply because the user being monitored contests it. This problem cannot be solved merely by technology or theory alone. Instead, we propose to bring the user into the loop. When a user, whether a legitimate user or an intruder, is queried for intent at the beginning of a session, this expressed intent becomes a certificate of normal user activity. Some obvious concerns may arise at this point. This technique can only be practical if the process of intent encapsulation is not very intrusive

by nature. Also, it becomes important to do it in a way that captures maximum
information with minimum effort. Intent encapsulation has been suggested as
an effective alternative to formal verification of chip design [2]. As in the intent-
driven verification in the form of *expressed* and *implied*, intent encapsulation in
our case can be achieved by a direct query which is *explicit* or in indirect ways
which is *implicit*; each has its advantages and disadvantages.

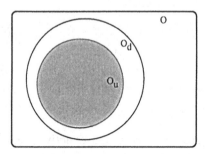

Figure 8.4.   Illustration of Effects of Implicit and Explicit Intent Encapsulation

Let us assume that the entire superset of operations is O as shown in Fig.8.4.
This is the entire set of operations supported on a computer system that any
user can attempt to execute.

Implicit Intent Encapsulation.   By using Guideline 2 (§ 3) and observing
that certain intents can be inferred directly from the context, we define a default
bracket of privileges corresponding to a user's user-id and his role (based on
the RBAC methodology). For example, a teller in a bank may have a different
job description than that of a manager, therefore requiring a different set of
privileges. This bracket O_d (Fig. 8.4) can be considered as the hard coded intent
of the user. This technique has been widely used in commercial databases and
has been successful. RBAC works well when the transactions and the ways in
which they are accomplished are few and clearly defined.

Explicit Intent Encapsulation.   RBAC based technique suffers from the
limitation that these bracket of privileges are static and pre-defined. This results
in a very general profile for the users and leads to poor performance.

By explicitly querying the user for intent, it is possible to define a smaller and
personalized bracket of privileges or jobs for each user. Let the set of operations
that a user defines to be his session-scope be O_u. If this set is bounded only by O,
then this technique is not very different from the known statistical techniques for
detecting insiders and masqueraders. However, by bounding O_u by O_d instead
of O, the user can express intent up to the set defined by his user-id. Such a
controlled intent extraction occludes questions such as "What if the user lies?"
because the user is allowed to choose only from what he is given. This subset

of jobs that are chosen forms the baseline for monitoring through the various sessions. Since this reference line is very focused and small, it becomes feasible to perform online and real-time monitoring which results in a low latency of detection and also lower false positives.

Variations of this technique included querying the user at the beginning of *every* session. This has the advantage that it can accommodate drastic changes from one session to the other. Its shortcoming is that it is very intrusive by nature. A slightly passive technique involves querying the user only at the beginning of his first session and then invalidating this intent only when some event occurs that warrants another query. For example, a student's activity involving the use of tools for his courses remain unchanged till the end of the current semester. This is less intrusive by nature and is perhaps adequate for most environmental settings.

Summary. The major advantage of intent encapsulation is that it can be done very specific to the environment making anomaly detection very effective. Also, by making the profiles very personalized, it becomes easier to establish the user's identity by way of differences in the choice of jobs and the choice of operations henceforth.

5. A BASIC ALGORITHM AND ENHANCEMENTS

Definitions

DEFINITION 8.1 *An **intrusion or anomaly** is defined as any deviation from a known normal operational behavior.*

The prior determination of legitimate operations or a sequence of operations is done based on certain criteria. Details of the criteria are not elaborated here, but for most operations, the determination of legitimacy should be simple ([27]). This definition of intrusion includes such activities as masquerading, legitimate user penetration, and legitimate user leakage ([5]), internal abuse, and illegal resource access such as buffer overflow attacks. Our IDS is not designed to handle external network level attacks, such as IP spoofing and remote exploits. Hence, these are not a part of the intrusion model.

DEFINITION 8.2 *A **watchdog** is a process that continuously monitors user commands typed in from a keyboard, submitted in the form of a script or a macro or input by mouse clicks.*

A watchdog process is spawned immediately following a user-id and password submission, and the creation of a user session. Only one watchdog process per user-id is created. The watchdogs are implemented to take into account the various ways user level commands can be submitted (globbing, aliasing, etc.). This watchdog process is active as long as the user sessions are active.

DEFINITION 8.3 **Session-scope** *is a file containing a list of intended activities submitted by a user at the beginning of a session. The session is assumed to be of bounded duration. Long periods of inactivity are considered as the end of a session. The session may then be locked or logged out. Regardless, it is a good security measure to avoid open sessions remaining unattended for long periods of time.*

This file, which encapsulates the owner's intent, is a high level description of user operations in a specific format. Since only one monitor session is set up per user account, only one session-scope is accepted per user account even if multiple sessions are opened on a given user account. The session-scope, once submitted, is treated as a secure document and is not accessible to anyone. Having one session-scope per user-id over a given period of time facilitates easy monitoring and also leads to low overhead and better coverage.

DEFINITION 8.4 *A* **verifiable assertion** *is a quadruple which associates a user with the intended operation over a given period of time.*

The format of the assertions is as follows.

$$(subject, \ action, \ object, \ period) \tag{8.1}$$

where "subject" is a user (along with additional IDs such as terminal identification, IP address etc.), "action" is an operation performed by the subject, such as login, logout, read, execute, "object" is a recipient of actions such as files, programs, messages, records, terminals, printers, etc., and "period" signifies the time interval for the usage of an action. These verifiable assertions are generated in advance for each user event specified in the session-scope file and forms a small and bounded set.

DEFINITION 8.5 *A* **sprint-plan** *(Signature Powered Revised INstruction Table) is a collection of verifiable assertions.*

This is a table automatically generated as a response to a user's session-scope file. The sprint-plan can also be viewed as a signatured stream of atomic operations (commands) that is generated for the purpose of on-line monitoring. The preparation of an accurate *sprint-plan* at the beginning of a session is a one-time effort as indicated in Figure 8.2. The effort in generating the sprint-plan is mostly dependent upon the session-scope. If the session-scope file is too cryptic or imprecise, it is possible to interpret legitimate use as an intrusion, giving rise to false positives. An important user requirement is the availability of enough flexibility to work on a session on a user's own workstation. This adds some burden on the sprint-plan generator. The assertions are currently derived with the information based on observation of user activity and specific requirements of jobs similar to the rule generation in ([2]). It can be further supplemented by certain techniques such as accounting checks or reasonableness checks ([20]; [27]) as well as systematic methods based on finite automata and Markov graphs ([4]).

A Sketch of the Algorithm

The user is queried for a session-scope at the beginning of the session. He is also given the choice of choosing whether multiple simultaneous user sessions should be allowed. The user is then allowed to continue with the session with no further interruption from the IDS. The user input line in the form of a singular command, command alias, macro or a script is monitored as a set of atomic operations by the per user watchdog, irrespective of whether it is an interactive or a batch submission. These atomic operations will have the subjectID resolved based on run-time characteristics. One can choose to monitor every single user command or set a particular monitoring rate depending upon parameters like system load and specified security levels. If the atomic operations are found in the previously generated sprint-plan, the session continues without interruption. If there is a mismatch, further examination is conducted to see if there is a subject ID violation. If so, an intrusion is obvious and appropriate signals will be sent to a *master* watchdog. Otherwise, the mismatch is interpreted simply as a deviation from the original plan and the count on permissible unplanned commands is incremented. If this count reaches a tolerance limit, then an intrusion is flagged and appropriate action is initiated.

Intrusion Scenarios and Enhancements

We now consider various intrusion scenarios and analyze the methodology. The sessions belong to either a legitimate user or an intruder.

- Case 1: A legitimate user logs in.

  This is the most innocuous case. The user logs in, expresses his intent and proceeds to work.

- Case 2: An intruder logs in.

  Since the system cannot readily distinguish between legitimate user and an intruder, an intruder would also be routinely presented with a session-scope query. An intruder is more likely to choose the largest possible set for it gives additional flexibility to carry out malicious operations. However, this set is constrained by O_d. Moreover, each operation submitted by the intruder is examined by the per user watchdog. While this may not totally eliminate intrusions, it does effectively restrict the intruder.

- Case 3: Two legitimate logins in some sequence in time.

When a user starts a session from his desktop and later starts another session while the first one is alive perhaps from a different machine. For example, a user may be working in his office and then remotely logs in from his lab. This is the normal case of simultaneous logins and we do not expect to have too many deviations.

- Case 4: The first login is from the legitimate user and the second login is from an intruder.

  If the first login is from the legitimate user then he is presented with the session-scope query. If an intruder logs in before the user's session is terminated, he is not queried for a session-scope and he must emulate the user precisely to avoid detection. His operations are restricted just as in Case 2.

- Case 5: The first login is from an intruder and the second login is from the legitimate user.

  The intruder is likely to specify the broadest session-scope possible. He is still restricted by O_d. In this case, the legitimate user who logs in will not be queried for a session-scope. If it is his first session then it should raise strong suspicion. If not, the variations between the intruder's and user's operations are going to culminate in an intrusion sooner or later.

- Case 6: Two intruders log in.

  This is a variation of Case 5 except that the second intruder does not expect a query and continues to work in his session. Unless their actions are concerted, deviations are bound to occur which result in an intrusion signal.

Enhancements

Several refinements to the basic algorithm are possible to enhance the robustness and efficacy of intrusion detection.

Profiling User Operations. Currently, very limited profiling is done by the basic algorithm. However, the detection technique can be made more effective if there is a better profiling scheme. Profiling on a per user basis within the bracket of activity defined by the session-scope generates an identity for the user while retaining the default restrictions imposed by the bracket. Profiling can be done by taking into consideration not only the frequency distribution of operations but also the temporal characteristics of system usage.

Dynamically Updating Session-scope. Although a user may specify a relatively broad session-scope, over time it may be possible to detect those operations that very rarely appear and then shrink the session-scope to eliminate these operations. A non-intrusive version of this enhancement would be to assume a default intent of O_d instead of querying and then performing the elimination of operations. However, this is a more passive approach and may require a long learning process.

6. IMPLEMENTATION DETAILS

Architecture

Our intrusion detection model is amenable to hierarchical monitoring where the lowest level of hierarchy is the user-session level monitoring. Hierarchical arrangement of watchdog monitors is highly effective in distributed systems as evident from other intrusion detection schemes such as COAST ([24]), EMER-ALD ([19]) and HUMMER ([17]).

A watchdog process is set up for each user on a given node. However, the process remains dormant until a user starts a session on a node. These watchdogs are essentially instances of the same process, monitoring the various user sessions. They remain restricted to the local nodes, but once operational, interact with a master watchdog which is responsible for coordinating distributed and concurrent system monitoring. This extends the whole security system from a host level system to a network level intrusion detection system.

In addition to the user watchdogs and master watchdogs, each local network has a separate watchdog called a File Watchdog. The function of the file watchdog is to monitor accesses to secure files on the file server. The file watchdog will interact with the master watchdog on the individual nodes to coordinate the dissemination of intrusion detection and to initiate recovery. The architecture of the individual user watchdog is shown in Figure 8.5.

The watchdog process receives input from the User Command Buffer and/or from the OS. The Atomic Operation generator converts user command lines into an on-line assertion statement. The Inclusion Checker module verifies if the assertion statement generated on-line is in the set of previously generated verifiable assertions. The optional blocks in the figure represent enhanced features.

In order to test our basic ideas, we built a preliminary prototype. The session-scope can be fed into the system in a variety of ways. We use a graphical user interface (GUI) to simplify the process of the user input. This makes it possible to perform the process of intent encapsulation in a controlled manner.

If the login is valid, the watchdog queries the user about the applications the user is going to work in that particular session. Based on the applications a preselected list of inputs containing the system resources available for the user is provided in a GUI, from which the user can select the scope of the session. The watchdog also queries the user about his multiple login intent. If the user wishes to open multiple sessions, a list of all the hosts a user can connect to in

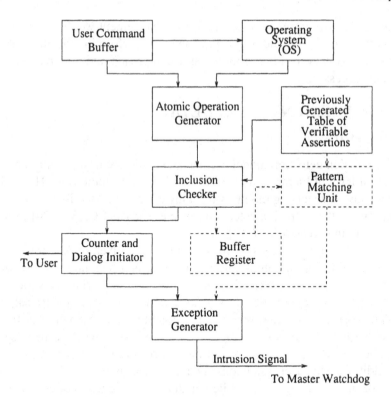

Figure 8.5. Block Schematic of the Watchdog Process

the network is generated. The scope-file thus obtained is given to a converter, which is built into the watchdog. The converter converts the scope-file into a sprint-plan consisting of verifiable assertions. A formatter formats this spring-plan into a format that can be used for comparison.

Once the sprint-plan is generated which is a one-time monitoring effort, the user is allowed to proceed with his normal operations. Every user operation on the system is monitored and converted to an atomic operation by the watchdog's preprocessor. This is done using *ptrace(2)*. By forcing the process to stop at *exec(2)* and subsequent system calls, it is possible to determine which command is being executed and the resources it uses. The output of the preprocessor is similar to the sprint-plan, and is used by the watchdog for comparison with the reference sprint-plan. Site-specific details, if any, are also given to the

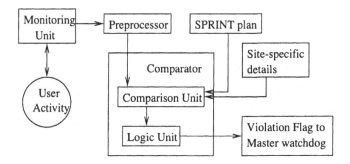

Figure 8.6. Monitor/Comparator Unit

comparator. Any violation is reported to the master watchdog. The architecture of the monitor/comparator unit is shown in Figure 8.6.

The comparator consists of a comparison unit and a logic unit. The comparison unit does all the comparisons and if there is a mismatch then it is passed to the logical unit, which determines the violation flag level.

Verifiable Assertions

Verifiable assertions are basically an access control mechanism to enforce the bracket of activity of the user defined by his intent. They are mainly in the form of *do's* and *dont's*. These assertions typically govern file system objects such as files and directories. They are currently derived manually. Fig. 8.7 shows an example of such assertions in a simplified form.

ProgramDevelopmentJob:
commands: emacs, vim, xemacs
file system objects: home dir – allow all, /usr/lib/, /lib, – read–only

MailJob:
commands: pine, elm, emacs
file system objects: home dir – allow all, /var/mail/username – allow all

AcademicCourse:
commands: matlab, mathematica
file system objects: home dir – allow all, /usr/lib, /lib – read–only, app specific libs – read–only

■■■

Figure 8.7. A Sample of Verifiable Assertions

7.   SIMULATIONS AND RESULTS

We chose a student/faculty user academic environment for the purposes of testing. This environment has fewer security controls in place and allows greater freedom for the users and hence makes a good test bed to study the efficacy of our technique. We could also consider a regulated system such as web-enabled banking to estimate the feasibility and impact on a more general and commercial setting.

Simulating a University Environment

The basic architecture is client-server based. Such a setup allows us to derive some test cases from the published descriptions of well known attacks and in developing site-specific test cases based on the security policy. It also helps us to consider both sequential and concurrent intrusions. In a sequential intrusion, a single person issues a single sequence of commands from a single terminal or a workstation window. In concurrent intrusion, one or more intruders issue sequences of commands from several terminals, computers or windows. The command sequences work cooperatively to carry out an attack. For example an intruder can open multiple windows on a workstation and connect to a target computer from each window and try to distribute his intrusive activities among them. The platform allows us to simulate basic sessions such as telnet, ftp etc. Synchronization can be achieved which lets us specify a fixed execution order of events.

When the student/faculty user logs in with a user-id/password submission, password verification is done first. If the user is authenticated to login he will be provided with a series of GUI windows to specify the scope of the session. The user selects the application he is going to work on. If, say, the user selects Research as the application, the user is provided with a preselected input list containing various categories such as simulators, design tools, operating systems, programming languages, scripts, documentation and miscellaneous items such as ftp, rlogin etc.

The user just needs to check the tasks he intends to perform. Once this is done the watchdog queries the user if he intends to perform any other activities that are not present in the predetermined list. The user is also queried if he intends to open multiple sessions.

The various components of the sprint-plan are combined together by a formatter to obtain the final sprint-plan. Figure 8.8 shows a run-time monitoring setup for a 1-user, 2-hosts system on a single server and is explained below.

The sprint-plan generated for the user is stored at a secure location on the server. As soon as the user logs in to a host, the watchdog checks to see if there is a sprint-plan already existing for the user, if there is none, it generates a new one. If a sprint-plan already exists, the user is allowed to proceed with his normal activity. The watchdog continuously monitors the user and compares it with the sprint-plan.

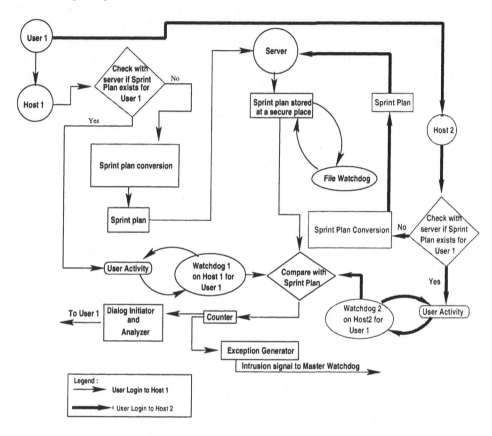

Figure 8.8. Run-time Monitoring Setup

Test Cases and Attack Scenarios

The test data is based on user activity collected over a period of two months. We required the test data to be confined within the same semester. We used this data to derive the verifiable assertions and then test the strength of the scheme by subjecting it to a few test cases and attacks.

There is usually no simple procedure to identify appropriate test cases for an intrusion detection system. A variety of intrusion scenarios are considered based on some common practices of system usage. These scenarios are grouped into four categories, viz., one-user without multiple logins, one-user with multiple logins, multiple users without multiple logins and multiple users with multiple logins. Two set of experiments are performed in each of these categories, first with the worst case, where a user selects all the entities provided in the session-scope GUI by the watchdog and the second where a user selects only a few entities. The tests are performed by treating the logins as four different cases, with up to two users at a given time. The first case is where both logins are legitimate. In the second case, the first login is from a legitimate user and the second login is from an intruder. In the third case, the first login is from the intruder and the second login is from the user and finally the fourth case where both logins are from intruders.

We performed a total of 32 attacks and they were of two types. One category represented very obvious and apparent attacks such as transferring the /etc/passwd file from one host to another, password-cracking by comparing the entries in the /etc/passwd file to entries in another file, using a dictionary file for the same, and exploiting the vulnerabilities such as rdist, perl 5.0.1, etc. The system is able to detect all the intrusive activities and terminate the connection for the logins of intrusive users. The second category involved more subtle attacks similar to mimicry attacks ([30]). Even in such cases, since we monitor both the operations and the file system accesses, we are able to restrict the damage caused by the intruder. The intruder is only able to cause damage within the user's login and home directory. In the worst case scenarios of one-user with multiple logins and multiple users with multiple logins, a relatively larger number of intrusive activities was not detected. The system has also generated a few false positives, flagging an intrusion when normal user activity is taking place. This happens when the user selects only a few entities from the session-scope. The results are summarized in Table 8.1 where detection latency is reported in terms of average number of user operations. The metrics shown in the table are consistent with the predictions made on the intrusion cases in § 5.

System Overheads and Performance Impact

Since Java is used for implementation, moderate impact on system performance is expected. When new connections are made or more users login, the system load increases. However, this increase is only marginal because there is no need to maintain any large data structures for each user or connection. The main server on which our intrusion detection system is running is a Sun Ultra Enterprise 450 Model 4400 and the clients are Sun Ultra 5's running Solaris 2.7.

A normal user in a university environment is assumed to have about six to eight processes running on the system at a given time. There is one watchdog dedicated for each user which makes it one more process per user on the system.

Sessions	Metrics	1 User, No Multiple Logins	1 User, Multiple Logins	2 Users, No Multiple Logins	2 Users, Multiple Logins
User	Detection	–	78.6%	74.90%	91.90%
and	Latency	–	35	36.1	29
User	False Positives	–	21.4%	25.1%	8.1%
	False Negatives	–	0%	0%	0%
User	Detection	98%	89.0%	100.0%	94.7%
and	Latency	0	11	0	9.6
Intruder	False Positives	0%	0%	0%	0%
	False Negatives	2%	11%	0%	5.3%
Intruder	Detection	99%	100%	98.2%	100%
and	Latency	0.4	0.7	0.6	0.5
User	False Positives	0%	0%	0%	0%
	False Negatives	1.4%	0%	1.8%	0%
Intruder	Detection	58%	81.3%	77.4%	91.5%
and	Latency	15.9	14.8	17	27
Intruder	False Positives	0%	0%	0%	0%
	False Negatives	44%	18.7%	22.6%	8.5%

Table 8.1. Summary of Preliminary Simulation Results

This watchdog process does not use many run-time resources and hence may not become an overhead to the system. However, when several users are logged in and are being monitored, the system may see some performance loss. In order to study this overhead, we eliminated all unrelated activities in the test environment, started the intrusion detection system and allowed the users to log in. We analyzed the average load per minute (no. of jobs in the run queue on Unix) and the storage overhead in kB against the number of users on the system. At this particular stage of implementation without much optimization, the operation is very stable for about 15 users. The load on the system tends to increase as the number of monitored users increases beyond 15. The storage overhead (325 kB for a single user) increases at a constant rate with the number of users. When the session-scope is large, the watchdog maps it to a huge sprint-plan. The storage used by the IDS in our study corresponds to the worst case scenario where a user selects all the entities from the session-scope provided by the watchdog in a GUI.

8. DISCUSSION

The proposed intrusion detection technique is very effective in detecting intrusions in user sessions. This is because the intruder's operations are likely to result in large deviations from the intended session-scope of the user. In the event that an intruder is able to compromise an account, he is still restricted by the defined bracket of activity.

The watchdog process which performs user session-level monitoring is the core module of the distributed concurrent intrusion detection scheme described in this chapter. Our scheme is not intended to be a replacement to other intrusion detection tools such as pattern matching and rule-based systems built to work on audit trail data. The concurrent monitoring watchdog described here can be used in conjunction with other distributed intrusion detection schemes to provide a higher detection resolution. For instance, the watchdog can be added as a third party security module in EMERALD's monitor ([19]).

Intrusion detection based on the encapsulation of owner's intent as described in this chapter will be more effective in detecting command level intrusions and internal system misuse. A user's course-of-action (COA) can be influenced by the balance between the user affirming the truth while the system checks for a hidden intent to deceive. This close interaction between the user's thoughts and the system's corresponding actions opens up new areas in information assurance related to COA [3].

The proposed scheme has certain limitations. There will be some performance loss due to the running of the watchdog monitors for each user. The watchdog processing time will increase with the size and vagueness of the session-scope and so it is important that users express a focused session-scope. We have implicitly made a simple cost/benefit statement to the user by requiring them to cognate some about what they are going to do and then state it in the form of session-scope. Lack of cognition on the user's part followed by a vague statement of intent has a cost. To deal with this cost, the weight of system complexity will have to bear down on the user (to track the vague intent). The cost accrued by the user will be lower quality of service and this aspect can be built into future versions of our IDS. Further, Our IDS can by no means provide a comprehensive solution to intrusion detection. For example, malicious code attached to programs or network level attacks may not be detected since no execution level monitoring is done in this approach. Profiling on user sessions becomes infeasible if the user activity has a large entropy. In such cases, the only defense is static monitoring using verifiable assertions and confining the user activity within the bracket defined by the intent.

9.   CONCLUSION

In this chapter, we have presented a new approach to intrusion detection using verifiable assertions. We have developed this scheme by leveraging some of the successful concepts from the fault tolerance domain. The main feature of our technique is that detection occurs concurrently with user operations and in real-time. The low latency detection of our technique can potentially speed up the recovery of affected systems. This is a significant benefit compared to the schemes based on audit trail analysis.

We have given a basic architecture and sketched an algorithm for intrusion detection. Several enhancements to the basic scheme are also presented. The technique is flexible in that changes or updates to the intended plan can be made easily. Also, every time a fresh session is started, a new set of verifiable assertions is generated. The finite length of a given user session helps to keep the sprint-plan to a small and bounded set.

The concurrent intrusion detection prototype described in this chapter is preliminary. Our simulation shows that on-line intrusion detection using assertion checking is feasible, that is, low performance overhead and good detection coverage. More detailed experiments with complex intrusion scenarios is desired. This requires further enhancements to the sprint-plan generation and consideration of structural and temporal sequence checking.

10. FUTURE WORK

The intent of this chapter is to present a practical implementation of an online intrusion monitoring scheme and its technical details. The following extensions are easily conceivable.

- Sequences of Operations and Improved Profiling

    It will be useful to consider sequences of operations to flag intrusions in addition to considering the set inclusion checks. See the optional blocks in Figure 8.5. This will enable the detection of more complex intrusions that are orchestrated by concocting sequences of benign operations. An analytical framework for reasoning about intrusions in such scenarios is already in place ([27]).

- Network Level Attacks

    When multiple sessions are allowed, it may be possible to mount a distributed attack. Issues related to computer networks and abuse of network servers could be addressed as future work.

- Automated Assertion Generation

    The generation of assertions can be automated using formal techniques such as accounting checks or reasonableness checks ([20]). Some preliminary reasoning work has been reported in ([27]).

ACKNOWLEDGMENTS

The research is supported, in part, by the US AFOSR Grant F49629-C-0063, AFRL Contract F30602-00-10507 and a seedling grant from DARPA. A preliminary version of this work was presented in SPECTS 1999.

Notes

1. Trusted Computer Security Evaluation Criteria, DOD 5200.28-STD, Department of Defense, 1985

2. This technique has been used by Real Intent, a company that develops formal verification based products. As of 2002, the white paper is available at:
http://www.realintent.com/products/idv_white_paper.html

3. DARPA has undertaken a Course-of-Action Challenge project to aid in the military decision making process. Details can be found at the URL:
<http://www.iet.com/Projects/RKF/COA%20CP-spec-v0.3.htm>

REFERENCES

[1] Alkhalifa, Z., Nair, V. S. S., Krishnamurthy, N., and Abraham, J. A. (1999). Design and evaluation of system-level checks for on-line control flow error detection. *IEEE Transactions of Parallel and Distributed Systems*, 10(6).

[2] Chari, Suresh and Cheng, Pau-Chen (2002). Bluebox: A policy-driven host-based intrusion detection system. *Network and Distributed System Security Symposium (NDSS'02)*.

[3] Clyde, A.R. (Sept. 1987). Insider threat identification systems. *Proc. 10th National Computer Security Conf.*

[4] Debar, H., Dacier, M., Wespi, A., and Lampart, S. (1997). An experimentation workbench for intrusion detections systems. *Research Report, IBM, Zurich Research Laboratory*.

[5] Denning, D.E. (1987). An intrusion-detection model. *IEEE Transactions on Software Engineering*, SE-13(2):222–232.

[6] Ferraiolo, D. and Kuhn, R. (1992). Role based access control. *15th National Computer Security Conference*.

[7] Ghosh, A. K., Schwartzbart, Aaron, and Schatz, Michael (1999). Learning program behavior profiles for intrusion detection. *1st USENIX Workshop on Intrusion Detection and Network Modeling*.

[8] Hochberg, J., Jackson, K., Stallings, C., McClary, J., DuBois, D., and Ford, J. (1993). NADIR: An automated system for detecting network intrusions and misuse. *Computers & Security*, 12(3):253–248.

[9] Ilgun, K., Kemmerer, R.A., and Porras, P.A. (1995). State transition analysis: A rule-based intrusion detection approach. *IEEE Trans. on Software Eng.*, 21(3):181–199.

[10] Ko, C., Ruschitzka, M., and Levitt, K. (May 1997). Execution monitoring of security-critical programs in distributed systems: A specification-based approach. *1997 IEEE Symp. on Security & Privacy*, pages 134–144.

[11] Krings, A.W., Harrison, S., Hanebutte, N., Taylor, C., and McQueen, M. (2001). Attack recognition based on kernel attack signatures. *to appear in Proc. 2001 Internations Symposium on Information Systems and Engineering, (ISE'2001)*.

[12] Kumar, S. and Spafford, E.H. (October 1994). A pattern matching model for misuse intrusion detection. *Proceedings of the 17th National Computer Security Conf.*, pages 11–21.

[13] Lane, Terran and Brodley, Carla E. (1997). Sequence matching and learning in anomaly detection for computer security. *AAAI-97 Workshop on AI Approaches to Fraud Detection and Risk Management*, pages 43–49.

[14] Lunt, T.F. (1993). A survey of intrusion detection techniques. *Computers and Security*, 12:405–418.

[15] Maxion, Roy A. and Tan, Kymie M. C. (2000). Benchmarking anomaly-based detection systems. *Int'l Conf. Dependable Systems and Networks*, pages 623–630.

[16] Maxion, Roy A. and Townsend, Tahlia N. (2002). Masquerade detection using truncated command lines. *Int'l Conf. Dependable Systems and Networks*, pages 219–228.

[17] McConnell, J., Frincke, D., Tobin, D., Marconi, J, and Polla, D. (1998). A framework for cooperative intrusion detection. *21st National Information Systems Security Conference*, pages 361–373.

[18] Namjoo, M. (1982). Techniques for concurrent testing of VLSI processor operation. *Proc. International Test Conference*, pages 461–468.

[19] Porras, P.A. and Neumann, P.G. (Oct. 1997). EMERALD: Event monitoring enabling responses to anomalous live disturbances. *National Information Systems Security Conf.*, pages 353–365.

[20] Pradhan, D.K. (1996). *Fault tolerant computer system design*. Prentice-Hall.

[21] Roesch, M. (1999). Snort: Lightweight intrusion detection for networks. *USENIX LISA Conference*.

[22] Schuette, M.A. and Shen, J.P. (1987). Processor control flow monitoring using signatured instruction streams. *IEEE Transactions on Computers*, C-36(3):264–276.

[23] Snapp, S.R., Smaha, S.E., Grance, T., and Teal, D.M. (June 1992). The DIDS Distributed intrusion detection system prototype. *USENIX, 1992 Technical Conference*, pages 227–233.

[24] Spafford, Eugene H. and Zamboni, Diego (2000). Intrusion detection using autonomous agents. *Computer Networks*, 34(4):547–570.

[25] Spyrou, T. and Darzentas, J. (1996). Intention modeling: Approximating computer user intentions for detection and prediction of intrusions. *Information Systems Security*, pages 319–335.

[26] Staniford-Chen, S., Cheung, S., Crawford, R., Dilger, M., Frank, J., Hoagland, J., Levitt, K., Wee, C., Yip, R., and Zerkle, D. (1996). GrIDS – A graph-based intrusion detection system for large networks. *19th National Information Systems Security Conference*.

[27] Upadhyaya, S., Chinchani, R., and Kwiat, K. (2001). An analytical framework for reasoning about intrusions. *20th IEEE Symposium on Reliable Distributed Systems*, pages 99–108.

[28] Upadhyaya, S.J. and Ramamurthy, B. (1994). Concurrent process monitoring with no reference signatures. *IEEE Transactions on Computers*, 43(4):475–480.

[29] Wagner, David and Dean, Drew (2001). Intrusion detection via static analysis. *IEEE Security and Privacy Conference*.

[30] Wagner, David and Soto, Paolo (2002). Mimicry attacks on host-based intrusion detection systems. *ACM CSS*.

Chapter 9

TOPOLOGICAL ANALYSIS OF NETWORK ATTACK VULNERABILITY

Sushil Jajodia, Steven Noel, Brian O'Berry
Center for Secure Information Systems, George Mason University

Abstract: To understand overall vulnerability to network attack, one must consider attacker exploits not just in isolation, but also in combination. That is, one must analyze how low-level vulnerabilities can be combined to achieve high-level attack goals. In this chapter, we describe a tool that implements an integrated, topological approach to network vulnerability analysis. Our Topological Vulnerability Analysis (TVA) tool automates the labor-intensive type of analysis usually performed by penetration-testing experts. It is ideal for inexpensive what-if analyses of the impact of various network configurations on overall network security. The TVA tool includes modeling of network security conditions and attack techniques (exploits), automatic population of models via the Nessus vulnerability scanner, and analysis of exploit sequences (attack paths) leading to specific attack goals. Moreover, the tool generates a graph of dependencies among exploits that represents all possible attack paths without having to enumerate them. This representation enables highly scalable methods of vulnerability analysis, such as computing network configurations that guarantee the security of given network resources. Finally, this chapter describes some of the open technical challenges for the TVA approach.

Keywords: Network vulnerability analysis, network attack modeling, network hardening.

1.   INTRODUCTION

There are a number of tools available that can scan a network for known vulnerabilities. But such tools consider vulnerabilities in isolation, independent of one another. Unfortunately, the interdependency of vulnerabilities and the connectivity of networks make such analysis limited.

While a single vulnerability may not appear to pose a significant threat, a combination of such vulnerabilities may allow attackers to reach critical network resources.

Currently available tools generally give few clues as to how attackers might actually exploit combinations of vulnerabilities among multiple hosts to advance an attack on a network. After separating true vulnerabilities from false alarms, the security analyst is still left with just a set of known vulnerabilities. It can be difficult even for experienced analysts to recognize how an attacker might combine individual vulnerabilities to seriously compromise a network. For larger networks, the number of possible vulnerability combinations to consider can be overwhelming.

In this chapter, we describe a tool that implements a powerful topological approach to global network vulnerability analysis. Our Topological Vulnerability Analysis (TVA) tool considers combinations of modeled attacker exploits on a network and then discovers attack paths (sequences of exploits) leading to specific network targets. The discovered attack paths allow an assessment of the true vulnerability of critical network resources. TVA automates the type of labor-intensive analysis usually performed by penetration-testing experts. Moreover, it encourages inexpensive "what-if" analyses, in which candidate network configurations are tested for overall impact on network security.

In implementing TVA, we collect extensive information about known vulnerabilities and attack techniques. From this vulnerability/exploit database, we build a comprehensive rule base of exploits, with vulnerabilities and other network security conditions as exploit preconditions and postconditions.

In the network discovery phase of TVA, network vulnerability information is automatically gathered and correlated with the exploit rule base. In the analysis phase, we submit the resulting network attack model to a custom analysis engine. This engine models network attack behavior based on exploit rules and builds a graph of precondition/postcondition dependencies among exploits. The result is a set of attack paths leading from the initial network state to a pre-determined attack goal.

The next section describes the network attack problem, and Section 3 reviews related work. Section 4 describes how TVA specifically addresses the network attack problem. Section 5 applies TVA to the optimal hardening of a network, and Section 6 discusses some of the TVA technical challenges. Section 7 summarizes and concludes this chapter.

2. NETWORK ATTACK PROBLEM

We consider the complex problem of analyzing how attackers can combine low-level vulnerabilities to meet overall attack goals. Solving this problem involves modeling networks in terms of their security conditions, modeling atomic attacker exploits as transition rules among security conditions, and computing combinations of atomic exploits that lead to given network resources.

In this problem, we model the various security conditions a_i of a network as binary variables. In particular, the values model the conditions necessary for the attacker's success. For example, if some a_i represents a vulnerable version of a particular software component, $a_i = 1$ means the component exists and $a_i = 0$ means it does not. Under an assumption of monotonicity[1], a condition may transition from false to true but not back to false. That is, once a condition contributes to the success of an attack, it will always do so.

Next, we model the success of some attacker exploit $s_j \equiv s_j\left(a_{i_1}, a_{i_2}, \ldots, a_{i_k}\right)$ as a Boolean function of some set of conditions. For simplicity and without loss of generality, we model s_j as a conjunction, i.e., $s_j\left(a_{i_1}, a_{i_2}, \ldots, a_{i_k}\right) = a_{i_1} \wedge a_{i_2} \wedge \cdots \wedge a_{i_k}$. If an exploit involves disjunction (e.g. more than one version of a vulnerable program), we simply divide the disjunctive portions into separate conjunctive exploits. The success of an exploit s_j then induces some set of new conditions to become true, i.e., $s_j\left(a_{i_1}, a_{i_2}, \ldots, a_{i_k}\right) = 1$ implies $a_{p_1} = 1, a_{p_2} = 1, \ldots, a_{p_q} = 1$. In other words, s_j is a mapping from $s_j^{\text{pre}} = \left\{a_{i_1}, a_{i_2}, \ldots, a_{i_k}\right\}$ (s_j's *preconditions*) to $s_j^{\text{post}} = \left\{a_{p_1}, a_{p_2}, \ldots, a_{p_q}\right\}$ (s_j's *postconditions*) such that if all the preconditions in s_j^{pre} are true then all the preconditions in s_j^{post} become true.

Given a network attack model, the next step is to determine how the application of exploits (in terms of security conditions) impacts network vulnerability. This step involves discovering combinations of exploits that lead to the compromise of a given critical resource. That is, some security condition a_{goal} is designated as the goal of the attack. An *attack path* is then a sequence of exploits $s_{j_1}, s_{j_2}, \ldots, s_{j_l}$ that leads to a_{goal} becoming true. Of particular interest are *minimal* attack paths, such that all exploits in the path are necessary for achieving the attack goal.

Attack paths can help network administrators determine the best way to harden their networks. To ensure complete security, all attack paths must be accounted for. Some approaches in the literature do not report all paths, while other approaches explicitly enumerate all of them. For scalability, what is needed is a representation that allows the (implicit) analysis of all possible attack paths without explicitly enumerating them. For example, in terms of network hardening, it is sufficient to know that a particular exploit is required for all possible paths, without explicitly generating all of them.

In network hardening, it is also necessary to distinguish between two types of network security conditions. One type appears only as exploit preconditions. The only way that such conditions can be true is if they are true in the initial network conditions, since they are postconditions of no exploit. These initial conditions are precisely the ones we must consider for network-hardening measures. The other type of condition appears as both exploit preconditions and postconditions. We can safely disregard such conditions for network hardening, since attacker exploits can potentially make them true despite our hardening measures.

Given a set of initial conditions $A_{\text{init}} = \{c_1, c_2, \ldots, c_k\}$, we therefore wish to compute assignments of condition values (hardening measures) in A_{init} that guarantee the safety of a set of goal conditions $A_{\text{goal}} = \{g_1, g_2, \ldots, g_p\}$, i.e., $g_i = 0, \forall i$. Moreover, we wish to compute hardening measures that minimize assignments of $c_i = 0$, since such assignments generally have some cost associated with them, e.g., the application of a security patch or the disabling of a service.

3.   PREVIOUS APPROACHES

Several aspects of the TVA problem have been studied previously. While these studies have tended to focus on specific TVA-related subproblems, our goal is to develop TVA to its full potential.

For example, Swiler *et al.* [5] presents a tool for generating network attack graphs. In our TVA tool, we apply an alternative attack graph representation that is considerably more efficient, making the graphs feasible for larger networks. Templeton and Levitt [6] and Daley *et al.* [7] describe approaches for specifying attacks that are similar in spirit to our exploit modeling. These approaches focus primarily on modeling, but we include a subsequent analysis phase.

The application of model checking for network attack models was first proposed by Ritchey and Ammann [8]. More recently, Sheyner *et al.* [9] modified the Symbolic Model Verifier (SMV) model checker to find all possible attack paths rather than a single attack path.

We experimented with SMV as an initial TVA analysis engine, because we could deploy it off the shelf. But scalability problems with SMV led us to develop a custom analysis engine. Our analysis engine applies an efficient graph-based representation of exploit dependencies, as described in Section 4.2. The application of such a representation to network vulnerability analysis was first described by Ammann *et al.* [10].

A central aspect of TVA modeling is connectivity among machines. A layered connectivity structure is needed to represent the various network architectures and protocols. Our connectivity model mirrors the Transmission Control Protocol/Internet Protocol (TCP/IP) reference model and is described in more detail in [11].

4. DESCRIPTION OF TVA TOOL

In this section we describe our TVA tool for analyzing vulnerability to network attacks. The description includes the modeling of network attacks and the analysis of network attack models for discovering attack paths to given critical resources.

Figure 9-1 shows the overall architecture of our TVA tool. There are three components: (1) a knowledge base of modeled exploits, (2) a description of a network of interest, and (3) a specification of an attack scenario (attacker target, initial attack control, and network configuration changes). The TVA analysis engine merges these three components and then discovers attack paths (exploit combinations) based on the merged model.

We model exploits in terms of their preconditions and postconditions. That is, each exploit is a rule in which the occurrence of a particular set of preconditions induces a particular set of postconditions. The resulting set of exploit rules comprises an attack knowledge base. The exploits in the knowledge base are generic, i.e., independent of any particular network.

A network discovery component gathers configuration and connectivity information to produce a TVA network description. Here we use "network discovery" in a more general sense, i.e., it may include traditional network discovery tools, vulnerability scanners, and code to convert such tool outputs to a TVA network description. The network description and exploit knowledge base share a common name space, which enables the mapping of generic exploits to actual network elements.

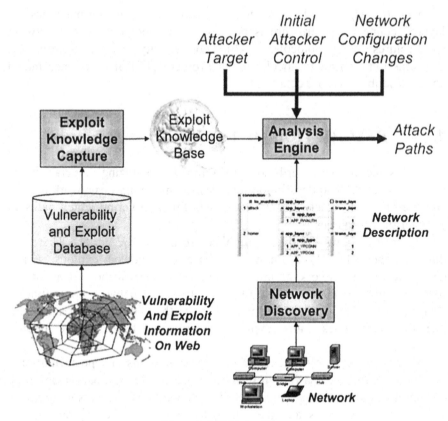

Figure 9-1. TVA Architecture

4.1 Modeling Network Attacks

Keeping pace with evolving threats and vulnerabilities requires an on-going effort in collecting information on network attacks that can be leveraged for TVA. The set of exploit rules in the TVA knowledge base must be comprehensive and up to date, since discovered attack paths will contain only those exploits that are actually included in the knowledge base.

Once raw information related to network attacks is gathered, we model it in terms of exploit preconditions/postconditions. For comprehensive and accurate results, this modeling requires a good understanding of attacker strategies, techniques, and tool capabilities. Exploit conditions can be any generic attributes that potentially impact network security.

Our TVA model structure is a hierarchical framework that serves as a taxonomy of model elements. The TVA model structure evolved as exploits were developed for various types of vulnerabilities. The evolving structure supports the effects of firewalls and other connectivity-related devices. Also important is the modeling of machine groups, such that a successful attack against one group member applies equally to other machines in the group[2].

In our experience, the TVA model structure in Figure 9-2 is flexible enough to address a full range of vulnerability types and network configuration variations. For example, we have implemented exploit rules for traffic sniffing, password capturing and cracking, file transfers, command shell access, X Window access, secure shell (ssh) public key authentication, buffer overflows that grant elevated user privileges, port forwarding, machine identity spoofing, and denial-of-service attacks.

In the next paragraph, we begin describing a way to automatically populate *network* models for TVA. However, it is much more difficult to automatically populate sets of modeled *exploits*. In particular, it is difficult to automatically capture the semantics needed for exploit preconditions and postconditions, because the vulnerability-reporting community has defined no standard formal language for specifying such semantics. Instead, databases of reported vulnerabilities usually rely on natural language text to describe vulnerabilities and ways of exploiting them. We have begun investigating how exploit semantics can be specified via web-based ontologies.

For TVA to be practical for real networks, it is important to automate the network discovery process. We have integrated our TVA tool with the open-source Nessus [1] vulnerability scanner. Nessus maps known vulnerabilities to network machines, reporting scan results using the eXtensible Markup Language (XML) [2]. The XML representation allows us to leverage the eXtensible Stylesheet Language (XSL) [3] to easily convert Nessus output to TVA input (which is also in XML).

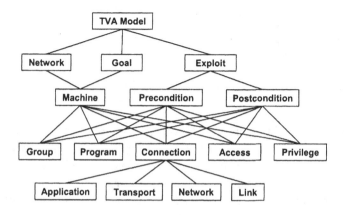

Figure 9-2. TVA Model Structure

To transform a Nessus report into a TVA network description, each reported Nessus vulnerability is cross-referenced against a list of known exploits. If a match is found, the Nessus vulnerability is applied as the name of a machine-connection precondition in the resulting network description. Nessus-based exploits may also have preconditions and/or postconditions for access type (e.g., execute or file transfer access) and privilege level (e.g., user or super user).

TVA maintains network connectivity details in separate tables that describe each machine's connections to the rest of the network. This means that firewalls don't have to be modeled directly because the individual host tables implicitly address their effects. However, multiple Nessus scans are required to correctly populate the connectivity tables when firewalls are present. In general, a separate Nessus scan is required for each network segment to which a firewall connects.

The network generation process merges the external and internal Nessus scans into a single coherent network description. The two-stage (external and internal) dataflow diagram for this process is shown in Figure 9-3. This process can be generalized in a straightforward fashion to handle arbitrary numbers of separate network segments.

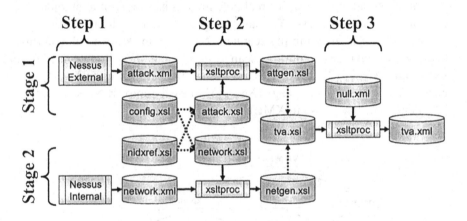

Figure 9-3. Generation of Network Description via Nessus

In the first step of this process, Nessus generates a vulnerability report for each network segment. In the second step, the Nessus report XML is processed against a Nessus cross-reference (nidxref.xsl), written in XSL. The second step optionally inserts configuration-specific information (contained in config.xsl) as specified by the TVA user. The nidxref.xsl stylesheet is produced by the Nessus exploit generation process described below. This stylesheet enables the network description to be optimized so that it contains only those Nessus connections for which exploits have been developed.

The last step merges the intermediate files from the second step into a single network description (tva.xml) that also incorporates an attack goal specification from the TVA user. The null.xml document is a dummy file that satisfies the XSL processor requirement [4] for an input XML file.

The process for generating TVA exploits from Nessus is shown in Figure 9-4. It begins with Nessus *plugins*, which contain the detailed information that Nessus needs for detecting vulnerabilities. We have developed a program (np2xp) to convert the Nessus plugins list into XML.

The resulting plugins.xml is then processed against the conditions.xsl stylesheet. This stylesheet is produced manually through researching the plugin information, e.g., consulting the relevant data in our vulnerability/exploit database. As we discussed earlier in this section, it is difficult to totally automate this manual step. The processing against conditions.xsl inserts the preconditions and postconditions developed through this exploit-modeling process. Finally, the resulting exploits.xml is transformed into Java modules and compiled into the TVA analysis engine. This process also generates the Nessus identification cross-reference file (nidxref.xsl) described earlier, which is in turn used to generate TVA network descriptions from Nessus scans.

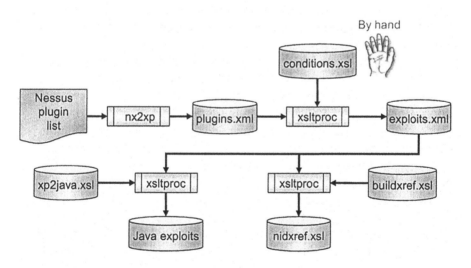

Figure 9-4. Generation of Exploits via Nessus

4.2   Network Attack Analysis

Given a particular TVA model (network description and set of exploits), we analyze the model to discover attack paths to critical network resources. From these attack paths we can then derive an expression for network safety in terms of the initial configuration. This safety expression in turn supports decisions about hardening the network against attacks.

We begin with a set of exploits $S = \{s_1, s_2, ...\}$ in terms of security conditions $A = \{a_1, a_2, ...\}$. These exploits and conditions conform to the modeling framework described in Section 4.1. The network attack model (network conditions and exploits) can be built by hand, automatically generated, or a combination of both.

The attack paths we compute are based on a directed graph of the dependencies (via preconditions and postconditions) among exploits and conditions. One way is to represent conditions as graph vertices and exploits as (labeled) graph edges. The dual of this representation is also possible, with exploits as graph vertices and conditions as labeled graph edges.

We employ a third representation that is a bit more flexible. This representation has both conditions and exploits as vertices. Edge labels then become unnecessary, with directed edges simply representing generic dependency. In this representation, a dependency edge $e = (a, s)$ going from condition a to exploit s means that s depends on a, i.e., a is a precondition of s. Similarly, a dependency edge $e = (s, a)$ going from exploit s to condition a means that a depends on s, i.e., a is a postcondition of s.

We build the dependency graph through a multi-step process. We first build the set of all exploits $S_{exec} \subset S$ that can be successfully executed by the attacker. Working from S_{exec}, we then build a dependency graph D_{init} starting from the initial condition exploit s_{init}. That is, we start from s_{init}, search S_{exec} for exploits whose preconditions match the postconditions of s_{init}, add exploit dependencies for any s_{found} found, and then remove s_{found} from S_{exec}. We continue by iteratively adding dependencies to D_{init} by searching S_{exec} and removing s_{found} from S_{exec}. The resulting graph D_{init} represents forward dependencies from s_{init}, i.e., exploits in D_{init} are those that are forward-reachable from s_{init}.

Next we do a backward traversal of the forward-reachable dependency graph D_{init}, starting from the attack goal exploit s_{goal}. The resulting dependency graph D includes exploits that are not only reachable from the initial conditions, but are also relevant to (i.e., reachable from) the attack goal. In fact, D comprises the necessary and sufficient set of exploits with respect to the initial and goal conditions, i.e., all exploits can be executed, and all exploits contribute to the attack goal. Thus D represents the set of minimal attack paths, in which no exploit can be removed without impacting the overall attack.

Given a dependency graph D, we then construct an expression that concisely represents all possible attack paths. This construction involves the recursive algebraic substitution of exploits (via precondition/postcondition dependencies) in the backward direction, starting from the goal-condition exploit s_{goal}. That is, we start from s_{goal} and algebraically substitute it with the conjunction of its preconditions, i.e. $s_{goal} \rightarrow \{a_{goal_1}, a_{goal_2}, \ldots, a_{goal_k}\}$.

We then substitute each of the goal-condition preconditions a_{goal_i} with the exploit that yields it as a postcondition, since these are logically equivalent. In the event that more than one exploit yields this postcondition, we form the disjunction of all such exploits, since logically any one of them could provide the postcondition independent of the others.

We continue in a recursive fashion, substituting the newly generated exploit expressions in the same way we treated the goal-condition exploit expression. In doing this recursive algebraic substitution, we make direct use of the exploit-condition dependency graph by traversing it breadth first. Once the dependency graph has been fully traversed, the result is a concise expression that represents all possible attack paths to the goal.

Initial-condition assignments of false mean that the corresponding network services are unavailable. It is desirable to choose assignments with minimal impact on network services. We can immediately choose one assignment over another if all of its disabled services also appear disabled in the other set. This choice is desirable because the selected set represents a comparative increase in available services. Moreover, this choice is neutral with respect to relative priorities of network services, since no service is disabled in the chosen set in comparison to the other.

This analysis yields all possible hardening measures (sets of initial-condition assignments) that have minimal impact on services. The analyst can now compare the various sets and select the one that offers the best combination of offered services.

5.   EXAMPLE TVA APPLICATION

In this section, we demonstrate by example how TVA combines vulnerabilities in a network to find attack paths to a particular goal. We then analyze the TVA results to determine the best way to harden the network against attack.

In this example, a restrictive firewall protects the machines that support public web and email services, as shown in Figure 9-5. This example shows how connectivity-limiting devices affect the TVA model and how vulnerable services on a network can be exploited even when direct access to services is blocked.

The firewall implements the following policy to restrict connectivity from the attack machine:

1. Incoming ssh traffic is permitted to both *maude* and *ned*, although only *ned* is running the service (this is a common practice under the assumption that it is safe because ssh is a secure protocol);
2. Incoming web traffic is permitted only to *maude*, which is running Microsoft's Internet Information Server (IIS);
3. Incoming email is permitted to *ned*, which is running the sendmail server;
4. Incoming File Transfer Protocol (FTP) traffic is blocked because *ned* is running the wu_ftpd server, which has a history of vulnerabilities;
5. All outgoing traffic is permitted (this is a common practice under the assumption that outgoing traffic won't harm the internal network).

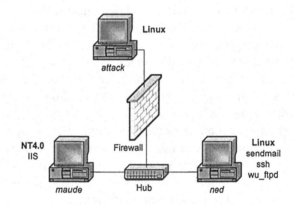

Figure 9-5. Network Diagram for Example TVA Application

The attack goal for this example is to obtain super user (root) access on *ned*. This is not directly possible because (1) no known exploits exist for the version of sendmail running on *ned*, and (2) the firewall blocks access to the vulnerable wu_ftpd service from the attack machine. The question now is whether the attack goal can be realized indirectly, i.e., through a sequence of multiple exploits.

The initial locus of attack is on the attack machine, since only that machine has user access and privilege defined as an initial condition, via the TVA network description. In general, the initial attack machine will also tend to have a complete set of programs used by the exploits in the model. Network connectivity is represented at the machine level by listing all possible connections from the given machine to all other destination machines in the network description. The effect of a firewall or other connectivity-limiting device is to reduce the size of each machine's connectivity table, but such devices generally will not appear as specific machines in the network description unless they run their own services to which other machines can connect. For this scenario, the firewall did not support any such services.

The attack goal is represented in the network description as a particular set of resources on a particular machine (the goal machine could appear elsewhere in the network description, with any set of initial conditions defined for it). In this example, we are only testing whether execute access (the ability to run programs) with super user (root) privilege can be obtained on *ned*. However, in general it is possible to test any other conditions, such as the appearance of any new connectivity or program in its configuration.

Figure 9-6 shows the resulting TVA attack graph for this example. For clarity, the specific exploit preconditions and postconditions are omitted from the figure, but they are described in Table 9-1.

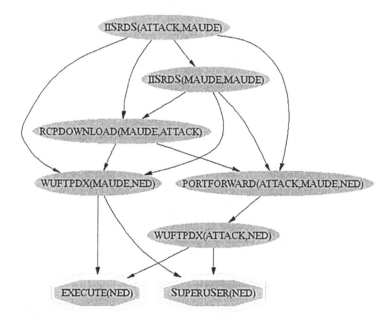

Figure 9-6. Attack Graph for Example Application of TVA

Despite the firewall policy designed to protect it, the external attacker obtains execute access with super user privilege on *ned*. The attack graph shows that the initial exploitation of the IIS vulnerability on *maude* ultimately leads to the compromise of *ned*, e.g., the following:

1. The IIS Remote Data Services (RDS) exploit enables the attacker to execute programs on *maude*;
2. Given the access provided by the IIS RDS exploit, the remote copy[3] (rcp) program on *maude* is executed to download a rootkit[4] from the *attack* machine;
3. A port-forwarding program from the rootkit is then executed to set up access from the *attack* machine through *maude* to the FTP service on *ned*;
4. Finally, the wu_ftpd exploit is executed through the forwarded connection against *ned* to obtain root access there.

Table 9-1. Exploits for Example Application of TVA

Exploit	Description	Preconditions	Postcondition
IISRDS	One of many exploits associated with Microsoft's Internet Information Server (IIS)	1. Execute access on attack machine 2. Attack machine has connectivity to IIS service on victim	Ability to execute programs on victim at super user privilege level
RCPDOWNLOAD	Binds rsh access to the ability to transfer programs (e.g., rootkits) from victim machine using the rcp program	1. Execute access on attack machine 2. rcp program on attack machine 3. Attack machine has connectivity to victim's rsh service	Copies victim machine's programs to attack machine
WUFTPDX	Yields super user on many Unix platforms that run the Washington University FTP daemon, wu-ftpd	1. Execute access on attack machine 2. wu-ftpd exploit program exists on attack machine 3. Attack machine has connectivity to FTP service on victim	Super user execute access on victim
PORTFORWARD	Enables attacker to work around firewall when foothold obtained on an internal machine. One of few exploits that implements "middleman" machine to direct exploits against victim machine.	1. Middleman and victim are different machines (implicit, not in attack graph) 2. Execute access on middleman 3. Port-forwarding program on middleman 4. Attacker connectivity to transport-layer (unused) port on middleman	Attacker acquires middleman's transport layer connectivity to victim

Finding such attack paths is a unique TVA capability. No commercial tool connected outside the firewall is currently capable of reporting more than an IIS vulnerability on *maude*. Connected inside the firewall, a commercial tool would also report the vulnerable wu_ftpd service, but human analysis would still be required to build an attack path from the outside through *maude* to *ned*. This would be an easy enough exercise for an experienced penetration tester working on such a small network. But it would be infeasible for networks in which voluminous outputs must be analyzed manually for large numbers of machines.

From a TVA attack graph, we can immediately compute an expression for the attack-goal conditions in terms of the initial conditions. This process involves traversing the attack graph in a backwards direction, algebraically substituting exploits with those exploits that satisfy their preconditions. This computation is done recursively, with the recursion ending when an exploit's precondition is an initial condition.

As we explained in Section 2, the only conditions relevant to network hardening are the initial conditions. An expression $g(c_1, c_2, \ldots, c_k)$ for the attack goal in terms of initial conditions $C_{init} = \{c_1, c_2, \ldots, c_k\}$ then provides a way to determine if a particular network configuration is guaranteed safe with respect to the attack goal. From the particular form of g, we can determine the safe assignments of A_{init}.

Figure 9-7 again shows the TVA attack graph for this example, this time with the initial conditions included. For convenience, the figure includes algebraic symbols that correspond to our analysis of network hardening. In particular, exploits are denoted by Greek letters, and initial conditions are denoted by c_i.

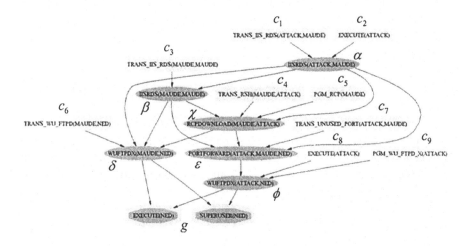

Figure 9-7. Attack Graph with Exploit Preconditions Included

By examining Figure 9-7, we can traverse the attack graph backwards, starting from the goal condition g, and recursively perform algebraic substitution according to precondition/postcondition dependencies.

$$
\begin{aligned}
g &= \delta + \phi \\
&= (\alpha + \beta)\chi c_6 + \varepsilon c_8 c_9 \\
&= (\alpha + \alpha c_3)\chi c_6 + (\alpha + \beta)\chi c_7 c_8 c_9 \\
&= \alpha(\alpha + \beta)c_4 c_5 c_6 + \alpha(\alpha + \beta)c_4 c_5 c_7 c_8 c_9 \\
&= \alpha c_4 c_5 c_6 + \alpha c_4 c_5 c_7 c_8 c_9 \\
&= c_1 c_2 c_4 c_5 c_6 + c_1 c_2 c_4 c_5 c_7 c_8 c_9 \\
&= c_1 c_2 c_4 c_5 (c_6 + c_7 c_8 c_9)
\end{aligned}
\tag{1}
$$

In terms of the problem domain, some initial conditions are outside the network administrator's control. In particular, the administrator has no control over conditions like programs and user access/privilege on the attacker's machine. Thus we have $c_2 = c_8 = c_9 = 1$, so that Eq. (1) becomes

$$
g = c_1 c_4 c_5 (c_6 + c_7)
\tag{2}
$$

From Eq. (2), four assignments of initial conditions are apparent that provide network safety. While other safe assignments are also possible, these four minimize the cost of hardening the example network:
1. Patch or disable the IIS RDS web server on *maude* ($c_1 = 0$);
2. Disable outgoing rsh from *maude* ($c_4 = 0$);
3. Remove the rcp program from *maude* ($c_5 = 0$);
4. Patch or disable wu_ftpd from *maude* to *ned*, and block all unused ports on *maude* ($c_6 + c_7 = 0$).

When considered separately, each of these four options has a minimal hardening cost, in the sense that no hardening measure can be ignored without jeopardizing the attack goal. The network administrator can then choose the option that has overall minimum cost, based on the relative costs of the individual hardening measures.

6.   TECHNICAL CHALLANGES

The TVA modeling framework supports the full range of network and exploit information needed for realistic scenarios. But to make TVA feasible for large networks, automatic model generation methods are needed.

As described in Section 4.1, we currently create TVA network descriptions via the Nessus vulnerability scanner. But Nessus lacks the ability to provide certain types of information. For example, with Nessus we must assume that firewalls enforce generic policies for the individual network segments. Although this may be an acceptable approximation of firewall effects, real policies often include host-specific rules.

While host-specific rules could be handled by individual Nessus scans from each machine in the network, this procedure is not very efficient. A more efficient solution would be to build TVA models directly from firewall filter tables. Also, while transport and application layer information is available from Nessus, additional topology information is needed to delineate between the link and network TCP/IP layers.

Although Nessus can guess a remote machine's operating system, it is not always correct and often cannot determine a specific version. Many exploits depend on detailed information about the operating system. Vulnerabilities are often removed by applying a patch to the applicable operating system or application. Patch-level information is therefore required for accurate exploit modeling.

Nessus scans for vulnerabilities from a remote location, so it can only detect network service information. However, many vulnerabilities are local and are not exploitable or detectable over a network. Processes are required to gather program-specific information from individual hosts, e.g., from host configuration files. For example, some trust relationship and group membership information is difficult to obtain remotely. This information is valuable for TVA, to determine whether an exploit is really possible or whether it affects machines other than the immediate target.

As one can imagine, TVA attack graphs might become huge for large, poorly secured networks. Analytical and visual methods are necessary for handling such (quadratic) attack-graph complexity, such as aggregating parts of the graph as summary information or culling parts of the graph not of immediate interest. We have developed a prototype drill-down visualization tool that shows great promise in solving the attack graph management problem.

A current bottleneck for TVA implementation is the process of modeling exploits manually. The problem is that much of the domain knowledge is available only as natural-language text. What is needed are exploit specifications written in a standard, machine-understandable language.

It appears that this requirement can be met by the emerging Semantic Web [12] under development by the World Wide Web Consortium. The vision is that web content of the future will be defined and linked in a way that it can be used for automation, integration, and reuse across various applications, not just for display purposes as with Hypertext Markup Language (HTML). With the Semantic Web, standardized rule-based markup provides the actual semantics (meaning) for web content.

TVA has potential application beyond penetration testing and network hardening. For example, it can be applied to the tuning of intrusion detection systems. In practice, network administrators must often balance the risk of attack against the need to offer services. Even with network hardening guided by TVA, administrators may still decide to tolerate some residual network vulnerability from services they absolutely need. The intrusion detection system could be configured to consider only this residual vulnerability and thus generate alarms only in the context of genuine threats to critical network resources.

At a minimum, vulnerabilities that do not significantly contribute to overall risk can be ignored, reducing the effective false-positive rate. It may also be possible to infer new intrusion signatures from TVA results, in turn increasing the number of true positive detections.

But there is a limit to what can be accomplished with network hardening and intrusion detection. The need to offer services is at odds with network hardening, and effective intrusion detection will remain challenging, particularly in the face of novel attacks.

To augment methods of avoidance and detection, TVA can be applied to attack response, both defensive and offensive. For defensive response, the network is dynamically hardened in the face of attacks. A less conservative approach is to launch an offensive counterattack in response to an attack against one's own network. While approach may be extreme, it could be the only available option for allowing a network to function after being attacked.

7.   SUMMARY AND CONCLUSIONS

This chapter describes a tool for Topological Vulnerability Analysis (TVA), a powerful approach to global network vulnerability analysis. The tool analyzes dependencies among modeled attacker exploits, in terms of attack paths (sequences of exploits) to specific network targets. While the current generation of commercial vulnerability scanners generates voluminous information on vulnerabilities considered in isolation, they give little clues as to how attackers might combine them to advance an attack.

The tool automates the type of labor-intensive analysis usually performed by penetration-testing experts, providing a thorough understanding of the vulnerabilities of critical network resources. It encourages inexpensive what-if analyses of the impact of candidate network configurations on overall network security.

Also, the tool employs a comprehensive database of known vulnerabilities and attack techniques. This database includes a comprehensive rule base of exploits, with vulnerabilities and other network security conditions serving as exploit preconditions and postconditions.

During TVA network discovery, network vulnerability information is gathered and correlated with exploit rules via the open-source Nessus vulnerability scanner. Our custom TVA analysis engine then models network attack behavior based on the exploit rules, building a graph of precondition/postcondition dependencies. This graph provides attack paths leading from the initial network state to a specified goal state. From the attack graph, we can determine safe network configurations with respect to the goal, including those that maximize available network services.

Our TVA tool provides powerful new capabilities for network vulnerability analysis. It enables network administrators to choose network configurations that are provably secure and minimize the cost of network hardening. TVA also has potential application to other key areas of network security, such as identifying possible attack responses and tuning intrusion detection systems.

ACKNOWLEDGEMENTS

We gratefully acknowledge the software development efforts of Michael Jacobs in support of this chapter. The work of Sushil Jajodia was partially supported by the Virginia Commonwealth Information Security Center (www.cisc.jmu.edu).

NOTES

1. In the context of network security, our assumption of monotonicity is quite reasonable. It simply means that once an attacker gains control of a resource, he need never relinquish it in order to further advance the attack. In other words, no backtracking is necessary.
2. An example of machine group effects is that guessing a Windows NT domain user password would probably allow login to all machines in the domain.
3. The rcp program is installed by default with Windows NT 4.0.
4. A "rootkit" is a hacker term that refers to tools an attacker often transfers to a compromised machine for the purpose of expanding access or escalating privileges.

REFERENCES

[1]   R. Deraison, *Nessus*, Retrieved from http://www.nessus.org, May 2003.
[2]   World Wide Web Consortium, *Extensible Markup Language (XML)*, Retrieved from http://www.w3.org/XML/, May 2003.
[3]   World Wide Web Consortium, *The Extensible Stylesheet Language (XSL)*, Retrieved from http://www.w3.org/Style/XSL/, May 2003.
[4]   World Wide Web Consortium, *XSL Transformations (XSLT) Version 1.0.*, Retrieved from http://www.w3.org/TR/xslt, May 2003.
[5]   L. Swiler, C. Phillips, D. Ellis, and S. Chakerian, Computer-attack graph generation tool, In *Proceedings of the DARPA Information Survivability Conference & Exposition II*, 307-321, 2001.
[6]   S. Templeton and K. Levitt, A requires/provides model for computer attacks, In *Proceedings of New Security Paradigms Workshop*, 19-21, 2000.
[7]   K. Daley, R. Larson, and J. Dawkins, A structural framework for modeling multi-stage network attacks, Presented at *International Conference on Parallel Processing Workshops*, 5-10, 2002.
[8]   R. Ritchey and P. Ammann, Using model checking to analyze network vulnerabilities, In *Proceedings of the IEEE Symposium on Security and Privacy*, 156-165, 2000.
[9]   O. Sheyner, J. Haines, S. Jha, R. Lippmann, and J. Wing, Automated generation and analysis of attack graphs, In *Proceedings of the IEEE Symposium on Security and Privacy*, 254-265, 2002.
[10]   P. Ammann, D. Wijesekera, and S. Kaushik, Scalable, graph-based network vulnerability analysis, In *Proceedings of 9th ACM Conference on Computer and Communications Security (ACM-CCS 2002)*, 217-224, 2002.
[11]   R. Ritchey, B. O'Berry and S. Noel, Representing TCP/IP connectivity for topological analysis of network security, In *Proceedings of 18th Annual Computer Security Applications Conference*, 156-165, 2002.
[12]   World Wide Web Consortium, *Semantic Web*, Retrieved from www.w3.org/2001/sw/, May 2003.

Chapter 10

ANALYZING SURVIVABLE COMPUTATION IN CRITICAL INFRASTRUCTURES

Yvo Desmedt

Computer Science Department, Florida State University

Abstract: For centuries, our society relied on mechanical technology. Today, it is being computerized to such an extent that we are becoming very dependent on computer technology. This makes cyber attacks a potential threat to our society. Heuristics is one approach to analyzing which infrastructures are critical and vulnerable. We will discuss several methods that can be used to analyze this topic more scientifically. The methods are independent of the type of attacks the enemy uses, whether, e.g. a traditional bomb or cyber terrorism.

Keywords: Critical Infrastructure, adversarial structure, flow, model, security, AND/OR graph

1. INTRODUCTION

The first industrial revolution made us very dependent on mechanical devices. Some mechanical devices played a more important role than others. Ballbearings were viewed as the most critical component.

Today, we are moving towards an information technology society. Computers (general purpose as well as dedicated ones) control and manage several aspects of our society. Examples are the use of computers for bookkeeping, in sensors and control units. In large plants, several dedicated computers as well as general purpose computers are commonly used. Computers are also deployed extensively in modern communication equipment, in database systems (e.g., airline reservation systems), etc. Essentially, our society has become quite dependent on computers.

When a home computer is maliciously shut down, the applications on the computer, such as word processing, are no longer available. The impact of unavailability (e.g., caused by a denial of service) may be much greater for one application than for another. For example, compare a word processor program used on a PC at home, versus computers used to manage the stock market, or used in airline reservation systems. Aside from direct impacts of shutdowns or incorrect computations (or other security failures), there are also indirect impacts. Indeed, a shutdown of a computer, e.g., one used to control mechanical, chemical and other processes, may have a ripple through effect on the economy as a whole.

Although there has been a lot of research on information security [2, 24], there are still several problems. Some research problems have not been sufficiently addressed. Indeed, computer viruses continue to pose a major threat today, as they did 15 years ago. Yet, there is no major effort anymore to develop a secure operating system [27]. So, it is unlikely we will see inexpensive computer security deployed on a large scale. This implies that in order to protect our critical infrastructure, we must identify which parts of the infrastructure are truly critical. Indeed, failure to do this correctly may result in "over-protecting" infrastructures that are in fact less critical, wasting resources and creating a false impression of security.

An important question is *how* to identify which infrastructures are critical. One approach is ad-hoc. That approach was used by the President's Commission on Critical Infrastructure Protection during the Clinton administration [26]. In that case, there was almost a one-to-one mapping between the infrastructures identified as critical and the employers of the members of the commission. So, unfortunately, the commission clearly failed to fully analyze which infrastructures outside their area of expertise should have been added to the list. For example, the food distribution and production industry is one of the many that clearly seems critical. It is now included in the list of President's National Strategy for Homeland Security [20]. However, how can we ensure that the list is now complete and the most critical infrastructures are identified? A different approach is, therefore, to find a more scientific method for identifying them.

In Section 2, we will discuss a method for modeling both the "mechanical" as well as the information technology aspects of our society. In Section 3, we will reflect and improve on the typical approaches used to model the enemy. The strength of the models used here is that these models are independent of the type of attack the enemy uses. In Section 4, we will survey how flow can be used to measure what is critical, and what results have been found so far using this method. A problem with the flow based method is that it does not allow for dealing with multiple applications that have different relative impacts. A method inspired by economics is surveyed in Section 5. In Section 6 we will end by examining open problems, and then conclude.

2.   HOW TO MODEL THE INFRASTRUCTURES

When talking to an industrial or a mechanical engineer, one discovers that the different sectors involved in making a product, like a car, are modeled using a PERT directed graph (digraph) [16]. PERT stands for *Program Evaluation and Review Technique*. A computer scientist models communication networks [18] by (directed) graphs. So, it seems that since both use graphs, we could easily merge our mechanical (chemical, etc.) world with our information technology one. Unfortunately, these two graphs are used in very different ways.

When a PERT digraph is used, an output, (a sink), often corresponds to a product/task that plays no role in other products/tasks. For example, in the production of a car, (where nodes correspond to a sector of the economy), the sink node corresponds to the production of cars and other nodes correspond to the tire manufacturing sector, the rubber sector, the steel sector, etc. The outgoing edges represent the products/tasks that are the output of the node, which is the corresponding infrastructure/task. A node can only produce an output provided that the required input(s) from *each* incoming input edge is available. For example a car needs 4 tires, *and* a motor, etc.

In a network directed graph, data can flow from one node A to a node B via *any* directed path from A to B (provided there is no congestion). So, when one compares PERT digraphs with network, one observes that the role of a node differs. In the PERT graph, the node corresponds to an "AND" in the sense that to produce the output all inputs are required. On the other hand, in a network graph, the node corresponds to an "OR." Indeed, a node can provide an output, provided an input is available from just one input. Note that this AND or OR should *not* be viewed as logical gates!

So, it seems that combining a mechanical society and an information technology one is more difficult. However, the Artificial Intelligence concept of AND/OR graph [25] permits the merging of these, as suggested in [5]. We will now survey this approach, focusing on the car production example.

While the PERT graph models infrastructures, it cannot deal with redundancy. Usually there is more than one factory that produces tires. So, a car manufacturing plant could choose tires from different tire manufacturing plants. This point is important when one tire manufacturing plant is shut down. So, a node labeled OR can be used to indicate this redundancy. A node labeled AND is used to indicate that all inputs are needed. A manufacturing plant corresponds in practice to a few AND/OR labeled nodes. This unifying approach obviously allows modeling PERT directed graphs, network directed graphs, and what one could call a redundant PERT graph [9]. Therefore, the model does allow for integrating data networks with a mechanically oriented society.

3.   MODELING THE POTENTIAL OF AN ENEMY

Now that we have described a unifying approach to model infrastructures, another question is how to model the enemy. For many years the enemy was viewed as an outsider [29]. Today, such a model is clearly outdated. Indeed, computer viruses, worms [2] and vulnerable operating systems where user-friendliness is viewed as more important than security, allow an enemy to take over several computers. So, it has become clear that insiders may be corrupted.

The first model that described this is the threshold model, used by Blakley and Shamir [3, 28]. This was studied in a narrow context. The problem was that one wanted to back up a secret in n safes, while being afraid that a number, let's say[1] up to t, is not trustworthy. One does not know in advance which of these safes may be corrupted. The same threshold idea was used in the context of secure distributed computing. The original problem [22, 12] deals with n computers selecting a bit (or a leader), however t may deviate from the prescribed protocol. The question regarding how reliable communication remains possible under such an attack was studied in [17], and privacy was discussed as well in [13] (see also [11]). The problem of secure distributed computation in general was studied in [14, 1, 6]. Note that these studies assume that the nodes are general purpose computers, which in infrastructures is often false. Indeed, they could play mechanical, chemical or other non-computer roles. Furthermore, even if they are computers, they could be dedicated ones instead of general purpose ones.

Unfortunately, the threshold approach no longer properly mimics the power of an enemy. Indeed, few operating systems are around today. Moreover, the number of different types of CPUs used is small. So, why would it be harder for an enemy to break into $t + 1$ computers running on the same platform compared to attacking t computers on very different platforms. This seems illogical, particularly when taking into account that an enemy who has found a weakness against one platform can easily exploit it against several computers on the same platform. An initial approach to dealing with this problem is to assign an adversarial structure[2] Γ_{adv} which is a list of sets of nodes the enemy can corrupt [19].

So, the model used here assumes the enemy *can* take over some nodes, as defined by the adversarial structure. This model is in sharp contrast with some other approaches in which one hopes to build trusted computers [2] and/or be able to detect any intrusion. The model used corresponds more to the current reality, where computer viruses and worms take over some, but not all, computers. This is one of the major advantages of the model used.

Clearly this model of an enemy is very general. The problem with this model is that the size of an adversarial structure may be exponential in size of the number of nodes, making it impractical to work with. Recently, a threshold-platform model was introduced [4]. This model is based on the assumption that the cost of breaking into all machines running the same platform is not much more than breaking into a single one. However, the cost to break into computers on different platforms is assumed to be sufficiently higher than the cost of corrupting computers that rely on the same platform. The threshold is not based on the number of computers, but on the number of platforms an enemy can penetrate. This model can be justified using the model described in Section 5. Evidently, both the threshold and threshold-platform model are special cases of general adversarial structures.

A problem with all these models is that they do not take into account the impact of the attack. The above delineates which nodes the enemy can potentially take over. While several modern hackers want to demonstrate the feasibility of an attack, a strike against a (computer automated) infrastructure may be planned by an adversary who wants to optimize the impact of the attack. The adversarial structure does not model which of these choices specified by Γ is the most optimal from the enemy's viewpoint. Modeling this aspect is rather new and different approaches have been taken. In sections 4 and 5, we will discuss some metrics the enemy could choose when optimizing the attack. In these approaches, the infrastructure or economy as a whole is modeled using an AND/OR directed acyclic graph.

4.   A MINIMUM FLOW BASED APPROACH

The survival of our society depends on the flow of goods and data through distribution networks. Typical examples are food, fuel and water distribution. If such flows fall below a critical value, our economy will suffer and people may die. For simplicity, we will focus on a single flow application. In Section 5 we discuss how different applications can be weighted. Note that the number of cars produced by a car manufacturing plant can also be modeled using a flow model. We will now discuss how this approach proceeds in [9].

Flow model

To each edge $e \in E$ in the AND/OR directed acyclic graph $G(V, E)$ let capacity $c(e)$ correspond. We assume the capacity is discrete [9]. (Even if it were continuous, when a computerized control system is used, the data is represented in a discrete matter.) The flow $f(e)$ going through an edge e must be less or equal to the capacity $c(e)$. When we speak about a capacity c and flow f, we are referring to, respectively, all the capacities $c(e)$ and all flows $f(e)$ over all edges e. Note that both c and f can be viewed as functions with, as domain E, the set of all edges.

We will now explain models used to study the relation in a node between incoming and outgoing flows. In a typical water distribution system, the total flow coming into a node must equal the total outgoing flow to maintain mass preservation. So, this model seems fit to be used to describe the relation between incoming flows and outgoing ones in an OR labeled node, which usually deals with flows of the *same type* (e.g. tires, water, etc.). When reconsidering the use of AND nodes, as described in Section 2, we see that *different types* are typically used. Indeed, as previously stated, a car needs 4 tires, a motor, etc. So, there is a correlation between the incoming flows and outgoing flows. This could be modeled as follows. If v is a node labeled AND, let v^- be the set of incoming edges and v^+ be the set of outgoing ones. We then require that for each $e \in v^- \cup v^+$ there is a constant $c_{v,e}$, such that:

$$\forall e_1, e_2 \in v^- \cup v+ : c_{v,e_1} * f(e_1) = c_{v,e_2} * f(e_2) \qquad (10.1)$$

In [9], a different type of flow relation was used for nodes labeled AND. The main difference is that it assumed that any outgoing flow of an AND node is always less or equal to any of its incoming flows. This model is, for example, utilized when the AND/OR graph corresponds to distributed computation.

An alternative relation between flows coming into an OR labeled node and its outgoing flows may be needed when we deal with data. As already observed by Martelli and Montanari [23], data can be copied. In this case, the outgoing flow of *each* edge must be less than or equal to the total incoming flow into the node. This model is often called "additive."

The enemy's impact

We will now discuss some metrics the enemy could use to optimize the attack. The AND/OR acyclic directed graph has "sinks," which means, nodes without outgoing edges. In practice, these correspond to output nodes, such as those representing the final factory where goods are manufactured (e.g. a car manufacturing plant), or to consumers that use the product, like water. So, the total flow coming in such sinks can be used to measure the performance of the system. We call this *total flow* $F_f(G)$. The f indicates the flow used in the graph satisfying the conditions discussed in Section 4.0 (such as the fact that $f(e) \leq c(e)$).

Since $F_f(G)$ depends on f one might wonder what the maximum value is over all possible allowable values of f. We speak about the maximum capacity of the graph $C_c(G)$ as being this maximum. The c indicates that this value is a function of the capacities of the edges and, evidently, of the model used that describes the relation between incoming and outgoing flows into nodes.

We now model the *impact* of the enemy. This will again be modeled *independently* of the method of attack the enemy uses. Let us compare this approach with, for example, intrusion detection [7]. A major difference is that intrusion detection is a method which is limited to computer security. The approach used here does not have such a limitation. The goals are also distinct. While intrusion detection wants to detect an attack, this study wants to analyze what damage an enemy can cause on the critical infrastructure, if the enemy succeeds in an attack.

We will now focus on an enemy that destroys one or more nodes. This could be done using e.g. bombs, or some other type of sabotage. This may also be achieved by breaking into the computers that control the plant and cause a shutdown, or even an explosion in the case of a chemical plant [8, p. 257]. So, the outgoing flows of such a node drop to zero. When the system has enough redundancy, the impact of such node destruction does not necessarily imply that the total flow drops to zero. We will now describe this.

When the enemy destroys all the nodes in a set $U \subseteq V$, their flow drops to zero. One describes the remaining AND/OR graph with the remaining nodes $\bar{U} = V \setminus U$ and remaining edges. This then naturally defines $C_{c_{\bar{U}}}(G)$, the remaining capacity of the graph. Evidently, if the enemy has unlimited power, the enemy can destroy all nodes, and the capacity drops to zero. The case where the enemy can only destroy up to t nodes is therefore more interesting to study. As follows from Section 3, in general the enemy could only have the power to destroy a set of nodes U in $\Gamma_{adv}(V)$ (V indicates that $\Gamma_{adv}(V)$ is a list of subsets of V). We will now discuss how the enemy can choose an "optimal" set, U, out of the potential sets he can destroy.

The enemy could choose two strategies. In the first case, the enemy tries to reduce the remaining capacity below a critical value C_{crit}. So, the enemy will choose a set $U \in \Gamma_{adv}(V)$ such that $C_{c_{\bar{U}}}(G) < C_{crit}$. We call this a winning strategy for the adversary. If no such U exists the best the enemy can do is to do as much damage as possible. In this context this mean choosing a set $U \in \Gamma_{adv}(V)$ such that for any other $U' \in \Gamma_{adv} \, C_{c_{\bar{U}}}(G) \leq C_{c_{\bar{U}'}}(G)$. The last strategy may be a "losing strategy," however, it is the best available in view of the limited resources of the adversary.

The results of more detailed studies on these flow problems are described in [9]. This work demonstrates that for certain flow models it seems computationally hard for the enemy to choose an optimal or winning strategy.

An example

Ball-bearings were viewed as the most critical component of a mechanical infrastructure, as can be verified using a PERT graph model of the mechanical world. In such a PERT graph removing the single node of the ball-bearing sector implies that several outputs (such as cars, planes, tanks, etc.) can no longer be produced. Therefore, Nazi Germany's factories involved in making ball-bearings were targeted by bombing campaigns during World War II.

A problem with the PERT model is that it does not take redundancy into account. If enough factories (more than t) can produce ball-bearings and the enemy has the resources to only bomb t of these factories, then the approach discussed allows, e.g. to analyze whether the capacity remaining after the destruction of t factories is above C_{crit}.

We will come back to this example in Section 5.0.

Limitations of this approach

The flow approach is a useful tool to analyze the vulnerability of one infrastructure. However, when multiple infrastructures are involved, it does not allow them to be compared. The following method averts this problem.

5.   AN ECONOMICS BASED APPROACH

We will now survey the work in [10].

Modeling what the enemy can attack

A problem with the models described in Section 3 is that they describe what the enemy can do in a very general context. Indeed, the adversarial structure permits describing any subsets of nodes as being vulnerable. The question, however, remains: how to choose this adversarial structure. Before answering this question, we have a criticism against the traditional adversarial structure [19].

The adversarial structure models the nodes the enemy can take over. However, even if the adversary is unable to take over any nodes, the enemy can still control edges (links). Note that originally, as in the study of cryptography [24], the enemy was assumed to attack the edges, not the trusted nodes. One might wonder why the traditional adversarial structure models do not account for this. In a computer network, it may make sense to assume that the adversary succeeds in taking control of some nodes. Then the adversary has full control of the corresponding edges. When cryptographic tools are available, privacy and authenticity of the communication can easily be guaranteed. So, it may seem that the remaining edges are protected. Unfortunately, this does not handle denial of service attacks. So from now on, we will view the adversarial structure $\Gamma_{adv}(V \cup E)$ as a list of subsets of nodes and edges [10].

The question now is how to choose this adversarial structure. One method is to assume that to any attack, there corresponds a cost, and that the adversary has a limited budget. So to each $S \subseteq V \cup E$ corresponds a cost c_S for the adversary to take control of all these nodes or edges in S. The enemy has a budget B_E and

$$\Gamma_{adv}(V \cup E) = \{S \mid c_S \leq B_E\},$$

which means the adversary can attack a set of nodes and edges within the budget B_E [10]. Note that $\Gamma_{adv}(V \cup E)$ describes what the enemy *can* attack.

However, it does not say anything about what is most optimal for the adversary to attack.

As usual, in economic studies the unit does not need to be monetary. Indeed, a hacker's budget could be expressed in the numbers of free hours available.

It is important to observe that c_S is not necessarily linear. So, if $S = S_1 \cup S_2$ and $S_1 \cap S_2 = \emptyset$, then c_S is not necessarily equal to $c_{S_1} + c_{S_2}$. Indeed, if similar platforms are used in S_1 and S_2, then c_S may be only slightly larger than the maximum of c_{S_1} and c_{S_2}.

Optimizing the attack

As in Section 4, flows will be used to describe what is the most optimal for the enemy to attack. However, a weighting factor is now used to indicate its importance. When we consider an application a, to it corresponds the nodes/edges involved, which we call T_a, being a subgraph of an AND/OR acyclic directed graph. Note that different applications may use overlapping nodes/edges, so if $a \neq a'$ then $T_a \cap T_{a'}$ is not necessarily empty. Indeed, the same freeways and computer networks are involved in multiple applications.

To T_a may correspond a flow F_{T_a}, satisfying rules as discussed earlier on. Moreover, there is a maximum flow, or capacity C_{T_a}.

To an application a corresponds its impact factor I_a. This impact factor is not necessarily measured from a monetary viewpoint. E.g. terrorists may be interested in the psychological impact. So, if we consider several applications, or even the economy as a whole, to it corresponds a weighted total flow $F = g_F(F_{T_{a_1}}, F_{T_{a_2}}, \ldots)$ and a weighted total capacity $C = g_C(C_{T_{a_1}}, C_{T_{a_2}}, \ldots)$. Note that g_F and g_C are not necessarily linear, so F is not necessarily $\sum_a I_a F_{T_a}$.

When $S \in V \cup E$, we now define $C_{\bar{S}}$ as the remaining weighted capacity after the removal of the nodes and edges in S. So, as in Section 4, an enemy, in order to optimize the attack, will choose a set S of nodes and edges that is in $\Gamma_{adv}(V \cup E)$ such that $C_{\bar{S}} < C_{crit}$, where C_{crit} is now the weighted critical capacity. We call this a winning strategy for the adversary.

One may think that this economic approach is less powerful than an application oriented one. Indeed, suppose there is more than one application with a critical capacity. How can one guarantee that each application with a critical capacity is reflected? Since the weighted total capacity function g_C is non-linear, it is possible that when the enemy succeeds in having the capacity of one application fall below the critical value that $C_{\bar{S}} < C_{crit}$. It should also be clear now that this generality of this particular model is also its weakness. In order for it to be useful, approximations will have to be made so that one can make predictions.

The example revisited

As already stated, the problem with the flow based approach of Section 4 is that it does not combine different applications. To illustrate this let us focus on the example discussed in Section 4.0.

In the example of Section 4.0, one focuses on an enemy that targets the ball-bearing industry. However, even if the enemy may fail to reduce the remaining capacity of the ball-bearing industry to below its critical value, the enemy may be able to reduce the flow of the production of cars and planes (which need ball-bearings) to a level that affects the economy as a whole. This could be achieved by using a combined attack targeting ball-bearing as well as other nodes (being factories producing other components).

Protecting

When a system is being designed, the designer has a budget B_D. Furthermore, a minimum required weighted total capacity C_D is expected from the system. The designer is asked to build an AND/OR graph G such that:

- the cost$(G) \leq B_D$, and

- the weighted total capacity $\geq C_D$, and

- the enemy cannot win. This means that there is not a winning strategy for the enemy (see Section 5.0 for the definition of a winning strategy and Section 4.0 for a discussion of strategies in general).

If this is impossible, the enemy will win, or the budget will need to be increased.

Evidently, this approach is very general. To be used in practice, it would require a relation between the cost of security (setting up secure nodes and edges) and the cost of an attack. Today, no methods exist to tackle this problem. However, the economic approach may be useful for demonstrating that some models, such as the threshold model for the enemy (see Section 3), are unrealistic. It can be used as the foundation for proposing alternative models.

6.   FURTHER RESEARCH AND CONCLUSIONS

These models and their use are the result of many years of research. If our society wants to identify which infrastructures are truly the most critical, more refined and alternative models will have to be presented. We will now suggest some paths that could be followed, taking into account:

the dynamic aspect of our society. The above models are very static. As is common in control theory, time aspects could be included. This permits dealing with buffers. The buffers guarantee that if the enemy shuts down nodes and edges in S, and that even if $C_{\bar{S}} < C_{crit}$, the society could survive for a while. Obviously, if the control of these buffers is computerized, the adversary can try to target it, making the buffers less useful.

Recovery is also a dynamic aspect that must be studied. Indeed, destroyed infrastructures can often be rebuilt.

Note that C_{crit} is dynamic, too. If the adversary were to succeed in an attack that reduced the population significantly, the new C_{crit} would be lower, making it harder, potentially, for the enemy to inflict a second serious blow.

Destruction of nodes and edges may also result in an unacceptable slow down in production. If the nodes and edges that were destroyed had a relatively low delay, replacing them may increase the time to go from the input to the output. This problem is well known in the study of critical paths of PERT graphs [16]. Similar studies for AND/OR graphs can be found in [9], but they do not discuss the impact of the enemy. Another question is how hard it is for the enemy to optimize which nodes to destroy in an AND/OR graph to slow down the process the most.

that damaged nodes are not necessarily destroyed. In this context, several issues are not currently modeled. These are, for example:

- In the flow model, if the enemy takes over a node, the capacity of the outgoing edges is reduced to zero. In other words, the node "shuts down." However, not all attacks correspond with a reduction to a zero flow. The enemy may only be able to reduce the flow.

- It may also be undesirable if an adversary could increase a flow. Indeed, that would imply a waste of resources. If the system contains buffers, such an undesired increase may decrease the capability of recovering from an attack. For example, the enemy, having control of the computer facility that manages the flow coming from a buffer, such as a dam, may cause a spill by opening the floodgates.

- Modeling the enemy as just being able to stop, reduce or increase the flow is obviously not sufficient. As is well known by the work on secure distributed computing (see Section 3 for a short survey), the output of a node could be faulty. The same problem may occur with non-data items. In the case of, for example, computer controlled robots, the impact of an adversary breaking into a node may lead to the production of products that do not satisfy the specifications. So, the result is the flow of faulty products. This, if not detected, may have a ripple through effect. The problem of detecting whether an output is faulty may actually be (computationally) hard. In secure distributed computing, this problem is solved by having the node prove in "zero-knowledge" [15] that the output satisfies the specifications. Its generalization to a mechanical society would be to convince the user that the specifications are satisfied without revealing such information as the production method used. However, generalizing this idea to outside the area of information security seems non-trivial.

There are many more different approaches that can be followed. Some researchers have suggested using a probabilistic viewpoint [30]. The problem with this approach is that security is inherently non-ergodic. Another problem is that while the probability that an attack of catastrophic proportions could happen may be very small, the damage caused by it would be very large. Unfortunately, the product of a function f_1, whose limit is tending towards 0 and a function f_2, whose limit is growing to infinity is, in general, undefined!

In conclusion, we have surveyed theoretical approaches used in secure distributed computation. The advantage of these approaches is that these abstract away the method used by the enemy to attack. We have argued that the approaches must be adapted for dealing with critical infrastructures. Nodes are not necessarily general purpose computers, and the traditional network model does not take the AND condition into account. Reduction in flow is one way of measuring the effect of an attack. If the impact on several applications needs to be studied, an economic model seems the most natural. We believe that this approach is just the start towards more precise models that can be used to study the potential impact of cyberterrorism or cyberwar, combined with more classical means of destruction. Whether such large scale attacks will ever be used depends on socio-political arguments that go beyond scientific discussions and have therefore not been taken into account.

ACKNOWLEDGMENTS

Partial funding provided by grant DARPA F30602-97-1-0205 and by NSF CCR-0209092. However, the views and conclusions contained in this paper are those of the authors and should not be interpreted as necessarily representing the official policies or endorsements, either expressed or implied, of the Defense Advance Research Projects Agency (DARPA), the Air Force, of the US Government.

Notes

1. In secret sharing it is custom to call the maximum number of untrusted insiders $t - 1$, while in network security one says that up t insiders can be corrupted. Since the discussion in this chapter is more closely related to network reliability and security, we use t in both contexts.

2. This idea originated from the work on secret sharing [21]. In this earlier work, an access structure is defined as the dual (complement) of an adversarial structure. Further details of access structures and secret sharing are beyond the scope of this paper and can be found in [21].

REFERENCES

[1] M. Ben-Or, S. Goldwasser, and A. Wigderson. Completeness theorems for noncryptographic fault-tolerant distributed computation. In *Proceedings of the twentieth annual ACM Symp. Theory of Computing, STOC*, 1–10, 1988.

[2] M. Bishop. *Computer Security*. Addison-Wesley, Reading, MA, 1993.

[3] G. R. Blakley. Safeguarding cryptographic keys. In *Proc. Nat. Computer Conf. AFIPS Conf. Proc.*, 313–317, 1979. vol.48.

[4] M. Burmester and Y. Desmedt. Hierarchical public-key certification: The next target for hackers? Submitted October 2001 to Communications of the ACM, accepted February 21, 2003.

[5] M. Burmester, Y. Desmedt, and Y. Wang. Using approximation hardness to achieve dependable computation. In M. Luby, J. Rolim, and M. Serna, editors, *Randomization and Approximation Techniques in Computer Science, Proceedings (Lecture Notes in Computer Science 1518)*, 172–186. Springer-Verlag, 1998.

[6] D. Chaum, C. Crépeau, and I. Damgård. Multiparty unconditionally secure protocols. In *Proceedings of the twentieth annual ACM Symp. Theory of Computing, STOC*, 11–19, 1988.

[7] D. E. R. Denning. An intrusion-detection model. *IEEE Transactions on Software Engineering*, SE-13(2), 222–232, 1987.

[8] Y. Desmedt, J. Vandewalle, and R. Govaerts. Cryptography protects information against several frauds. In *Proc. Intern. Carnahan Conference on Security Technology*, 255–259, 1983. IEEE.

[9] Y. Desmedt and Y. Wang. Analyzing vulnerabilities of critical infrastructures using flows and critical vertices in and/or graphs. *International Journal of Foundations of Computer Science*, 15(1), 107–125, 2004.

[10] Y. Desmedt, M. Burmester, and Y. Wang. Using economics to model threats and security in distributed computing. Workshop on Economics and Information Security, Berkeley, May 16-17, 2002,
http://www.sims.berkeley.edu/resources/affiliates/workshops/econsecurity/econws/33.ps.

[11] Y. Desmedt and Y. Wang. Perfectly secure message transmission revisited. In L. Knudsen, editor, *Advances in Cryptology — Eurocrypt 2002, Proceedings (Lecture Notes in Computer Science 2332)*, 502–517. Springer-Verlag, 2002.

[12] D. Dolev. The Byzantine generals strike again. *Journal of Algorithms*, 3, 14–30, 1982.

[13] D. Dolev, C. Dwork, O. Waarts, and M. Yung. Perfectly secure message transmission. *Journal of the ACM*, 40(1), 17–47, 1993.

[14] O. Goldreich, S. Micali, and A. Wigderson. Proofs that yield nothing but their validity and a methodology of cryptographic protocol design. In *27th Annual Symp. on Foundations of Computer Science (FOCS)*, 174–187. IEEE Computer Society Press, 1986.

[15] S. Goldwasser, S. Micali, and C. Rackoff. The knowledge complexity of interactive proof systems. *SIAM J. Comput.*, 18(1), 186–208, 1989.

[16] M. Gondran and M. Minoux. *Graphs and Algorithms*. John Wiley & Sons Ltd., New York, 1984.

[17] V. Hadzilacos. *Issues of Fault Tolerance in Concurrent Computations*. PhD thesis, Harvard University, Cambridge, Massachusetts, 1984.

[18] F. Halsall. *Data Communications, Computer Networks and Open Systems*. Addison-Wesley, Reading, MA, 1996.

[19] M. Hirt and U. Maurer. Player simulation and general adversary structures in perfect multiparty computation. *Journal of Cryptology*, 13(1), 31–60, 2000.

[20] Information analysis and infrastructure protection: Q's & A's.
http://www.ciao.gov/publicaffairs/qsandas.htm.

[21] M. Ito, A. Saito, and T. Nishizeki. Secret sharing schemes realizing general access structures. In *Proc. IEEE Global Telecommunications Conf., Globecom'87*, 99–102. IEEE Communications Soc. Press, 1987.

[22] L. Lamport, R. Shostak, and M. Pease. The Byzantine generals problem. *ACM Transactions on programming languages and systems*, 4(2), 382–401, 1982.

[23] A. Martelli and U. Montanari. Additive and/or graphs. In *Proceedings of the Third International Joint Conference on Artificial Intelligence*, 1–11. Morgan Kaufmann Publishers, Inc., 1973.

[24] A. Menezes, P. van Oorschot, and S. Vanstone. *Applied Cryptography*. CRC, Boca Raton, 1996.

[25] N. J. Nilsson. *Principles of Artificial Intelligence*. Tioga, 1980.

[26] Critical foundations, the report of the President's Commission on Critical Infrastructure Protection. 1997.
http://www.ciao.gov/resource/pccip/PCCIP_Report.pdf

[27] C. P. Pfleeger. *Security in Computing*. Prentice-Hall, Englewood Cliffs, New Jersey, second edition, 1997.

[28] A. Shamir. How to share a secret. *Commun. ACM*, 22, 612–613, 1979.

[29] U.S. Department of Defense. *Department of Defense Trusted Computer System Evaluation Criteria*, 1983.

[30] H. R. Varian. PBIs on economics of computer security history background. www.sims.berkeley.edu/~hal/Talks/security.pdf, 1998.

Chapter 11

ALERT MANAGEMENT SYSTEMS: A QUICK INTRODUCTION

Robert L. Grossman
Laboratory for Advanced Computing, University of Illinois at Chicago, and Open Data Partners

Abstract: We describe a type of data mining system designed to screen events, build profiles associated with the events, and send alerts based upon the profiles and events. These types of systems are becoming known as alert management systems (AMS). We give some examples of alert management systems and give a quick introduction to their architecture and functionality.

Keywords: data mining, alert management systems, events, profiles, alerts

1.   INTRODUCTION

In this chapter, we give an overview of systems designed to screen events, build profiles associated with the events, and send alerts based upon the profiles and events. These types of systems are becoming known as alert management systems (AMS). In this paper, we give some examples of alert management systems and give a quick introduction to their architecture and functionality.

Section 2 contains a brief description of related work. Section 3 contains the key definitions. Sections 4 and 5 describe the functionality and architecture of alert management systems. Section 6 describes several examples. Section 7 describes some alert management systems built by the author and Section 8 contains the conclusion. Skimming the examples in Section 6 first may make the paper easier to understand.

2.   BACKGROUND AND RELATED WORK

One of the best understood examples of alert management systems are systems designed to detect fraud. Descriptions of fraud systems can be found in [1], [4], [6], [7]. As far as we are aware of the idea of abstracting the concepts of events, profiles, and alerts and considering a class of systems that uses these concepts for scoring, matching, routing, and linking appears to be novel. On the other hand, as the large number of examples described in Section 4 shows, various examples of alert management systems have been around for quite a long time. Additional references can be found in the references of the work cited above.

3. EVENTS, PROFILES, AND UPDATES

Alert management systems are based upon three primitive concepts: events, profiles, and updates, which we now describe.

1 *Profiles*, abstracting feature vectors, are modeled as an (unordered) set of vectors $\{x_i \in \mathbf{R}^N : i \in \mathcal{I}.\}$ The indices $i \in \mathcal{I}$ are called profile ids.

2 *Events*, abstracting transactional data, are modeled as an ordered set of $\{e_j : j \in \mathcal{J}\}$, with the following properties:

    (a) there is a map $\theta(e_j)$ assigning a profile id $i \in \mathcal{I}$ to each event e_j, $j \in \mathcal{J}$.

    (b) events can be concatenated $e_j \cdot e_k$ and this concatenation is associative $(e_i(e_j e_k)) = ((e_i e_j) e_k)$;

    The indices $j \in \mathcal{J}$ are called transaction ids.

3 An *update* is given by an action of events on profiles $e_k \cdot x_i$ with the following properties:

    (a) for an event e_k and a profile x_i,

$$e_k \cdot x_i \in \mathbf{R}^N,$$

    (b) $x_i = e_k \cdot x_i$, in case $\theta(e_k) \neq i$

    (c) For all events e_j and e_k

$$(e_j \cdot e_k) \cdot x_i = e_j \cdot (e_k \cdot x_i).$$

In words: transactional data are modeled by events; profiles summarize state information derived and aggregated from their associated events; and events update profiles. The update action captures the aggregation and computation of derived attributes which is usually involved when one or more transactions are used to update their corresponding profile.

Given an initial collection of profiles, the effect of transactional event data is to move each profile along an orbit.

In the paper [9], a very similar set up, dual to the set up here, is used to model events, profiles and updates.

4. FUNCTIONALITY

Although different alert management systems can have quite different functionality, many of them share the following core functionality: scoring, matching, routing, and linking. In this section, we give brief descriptions of each of these.

Scoring

Scoring is a function mapping profiles to a continuous

$$f : \mathbf{R}^N \longrightarrow \mathbf{R}$$

or finite set of values or labels

$$f : \mathbf{R}^N \longrightarrow \text{Labels}.$$

Alert management systems are often used for real time scoring in the following way:

1 Let e_j be an event associated with a profile ID i, i.e., $\theta(e_j) = i$.

2 Let x_i be the profile associated with profile ID i and

$$x_i' = e_j \cdot x_i$$

be the result of updating the profile with the event.

3 With this data, $f(x_i')$ is the result of scoring the updated profile using a scoring function $f(\cdot)$.

In other words, the event data is used to update the corresponding profile, which is then scored. The goal is to detect bad behavior as soon as possible.

Finally, the term *signature* is sometimes applied to an updating rule in which the old profile or score is averaged with the new profile or score. More precisely, using the notation above, a signature based update uses an update of the form

$$y_i' = \theta f(x_i') + (1 - \theta)y_i,$$

where y_i is the previous, y_i' is the new score, $x_i' = e_j \cdot x_i$ is the updated profile, and $f(x_i')$, the corresponding score. Here $\theta > 0$ is a constant. Signature based methods are described in [2] and [3]. Signature based methods are commonly used in alert management systems since signatures "smooth" blend new event information with historical information stored in the profile, something which in practice is quite helpful.

Matching

Sometimes associating a profile ID i in $\mathcal{I}$ with an event is straightforward and sometimes it can be quite challenging. For example, given a credit card transaction or call detail record if the profile ID is the account number or the calling number, then the profile ID is immediately and unambiguously available from the event data. On the other hand, if the profile ID must be matched against another list, such as list of customers, this can be more difficult. For example, is John Smith, 121 Oak Road, San Francisco, CA the same as J. Smithe, Oak Avenue, San Francisco, CA 94701? As the amount of data grows, this problem becomes computationally challenging. Even more difficult is the problem of associating a profile ID to an individual who is deliberately trying to make this task difficult, such as an individual engaged in fraud or other inappropriate activities. In this case, multiple variants of names, addresses and phone numbers may be used.

Alert management systems using matching to normalize names, addresses and similar information and to check names, addresses and related information against various lists. Alert management systems often contain both bad and good lists, i.e. lists containing individuals which must be check more carefully (bad lists) and individuals which are known to the system and have already been vetted (good lists).

Workflow

Often after events and profiles have been scored and checked against good and bad lists, additional work is required. Further investigation may be warranted, checks against additional lists may be formed, various alerts may be sent, etc. For this reason, alert management systems often contain a workflow component containing rules describing the various types of further processing that is required. For example, workflow rules may be used to assign further investigative work to analysts based in part on the analysts current work load and area of expertise. In many cases, the impact of an alert management system is fundamentally dependent upon the quality of the workflow component. Even if the scoring component is extremely accurate with a very low false positive rate, nothing is gained unless the alerts produced by the score get to an individual analyst who can take the appropriate action at the appropriate time after having examined the appropriate auxiliary data.

Linking

Events and profiles can often times be linked by common shared attributes or by attributes which have some suspicious relationship with each other. A few examples will make this clearer. For example fraud rings sometimes stage a number of different accidents in order to collect insurance payments. The accidents, although seemingly unrelated, may share a common cell phone number (with different addresses), may all occur within a small physical region, may all use the same body shop, or the same doctor, etc. Of course, two accidents, neither of which are fraudulent, may also share common links or attributes. The goal of linking analysis software is to identify linkages which are suspicious in some way so that further investigation may be done. Sometimes link analysis software is also known as forensic software. Some examples of link analysis can be found in [11].

5.   ARCHITECTURE

In this section, we describe a common architecture for an alert management system. See Figure 11.1. In practice, actual alert management systems are usually much more complex. The functionality for an alert management system can be divided into three general areas. First, functionality which extracts, transforms, cleans, and loads the data. Second, functionality, for the off-line (i.e. non-real time) analysis of data. This includes data analysis, data mining, link analysis and related types of forensic activities. Third, functionality for the on-line or real time analysis, routing, and workflow.

The off-line analysis usually contains a data warehouse or data mart and various data analysis, data mining, and forensic analysis tools. From this off-line analysis, data mining models and profiles are often produced for the on-line system. In addition, the off-line analysis may involve extensive checking against various internal and third party databases, checking which may be too time consuming to take place on-line.

The on-line analysis usually contains one or more databases containing various watch lists which incoming events and profiles are compared to. In addition, scoring may be done using the data mining model produced from the off-line analysis. Finally, workflow and routing is usually done producing various alerts and reports.

Part of the complexity of alert management systems is that the extraction, transformation, cleaning and loading must be consistent for the both the off-line and on-line components. There is usually reporting which is part of both the off-line and on-line components of the system.

2. off-line modeling & analysis   **3. on-line deployment**

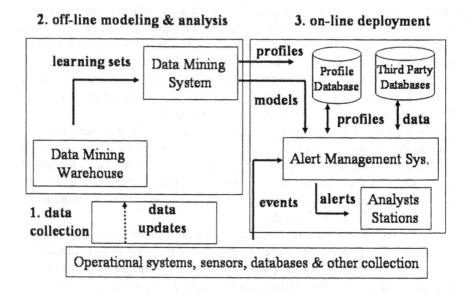

Figure 11.1. A typical architecture for an alert management system.

6. EXAMPLES

In this section, we give some examples of alert management systems. In most of the cases discussed below, there is a natural way to label a data set of events. For example, events may be labeled "good" or "bad"; "intrusion" or "no intrusion"; "normal" or "abnormal"; "threat" or "no threat"; "fraud" or "no fraud"; or "red" or "blue". For simplicity, we often refer to the labels simply as "bad" or "good," with the understanding that the particular meaning of these terms is dependent upon the particular example.

A labeled set of events can be used to label profiles in different ways. A common rule is to assume that profiles are initially labeled good until an event labeled bad is associated with them, after which they are labeled bad. Notice that this makes sense for credit card transactions and similar types of event data: a given credit card account can have a mixture of good and bad transactions. The goal is to detect when there are bad transactions and thereafter stop all transactions. Given a labeled set of events, we can use a variety of classification algorithms to construct a scoring function, which is simply a numerical function on state space R^N indicating the likelihood that a profile is bad.

Credit Card Transacations. One of the best examples of transactional data is provided by credit card transactions. The data in a credit card transaction is broadly based upon the ISO 8583 standard and includes the account number, the date and time of the transaction, the amount of the purchase, etc. By aggregating transactional data by account number, a profile can be built for each account number. A fraud model uses transactional data to update profiles and then scores each profile for the likelihood of fraud.

Perhaps the best known alert management system for detecting credit card fraud is the Falcon System developed by HNC [10].

Call Detail Records. A Call Detail Record (CDR) contains data about telephone calls, including the date and time of the call, the duration of the call, the calling number, the called number, the telephone number of the billed party, which may be different then the calling number (for example, with 800 numbers), and related data. By aggregating CDR data by the calling number, a profile can be created. A variety of models can be built using these profiles. As before, a fraud model can be built which updates profiles using CDR data and then scores the updated profiles for the likelihood of fraud. As another example, models can be built predicting the likelihood of customer attrition or churn, or predicting the lifetime value of a customer. For the latter two examples, models may be built based upon a single calling number, or by aggregating all calling numbers associated with a given individual, household, or business.

Alert management systems for detecting telephone fraud have been developed by several of the large telephone companies, for example by AT&T [3].

Passenger Name Records. A third example is provided by passenger name records or PNRs. The transactional data in a PNR includes the originating city, connecting cities, if any, the destination city, flight numbers, name and address of the passenger, frequent flyer number, and related information. Giving a collection of PNRs, profiles can be built for each passenger. Using these profiles, a risk assessment can be done for each airline passenger.

An example of an alert management system for PNRs is the Computer Assisted Passenger Screening System (CAPS) used by the TSA to screen airline passengers at airports.

Network Intrusion Systems. Another example is provided by network intrusion systems employing statistical methods. Network intrusion systems monitor events derived from system logs and other sources. These are used to update various internal feature vectors, which are used as the inputs to statistical models, whose outputs trigger alerts.

Today, the most common network intrusion detection systems, such as Snort [12], look for specific patterns in the data (which are also called signatures, but different than the signatures described above) and do not employ event-profile based techniques.

Suspicious Activity Reports. The Financial Crimes Enforcement Network or FINCEN, which is part of United States Department of the Treasury, collects reports from financial institutions about various types of suspicious financial transactions. These reports are called Suspicious Activity Reports or SARs. There are a number of criteria used for deciding whether or not to file a SAR. In addition, financial institutions are precluded from doing any business with certain individuals or business which have been placed on various watch lists. Larger financial institutions use alert management systems for comparing new accounts to the watch list, as well as for scoring transactions in order to decide whether or not it is necessary to file a SAR.

Automated Manifest System. The Automated Manifest System (AMS) is a system operated by the US Customs which provides inventory control and release notification for cargo entering the US. Carriers, port authorities, service bureaus, freight forwarders, and container freight stations can use the AMS to provide digital processing of manifest and waybill data. The AMS in turn can use manifest and waybill event data to build profiles about the users of their systems. Alert management systems associated with the AMS can score both event data (manifest and waybill data), as well profiles summarizing activities about carriers and other users of the system. Particularly important for systems like this is improving scoring by overlaying third party data over internal event and profile data.

Interagency Border Inspection System The US Customs Service and Immigration and Naturalization Service (INS) use the Interagency Border Inspection

System (IBIS) to screen individuals at ports of entry to the US. IBIS data is collected from a variety of sources and profiles generated by IBIS are shared by a over 20 US federal agencies. IBIS is used at ports of entry to clear expeditiously the majority of the traveling public, while allowing attention to be focused on a relatively small number of individuals. IBIS contains data on suspect individuals, businesses, vehicles, aircraft, and vessels.

7.   STATUS

During the period 1996-2002, Magnify developed an alert management system based upon its PATTERN data mining system [7]. PATTERN was a data mining system which was designed for mining very large data sets which did not fit into memory and was based upon the following ideas:

- PATTERN employed ensemble based modeling. Typically, ensembles were used to partition data into chunks which could fit into memory.

- PATTERN also employed boosting to improve the accuracy of the ensembles produced.

- PATTERN employed a column oriented data warehouse so that numerically intensive operations could be performed efficiently on large amounts of disk resident data.

- PATTERN was designed to run on both single workstations and clusters of workstations. MPI was used for message passing when employed on clusters.

- PATTERN used an XML representation for statistical and data mining models to provide a simple interface between the off-line data mining component and the on-line scoring or deployment of component of the system.

- PATTERN contained specialized libraries for data transformations and data aggregations so that large numbers of events could be aggregated into profiles efficiently.

This functionality was added over a period of time. During the period, 1995-1996, the alert management system consisting of a off-line data mining system which was used for scoring. An on-line scoring component was added during 1997-1998 following the architecture described in Figure 11.1. A component for transforming and aggregating data was added during the period 1999-2000. A workflow and routing component was added during the period 2000-2002 [8]. Simple matching and linking was done in an ad hoc fashion, dependent upon the particular requirements of of the application.

The alert management systems built over PATTERN were used for a variety of applications including: detecting credit card fraud, detecting insurance fraud, analyzing TCP packet data for network intrusions, and uncovering suspicous events and profiles in passenger name record data.

8. CONCLUSION

In this note, we have provided a quick introduction to alert management systems. We have introduced the primitive concepts of events, profiles, and updates. We have also given six examples of these types of systems; many more could be given. There are four key functions usually present in an alert management system: scoring, matching, linking, and workflow, which we have briefly described. Finally, we have given a brief description of a common architecture used by alert management systems. With the increased focus on homeland defense, alert management systems will no doubt grow in importance.

REFERENCES

[1] Dean W. Abbott, I. Phillip Matkovsky, and John F. Elder IV. An evaluation of highend data mining tools for fraud detection. In IEEE International Conference on Systems, Man and Cybernetics, 1998.

[2] C. Cortes, K. Fisher, D. Pregibon, and A. Rogers. Hancock: A Language for Extracting Signatures from Data Streams. In Proceedings of the Association for Computing Machinery Sixth International Conference on Knowledge Discovery and Data Mining, pages 9–17, 2000.

[3] C.Cortes and D. Pregibon, Signature-based methods for data streams, Data Mining and Knowledge Discovery, 2001.

[4] T. Fawcett and F. Provost, Adaptive Fraud Detection, Data Mining and Knowledge Discovery, Volume 1, Number 3, 1997, pages 291-316.

[5] T. Fawcett, and F. Provost, Activity monitoring: Noticing interesting changes in behavior, Proceedings of the Fifth International Conference on Knowledge Discovery and Data Mining, 1999, pages 53-62.

[6] R. L. Grossman, H. Bodek, D. Northcutt, and H. V. Poor, Data Mining and Tree-based Optimization, Proceedings of the Second International Conference on Knowledge Discovery and Data Mining, E. Simoudis, J. Han and U. Fayyad, editors, AAAI Press, Menlo Park, California, 1996, pp 323-326.

[7] PATTERN Data Mining System, Version 1.2, Magnify, Inc., 1997.

[8] PATTERN Data Mining System, Version 3.1, Magnify, Inc. 2000.

[9] R. L. Grossman and R. G. Larson, An Algebraic Approach to Data Mining: Some Examples, Proceedings of the 2002 IEEE International Conference on Data Mining, IEEE Computer Society, Los Alamitos, California, 2002, pages 613-616.

[10] HNC Software, a division of Fair Isaac Corporation, retrieved from http://www.fairisaac.com/fairisaac on August 20, 2003.

[11] Daryl Pregibon, Graph Mining: Discovery in Large Networks, CCR/DIMACS Workshop on Mining Massive Data Sets and Streams: Mathematical Methods and Algorithms for Homeland Defense, June 2002.

[12] Snort(tm), The Open Source Network Intrusion Detection System, retrieved from http://www.snort.org on August 20, 2003.

PART IV

CYBER FORENSICS

Chapter 12

CYBER FORENSICS: MANAGING, MODELING, AND MINING DATA FOR INVESTIGATION

Erin E. Kenneally, Tony Fountain
San Diego Supercomputer Center, University of California San Diego

Abstract: This chapter describes a collaborative project between the San Diego Supercomputer Center (SDSC) and the Automated Regional Justice Information System (ARJIS) entitled P³ELE (Public-Private-Partnership Enabling Law Enforcement). The project is focused on developing a model research infrastructure for the management, analysis and visualization of public and private multidimensional data. This includes addressing the technical and analytical models, methods, tools and techniques to effectively integrate and correlate law enforcement information with public, cyber-based information. This framework will enable researchers to study the impact of this expanded dimensional information on the efficient remediation and proactive capabilities of law enforcement, and ultimately, will enhance the operational capabilities of justice professionals in our digital society.

Keywords: Cyber forensics, law enforcement, management, analysis, visualization.

1.   INTRODUCTION

Law enforcement is an information-intensive process in which government agencies are called upon to collect and interpret large public data sets in an effort to serve and protect the citizenry, while at the same time maintain trust and reliability in fulfilling its mission. However, law enforcement is by its very nature reactionary to information contained within and derived from reports of criminal activity. As a result, the effectiveness of law enforcement is directly related to the quality of information reported and proficiency of the subsequent analyses. The process of law enforcement has thus far encountered technical, managerial and socio-legal barriers to integrating, correlating and interpreting intra-agency crime data with public, Internet-based data. The challenge lies in developing a systematic and scientifically-based framework to enhance the best available information upon which courses of action are based.

To address this need, collaboration between The San Diego Supercomputer Center (SDSC) and the Automated Regional Justice Information System (ARJIS), entitled P³ELE (Public-Private-Partnership Enabling Law Enforcement), is focused on developing a model research infrastructure for the management, analysis and visualization of public and private multidimensional data. This includes addressing the technical and analytical models, methods, tools and techniques to effectively integrate and correlate law enforcement information with public, cyber-based information. This framework will enable researchers to study the impact of this expanded dimensional information on the efficient remediation and proactive capabilities of law enforcement, and ultimately, will enhance the operational capabilities of justice professionals in our digital society.

P³ELE represents a mechanism through which data collection and analyses models developed by university-based intermediary researchers can facilitate the transfer of technology and knowledge to government entities seeking to manage, analyze and link public and private multidimensional data. This academic research on public and private data integration and correlation integrates knowledge in information retrieval, knowledge management, information visualization, artificial intelligence, decision theory, social informatics, data mining and forensic analysis.

By designing a path for public, open source data to be input into existing models used in investigation planning and decision making, the credibility and influence of justice research will be enhanced. P³ELE is an academic bridge to transport private sector technology into usable and civilly responsible law enforcement. Likewise, it will provide a forum for cross-pollination of teaching, training and learning between academia, industry and the government. Aside from enabling a transparent, reproducible, and objective system for integrating models from the public and private sectors, academic researchers will gain access to important problems and data in real-world large-scale contexts. This is critical to understanding and predicting the impact of these technologies on law enforcement agencies and services, governance, and the democratic process.

The significance of this integration will extend beyond its origins in southern California to include other public-private partnerships, demonstrating an applied instantiation of how to leverage the strengths of individual public, private and academic communities toward a better collective whole.

1.1   A Cyber Forensics Project: P³ELE: Public-Private-Partnership Enabling Law Enforcement

Just as residue from the ridge patterns on our fingers existed before science and technology was able to "uncover" them by latent fingerprinting methods, digital traces of criminal activities exist on the Internet, and consequently lay dormant because we lack the right tools and techniques to manage, model and mine answers to probing questions.

Cyber forensic investigations occur in varying degrees throughout the fields of computer security, law enforcement and private investigations and involve the recognition, recovery and reconstruction of investigatory leads and evidence. In the context of investigations, the sources of evidence and investigatory leads are often "siloed" into data from law enforcement reports, or data from investigations of individual computers involved in a crime. No longer is the stand-alone computer exclusively a target or tool used in criminal activity. The Internet itself has become a breeding ground for primary and secondary sources of evidence in the search for truth, as well as providing the seeds for predicting future malfeasance. Like other forensic sciences, fundamental methods of cyber forensics begin by collecting a large number of intensely diverse variables or attributes, and culminate in pattern matching among these variables to individualize evidence.

Computer security, network forensics, and increasingly law enforcement investigations involve working with heterogeneous datasets that contain remnants of human activity, oftentimes occurring across multiple environments. Pattern matching in this context consists of the recognition and correlation of digital evidence contained within and among various data sources such as web pages, computer logs, Internet newsgroups, online chat rooms, and corporeal case reports — each with different levels of granularity and context. Nevertheless, linkage of this data is becoming more important for the efficient administration of justice in a 21st Century society that is increasingly leading its collective lives in the digital realm.

2.   GAP ANALYSIS: WHAT IS THE PROBLEM AND RESEARCH NEEDED?

One of the most prevalent challenges facing law enforcement (LE) in our information society is to integrate public, Internet-based data with existing private data sets to enhance its duty to enforce laws as well as its mission to protect and serve the public citizenry. Fulfilling this expectation in isolation from other law enforcement entities and public data sources is no longer tenable, especially in light of information technology advances and pressure to enhance predictive capabilities. Although there have been a handful of approaches that allow law enforcement to integrate data within their agencies as well as from other jurisdictions, constructing new approaches that expand this data integration to encompass public, Internet-based data to produce better actionable information is a mounting priority.

To address this need, the San Diego Supercomputer Center (SDSC) is developing a research infrastructure for the management, analysis and visualization of public and private multidimensional data. This will include addressing the technical and analytical models, methods, tools and techniques to effectively integrate and correlate law enforcement information with public, cyber-based information to study the impact of this expanded dimensional information on the efficient remediation and proactive capabilities of law enforcement.

Law enforcement is an information-intensive process, beginning with initial data collection at the crime scene or via victim reporting, extending through evidence and intelligence gathering, and culminating in analysis of data to support the prosecution and aid in preventing criminal activities. However, LE is by its very nature reactionary to information contained within and derived from reports of criminal activity. As a result, the effectiveness of law enforcement is directly related to the quality of information reported and proficiency of the subsequent analyses. This quality is enhanced by collecting, processing, organizing and analyzing reports between agencies.

Nevertheless, there is a chasm between information contained in crime-related reports and the forensically relevant (who, what, when, where, how, why) data that exists independent of crime reports. The breadth of forensically relevant data available on the Internet can impact the quality of actionable information contained within existing private records maintained by LE.

The process of law enforcement has thus far encountered barriers to recognizing, accessing and utilizing this complementary dimension of information because of technical, managerial and socio-legal properties of information. The challenge lies in integrating, correlating and interpreting intra-agency crime data with public, cyber-based data to enhance the best available information upon which courses of action are based.

2.1   Technical, Managerial and Socio-Legal Problems

The Internet has emerged as a mainstream vehicle for global communications among persons, informal groups and public organizations, corporations and governments. Over three billion pages of information have been posted to the Internet using various protocols, including http, IRC/DCC

(Internet relay chat/direct client communications), ftp (file transfer protocol), Usenet (newsgroups), auctions and peer-to-peer services. Unfortunately, the same characteristics that have made the Internet so attractive for business and government — low cost, high-speed, anonymity, multi-media capabilities, etc. — have also made it highly useful for fraudsters, terrorists and organized criminal groups.

LE's exploitation of the Internet as an intelligence and investigative resource has been complicated by the lack of a readily trained cadre of government collectors and analysts, established operational processes and an accessible collection and analysis platform capable of supporting high-volume content collection, reduction, aggregation, analysis, reporting and assessment. The lack of such a platform has relegated cyber forensics to ad hoc, "hit-or-miss" efforts. Controlled, systematic collection has typically not been performed.

Technology should be employed to increase the scope and quality of the information upon which LE depends to ensure the public safety. As the persons engaging in unlawful activities grow increasingly dependent on the Internet as a tool (i.e. communication or transaction mechanism) and/or target (i.e. the use of the Internet to commit new crimes or old crimes in new ways) to facilitate their offenses they leave a trail of evidence and investigatory leads as a natural byproduct. From this vast and disparate well of publicly accessible data much can be uncovered and inferred.

Currently, the search, collection, and analysis of information evidence from the public Internet have been relegated to a few, highly specialized, and usually grant-funded law enforcement projects. It has been addressed, conceptually, as a new kind of high technology criminal problem. It is indeed that, but also much more. Cyberspace has become the neighborhood wherein law enforcement officers must regularly interact with their constituency. The previously specialized projects and investigation techniques confined to the non-budgeted criminal justice arena will certainly be deployed universally. Regular law enforcement reporting and records systems, evidence collection and analysis systems, and pro-active crime suppression activities must likewise be relocated to the virtual existence of cyberspace and scaled well beyond traditional jurisdictional barriers. The alternative is failure of law in society.

Integrating public data with justice data will prove helpful in gathering and exchanging information that can provide the hard data needed to assess various threats. The frequency (number of occurrences) and severity data may not find their way into LE reports because there may be no formal reporting requirements, but nonetheless, information needed to provide a meaningful assessment may certainly lurk informally on the Net. Furthermore, cases involving events related to the investigation at hand may be inaccessible or unverifiable for reasons ranging from out of court settlements to unpublished opinions.

Indeed, traditional investigation of that index on the individual, rather than querying on the criminal act itself may be problematic. This is where data mining and modeling can significantly enhance the ability to infer behavior and intent from patterns of acts (usage signatures). For instance, a query on a particular suspect who may carry out identity theft using the Internet under multiple aliases will largely fly under the radar of traditional investigations that do not make use of Internet-based information.

While models of certain types of criminals have been available for sometime, models of how these criminals may utilize the Internet to commit transgressions, as well as composites of persons committing cyber-based crimes are very immature. This project will start to collect and populate the requisite repository of data that does not yet exist. A corollary challenge that will be addressed is compiling the data and constructing the models needed for such a repository.

While the current Internet offers the benefit of a new dimension of information and unprecedented ability to interact with remote groups, it is not without potential dangers that must be a consideration in any management, analysis and visualization model. For example, the reliability and credibility of the links may need some degree of quantification and qualification. The credibility of the proposed relational model depends on the linkage between Internet-based data and current corporal-based report events. To further illustrate, the collection and entry of crime report data is facilitated by trained officers who observe traditional interactions where issues of competence, coercion, malice, or willingness are effectively evaluated. However, these traditional metrics may not be present when considering information obtained from impersonal computer-computer interaction on the Internet. In short, measuring the context of cyber data is a growing challenge.

2.2   The Need To Integrate Public and Private Data Sets

Recognizing the need to integrate private LE data sets, the Automated Regional Justice Information System (ARJIS) was formed and has successfully automated access to records and databases among its 50 local, state and federal member agencies. The ARJIS Joint Powers Agency marries reports from southern California-based LE agencies to effectively broker regional enterprise information. ARJIS' integrated database of LE records allows real-time data queries and notifications, thus eliminating multiple query operations. Furthermore, its knowledge management technology helps eliminate redundant data entry between various LE information systems.

A prominent objective for ARJIS is enhanced intelligence analysis through integration of justice and other public data, thus necessitating the identification of technologies to jointly analyze structured criminal justice data and various structured or unstructured data sets. Correspondingly, there is a need to identify analysis models, data sources and standards, and access requirements to enable the technical and managerial links between public and private (current LE records) data.

It has become clear that public, cyber-based information is an unstructured and dynamic data set where residue and patterns of LE-related information are constantly being created. In this respect, Internet-based data mirrors the forensic capabilities of corporally derived data: who (the person(s) involved or having knowledge of a crime); what (the criminal act itself); where (geographic location of the crime event); why (economic, political motivations, etc.) and how (method of perpetrating a crime). Furthermore, public datasets can create complex and diverse models, and large quantities of such data may be essential to a unified and efficient remediation of a crime.

Although ARJIS has made significant progress, the data upon which LE is acting is limited to structured, static, historic collections that make use only of corporally derived data (i.e. recorded interviews, witness reports, criminal records). If law enforcement is to enhance the quality of actionable information necessary to reach its goals of more efficient remediation and proactive enforcement, it must expand dimensionally and engage in studying and developing automated and systematic models and techniques to tap into publicly available data.

Each of the LE user groups- patrol officer, criminal investigator, counter intelligence/counter terrorism investigator and crime analyst- has developed models to manage and collect private LE data. Effective models define and streamline reproducible methodologies and techniques to key on oft times isolated and disconnected event data contained in the crime reports. The reality of crime, especially as it occurs using the Internet as a target or tool, is that artifacts of the crime are not disconnected. Yet, the quality of the data sample size and technique is a barrier to coordinated response, scalable management of knowledge, timely reaction and predictability. Consequently, P^3ELE aims to develop a research infrastructure that enables the complex feedback among artifacts and user groups at varying scales.

SDSC's collaboration with law enforcement and exposure to ARJIS thus far has revealed several important points: first, academic research on public and private data integration would benefit from access to and use of the tremendous capabilities that exist for querying and collecting public,

Internet-based information; and second, effective deployment of scientific research into the broader community depends, in part, on finding mechanisms through which data collection models developed by university-based intermediary researchers can facilitate the transfer of technology and knowledge into the models used for managing, analyzing and linking public and private multidimensional data.

3.   BRIDGING THE GAP: CYBER FORENSICS APPROACH

One overarching goal of this P³ELE project is to develop and deploy a connectivity framework that will enhance existing information collaboration between and among LE agencies, justice-related researchers and the public in southern California.   Integrating publicly available data with existing justice-related data sets may enhance the qualitative and quantitative value of information needed to protect and serve our society. To accomplish this goal, this project stands on the shoulders of recent advances in Internet searching capabilities, and criminal justice networking- pioneered by ARJIS, to develop a research infrastructure for the management, analysis and visualization of public and private multidimensional data.

3.1   A Framework For Cyber Forensics

Although ARJIS offers centralized storage and long-term maintenance of LE data, adopting a distributed approach to integrating public data from specialized Internet searches allows it to be accessed more dynamically. In this way, investigations models can be coupled, while allowing their design and maintenance to remain relatively autonomous. In order to accomplish integration in this way, the following general architecture will be assessed (Figure 12-1).

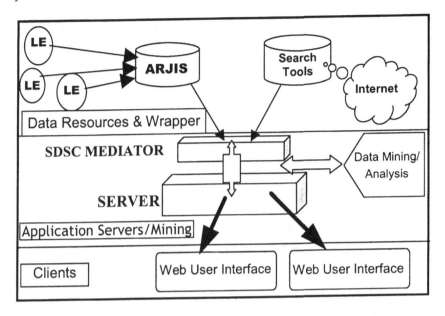

Figure 12-1. General architecture for the integration and analysis of public-private data sets

3.2   Approach Steps

3.2.1   Step 1:   Identify analysis requirements, data sources and model standards

This step in the activity schema consists of organizing project team members from SDSC, industry collaborator(s) and ARJIS who will define various problems in conjunction with ARJIS/LE case-based investigative needs, and about which open source data artifacts are sought. This will include an initial analysis of each entity's respective technical and substantive datasets and requirements. This will include an identification of some initial query terms and data collection strategies, and result in a set of data-input requirements and output products.

Deployment and feedback will be obtained by utilizing ARJIS member, CATCH (Southern California High Tech Task Force) in executing the proposed work and serving as a testbed.

3.2.2   Step 2.   Convert analyses requirements to collaborator workflow (search and collection); define search strategy and collection plan

This step involves federating the requirements analysis from the ARJIS dataset with the Internet query infrastructure to define a search strategy and collection plan for Internet-based data. This involves customizing the data display configuration and query result report format to fit the specification of the ARJIS client.

3.2.3   Step 3. Identify access needs for ARJIS for each client type

The compilation of ARJIS data and public data will carry with it the more strict legal controls assigned to the ARJIS law enforcement records. This project step will identify the access needs of the two kinds of typical users within the law enforcement community — investigators and analysts.

3.2.4   Step 4. Develop an information exchange platform — integrate public, Internet data with private, justice data

This activity involves marrying the query response artifacts from public, Internet-procured data with ARJIS client reports. We then develop query templates specific to the investigative need and resulting problem statement developed at the onset. The value here is in defining a "common currency" between structured, justice report data and unstructured, cyber data based on model metadata language.

We will investigate and adapt relevant XML standards for security data and analysis. We expect to define model metadata to discover, locate and evaluate models suitable for specific LE investigations and intelligence needs, and describe the data-input requirements and output products. In so doing, we develop searchable models and data requirements using XML (eXtensible Markup Language) schemas for encoding model and application metadata, which will allow us to register and document the various models that are developed. This step is designed to develop a crosscutting search mechanism model that relates structured, LE report data with unstructured, Internet data and to identify their function, design, and suitability to answer the problem. The teams will identify input requirements of models such as type of event variables (person, geography, and/or motivation key words), data quality requirements, and classification metrics.

Where possible, we will leverage the current cyber infrastructure developments at SDSC, including exploring the applicability of Web Services to LE information integration and analysis.

3.2.5 Step 5. Develop operational and technical criteria for analysis tools- blending technology with people

This phase consists of the development of tools to recognize, reconstruct and automate domain knowledge decision support patterns. This involves recording expert domain knowledge about investigations as scripts that allow us to set up expectations and perform inferences.

In addition, we will investigate supervised and unsupervised machine learning approaches to pattern discovery and modeling, including probabilistic models, decision trees, and support vector machines. This includes research into compute-intensive statistical and machine-learning approaches to pattern discovery and modeling, and software development to ensure that these results are incorporated into the overall system.

Tools will be tested and reviewed in an effort to assess reliability and establish baseline metrics for the management of public-private data. Furthermore, team members will define models for optimal visualization schemas of the integrated data set. We will experiment with various visual designs to best capture the domain knowledge of the LE investigator/analyst in a client interface.

3.2.6 Step 6. Implement analysis tools in small scale, real-world law enforcement environments

Here the objective is to beta-test the analytical tools in specialized law enforcement and intelligence environments capable of evaluating their effectiveness by comparison with traditional investigative support tools.

3.2.7 Step 7. Evaluate Findings

The final step consists of evaluation and iteration of the earlier research stages with the intent of refining the templates, models and metrics. As described, we will develop the information exchange platform and the model metadata standards to include a wide range of data and model types, as well as meet the access and security needs of diverse LE agencies. This evaluation will encompass the analytical process of identifying the cyber-based data artifacts, assessing the value of those artifacts as it relates to the overall case report, and developing a methodology to extend the investigation and collection of justice report data to include cyber-based data.

3.3   Follow-on Questions and Issues

Some of the other questions to be posed and potentially answered address security and legal concerns. These include, but are not limited to the following:

- What are the benefits (positive consequences) of information integration (in the form of data sharing) to the public? What are the warning signals about the negative consequences of information integration?
- How does this information integration affect the public sector concerns related to data sharing: Is it restricting/enabling privacy infringement? What decision-making processes might profiling information be used?
- How can existing public data be used to further LE's mission?
- Will the access to and use of publicly available data encourage private sector to share higher quality data with LE?
- What are the relationships between static, law enforcement records (ARJIS records), dynamic, public behavioral data (specialized Internet searches), and transactional, network history and traffic data (security logs)?
- What is the cost-benefit of integrating public information with LE data sets?

In terms of cost-avoidance related to information location cost (time spent identifying potential sources of information, accessing those information sources, purchasing external data)? Information interpretation costs (cost to follow up and validate; cost of misinterpreting information; cost of relying on inaccurate data)? Information integration and reorganization costs?

4.   IMPACTS OF CYBER FORENSICS FOR LAW ENFORCEMENT

4.1   Significance of Integrating Information from Public and Private Multidimensional Data

The potential network for collaboration in justice operations and research in southern California is extensive. The ARJIS Joint Powers Agency represents San Diego and Imperial county regions, and is partially interfaced with Los Angeles County. The 50+ ARJIS member agencies that form this distinctive justice information brokerage comprise over 7,000 local, state and federal LE professionals with a service population of approximately 3.1

million people living in a geographical area of nearly 9,000 square miles, and with a very active international border and port of entry.

The resources available within the LE community that are of value to investigative officers, analysts, criminal justice administrators and forensic researchers include both primary datasets and models. The San Diego Supercomputer Center has developed a unique partnership among high technology law enforcement by way of knowledge and technology transfer, as well as providing a forum for cross-pollination of teaching, training and learning between applied security research and operational law enforcement. This institutionalized trust between law enforcement and academia is rare and valuable.

Developing a formal framework for sharing data and models with the research, management and investigative operations will benefit ARJIS and other SDSC cyber-forensic projects that seek to incorporate dynamic, real-world, social and economic parameters into data sharing models. As these models (tools, techniques, methodologies) mature, the infrastructure will make the models accessible and deployable to other researchers, policymakers, investigative professionals and justice planners. The significance of this integration will extend beyond the southern California region to include other public-private partnerships, demonstrating an applied instantiation of how to leverage the strengths of individual public, private and academic communities toward a better collective whole.

By designing a path for open source data to be input into existing models used in investigation planning and decision making, the credibility and influence of justice research is enhanced among audiences that are often mislead by erroneous and sensationalized information from the popular media.

4.2   Enabling Public and Private Technology Transfer

The P^{3}ELE model serves as an academic bridge translating private sector technology into usable and civilly responsible law enforcement. Likewise, it provides a forum for cross-pollination of teaching, training and learning between academia, industry and the government. Aside from enabling a transparent, reproducible, and objective system for integrating models from the public and private sectors, academic researchers will gain access to important problems and data in real-world large-scale contexts. This is critical to understanding and predicting the impact of these technologies on law enforcement agencies and services, governance, and the democratic process.

4.3   Value to Traditional, Broader LE Community

Although the immediate application of this project is to integrate private, LE data with open Internet-wide data within southern California, it is expected that the products (tools, techniques, methodologies) developed in this project will have much broader applicability. For instance, we anticipate that the basic design for implementing data as Web Services will have similar portability to other information aggregation, correlation and crime mapping research efforts.

This research empowers LE in its role as a collector, interpreter and custodian of large public data sets to manage large-scale data and information acquisition. Furthermore, by using open standards it enables a more transparent and scientific assessment of technological impact on LE investigations and decision-making so that data, networks and architectures can interoperate without running afoul of security, privacy and information assurance requirements.

P³ELE will help fulfill the global information needs of LE more efficiently to enhance response and proactive protection. Although LE has trained public servants skilled in using the Internet and cyber-based data to enhance investigations, the problem is these officers represent a small fraction of law enforcement. The reality is that the vast bulk of police officers do not have the skills, resources, or time to effectively locate data from the Internet and integrate it into their investigation. The proposed project holds the promise of lowering the barrier to entry for those technically challenged investigators, while expanding the scope of public servants capable of utilizing digital traces of crime.

4.4   Significance To Computer Security Community

The research conducted and goals attained through P³ELE will offer complementary benefits to the current computer security and computer forensic research within and between academia, the private sector and government. Geared toward quantifying various security risks, the technology developed will inform better metrics regarding threat assessment, operational vulnerabilities and defense-response actions such as:

- An understanding of system vulnerabilities, including hardware, software and human, and particularly as seen through the eyes of known hacker communities,
- An awareness of the relative availability of software tools that present a direct threat to codes, content, or network access.

- Indications and warnings of specific internal or external hacker challenges, or hacker community projects that suggest attacks may be imminent or underway.

Furthermore, P³ELE framework will enable computer security research aimed at correlating information security logging data and real world events. For instance, the investigation of issues related to windows of vulnerability optimal disclosure and release of system patches must be addressed by our information society in a more empirical way. By coupling behavioral data — public searches of patch releases, vulnerability announcements, and exploit releases — with transactional data from security logs showing attempted and successful exploits, we can enhance the efficient identification and remediation of actual threats to our cyber infrastructure.

4.5   Comparison to Other Efforts

There are several projects underway that attempt to integrate and search different LE databases to allow LE to share information from their operational databases (CopLink, CrimeSoft, ISYS, RISS). Insofar as these are valuable efforts, they all lack several features that are defining capabilities within the P³ELE infrastructure. None of the aforementioned projects are designed to include the domain of open source, public, Internet data in pool of justice information used to make associations for investigations and intelligence. P³ELE is further distinguishable because it stands on the shoulders of an established framework for integrating justice data spanning the breadth of 50+ local, state and federal agencies. Other efforts connect only a handful of agencies that share private, structured LE data only.

Furthermore, these efforts do not make significant progress toward solving the lack of metrics problem in data sampling: data in reports is uncoordinated, unautomated, and not scalable. This results in investigations (link analysis) that are limited, remediation (responding to incidents and predicting/preventing future incidents) that is suboptimal (uncoordinated), and resulting statistical analysis that is inaccurate (gap). P³ELE's data mining and web services approach to integrate unstructured, Internet data promises a novel approach to this quantification effort.

Finally, the P³ELE approach enables LE and researchers to correlate cyber and real world events by uncovering correlations between static, law enforcement records (ARJIS records) with dynamic, public behavioral data (Internet data), along with transactional, network history and traffic data (security logs).

5. CONCLUSION: P³ELE AS A CYBER FORENSICS PROJECT FOR MANAGING, MODELING AND MINING DATA FOR INVESTIGATION

Cyber crime will not "cease and desist" in deference to LE's ability to utilize the artifacts it leaves behind. The rapid pace of technological development has not only fostered new criminal acts (i.e. the spread of computer virii, unauthorized access to a computer system, possession of access control devices, etc.), but in fact has spawned novel means to conduct old crimes (i.e. online fraud, internet gambling, copyright infringement, etc.).

Therefore, the question is not whether evidence exists, but rather, whether LE can uncover, contextualize and integrate cyber evidence with predication data from traditional case reports. P³ELE is focused on developing a model research infrastructure for the management, analysis and visualization of public and private multidimensional data so as to generate more actionable knowledge from various data sets. Ultimately, this research will be applied to enhance LE operations to more efficiently serve and protect society in our information age.

NOTES

1. For the purposes of this Chapter, "public" and "private" are used to distinguish the two broad categories of data sets upon which this project focuses. "Public" refers to the cyber-based data available openly on the Internet, whereas "private" refers to law enforcement-related data sets administered by justice officials.

2. For the purposes of this Chapter, "cyber forensics" is used by the authors to refer to the novel subcategory of "Internet forensics," defined as repeatable techniques and methodologies to collect, preserve and analyze digital data on the Internet for investigation purposes. Note that, "computer forensics" is the principles applied to the collection, preservation and analysis of computer-derived evidence to ensure its admissibility as evidence in a legal proceeding.

3. E-commerce, email and VOIP (voice-over-Internet-protocol) communications are a few prominent examples of the ubiquity of computer-based transactions in modern society.

4. Computer Science and Telecommunications Board. Cyber-Security and the Insider Threat to Classified Information. 2000 December.

5. Lasser, Jon, Irresponsible Disclosure. Security Focus; 2002 June 26.

6. Lamont, Judith, KM Aids and Abets Law Enforcement. KM World, 2002 March.

7. Coplink <http://www.coplinkconnect.com/>; CrimeSoft <http://www.crimesoft.com>; RISS — Regional Information Sharing System <http://it.ojp.gov/ process_links.jsp?link_id=LI-00245>; ISYS <http://www.isys.com>.

8. Cisco Systems. Network Based Transformation for Justice Systems. 2002.

REFERENCES

[1]   Computer Science and Telecommunications Board, Cyber-Security and the Insider Threat to Classified Information, 2000.

[2]   J. Lasser, Irresponsible Disclosure, *Security Focus*, 2002.

[3]   J. Lamont, KM Aids and Abets Law Enforcement, *KM World*, March 2002.

[4]   Cisco Systems, *Network Based Transformation for Justice Systems*, 2002.

Chapter 13

CYBER FORENSICS: ISSUES AND APPROACHES

Jau-Hwang Wang
Central Police University, Taiwan, ROC

Abstract: This chapter introduces the concept of cyber forensics, digital evidence, and computer forensic process. Cyber forensics is defined as the application of computer science to laws – to process and analyze digital evidence, to reconstruct a crime, and to provide links among the offender, the victim and the crime scene. Basically Digital evidence includes all digital data, which can be used to establish that a crime has been committed or can provide a link between a crime and its victim or a crime and its perpetrator. The forensic process of digital evidences includes evidence recognition, collection, preservation, and analysis for crime reconstruction.

Keywords: Cyber Forensics, Digital Evidence, Crime Investigation.

1.   INTRODUCTION

Since the introduction of the first electronic computer in 1946, computer and its storage devices have created a trend to process and store information in digital format. It is relatively easier and less expensive to create and store digital information compared to traditional information processing techniques, such as writing and punch cards. As a result, more and more information is created, processed, and stored on computer storage devices, such as magnetic disks. The trend is further accelerated by the introduction of computer network in 1969 and personal computer in 1981. Nowadays, computer and computer network are ubiquitous within our society and used in every facet of modern society. For example, computer and computer network are commonly used to edit and send messages, transfer funds, purchase stocks, compute financial data, make reservations, and access worldwide information online. Consequently, the amount of information, such as financial, military, proprietary business data, and personal communications stored and transmitted by computer and computer network has increased tremendously. Consider the facts that there are more than 3 billion indexed Web pages are on the world wide web (WWW), more than 550 billion documents are available on-line, and billions of messages are sent and received daily through computer network [1]. Furthermore, a microcomputer nowadays may often have disk with 60-GB or more storage capacity and store thousands of files. In general the widely application of computer related technologies benefited our society. However it is inevitable that computer and computer network may also be used in illegal activities.

Computer network was originally designed for connecting computers in academic environment and thus the security was not among the top design issues. Therefore, computer networks are vulnerable to unscrupulous attacks. The problem is worsened by the prevalence of the WWW technology. Nowadays, computer and computer network have been widely used for enterprise information processing and E-Commerce. E-commerce, such as business-to-business (B2B), business-to-customer (B2C) and customer-to-customer (C2C), has become common business practice and Internet connection has become a commodity for general public. Furthermore, the efficient computation and the effective control capability of computer have made it an excellent mechanism for controlling a wide range of facilities and devices, such as power plants, robots, and information appliances (IA). Many facilities and assets are controlled either directly or indirectly using computers. As a result, the computer and computer network may become targets of criminal activities, such as thief, vandalism, espionage, or even cyber war[1]. For example, computer is often used as a weapon to attack other computers, such as spreading computer virus and blocking network services. Some highlights of the sixth annual "Computer Crime and Security Survey" for 2002[2] published by the Computer Security Institute are: ninety percent of respondents detected security breaches within the year 2002, eighty percent acknowledged financial losses, 223 respondents reported $455,848,000 in financial losses, and so on.

The problem will be getting worse as a result of the continuous expansion of computer applications. It is often stated that computer crime investigation will become one of the top challenges for the law enforcement agencies in

---

[1] *Cyber war or information warfare* is defined as the *offensive* and *defensive* use of information and information systems to deny, exploit, corrupt, or destroy, an adversary's information, information-based processes, information systems, and computer-based networks while protecting one's own. Such actions are designed to achieve advantages over military or business adversaries. (**Ivan K. Goldberg**, *"Glossary of Information Warfare terms"*, http://www.psycom.net/iwar.2.html)

[2] http://www.gocsi.com/press/20020407.html

the 21st century. One of the most fundamental aspects of computer crime investigation is *computer forensics* or *cyber forensics*, which deals with the *recognition, collection, preservation, comparison and identification*, and *documentation* of digital data from computers and computer networks. This chapter introduces the concept of computer forensics and its processes. The organization of this chapter is: section 2 gives the concept of computer forensics and digital evidence, section 3 describes the computer forensics processes, section 4 and section 5 address the evidence searching issues in computer systems and computer networks, section 6 discusses the research and development issues, and section 7 gives the conclusions.

2. COMPUTER FORENSICS AND DIGITAL EVIDENCE

2.1 Computer Forensics

Forensics is defined as the application of science to laws enforced by police agencies in a criminal justice system [2]. In general, any scientific principle or technique that can be used to identify, recover, reconstruct or analyze evidence during a crime investigation can be considered as part of forensic science. Similarly, *computer forensics* can be defined as the application of *computer science* to laws — to *process and analyze digital evidence, reconstruct crime, and provide links among the offender, the victim and the crime scene*. Although forensic practice can be traced back to 18th century [3] and comparatively computer forensics has a brief history, the basic methodologies in determining the evidential value of crime scene and related evidence mostly remain consistent. While traditional forensic professionals use fingerprints, DNA typing, and ballistic analysis to make their cases, computer forensic professionals have to develop sophisticated tools for collecting, preserving, examining, extracting, and evaluating digital evidence in an effort to establish intent, culpability, motive, means, methods, and loss resulting from cyber crime. According to Locard's Exchange Principle [4], any one or any thing, entering a crime scene takes something of the scene with him, and leaves something of him behind when he departs. An offender might leave fingerprints at the scene in a traditional crime. Similarly a computer criminal might inadvertently leave "electronic trails" in computer or computer network storage devices during an offence. "Electronic trail" is similar to fingerprint in traditional crime scene — only that it is relatively soft, highly volatile, less tangible, and much harder to find and recover.

2.2   Digital Evidence

Evidence is defined as "testimony, writing, material objects, or other things presented to the scene that are offered to prove the existence or non existence of a fact" [5]. Digital evidence is defined as "all digital data that can establish that a crime has been committed or can provide a link between a crime and its victim or a crime and its perpetrator" [6]. Essentially, digital evidences are binary data that present information of various kinds, such as text, audio, images and video. For examples, e-mail messages, registry entries in Windows systems, system event logs, forged e-mail headers, virus codes and infected files, etc, all may provide important clues for crime investigation. The evidences recovered can be used to determine the relational, functional, and temporal aspects of crime acts. With the increasing use of computers and the prevalence of computer networks, it is inevitable that people's daily life, so as illegal activities, may be involved with computers and computer networks. Furthermore, in this paperless information era, the pieces of data stored on a computer disk may often be the only information available for a crime investigation. Thus, digital evidence has become more and more important to today's investigative maneuver.

3.   COMPUTER FORENSIC PROCESS

Forensic scientist functions include analyzing physical evidence, providing expert testimony, and furnishing training in the proper recognition, collection, and preservation of physical evidences [2]. According to this definition, the techniques used in forensic science can be categorized into two aspects: processing of forensic evidences, which includes evidence recognition, collection, preservation and analysis; and providing expert testimony. Although the traditional forensic principles are still applicable in computer forensics, the processing of digital evidence needs more precautions. Firstly, digital evidence is binary data stored and represented by magnetic domains and can only be interpreted by proper devices, such as disk drives. It is less tangible, highly volatile and relatively easier to be tampered compared to physical evidence. Secondary, to search for digital evidence in a computer system without any tool is similar to find a needle in a haystack since a typical hard disk may contain huge amount of data[3]. Finally, due to pervasive Internet connectivity, the scope of computer crime incidents is often across enterprise or national boundaries and computer

---

[3] A typical hard disk today can store more than 60GB of data and contains thousands of files. Furthermore, the capacity of hard disk may increase to terabytes in the near future.

forensic professionals often have to trace offenders across the cyber world. Thus, computer forensic professionals need to develop new methodologies in order to acquire the evidence without damaging the original, to authenticate that the evidence as the one originally sized, and to analyze the evidence without incurring any alteration or damage [7]. From the forensic science perspective, there are four major key aspects to processing and examining digital evidences [6,8]: evidence recognition, evidence preservation, collection and documentation, evidence classification, comparison and individualization, and crime reconstruction.

3.1   Evidence Recognition

The crime scene of a computer related crime consists of two spaces: the physical world and the cyber world. Thus, the process of recognizing digital evidence also includes two folds: firstly to recognize the hardware, such as computers, disks, network connections, and printouts for case related information, and secondary to search for relevant digital data, such as e-mail messages, system log files, web pages, and so on. Since a typical hard disk may contain 60GB or more data, in practice it is unlikely to exhaustively examine every file stored on the computer system. In addition, the computers involved may be located in different locations, such as across networks or countries, it may not be possible to collect and search all related information. Thus, the scope of examination is limited to well-identified probative information, i.e., is the information related to a certain case. Often a list of key words are usually created and used to search case related information from huge groups of files on a computer system.

3.2   Evidence Preservation, Collection and Documentation

Videotaping, and photographing are often used to freeze the crime scene, such as the relative positions of hardware components, the display on the monitor of a workstation, and the status of connections between devices. These are all very useful for crime scene reconstruction and evidence authentication. Since the hard copy of information is usually more admissible in court than the digital file, in practice files are printed out, dated, and signed as much as possible. The crime scene and the investigative activities should be documented in detail by drawing crime scene diagrams and taking notes for each collection, such as the position of the evidence, who collects the evidence, and at what time. If an entire computer needs to be collected, all of its peripheral devices, such as printers and scanners, should be also sized if they were possibly used in committing the crime. If only some hardware components need to be collected, the *independent component doctrine*[4] [9] should be followed and the serial number of each component should be documented.

The digital evidence should be unaltered and authentic in order to be admissible in court. Thus, the state of digital evidence must be preserved as it originally sized. There are commercial available tools and techniques to properly collect and preserve digital evidence such that it will be admissible. For example, message digests of files can be created to verify that they are not altered. A message digest program accepts a digital object and produces a number, the *message digest*, often also called *hash value* or *digital fingerprint*. If data is slightly modified or tampered, the message digest thus created will be significantly different from the original. The most commonly used message digest algorithms are MD5 and SHA[5].

Besides authentication, computer records must also satisfy the following criteria to be admissible [10]: (1) they are produced, used, and maintained in the regular course of business operation, (2) they must be the best evidence available, and (3) they are collected by people who have the necessary expertise. For example, if a log file is related to a case, instead of just retrieving the related event log entries, the entire log file should be collected.

Bit-stream copy algorithms are usually desirable to fully backup the contents from computer hard disks. Also, all the files collected and the message digests for each file should also be listed, printed, and signed. Finally, the current date/time and that on the computer, the name of the person who collects the file, the operating system used, the software used to copy the file, and the type of information possibly contained in the file should be documented in detail.

3.3   Evidence Classification, Comparison and Individualization

Evidence classification refers the process of finding the characteristics of the evidence and describing it in general terms, and further determining the application software used to create it. Comparison and individualization refer to examining and revealing characteristics of digital evidence and comparing the evidence with control specimen in order to identify the source of the evidence. Individualization is often based on the randomly created flaw in particular computer equipment. For example, a document created by Word 97 software on a computer contains the computer's Ethernet address

---

[4] Independent component refers to the component can articulate an independent basis for search or seizure.

[5] Some other messages digest software are HAVAL, and SNEFRU.

(Media Access Control, or MAC address)[6] in a line headed by _PID_GUID within the document.

3.4   Crime Reconstruction

The ultimate goal of a crime investigation is to know what happened, when did it happen, who was involved, how it was carried out, and why, for each activity in a crime, besides the facts that someone is injured and a computer is broken into. Crime reconstruction process includes discovering evidences or recovering damaged evidences and determining the actions of a criminal act based on the evidences. The evidences recovered can be used to determine the relational, functional, and temporal aspects of crime acts. For example, the modified, accessed, and created times of a file, the logs of system events, the timestamps of e-mail messages, and etc, all can be used to reconstruct the sequence of activities of a crime act.

4.   DIGITAL EVIDENCE IN COMPUTER SYSTEMS

Computer systems are ubiquitous in modern society. The vast varieties of network stations are mostly general computer systems. The network nodes, such as gateways and routers, are dedicated computers, which control and provide the functioning of the network. Both kinds of computers provide huge data storage capacity besides their computing power. In general, the hierarchy of computer data storage consists of registers in the central processing unit (CPU), random access memory (RAM), online secondary storage, and offline storage. The data in the CPU registers are highly dynamic and volatile. It will be very difficult if not impossible to recover data from CPU registers. However, the RAM might keep a copy of some register data, which can then be recovered. Modern computers use magnetic disks as their primary on-line secondary storage devices. Data are abstracted as files and mapped onto physical devices by the operating system. Offline magnetic storage devices are rather static and the data recovering techniques are very similar to recovering data from on-line magnetic secondary storage. In this section, the digital evidence recoverable from the random access memory (RAM), the file system, and the physical media are described in detail.

---

[6] The MAC address is the same as the serial number of the network interface card. Viewing the Word 97 document using NotePad or other text editors can easily reveal the information.

4.1   Digital Evidence in Random Access Memory

It may be necessary to recover programs or data from main memory for forensic analysis. For example, an intruder may leave a back door process with it source codes as well as its executable removed to cover his trails. Some modern UNIX systems, such as Solaris, FreeBSD, and Linux, keep a copy of the executable files, current directory, and process memory of a running process in a /proc file system [11], as shown in Table 13-1. The information of a process is stored in the directory /proc/pid, where pid is the process identification number and the attribute of the process is specified by the /proc/pid/filename. For other systems, the TCT's[7] pact utility can be used to recover process memory, including code, data, and stack.

Table 13-1. Process attributes and their correspond files in /proc

Attribute of Process	Solaris	FreeBSD	UNIX
Executable Code	/proc/pid/object/a.out	/proc/pid/file	/proc/pid/exe
Process Image	/proc/pid/as	/proc/pid/mem	/proc/pid/mem
Memory Map	/proc/pid/map	/proc/pid/map	/proc/pid/maps

4.2   Digital Evidence in File Systems

A file system can be divided into two main components: namely the logical file system and the physical file system. The logical file system is further consisted of two parts: a collection of files and a directory structure. A file is the logical storage unit abstracted from the physical properties of its storage devices by the logical file system. The directory structure, which provides information about files in the system, is also abstracted and mapped onto physical devices by the logical file system. From a user's perspective, a file is the primitive allotment of secondary storage, and it is a named collection of related information that is recorded on secondary storage. The name of a file consists of two parts: primary file name and secondary file name, separated by "dot". Usually, the primary file name reflects the content of the file and the secondary file name indicates its type. Other file attributes include identifier, location, size, protection, time, date, and user identification [12]. The physical file system consists of the data structures recorded on the disk by the operating system for the purpose of disk space management. The operating system needs to do two tasks before storing files on a disk. Firstly, the operating system partitions the disk into one or more groups of cylinders, called partitions, and treats each partition as a separate disk. Secondly, the operating system needs to store the initial file system

---

[7] http:/www.fish.com/forensics

data structures onto the disk, such as an initial directory and the map of free and allocated space for each partition. Magnetic disk is one of the major storage media in computer system. A typical disk set consists one or more platters. Each platter surface is further divided into several tracks. Tracks, which are at the same position on different platter surfaces, form a cylinder. Each track is further divided into many sectors. A typical sector consists of 512 bytes. The organization of a typical disk platter is shown in Figure 13-1.

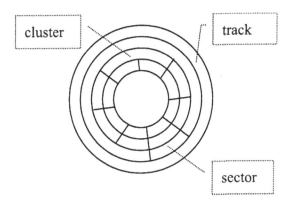

Figure 13-1. The Organization of a Disk Platter

While disk sector is the basic storage unit, the allotment of disk storage to files is often by cluster, which typically consists of several sectors. The number of sectors in a cluster is depended on the storage capacity of a disk. For example, a cluster in a 256MB disk using FAT16 may have 8 sectors, while in a 512MB disk the number of sectors per cluster is 16.

4.2.1 Recovering Deleted Files

In a Windows environment, when a file is deleted the first character of the directory entry is changed to hex value "E5" for distinction and the entries assigned to the deleted file in the FAT are changed to zero. The actual data stored on the disk clusters remained intact if the clusters are not reassigned and overwritten by other files. Thus, the deleted file can be recovered by putting the fragmented clusters together. There are some tools available for recovering deleted file in certain operating system. For example, PowerQuest's[8] Lost & Found utility can be used to recover deleted file in DOS FAT systems and RecoverNT[9] can be used to recover deleted files in Windows NTFS or 2000 systems.

---

[8] http://www.powerquest.com/
[9] http://www.lc-tech.com/Forensicsuit.asp

A typical UNIX system partitions an entire disk into several partitions, which is further divided into several zones, and each of which contains its block allocation bitmap, data blocks, and I-node blocks, as shown in Figure 13-2.

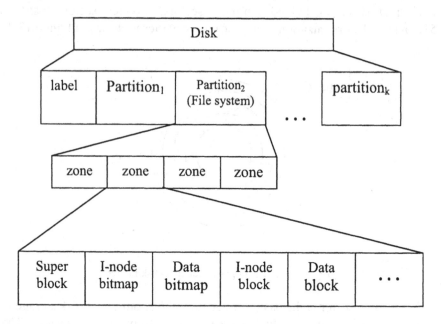

Figure 13-2. Disk Layout for a Typical UNIX File System

Thus, the data blocks of a small file are normally stored on the same zone and good file locality allows the contents of a deleted file to survive long after it is deleted. When a file is deleted, the system makes following changes [13]:

- The directory entry is marked as unused, but the name of the file still can be found by search the directory with the "strings" command.
- The I-node block is marked as unused in the block allocation bitmap. Some of the file attributes (information stored in I-node) are destroyed but a lot of them are preserved, such as owner, group ID, last read access timestamp and last write access timestamp. In particular, Linux also preserved the first 12 data block pointers and the deleted file can be recovered up to 12 data blocks by chasing the data block pointers.
- Data blocks assigned to the file are marked as unused in the block allocation bitmap. The actual data stored on the data blocks remained intact unless the data blocks are reassigned to save other files. Thus, the deleted file can still be recovered by putting the fragmented data blocks together.

The icat utility from the Coroner's Toolkit[10] can be used to recover parts of the information from deleted files in UNIX or Linux systems

4.2.2   Recovering Data on Slack and Unused Disk Space

The unit allotment of memory chunk that file system allocates to files is by block or cluster. A cluster normally consists of several sectors. In general, the size of a file is not exact multiple of cluster size, thus the last disk cluster allocated to a file may not be fully occupied and overwritten completely. The fraction of the last cluster which is not overwritten, often called slack space, may contain contents of a preexist file. Similarly, unused disk space may contain contents of previously deleted files. Therefore, it is important in forensic practice to recover these hidden files. There are several tools available for recovering hidden files, such as Guidance's[11] EnCase, NTI's [12] getslack and getfree utilities, and Ontrack[13].

4.3   Data Recovery from Physical Storage Medium

The user's view of files and the directory hierarchies and disk blocks are all abstractions provided by the operating system. At the physical medium level, every bit of information is recorded as a magnetic domain. Although it is relatively easy to delete a file from the file system, it is very difficult to destroy its contents in physical medium [14,15,16]. Firstly, when data is written to the physical medium, the read-write head sets the polarity of most of the magnetic domains, but not all, due to the inability for the device to precisely position the read-write head at the exactly same location each time and the variations in medium sensitivity and field strength difference over time and among devices. Secondary, when a "0" is written to disk the medium stores a "0" by setting the strength of the magnetic domain to a certain value, say 0, and when a "1" is written the strength of the magnetic domain is set to 1. However, in reality the actual effect is closer to 1.05 when a "1" is overwritten with a "1", and 0.95 when a "0" is overwritten with a "1". Although the read-write head of a disk is set up to read both values as a "1", these differences can be detected by using magnetic force microscopy (MFM) techniques. It turns out that the magnetic medium contains an image of everything ever stored on it. Thus, data can still be recovered even after which has been overwritten by an arbitrarily large number of times. This makes it very difficult to "truly" remove information

---

[10] http://www.porcupine.org/forensics
[11] http://www.guidancesoftware.com
[12] http://www.forensics-intl.com
[13] http://www.ontrack.com

from magnetic storage simply by overwriting or disk wiping. Although it is possible to recover layers of overwritten data when armed with MFM techniques, it is a very complex process to piece bits of information together. Thus, MFM is only used as a last resort in computer forensics.

5.   DIGITAL EVIDENCE IN NETWORKS

The threats to information systems were at approximately 80% internal and 20% external in early 1990s. However, with the integration of telecommunications and personal computers into the Internet, the threats appeared to be approaching an equal split between internal and external agents in the year of 2000 [17]. Furthermore, the sixth annual "Computer Crime and Security Survey[14]" for the year 2002 published by the Computer Security Institute showed that 74% of the respondents cited that more attacks are from the internet connections than from their internal systems. Seeing this trend, we believe that in the near future, the Internet will become one of the most important areas for crime investigation, and to search digital evidence in the computer networks will also be one of the most challenging tasks as well.

5.1   Network Architecture

The network subsystem of a modern computer system is designed and organized as a series of layers. Each layer offers certain services to the higher layer and shields the higher layer from the detail implementation of its services. The services between two adjacent layers define an interface between them. A computer network is normally characterized by the number of layers, the contents, and the functionality of each layer. The communication between layer n on two different machines is governed by a set of rules and conventions, collectively called *protocols*. The International Standard Organization defined an Open Systems Interconnection Reference Model [18], which has seven layers, namely *physical, data link, network, transport, session, presentation, and application layers*. One of the most widely implemented network protocols is the TCP/IP suite. TCP/IP is a four-layer network, as shown in Figure 13-3. The four layers mainly correspond to the physical layer, data link, network, and transport layers in OSI reference model and above the top TCP/IP layer is the application layer.

---

[14] http://www.crime-research.org/eng/library/Cybercrime_Stat.htm

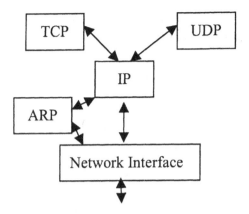

Figure 13-3. A Conceptual TCP/IP Architecture

The functions of the transport layer are managing the delivery of data and session management, such as establishing and terminating connections. The network layer is mainly responsible for routing message to its destination according to its addresses. The data link is responsible for establishing connection for data transmission between computers that are connected to each other. In addition to provide network functionalities, each layer usually maintains some housekeeping data. For example, a router usually keeps a routing table for determining the outgoing link for each message it received according its destination addresses.

On top of the network system, various applications are implemented to provide interfaces between users and networks. For example, mail server enables us to exchange e-mail, web server allows us to view web pages, and so on. The architecture of network services is shown in Figure 13-4.

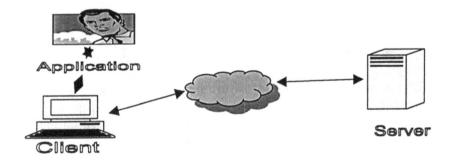

Figure 13-4. The Architecture of Network Services

Since a message needs to travel through many layers before being sent through communication media to its destination, it often leaves some trails behind in certain layers. Thus, it is often possible to recover links to network from a computer, as shown in Figure 13-5.

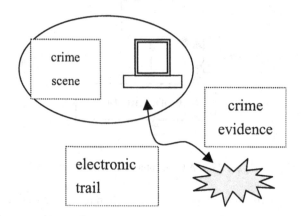

Figure 13-5. The Relationship between a Crime Scene and Network

5.2   Evidence in Application Layer

Most people use the network services through application programs, such as Internet Explorer (IE) or Netscape Navigator, bulletin board server (BBS), world wide web server (WWW), internet relay chat server (IRC), news server, e-mail server, and etc. Since the application layer is essentially the mostly widely used interface to computer networks, many trails may be left in this layer. Also many sources of digital evidence are created by applications. For example, the user's workstation may keep a copy of each e-mail message sent or received by the computer, the Cookies[15] may keep records of web sites visited, and so on.

5.3   Evidence in Transport and Network Layers

The process in the application layer often generates associated logs on the transport and network layers. For example, when a web page is surfed, very often the IP address and the connection time are logged on the web server. Similarly, the timestamp and IP address used to send an e-mail message are usually logged on the e-mail server when a message is sent or

---

[15] Cookie is a file stored within a web browser's file area for a user. Cookie is a text file and typically holds the following information: user name and password for a given web site, any custom settings for a given web site, the web sites visited by the user, and anything the web site has been programmed to store there.

received. The log files of a UNIX system normally include *acct* or *pacct*, *aculog, lastlog, loginlog, messages or syslog, sulog, utmp and utmpx, wtmp and wtmpx, vold.log,* and *xferlog.* Most of the log files are stored in /var/adm or /var/log directories and can be viewed directly with a text viewer, such as "*more*" or "*vi*". The two log files, utmp and wtmp may be stored in /etc and can be viewed by "*who*" and "*last*" commands respectively. The log entries in Windows keep records of application usage, activities that have security implications, and system events (such as shutdown), and can be displayed by using the Event Viewer. Another source of digital evidence in transport and network layers is the state tables, which contain information about current or recently terminated TCP/IP connections. The list of recently terminated and current connections can be listed by typing "netstat" command on UNIX and Windows environment. Additionally, RADIUS/DHCP servers usually log the records of IP assignment. Firewalls and routers may also be configured to keep records of TCP/IP packets passed through them. The logs and state tables in computer network are shown in Figure 13-6. These are all wealthy sources for digital evidences.

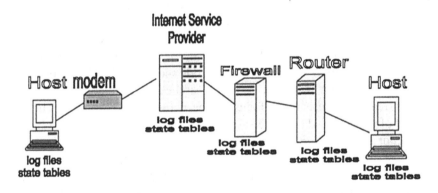

Figure 13-6. Network Log files and State Tables

5.4   Evidence in Data Link Layer

Data link layer is responsible for enabling communication between computers on the same network. A message in this layer is identified by its Media Access Control (MAC) address, which is directly associated with the identification number of the Network Interface Card (NIC) in a computer. However, the source and destination addresses of any outgoing message from a network router have to be translated into IP addresses using Address Resolution Protocol (ARP) before they are sent to the Internet. Thus, the router often caches a MAC/IP address translation table for address resolution. The mapping information can be retrieved by typing "arp –a" command on the router console. However, a record in the cache will be deleted if it is not used for a period of time between 20 minutes and 2 hours [6]. Furthermore, network management software, such sniffers, can be used to configure the NIC into "promiscuous mode" and force it to listen in and capture all network packets for forensic analysis.

6.   RESEARCH AND DEVELOPMENT ISSUES

Recognizing or search crime related information from computer disks could be a challenge for cyber forensics. Often a list of key words related to a crime are generated and used as the surrogates for the case. A full text scanner then searches the disk for matches with the surrogates. However, the search results may still contain too much information for human examination. Thus, it is critical to develop better search methods to precisely search the disk. Furthermore, evidence collected from a computer crime may contain a huge number of files. It may take months for human expert to classify and analyze these files, thus automatic document clustering and analyzing techniques need to be developed for supporting such applications.

Most of the forensic techniques were designed for known post-attack analysis. However, compared to real world, the activities in cyber space are less detectable. Automatic detection methods should be developed to address this issue. Although there are many researches on intrusion detection and related area, most researches focus on the network defense area. The huge amount of cyber world activities are mainly left free. Research must be done to monitor and detect unknown crime or trans-attacks in computer network. The huge amount of web sites, web pages, online documents, and etc, may need to be analyzed and monitored by techniques based on data mining technology under "right to monitor" environment. Again many of the issues remain opened.

There are a large number of forensic tools developed by individuals from academia and law enforcement. However, standards to ensure the quality and interoperability of these tools have not been established. Furthermore, most of the commercially available tools were designed for gathering evidence in a single computer system. The evidence gathering process in computer network still mainly relies on the network utilities. Techniques and tools for searching and gathering digital evidence from computer network shall be developed to address this problem.

Quick data recovery after attack is also a critical issue. An attack may damage a huge amount of files in a computer system or in many computers across networks. Efficient techniques, such as integrity checksum, should be developed to quick detect the damages and restore data to their original states before the attack.

7.   CONCLUSIONS

Our society has become more and more dependent on computer and computer network as the continuous expansion of computer applications. Consequently, more and more information, such as financial, military, proprietary business data, and personal communications are stored, processed and transmitted electronically. As our day-to-day life becomes more dependent on computer and computer network, it is inevitable that criminal activities will also be involved with the usage of computer and computer network. As a result, effective computer crime investigation will become an important challenge for law enforcement agencies. It is fundamental to develop valid and robust methods to recover digital evidences from computers for crime investigation. The methods must ensure that all probative information is collected in a way such that it is admissible, and ensure that nothing was added, altered and deleted from the evidence originally sized in the forensic processes. Furthermore, current commercially available forensic tools were designed for post attack analysis, and only good for searching case related information from a single computer system. Forensic tools in the future should also be able to detect unknown attacks, search across computer networks, monitor on-line traffics, and recover data from attacks in a timely manner. Standards to ensure the quality and interoperability of these tools should also be established.

REFERENCES

[1]   J. Marcella and R. S. Greenfield. Cyber Forensics: *A Field Manual for Collecting, Examining, and Preserving Evidence of Computer Crimes*, Auerbach Publications, 2002.

[2]   R. Saferstein, *Criminalistics—An introduction to Forensic Science*, 2nd edition, Prentice Hall, 1981.

[3]   S. F. Galton, Personal Identification and Description – I, *Nature*, 1888.

[4]   R. Saferstein, *Criminalistics—An introduction to Forensic Science*, 6th edition, Prentice Hall, 1998.

[5]   K. Graham, J. R. Evidence, CASENOTE Law Outlines, 2000.

[6]   E. Casey, *Digital Evidence and Computer Crime: Forensic Science, Computers and the Internet*, Academic Press, 2000.

[7]   W. G. Kruse II and J. G. Heiser, *Computer Forensics: Incident Response Essentials*, Addison-Wesley, 2002.

[8] H. C. Lee, *Crime Scene Investigation*, Central Police University Press, Taoyuan, Taiwan, ROC.

[9] US Department of Justice. *Federal Guidelines for Searching and Seizing Computers*, [http://www.usdoj.gov/criminal/cybercrime/search_docs/toc.htm], 1994.

[10] D. Icove, K. Seger, and W. VonStorch, *Computer Crime - A Crimefighter's Handbook*, O'Reilly & Associates, 1995.

[11] W. Venema, Strangers in the Night, *Dr. Dobb's Journal*, [http://www.ddj.com/documents/s=879/ddj0011g/0011g.htm], November, 2000.

[12] A. Silberschatz, P. B. Galvin, and G. Gagne, *Operating System Concepts*, John Wiley & sons, 6th ed, 2003.

[13] W. Venema, File Recovery Techniques, *Dr. Dobb's Journal*, [http://www.ddj.com/documents/s=878/ddj0012h/0012h.htm], December, 2000.

[14] D. Farmer and W. Venema, *Forensic Computer Analysis: An Introduction. Dr. Dobb's Journal*, September, 2000.

[15] P. Gutmann, Secure Deletion of Data from Magnetic and Solid-State Memory. *Proceedings of the Sixth USENIX Security Symposium*, San Jose, California, July 22-25, 1996.

[16] S. L. Garfinkel and A. Shelat, Remembrance of Data Passed - A Study of Disk Sanitization Practices, *IEEE Security & Privacy*, Vol. No. 1, 2003.

[17] G. L. Kovacich, and W. C. Boni, *High-Technology Crime Investigator's Handbook*, Butterworth Heinemann, 2000.

[18] A. S. Tanenbaum, *Computer Networks*, 2nd ed., Prentice Hall, 1988.

[19] E. Casey, *Handbook of Computer Crime Investigation*, Academic Press, 2002.

[20] K. Mandia and C. Prostise, *Incident Response: Investigating Computer Crime*, Osborne/McGraw-Hill, 2001.